"This well-researched and engaging study makes a provocative case that Brazilian developmentalism had heretofore unidentified political consequences that shaped the nation throughout the second half of the twentieth century and beyond. Ioris turns the conventional wisdom on its head by locating the origins of the 1964 military coup in the developmentalism of the 1950s. This innovative argument will no doubt spark debate on twentieth-century Brazilian and Latin American political economy."

—**Joel Wolfe,** *University of Massachusetts*

"Rafael Ioris properly dispels the notion of late 1950s Brazil as embodied in the image of a smiling Juscelino Kubitschek overseeing the construction of Brasília and a dispute-free march towards national development. Ioris delves into the era's ideological debates and the lives of working-class people to provide us with a more realistic view of the challenges inherent in transformative human endeavors. Ultimately, Ioris sheds critical light on the years leading up to one of the most intriguing yet tragic developments of modern Latin America: the overthrow of Brazil's democratically elected government in 1964. Ioris's work is a must-read for anybody wishing to comprehend Brazil's subsequent efforts to further project itself globally."

—**Kenneth P. Serbin,** *University of San Diego*

"Drawing on a vast array of published and archival sources, Rafael Ioris has produced a sophisticated analysis of the debates about national development in postwar Brazil. This study offers fresh insights into the hopes and dreams of an impressive array of interest groups—including politicians, technocrats, labor leaders and many others—who sought to make the 'country of the future' into a developed nation."

—**Marshall C. Eakin,** *Vanderbilt University*

Transforming Brazil

In this book, Rafael R. Ioris critically revisits the postwar context in Brazil to reexamine traditional questions and notions pertaining to the nature of Latin America's political culture and institutions. It was in this period that the region lived through some of its most intense and successful experiences of fast economic growth, which was paradoxically marred by heightened ideological divisions, political disruptions, and the emergence of widespread authoritarian rule.

Combining original sources of political, diplomatic, intellectual, cultural, and labor histories, Ioris provides a comprehensive study of the fruitful debates concerning national development in postwar Brazil, a time when the so-called *country of the future* faced one of its best moments for consolidating political democracy and economic prosperity. He argues that traditional views on political instability have been excessively grounded on an institutional focus, which should be replaced by in-depth analysis of events on the ground. In so doing, he reveals that as national development meant very different things to multiple social segments of Brazilian society, no unified support could have been provided to the democratically elected political regime when things rapidly became socially and politically divisive early in the 1960s.

Innovating in its multidimensional analytical scope and interdisciplinary focus, *Transforming Brazil* provides a rich political, cultural, and intellectual examination of a historical period characterized by rapid socio-economic changes amidst significant political instability and the heightened ideological polarization shaping the political scenario of Brazil and much of Latin America in the Cold War era.

Rafael R. Ioris is an assistant professor of Latin American history at the University of Denver. He holds a Ph.D. from Emory University in Latin American history with a concentration on Modern Brazil. His research interests include the history of political ideologies and comparative development in Latin America and U.S.-Latin America relations. He has authored and co-authored articles published in various prestigious journals including the *Journal of Latin American Studies, Journal of Iberian and Latin American Research, Brazilian Journal of Political Economy,* and *Foro Internacional.*

Routledge Studies in Latin American Politics

1 **Research and International Trade Policy Negotiations**
Knowledge and Power in Latin America
Edited by Mercedes Botto

2 **The United Nations in Latin America**
Aiding Development
Francis Adams

3 **Fear and Crime in Latin America**
Redefining State-Society Relations
Lucía Dammert

4 **Populism in Venezuela**
Ryan K. Brading

5 **Civil Society and Participatory Governance**
Municipal Councils and Social Housing Programs in Brazil
Maureen M. Donaghy

6 **Representation and Effectiveness in Latin American Democracies**
Congress, Judiciary and Civil Society
Edited by Moira B. MacKinnon and Ludovico Feoli

7 **Lula, the Workers' Party and the Governability Dilemma in Brazil**
Hernán F. Gómez Bruera

8 **Transnational Activism and National Movements in Latin America**
Bridging the Divide
Edited by Eduardo Silva

9 **Democracy, Revolution and Geopolitics in Latin America**
Venezuela and the International Politics of Discontent
Edited by Luis Fernando Angosto-Ferrández

10 **Transforming Brazil**
A History of National Development in the Postwar Era
Rafael R. Ioris

Transforming Brazil

A History of National Development in the Postwar Era

Rafael R. Ioris

Routledge
Taylor & Francis Group
NEW YORK AND LONDON

First published 2014
by Routledge
711 Third Avenue, New York, NY 10017

and by Routledge
2 Park Square, Milton Park, Abingdon, Oxfordshire OX14 4RN

First issued in paperback 2016

Routledge is an imprint of the Taylor & Francis Group, an informa business

Library of Congress Cataloging-in-Publication Data

Ioris, Rafael Rossotto.
Transforming Brazil : a history of national development in the postwar era / by Rafael R. Ioris.
pages cm — (Routledge studies in Latin American politics ; 10)
1. Brazil—Economic policy—20th century. 2. Brazil—Economic conditions—1945–1964. 3. Brazil—Politics and government—1945–1954. 4. Brazil—Politics and government—1954–1964. 5. Economic development—Brazil—History—20th century. 6. Political culture—Brazil—History—20th century. I. Title.
HC187.I67 2014
338.981—dc23
2013049217

ISBN 13: 978-1-138-65150-0 (pbk)
ISBN 13: 978-1-138-77689-0 (hbk)

Typeset in Sabon
by Apex CoVantage, LLC

Contents

Acknowledgments

This book is the result of many years of hard work, patience, and perseverance not only on my part, but also from those around me who not deservingly were forced to be involved in its making. Naturally, this affected more directly my immediate family, to whom this work is dedicated, but similarly extended relatives and friends, in Brazil and in the U.S., whose support during this entire process was also essential. I am deeply appreciative of their continued encouragement and I hope this piece is worthy of their trust and understanding.

Investigating the history of Brazil within the Latin America context is the culmination of my own, not always coherent, personal trajectory, which expanded into different fields and areas of interest. I hope this work can live up to the expectations of so many who have generously guided me throughout this entire path, which started long ago in Brazil and could not have been pursued without the examples and unconditional support provided by my parents and family. Also of special relevance, the continued intellectual guidance and personal kindness provided by Jeff Lesser, Susan Socolow, Walter Adamson, and Bianca Premo proved invaluable and always inspiring. I am also especially grateful for the reiterated friendship and encouragement provided by Antonio A. R. Ioris and my colleagues in the history department at the University of Denver.

Many of the ideas advanced here were first presented to my students, particularly those taking my advanced seminar in development promotion in Latin America, whose insightful input always made me further question my own assumptions. Also crucial were the always attentive suggestions on the narrative style of the book provided by Joyce Anitagrace. Similarly, James Woodard, Paulo Fontes, Oliver Dinius, John French, Joel Wolfe, Ken Serbin, Aaron Schneider, Robert Pastor, Tony Pereira, John French, Brian Owensby, Maria Clara Dias, Carol Helstosky, Beth Karlsgodt, Jodie Kreider, Jonathan Sciarcon, and Ingrid Tague have thoughtfully commented on different portions of the work. I have tried my best to incorporate their valuable points and hope the book can do justice to their time and the quality of their suggestions. An abridged version of Chapter Six was originally published in the *Journal of Latin American Studies* (Vol. 44, Issue 2, May 2012) and is being reprinted with permission here. I am very thankful to Cambridge University Press for allowing me to do this.

As a final point, even though I cannot assess how this book may ever impact them, it was in the hope that the work could provide some guidance in helping Brazil become a more just and inclusive society for upcoming generations of *brasileirinhos*—including my beloved children, Taís and Daniel—that I took the time to write it. I hope one day they may see that this is indeed so. Finally, without the unyielding support and partnership of my wife, Renata, none of this would have ever been possible. Thank you!

Introduction

Brazilian Development in Historical Perspective

Renowned worldwide for its visually exuberant soap operas, Globo TV, Brazil's most watched television station, broadcasted in January 2006 a Hollywood-style celebratory miniseries on the life of Juscelino Kubitschek de Oliveira, the country's president between 1956 and 1961. Simply called *JK*, the usual way Brazilians refer to the president, the well-reviewed show attracted the attention of the media as soon as filming began. Interviewed at the time, the miniseries' creator stated that in light of the recent corruption scandals and political divisions plaguing the nation, she had found comfort in the life of JK, the political leader who helped redefined the country's self-image by successfully promoting the long-sought dream of national development.[1]

The act of representing Brazil's so-called golden years in such an essentially congratulatory fashion is noteworthy for selectively effacing from living memory the many difficulties Kubitschek faced in his own time, which included three attempted military coups, corruption charges daily displayed in the national media, rising inflation rates and associated deteriorating living conditions for the urban poor, and a wave of massive labor stoppages in key industrial centers.[2] Ironically, when the first episodes of the series aired in the first months of 2006, Brazil had embarked upon a new experience of economic prosperity under the stewardship of the metalworker-turned-president Luis Inácio Lula da Silva, whose administration would add more than forty million Brazilians to the middle-income social stratum by the end of the decade. The recent achievements of the Lula administration (2003–2011) have called attention to the country's economic prospects and the sense of optimism that marked the end of his term in office, just as Brazil celebrated fifty years of the so-called JK Years. Inspired by the many, not always apparent, contrasts and similarities existing between recent and mid-century events associated with rapid state-led economic development, this book critically reflects on the paradigmatic phase of accelerated reforms that helped shape Brazilian society in the postwar years.

This was a time when the so-called country of the future had approximately 52 million inhabitants living in an economy still overwhelmingly defined by the production and exporting of agriculture commodities, particularly coffee. It was during those same years, however, that the country experienced profound economic, political, social, and cultural changes as many different social segments pushed for substantial redefinitions in the nation's traditional agrarian path, thus fostering a fruitful debate on which strategies the country should pursue in order to secure long-term economic prosperity. Beyond its comprehensive examination of some of Brazil's most transformative experiences, the book revisits the broader context of Latin America in the postwar era, a time when the developmental path Brazil followed in mid-century represented a potentially more moderate course towards socio-economic advancements for a region constrained by recurrent authoritarian rule and revolutionary upheavals.

An up-beat cultural outlook defined much of the second half of the 1950s in Brazil, a general sentiment that was further bolstered by the country's first soccer World Cup victory in 1958, the same year that the new and exciting musical style of Bossa Nova was introduced to world audiences. Likewise, in April 1960, his final year in office, JK inaugurated Brasília, the country's futurist-looking new political capital situated in the heartland of Brazil's vast territory, as domestically produced automobiles began circulating through the country's growing number of highways. It was also in the 1950s that, after the turbulence and authoritarianism of the war years, Brazilians experienced flourishing democratic life, remarkable economic growth, and an accelerated path of industrialization.

Shaping the political, economic, intellectual, and cultural lines of the postwar years in the country, the goal of rapidly transforming Brazilian society by means of state-planned industrialization mobilized different sets of government officials, nationalist intellectuals, leading business associations, and influential sectors of organized urban labor into a prolific, original, and creative discussion about the meanings of national development. The large and widespread initial enthusiasm notwithstanding—and in spite of the active involvement of these multiple socio-political actors in some of the country's most intense, original, and influential debates pertaining to how best shape the nation's future—in the end, a narrowly defined developmental strategy centered on absolute rates of economic growth prevailed, to the detriment of more socially inclusive and publicly debated policies.

It is not surprising, therefore, to see that although at first supportive of the moderate developmental path followed by the federal administration, as the 1960s dawned on Latin America's largest country, growing numbers of Brazilians were increasingly frustrated with the achievements of the period and, consequently, looked left and right in search of political and economic alternatives that, in their views, better advanced their interests and needs. What is rather surprising is to see that despite the short- and long-term negative consequences of the labor-saving—and foreign capital-dependent industrial modernization pursued in the middle of the twentieth-century—much of the still-prevalent historiography on the period is largely defined by a very positive portrayal of what is now referred to in Brazil as the "developmentalist decade." The much-praised JK Years, in particular, have been recurrently described as a time of widespread optimism, rapid economic growth, efficient governmental planning, broad levels of support for the goals pursued by the federal administration, and unprecedented levels of political democracy.[3]

Undoubtedly the country's most influential political figure of his time, Juscelino Kubitschek de Oliveira, was elected president of Brazil in October 1955 on the basis of an aggressive campaign that promised fifty years of economic growth during the five years of the presidential term, and "fifty years in five," the informal slogan of the candidate's political platform, came to define his administration.[4] Along these same political lines, JK assertively sought to implement an ambitious plan of accelerated economic growth centered on industrial promotion largely by resorting to a creative alliance established between domestic, international, private, and governmental sources of capital. Kubitschek's core policies came to be known as the Targets Plan, as it included a list of thirty areas of the national economy assigned to receive preferential treatment from public and private economic agents so that accelerated economic growth could take place.

The plan exerted a significant impact over the economic infrastructure of the country and consolidated the path of industrialization of the preceding years. Moreover, the implementation of the plan fostered a genuine interest and associated debates across Brazilian society about the very idea of fast-paced national development, as is demonstrated in the different sections of the present book.[5] A good indication of the important economic transformations of the period is that in the 1950s the Brazilian economy expanded on an average of about 7.5 percent a year, with an annualized industrial growth of 11 percentage points.[6] Despite these ambitious economic goals and their associated significant achievements, at the decade's end Brazil witnessed heightened ideological polarization and a growing distrust in much of the democratic institutions—a political trend that ultimately helped pave the way to the right-wing military coup of March 1964 and the ensuing twenty-one years of authoritarian rule and encroaching exclusionary economic policies.[7]

This final outcome is particularly relevant as the developmental policies pursued not only in Brazil but in other parts of Latin America at the time had been largely framed along the lines of what came to be known as the Modernization Paradigm. Grounded in late nineteenth-century European social thought but more clearly articulated in the mid-century politics of the U.S., one of its core tenets was the notion that self-sustaining economic growth would eventually spill over into other societal dimensions, such as the political system. Along these conceptual lines, economic prosperity was seen as the most expeditious step toward a stable social order and a democratic political regime; thus, industrial promotion became a priority for the political and intellectual agendas of mid-century Latin America.[8]

In Brazil, the complexity of transitioning to an urban, industrialized society was a major challenge for the country's political regime, particularly after the economic debacle faced by its agrarian base brought about by the world depression of the 1930s. As a result, the central government emerged as the only political player capable of formulating and enacting new strategies of capital accumulation while also controlling the conflicting interests being mobilized under a process of rapid social and economic transformation.[9] Further contributing to the industrial drive of the postwar era, mid-century Brazilian economic thought manifested a largely pragmatic orientation, especially in light of the growing need to move away from the country's historic dependence on agrarian exports. This was particularly true in the case of the much-debated goal of substitutive industrialization, which received innovative and groundbreaking conceptual strength in the formulations produced by the United Nations-sponsored Economic Commission for Latin America (ECLA) in the late 1940s and early '50s.

A founding member of the ECLA, Brazilian economist Celso Furtado applied the agency's framework to explain how industrial growth had gained momentum in Brazil in the late 1930s. In his view, the process was largely grounded on the need to produce traditionally imported goods domestically, given the world recession and the global military operations of the period.[10] Adding to Furtado's original studies, later examinations of the emerging industrial activities taking place at the turn of the century (particularly in the state of São Paulo) have similarly emphasized the importance of capital accumulation obtained on the basis of commodity exports.[11] Debates pertaining to the origins of the process of industrialization notwithstanding, most scholars agree that the 1950s represented a new, fundamentally different phase in the industrial evolution of the country. It was then that the involvement of the national government reached new grounds in its planning, regulating, and financing of economic functions and industrial activities expanded beyond the traditional areas of steel and chemical production to include the manufacturing of (potentially) mass-consumable, durable goods, such as automobiles.[12]

The impact of industrial growth on the consolidation of the modern Brazilian state is another especially relevant theme in the scholarly literature on the war and postwar years. The bulk of these analyses centers on the role the central government played in promoting and directing the mid-twentieth century industrial drive. Earlier studies characterized the federal government as performing an essential and unmatched task in the promotion of industrialization and the political modernization of the country, particularly after the mid-1930s.[13] Later works conversely emphasized that throughout this entire process the structures of the national government did not act alone but were rather permeated by interest groups that allied themselves with policy-makers in order to implement a new developmental course for the country.[14] But although disagreements pertaining to the bureaucratic nature of the federal government may remain, most scholars accept the notion that, by the second half of the 1950s, the goal of industrial expansion became a broadly shared position among the majority of the most politically relevant and active sectors of the Brazilian elite. What is more, as is further detailed in the following chapters, new technocratic agencies (e.g., the Council of Industrial Development in the first half of the decade and the National Council of Development in the second), tied to the presidential office and providing direct links between policy-makers and business groups in both the Vargas (1951–1954) and Kubitschek administrations, have been seen as especially relevant for the deployment of key industrial policies of the period.[15]

Some of the most profound and lasting experiences concerning development promotion in Brazil indeed occurred in the postwar years, particularly during the implementation of the Targets Plan, when the majority of the industrial undertakings that eventually converted the country into a regional industrial powerhouse were initially established. But despite the significant economic achievements of the period, at the end of the decade Brazil remained essentially underdeveloped for the vast majority of its people, who endured challenging living and working conditions on a daily basis. And even in major urban industrial centers, where the main achievements of the transformative years of the period were felt most concretely, nominal gains for industrial salaried workers (a privileged labor segment by most standards) were rapidly depleted by the rising costs of living and persistently high inflation rates.[16]

In light of these broad, multi-dimensional, and many times disruptive socio-political and economic scenarios, and by closely probing the developmental experiences being carried out in Brazil in the 1950s, this examination provides a more comprehensive review and critical understanding of how political and ideational negotiations on the topic of national development impact socio-cultural, economic, and political realities in societies undergoing a broad and accelerated path of transformation. Similarly, by situating Brazil's developmental experiences within the regional, hemispheric, and global dynamics of the time, this book offers a comparative reflection on the nature, means, and potential challenges of similar experiences in late-industrializing societies.

State-led policies of rapid economic development were not unique to the Brazilian context, especially in the 1950s, a period defined by the dissemination of the goal of industrial promotion and its purportedly related political autonomy.[17] Primarily focused on the Brazilian case, the present study therefore speaks to historical experiences beyond the particular context of this important regional economy as the goal of accelerated industrialization mobilized governments and societies in several agriculture-based economies throughout much of the twentieth century, particularly in Latin America. In the majority of these cases, complex political and ideological debates about the meanings of national development unfolded and questions pertaining to how development should be pursued, who should conduct the process, and who should benefit from such endeavors became objects of intense political negotiations.[18]

Indicative of these same historical dynamics, the variegated nature of the interaction between state policies and affected social sectors in the context of a fast-industrializing country was exemplarily displayed in the experiences associated with the formulation and implementation of the Targets Plan. Examining these transformative events is, therefore, revealing not only of important aspects in the historical trajectory of Brazil, but also of broader dynamics taking palace in Latin America during the context of the Cold War. It was during this turbulent period that different portions of the continent witnessed some of their most intense experiences of economic growth and industrialization, which were nonetheless counterpointed by heightened ideological divisions, radical political experimentation, political disruption of democratic rule, and, in most cases, ensuing authoritarianism.

Regrettably these were also years of growing mutual disappointment, resentment, and dispute between Latin America and its most influential and powerful northern neighbor, as well as of several missed opportunities for advancing more constructive patterns of interaction in the Western hemisphere. Conversely amidst this increasingly unstable regional scenario, Brazil, Latin America's largest country and economy, seemed to offer a more hopeful scenario, particularly in the mid-1950s. In effect, during much of its so-called developmental decade, Brazil appeared to be particularly well-positioned to embark upon a historical path that promised to reshape the face of the nation in significant and largely positive ways. Much of this was predicated on the notion that growth would reinforce the blossoming, yet still fragile, political arrangements of the period.

Along these lines, beyond the laudatory tone applied to the JK Years, much of the political literature on the 1950s has traditionally advanced the concept of populism (as well as that of the Populist Republic) to characterize the mid-century political context of the country. In a general sense, both terms seek to describe the inherently unstable, corporatist-like social pact said to exist in mid-century Brazil (and many other parts of Latin America) and which is nonetheless seen as instrumental in sustaining a path of industrialization.[19] In effect, by equating the consolidation of a vast national industrial base with the long-sought dream of modernization, much of the literature on the 1950s sees JK as the quintessential developmental leader who held a fragile political situation in balance by helping disseminate a true ideology of national development.[20] This extensive and, in many ways, still relevant scholarly contribution notwithstanding, the widespread and growing political activism marking the final years of the 1950s is a case of rising disenchantment amidst an experience of accelerated economic growth still in need of a more satisfactory historical account. Thus, critically adding to the existing historiography, this work advances the notion that no consensual definition of national development existed in Brazil during the so-called Populist Republic (1945–1964). Likewise, by providing a detailed analysis of the rich cultural debates pertaining to development promotion in Brazil, the present work offers a new look at the very nature of the so-called Latin American populist state.

In fact, in lieu of the still prevalent accounts positing that the rapid and mostly unopposed demise of the Brazilian democratic regime of the mid-century derived from either the "exhaustion of the easy phase of industrialization,"[21] or the "democratic overload" placed on the political system by excessive demands from rising popular segments,[22] this examination demonstrates how the roots of the growing political polarization of the early 1960s are better found in the fact that different social segments involved in the many political, intellectual, and cultural debates of the 1950s advanced their own conceptions of national development, which were not evenly incorporated in the developmental efforts of the time.[23] By the same token, along the alternative analytical lines advanced here, the collapse of the political regime then in place is seen as largely grounded in the ideological polarization caused by the lack of willingness on the part of the federal administration to effectively incorporate the diversity of developmental views into the many ambitious policies it pursued, as well as the myopic developmental conceptions it espoused. What is more, the ultimate demise of the democratic order in the mid-1960s should be, therefore, considered as inextricably associated with the developmental policies of the preceding years, particularly with the ways in which they were conducted, i.e., by trying to reform key elements of the economic structure of the country while largely maintaining the main contours of its social structure and political system.

Any successful new examination of the historical experiences of the fast-paced development promotion of mid-century Brazil needs to take into account a range of recent investigations on the status of the developmentalist experience in Latin America. On the one hand, comparative analyses of the Southeast Asian economic miracle of the third quarter of the twentieth century have almost unanimously framed similar undertakings in Latin America, and above all in Brazil, as devoid of the bureaucratic efficiency found in the Japanese-modeled, farsighted, and politically insulated developmental state.[24] On the other hand, culturally driven critical studies have emphasized the hubris and authoritarian nature of similar initiatives in Latin America, particularly in the postwar era, as ways to call attention to the multiple voices and alternative notions of development suppressed in the pursuit of allegedly neutral, male-centered, economically focused, state-led projects.[25]

Inspired by the rich historiographical reflection on mid-century Brazil and Latin America and on the important inter-disciplinary analytical lenses advanced in the field of comparative development briefly reviewed above, the present work scrutinizes how a pro-development agenda loosely described as widely supported in Brazilian society was actually perceived, interpreted, and re-conceptualized by specific social sectors, including different groups of government officials, nationalist intellectuals, business elites, and important segments of organized labor. By the same token, even though scholars have long debated the concept of development, this study examines how different concrete historical actors thought of and acted to advance their own, at times divergent, positions on the topic that had come to define much of the 1950s in Brazil and large portions of Latin America. In doing so, this book also suggests how a less divisive political course could have been sought had a more socially grounded, rather than technocratic, definition of development informed the actions of the federal Brazilian state. This analysis is based on a diverse and largely original set of materials—including official government documents, intellectual works, business publications, and labor newspapers—brought together under the overarching goal of reconstructing, from several different angles, the rich socio-cultural mosaic that defined the 1950s in Brazil. With this goal in mind, the book is structured as follows:

Chapter One revisits the established reflection on economic development promotion in Brazil and provides a general characterization of the period in order to set the stage for the examinations presented in subsequent chapters. The emergence of a developmental awareness defined by a sense of optimism for the feasibility of the goal of industrialization and the creation of the institutional means to pursue this new historical path are central elements of the analysis provided. Finally, the chapter situates Kubitschek's key developmental policies in the broad context of Brazil's developmental path in the twentieth century.

Moving beyond the domestic scenario, *Chapter Two* offers a comparative examination of similar developmental initiatives taking place elsewhere in the world in the same period and examines how the Brazilian government tried to promote its developmental goals by engaging in innovative foreign policy projects (e.g., Operation Pan-America). The core argument presented is that there was a clear convergence at the time between the developmental debates taking place domestically and important international diplomatic initiatives proposed and conducted by recently emancipated nations on a truly global scale.

Chapter Three reveals how state-led development promotion became an acceptable notion within the structures of the Brazilian government. In specific terms, I examine the experiences of the Council of Development, the governmental agency created to implement the Targets Plan, and review the process of setting up an automotive industry in the country in order to showcase the ways in which the council operated. As a whole, the chapter indicates that while national development mattered to multiple segments of Brazilian society, very specific social sectors were favored by the very narrow developmental conceptions underpinning the implementation of such an important and transformative industrial path.

Chapter Four scrutinizes the broader socio-political, ideological, and intellectual context of the period, particularly its second half, mostly by reviewing key intellectual formulations and corresponding political debates regarding the topic of national development. This investigation centers on the experiences of the Higher Institute of Brazilian Studies (ISEB), the most important body of intellectual reflection on national development during Kubitschek's tenure. The core argument advanced is that while ISEB members thought of national development as a state-centered and socially inclusive goal, the main intellectual formulators of the administration tended to argue in favor of market-oriented industrial projects.

Chapter Five reflects on the emergence of a Brazilian version of a culture of mass consumption and its impacts on the political events and instability of the period. The chapter is centered on the analysis of two additional actors involved in the process of accelerated industrialization: business and technocratic elites. I probe how different influential business associations of the largest urban and industrial centers of the country conceived of and responded to the main developmental trends of the period.

Similarly, I examine the positions on national development posited in some of the most influential professional publications of the time. As a whole, the piece shows that though supportive of the main goals pursued by the federal administration, particularly under JK, business groups and technocratic cadres were nonetheless increasingly prone, and assertively acted to prevent any developmental path grounded on broader socio-political concerns. Alternatively, these ever more vocal political actors became increasingly active in espousing an alleged neutral (i.e., science-driven) position strictly focused on economic growth.

Chapter Six focuses on the lived experiences of the metalworkers of São Paulo and Rio de Janeiro. I closely scrutinize printed materials (e.g., newspapers, minute-books, conference manifestos, etc.) as well as concrete acts of collective mobilization (e.g., strikes and marches) performed by this increasingly important labor segment in order to assess the notions, views, and propositions on national development that industrial workers advanced in those years. In the end, the piece demonstrates that while the federal administration strove to promote a plan of national economic development based on market-oriented notions that favored multinational industrial companies and their locally associated domestic business groups, workers alternatively conceived of national development as an inclusive social project that had to be coordinated by a politically responsive and economically interventionist central government to produce tangible results.

Many things have undoubtedly changed since the middle of the twentieth century. Brazil is no longer the same country as the one that Vargas and Kubitschek encountered in the 1950s. Its economy is many times larger, with a much more significant industrial base, and its society is much more urban and complex. Brazil's political structures are also more democratic and stable, there is a much higher degree of social inclusion, and the country's civil society is much more dynamic, with a more sophisticated degree of mobilization of its many social movements. These important differences notwithstanding, Brazil remains a highly exclusionary society with an economy still substantially dependent on commodity exports and thus, like in the 1950s, closely tied to the whims of global economic demands. Furthermore, in the rapidly changing experiences of the 1950s, similar to those of today, development was not a monolithic, univocal project, but rather a central topic of debate and a matter of intense political engagement for multiple social segments.

Examining the developmental experiences of these transformative years should therefore offer valuable guidance for assessing some of the current challenges the country faces. In fact, even though high rates of economic performance have recently been achieved, only marginal changes in the social structure have been seen and these are largely due to a derivative enlargement of the urban middle classes. In addition to the consolidation of the process of the return to a democratic regime after a long period of military dictatorial rule and some levels of social inclusion produced by targeted poverty alleviation programs, some of most important political innovations witnessed in Brazil in recent years are found in the field of international diplomacy. In effect, it has become noticeable that as the country has progressively become more politically democratic, economically sound, and a bit more socially inclusive, its political leadership has simultaneously tried to promote a more autonomous and assertive course of foreign policy, a historical trend which also finds resonance in the ambitious international diplomatic propositions advanced by Brazilian political leaders in the 1950s.[26]

While economic and political dynamics unfolding in the middle of the twentieth century in Brazil have been researched for some time, no broad and systematic examination of the developmental efforts of the period, particularly of its impacts on different organized social segments currently exists. Thus, in addition to carrying out a detailed review of the extensive literature dealing with the complex political and economic realities of the 1950s produced in the fields of history and the social sciences in Brazil and the United States, I conducted an extensive primary source research in numerous archival and research-based institutions. In concrete terms, I have scrutinized a long list of published and unpublished government documents on the domestic and international political and economic projects deployed, as well as some of the most important intellectual, business and, labor-based publications of the period.

Worthy of note, I examined the collection of documents produced by the Council of Development available at Arquivo Nacional (AN) in Rio de Janeiro in order to assess core developmental goals and institutional means of the federal Brazilian state. I also consulted the rich documentation available at the Centro de Pesquisa e Documentação de História Contemporânea do Brasil (CPDOC) and at the Mario Henrique Simonsen Library, both at the Getúlio Vargas Foundation in Rio de Janeiro. These materials proved especially relevant for assessing key bureaucratic, diplomatic, and intellectual notions, formulations, and policies of the time.

Aimed at uncovering the developmental ideas advanced by business associations and influential technocratic cadres of the federal bureaucracy, I have turned to their own professional publications available at the Biblioteca Histórica do Ministério da Fazenda (BHMF), in Rio de Janeiro. Similarly, in addition to the vast secondary bibliography in Portuguese, the general characterization of the 1950s, particularly Kubitschek's political trajectory was also based on archival work conducted at the Public Archive of Minas Gerais (ArqPMG), Biblioteca Pública Estadual Luis de Bessa, Biblioteca da Fundação João Pinheiro, and archives of the Instituto Cultural Amilcar Martins (ICAM) in the city of Belo Horizonte.

In order to construct a portrayal of the ever more market-oriented consumer culture of the late 1950s, I have examined the underlining views on Brazilian society articulated by North-American marketing professionals available at the John W. Hartman Center for Sales, Advertising and Marketing History located in Duke University's Rubenstein Rare Books and Manuscripts Library. Much in the same way, seeking to understand how industrial workers conceived of and reacted to the main events and policies of the period, I have conducted extensive research at the Centro de Documentação e Memória (Cedem) at the State University of São Paulo, the private archive of the Metalworkers' Union of the city of São Paulo (SindMet/SP), and the Public Archive of the State of São Paulo (ArqPSP) in the city of São Paulo. I have also examined the extensive labor and political documentation on the period available at the Edgar Leuenroth Archive (AEL) at the University of Campinas, the Arquivo de Memória Operária do Rio de Janeiro (AMORJ), the Núcleo de Estudos sobre Trabalho e Sociedade (NETS) both at the Federal University of Rio de Janeiro, and the Public Archive of the State of Rio de Janeiro (ArqPRJ) in the city of Rio de Janeiro.

Beyond my sincere debt of gratitude to all of those working in these various research institutions who assisted me in my, at times, scattered yet persistent search for relevant materials, I am also appreciative of the many opportunities I had to conduct research in the rich collections of the following public and private libraries in Brazil and the United States. These include the Central Libraries of the Catholic (PUC) and Federal Universities (UFRJ) of Rio de Janeiro, the Social Sciences Library at the Federal University of Minas Gerais (UFMG), the Robert W. Woodruff Library at Emory University, the Latin American Library of the Howard-Tilton Memorial Library at Tulane University, and the Penrose Collection at the University of Denver.

This extensive and diverse set of source materials allowed me to propose this new reexamination of the historical experiences involved with national development promotion as manifested in the 1950s in Brazil. None of this would have been possible, however, without the generous support provided by important academic institutions and initiatives, including the Laney Graduate School of Arts and Sciences at Emory University, the Andrew W.

Mellon Foundation, the Office of Internationalization and the Faculty Senate at the University of Denver, and the UNC-Duke Consortium in Latin American and Caribbean Studies.

Thus, grounded on key political events, intellectual notions, and ideological positions of the developmentalist era in Brazil, the present book seeks to advance a new, inter-disciplinary, and multi-dimensional analysis of some of the most relevant political, intellectual, cultural, and labor debates of the time. All of this is done in the hope of advancing a more nuanced, comprehensive, balanced, yet still critical interpretation of the complex, important, and, above-all, fascinating historical events shaping the mid-twentieth century in the country, as well as of their continued relevance to today's society. All translations from Portuguese into English are my own, so is any possible merit, as well as the certainly more evident shortcomings, of the study.

NOTES

1. Maria Adelaide Amaral, interviewed by Martha Mendonça, published in *Revista Época*, no. 387 (Oct 17, 2005), accessed on June 15, 2013, http://revistaepoca.globo.com/Epoca/0,6993,EPT1052813-1666,00.html.
2. Essential works on the broad political context of the period include Maria Victoria de Mesquita Benevides, *O governo Kubitschek: desenvolvimento econômico e establidade política, 1956–61* (Rio de Janeiro: Paz e Terra, 1976); Edgar Carone, *A Quarta República, 1945–1964* (São Paulo: Difel, 1980); and Thomas E. Skidmore, *Politics in Brazil, 1930–1964—An Experiment in Democracy* (Oxford: Oxford University Press, 1967).
3. The list of works describing the JK Years as uniquely democratic, optimistic, and stable in the history of the country is extensive, with special note to Robert J. Alexander, *Juscelino Kubitschek and the Development of Brazil* (Athens: Ohio University Center for International Studies, 1991); Francisco de Assis Barbosa, *Juscelino Kubitschek, uma revisão na política brasileira* (Rio de Janeiro: José Olympio, 1960); Cláudio Bojunga, *JK: O Artista do Impossível* (Rio de Janeiro: Objetiva, 2001); Carlos Heitor Cony, *JK, como nasce uma estrela* (Rio de Janeiro: Record, 2002); Ronaldo Costa Couto, *Brasília Kubistchek de Oliveira* (Rio de Janeiro: Record, 2001); Amaury Santos Fassy, *JK: O Maior Estadista do Século XX* (Brasília: Thesaurus, 2000); José Louzeiro, *JK: o otimismo em pessoa* (Rio de Janeiro: Ediouro, 1996); Aluízio Napoleão, *Juscelino Kubitschek: audácia, energia, confiança* (Rio de Janeiro: Bloch, 1988); José Aparecido de Oliveira, *JK: O Estadista do Desenvolvimento* (Brasília: Memorial JK, 1991); Joaquim Ferreira dos Santos, *Feliz 1958: O ano que não deveria terminar* (São Paulo: Record, 1997); Pedro Augusto Gomes Santos, *A classe média vai ao paraíso: JK em Manchete* (Porto Alegre: EDIPUCRS, 2002); and Hélio Silva & Maria C. R. Carneiro, *Os Presidentes: Juscelino e o Desenvolvimentismo 1956—1961* (Rio de Janeiro: Grupo de Comunicação Três, 1983).
4. For details on Kubitschek's presidential campaign and how it was used to promote his developmental agenda, see Edward A. Riedinger, *The Making of the President, Brazil 1955: The Campaign of Juscelino Kubitschek* (Chicago: University of Chicago Press, 1978) and João Carlos Picolin, "Juscelino para presidente: as estratégias de comunicação política na campanha eleitoral de JK em 1955" (paper, Twentieth National Conference of Communication Sciences, Salvador, 2002).

5. The Targets Plan is one of guiding concepts of this study and will be examined in detail in Chapters One and Three. For additional works on the topic see Clóvis Faro and Salomão da Silva, "A Década de 50 e o Programa de Metas," in *O Brasil de JK*, ed. Angela de Castro Gomes (Rio de Janeiro: FGV, 1991), 44–70; Celso Lafer, *JK e o Programa de Metas (1956–1960): Processo de planejamento e sistema político no Brasil* (Rio de Janeiro: FGV, 2002); and Carlos Lessa, "Fifteen Years of Economic Policy in Brazil," *Economic Bulletin for Latin America* 9, no. 2 (Nov 1964), 153–214.
6. Ministério do Planejamento, *Índices de crescimento econômico médio do produto real na indústria*, (Brasília: 1967), 1:32, tab. 1; and Presidência da República, *Relatório Geral do Conselho do Desenvolvimento* (Rio de Janeiro, 1960), 4:5.
7. Brazil also experienced high rates of economic growth amidst a deeper process of wealth concentration in the early 1970s, under what became known as the country's "economic miracle." Given the militaristic, repressive, exclusionary, and authoritarian nature of the state at the time, and the fact that this experience was premised on some important diverging notions (e.g., geopolitics), a comparison of the two periods would entail a significantly different focus from the one proposed here and is not part of the present study. Details can be found in Cláudio Salm, "Estagnação Econômica, Desemprego e Exclusão Social," in *Novo-desenvolvimentismo: um projeto nacional de crescimento com eqüidade social*, ed. João Sicsu, et al. (Rio de Janeiro: Fundação Konrad Adenauer, 2005), 189–216; and José Pedro Macarini, "A política econômica do governo Médici: 1970–1973," *Nova Economia* 15, no. 3 (Sep–Dec 2005), 53–92.
8. One of the more representative works conveying the logic espoused by what is called the Modernization paradigm is Walt W. Rostow, *The Stages of Development: An Anti-Communist Manifesto* (Cambridge: Cambridge University Press, 1960). Additional works include Seymour M. Lipset and Aldo Solari, eds., *Elites in Latin America* (New York: Oxford University Press, 1967); Daniel Lerner, *The Passing of the Traditional Society* (Glencoe, Ill.: The Free Press, 1958); and W.A. Lewis, *The Theory of Economic Growth* (London: Allen & Unwin, 1955); and in the Latin American context Gino Germani, *Política y sociedad en una época de transicion: de la sociedade tradicional a la sociedad de masas* (Buenos Aires: Paidos, 1962).
9. On the format of the so-called Compromise State, leading to the process of import substitute industrialization in Brazil, see Octávio Ianni, *Industrialização e desenvolvimento social no Brasil* (Rio de Janeiro: Civilização Brasileira, 1963) and *Estado e planejamento econômico no Brasil* (Rio de Janeiro: Civilização Brasileira, 1986); and Francisco C. Weffort, *O populismo na política brasileira* (Rio de Janeiro: Paz e Terra, 1978).
10. Celso Furtado, *Formação Econômica do Brasil* (São Paulo: Fundo de Cultura, 1959).
11. Warren Dean, *The Industrialization of São Paulo*: 1880–1945 (Austin: University of Texas Press, 1969) and Carlos Manuel Pelaez, *História Econômica do Brasil* (São Paulo: Atlas, 1979).
12. Wilson Cano, *Raízes da concentração industrial em São Paulo* (São Paulo: Difel, 1977); and João Manuel Cardoso de Mello, *O Capitalismo Tardio: constribuição à revisão crítica da formação e desenvolvimento da economia brasileira* (São Paulo: Brasiliense, 1982); Maria da Conceição Tavares, *Da Substituição de importações ao capitalismo financeiro* (Rio de Janeiro: Zahar, 1973; Wilson Suzigan, *Indústria Brasileira: Origem e Desenvolvimento* (São Paulo: Hucitec, 2000).
13. The list of these works is vast, including important titles such as Werner Baer, *Industrialization and Economic Development in Brazil* (Homewood, Ill: Irwin,

1965); Sonia Draibe, *Rumos e metamorfoses: um estudo sobre a constituição do estado e as alternativas da industrialização no Brasil, 1930–1960* (Rio de Janeiro: Paz e Terra, 1985); Raymundo Faoro, *Os Donos do Poder.* (Porto Alegre: Ed. Globo, 1984); Florestan Fernandes, *A revolução burguesa no Brasil: ensaio de intepretação sociológica* (Rio de Janeiro: Zahar, 1981); Celso Furtado, *Formação Econômica da América Latina* (Rio de Janeiro: Lia Editores, 1969); Albert O. Hirschman, *The Strategy of Economic Development* (New Haven: Yale University Press, 1965); and Nathaniel Leff, *Economic Policy-Making and Development in Brazil, 1957–1960* (New York: Wiley, 1968). Authors stressing the role played by the federal state in an incipient industrialization prior to the 1930s include Steven Topik, *The Political Economy of the Brazilian State, 1989–1930* (Austin: University of Texas Press, 1987) and Marian O. Versiani, "Cotton Textile Industry of Minas Gerais, Brazil: 1868–1906" (PhD diss., University College of London, 1991).

14. Caren Addis, *Taking the Wheel: Auto-Parts Firms and the Political Economy of Industrialization in Brazil* (University Park: Pennsylvania State University Press, 1999); Renato Boschi, *Elites Industriais e Democracia* (Rio de Janeiro: Graal, 1979); Fernando Henrique Cardoso, *Empresário industrial e desenvolvimento econômico* (São Paulo: Difel, 1964); Eli Diniz, *Empresario, Estado e Capitalismo no Brasil, 1930–1945* (Rio de Janeiro: Paz e Terra, 1978); Maria A. Leopoldi, *Política e Interesses na Industrialização Brasileira: As associações industriais, a política econômica e o Estado* (São Paulo: Paz e Terra, 2000); Luciano Martins, *Industrialização, burguesia nacional e desenvolvimento* (Rio de Janeiro: Saga, 1968); and Helen Shapiro, *Engines of Growth: The State and Transnational Auto Companies in Brazil* (Cambridge: Cambridge University Press, 1994).
15. In addition to Lafer, *JK e o Programa de Metas*, see Leslie E. Armijo, "Public Policymaking in a Semi-Autonomous State: Brazilian Financial Modernization, 1950 to 1987" (PhD diss., University of California Berkeley, 1989); Barbara Geddes, *Politician's Dilemma: Building State Capacity in Latin America* (Berkeley: University of California Press, 1994); and Eliza J. Willis, "Explaining Bureaucratic Independence in Brazil: The Experience of the National Economic Development Bank," *Journal of Latin American Studies* 27, no. 3 (1995), 625–61.
16. This can be clearly seen in the statistics showing the cost of living increases in the capital city of Rio de Janeiro during these years. During the Kubitschek administration (1956–1961) alone, the rate of purchasing power vis-à-vis the cost of living for the average worker in the city eroded from 77 percent to only 22 percentage points between the years of 1956 and 1961. Detailed information can be found in the February 1962 through January 1964 editions of the journal *Desenvolvimento & Conjuntura* published by the National Industrial Confederation (*Confederação Nacional da Indústria,* CNI).
17. A non-exhaustive list of some of the most important, classic works on the promotion of industrialization under the auspices of the central government in late industrializing economies includes Alexander Gerschenkron, *Economic Backwardness in Historical Perspective* (Cambridge: Belknap,1962); by Albert O. Hirschman, *Journeys Toward Progress: Studies of Economic Policy-Making in Latin America* (New York: W.W. Norton, 1963) and *The Strategy of Economic Development* (New Haven: Yale University Press, 1965); and Gunnar Myrdal, *Economic Theory and Underdeveloped Regions* (London: Duckworth, 1964). Details on these authors and the notion of a late-coming economy will be provided in Chapters One and Two.
18. See Enrique Cardenas, José Antonio Ocampo, Rosemary Thorp, eds., *An Economic History of Twentieth-Century Latin America: Industrialization and*

the State in Latin America: The Postwar Years (London: Palgrave Macmillan, 2000), vol. 3; Adam David Morton, *Revolution and State in Modern Mexico: The Political Economy of Uneven Development* (London: Rowman & Littlefield, 2011); Jenkins Rhys Owen, *Dependent Industrialization in Latin America: The Automotive Industry in Argentina, Chile, and Mexico* (New York: Praeger, 1977); Yovanna Piñeda, *Industrial Development in a Frontier Economy, The Industrialization of Argentina, 1890–1930* (Palo Alto: Stanford University Press, 2009); John Sheahan, *Early Industrialization and Violent Reaction: Argentina and Brazil*, Discussion Paper 176 (University of Sussex: Institute of Development Studies, 1982); Kathryn Sikkink, *Ideas and Institutions: Developmentalism in Brazil and Argentina* (Ithaca: Cornell University Press, 1991); Célia Szusterman, *Frondizi and the Politics of Developmentalism in Argentina, 1955–62* (Pittsburgh: University of Pittsburgh Press, 1993); Arnulfo Valdivia-Machuca, *State and Business Groups in Mexico: The Role of Informal Institutions in the Process of Industrialization, 1936–1984* (New York: Routledge, 2005).

19. See Michael Conniff, ed., *Latin American Populism in Comparative Perspective* (Albuquerque: University of New Mexico Press, 1982); Kenneth P. Erickson, *The Brazilian Corporative State and Working-Class Politics* (Berkeley: University of Californai Press, 1977); Marly Rodrigues, *A década de 50: populismo e metas desenvolvimentistas no Brasil* (São Paulo: Atica, 1994); and Francisco C. Weffort, *Origens do sindicalismo populista no Brasil: a conjuntura do após-guerra* (São Paulo: Estudos Cebrap, 1973), no. 4.
20. In addition to the authors on note #2 above, see Miriam Limoeiro Cardoso, *Ideologia do Desenvolvimento,Brasil: JK-JQ* (Rio de Janeiro: Paz e Terra, 1978).
21. David Collier, ed., *The New Authoritarianism in Latin America* (Princeton: Princeton University Press, 1979); Guillermo O'Donnell, *Modernization and Bureaucratic-Authoritarianism: Studies in South American Politics* (Berkeley: University of California Press, 1973); and Alfred Stepan, ed., *Authoritarian Brazil* (New Haven: Yale University Press, 1973).
22. Samuel P. Huntington, *Political Order in Changing Societies* (New Haven: Yale University Press, 1968). A related argument explaining the collapse of democracy in 1964 on the basis of a lack of willingness of all parties involved to continue to support the rules of electoral politics can be found in Argelina Cheibub Figueiredo, *Democracia ou Reformas? Alternativas Democráticas `a Crise Política, 1961–64* (São Paulo: Paz e Terra, 1993).
23. Michael Wallerstein was one the first to call attention to the fact that the political crisis of the mid-1960s needs to be understood as the end result of a series of economic transformations promoted by the Kubitschek administration. While this book corroborates this view, the analysis herein advanced goes beyond the economic argument proposed by Wallerstein in "The Collapse of Democracy in Brazil: Its Economic Determinants," *Latin American Research Review* 15, no. 3 (1980), 3–40.
24. On the original notion of the *developmental state*, see Chalmers Johnson, *MITI and the Japanese Miracle: The Growth of Industrial Policy, 1925–1975* (Stanford: Stanford University Press, 1982). Later studies include Alice Amsden, *Asia's Next Giant: South Korea and Late Industrialization* (New York: Oxford University Press, 1989); Stephan Haggard, *Pathways from the Periphery: The Politics of Growth in the Newly Industrializing Countries* (Ithaca, NY: Cornell University Press, 1990); Robert Wade, *Governing the Market: Economic Theory and Role of Government in East Asian Industrialization* (Princeton: Princeton University Press, 1990); and Meredith Woo-Cumings, ed., *The Developmental State* (Ithaca: Cornell University Press, 1999).

25. A groundbreaking critical analysis was presented by Arturo Escobar in *Encountering Development: The Making and Unmaking of the Third World* (Princeton: Princeton University Press, 1995). His more programmatic take on these events can be found in "Imagining a Post-Developmental Era? Critical Thought, Development and Social Movements," *Social Text*, no. 31/32, Third World and Post-Colonial Issues (1992), 20–56. Additional conceptual critiques of the excesses of the developmental state can be found in H.W. Arndt, *Economic Development: The History of an Idea* (Chicago: University of Chicago Press, 1987); Suzanne Bergeron, *Fragments of Development: Nation, Gender, and the Space of Modernity* (Ann Arbor: University of Michigan Press, 2004); Rajesh Bhattacharya, "Ethics and Economic Development: Why Developmentalism Prevails as an Ideology," in *Beyond Developmentalism*, ed. Nilanjan Dutta (Kolkata: Sherya Publications, 2010), 23–50; Colin Leys, *The Rise and Fall of Development Theory* (Bloomington: Indiana University Press, 1996); and James C. Scott, *Seeing Like a State: How Certain Schemes to Improve the Human Condition Have Failed* (New Haven: Yale University Press, 1998). Especially relevant for the Latin American experiences, see also Maria Josefina Saldana-Portillo, *The Revolutionary Imagination in the Americas and the Age of Development* (Durham: Duke University Press, 2003).
26. Paulo Roberto de Almeida, "Uma política externa engajada: a diplomacia do governo Lula," *Revista Brasileira de Política Internacional* 47, no. 1 (2004), 162–84. See also by the same author *Brazil as a Regional Player and an Emerging Global Player*, Friedrich Ebert Stiftung Briefing Papers No. 8 (São Paulo, 2007). See also Adriano de Freixo, et al., *Política externa brasileira na era Lula: um balanço* (Rio de Janeiro: Apicuri, 2011); and Túlio Vigevani and Gabriel Cepaluni, "Lula's Foreign Policy and the Quest for Autonomy through Diversification," *Third World Quarterly* 28, no. 7 (2007), 1309–26.

1 State Planning and National Development

Political Devices for Turbulent Times

INTRODUCTORY NOTES

The 1950s in Brazil were characterized by rapid transformations amidst rising ideological polarization. The country witnessed high rates of economic and demographic growth, fast-paced urbanization, sustained industrialization, and the creation of an ever expanding consumer market within a context defined, however, also by continued social exclusion and persistent insufficiencies in the areas of infrastructure, education, and public health. Protracted socio-economic challenges notwithstanding, these were years of abundant intellectual, political, and cultural innovations developed essentially on the basis of the persistent search for a new historical course for the nation. This was process that had begun in a less consistent fashion late in the 1930s, when Brazilian society started undergoing profound institutional and socio-economic changes.

Leading the way, the federal government deepened the path of industrialization, expanded and professionalized its own bureaucratic structure, and gradually opened up the realms of urban political participation. Socially and culturally the country experienced the enlargement of middle-income sectors, mostly tied to the activities of the central government and burgeoning industrial initiatives, and the rapid growth and intense mobilization of urban industrial labor. In fact, though still largely defined by the corporatist framework created under the dictatorial regime known as "Estado Novo" (1937–1945), the industrial expansion of the time helped foster a better organized and ever more active workers movement that consistently pushed the boundaries of the legal and political systems.

World War II proved to be another important turning point in the recent history of the country, particularly at its aftermath when Brazil faced the challenge of moving beyond the experiences of authoritarian rule while sustaining the socio-economic achievements of the preceding years. Brazil was Latin America's most actively involved nation in the Allied war effort. The country provided important raw materials, logistical support that included the temporary cession of territory for military installations, and personnel to European operations coordinated by the U.S. military. Moreover, the concern about a protracted global war had convinced even its more reluctant political leaders that their country had to be more assertive in the goal of state-supported industrialization given the heightened risks of not having a national industrial base amidst a global economic blockade. In the end, despite the human cost involved, overall the country benefitted from its participation in the war, and Brazil's most important postwar industrial complex (and Latin America's largest steel mill), the Companhia Siderúrgica Nacional (CSN) was, in fact, a direct result of the country's close alignment with United States.

When postwar economic and political reconstruction got underway Brazil became an active participant in some of the most important newly created agencies and institutions of the UN system, providing enthusiastic diplomatic support for the cause of global economic liberalization. In the immediate postwar years the national economy was indeed in a privileged economic position given the large amounts of accumulated foreign reserves from exports associated with the war effort. These economic assets would be soon depleted, however, by rising levels of manufactured imports, a trend clearly indicative of the long-term structural weaknesses of an economy still marred by deep inefficiencies in the areas of energy production and transportation.

These shortcomings posed serious difficulties for the continuous growth that ruling elites increasingly saw as a *sine qua non* condition for sustaining the controlled path of economic inclusion that had taken place in the preceding years.[1] The challenge of delivering high rates of growth while responding to the growing mobilization of urban working- and middle-income groups within an increasingly complex and culturally diverse society therefore defined much of the developmental experiences of the 1950s in Brazil. It was amidst this changing, often-turbulent general scenario that one of the most promising periods of growth, political stability, and social inclusion in the history of the country unfolded.

In order to start assessing these many complex historical dynamics, the present chapter revisits the established literature on economic development promotion in Brazil and reconstructs the domestic political environment of the country. It begins by examining the role of the national state in the main developmental efforts conducted in the transformative years of the 1950s. In fact, no longer determined by the authoritarian laws of the Estado Novo, the mid-century political order was nonetheless largely defined by limited socio-economic inclusion and the persistent tutelage of a corporatist state apparatus and political logic still at work.

INDUSTRIAL PROMOTION AND THE PERSISTENT ROLE OF THE FEDERAL GOVERNMENT

Significant state and private investments recently made in different areas of industrial activity notwithstanding, in the aftermath of World War II the

Brazilian economy was still fundamentally defined by produce-exporting activities and the country remained largely dependent on coffee exports for obtaining convertible currencies used to purchase foreign manufactured goods.[2] Complicating matters further, the country faced growing challenges from the larger availability of agricultural goods offered in ever more integrated global markets defined by declining commodity prices. Coffee exports represented about 62 percent of all foreign trade revenues obtained in 1950, and throughout the entire decade these sales amounted to at least half of all gains associated with foreign trade, the intense price fluctuation of the time notwithstanding.[3] In fact, even though in its first years the Korean War helped push global commodity prices upward, by the end of the decade Brazil faced tremendous difficulties in obtaining the strong foreign reserves needed to support its balance-of-payment accounts. These problems were also grounded in the mid-decade, politically driven commercial boycott implemented by the U.S. Congress against Brazilian coffee exports, as well as on the rapid decline in global prices occurring in the second half of the decade.[4]

The importance of coffee exports for the mid-century economic soundness of the country was such that even the Kubitschek administration (1956–1961), despite being primarily focused on implementing an ambitious agenda of industrial development, was regularly forced to subsidize coffee production in the form of price guarantees and the purchase of significant portions of the annual harvests in order to stabilize global prices. Indeed, expenditures associated with coffee policies carried out in the second half of the decade amounted to the staggering figure of an estimated total of about 8 percent of the country's GDP.[5] Aggravating the situation, international prices dropped to the lowest levels of the decade in 1958 and the International Coffee Study Group of representatives of Latin American and African producers decided to set quotas for upcoming harvests—a decision that reduced, for the first time, the Brazilian share of global production to below 50 percent.[6] Thus, though decreasingly influential, the historically powerful large coffee growers of the southeastern portion of the country continued to hold considerable political power over the nation's decision-making process, forcing JK to take these interests into account while deploying his ambitious industrial plans.[7]

Such a challenging economic scenario defined by growing trade and balance-of-payment shortfalls was to become one of the main structural reasons behind the fact that promoting accelerated growth by means of fast-paced industrialization would become a central political theme in the 1950s. It should be noted, however, that though pursued in a less assertive and coordinated fashion, the goal of industrialization had shaped broad socio-political, economic, and even cultural dynamics in Brazil even before the developmentalist years of the 1950s.[8] It is worth recalling that the authoritarian Estado Novo had been at least partially justified in the expediency of imposing the needed political stability required for promoting a profound reordering in the country's economy.[9] The regime had been put in place when Vargas—who had come to power in 1930 based on a platform of traditional Latin American liberal political reforms typical of the first quarter of the century (i.e., fair elections and restricted recognition of labor unions) implemented a "self-coup" in November 1937 that forcefully closed the doors of the national congress, imposed widespread censorship, and centralized political rule. Coherent with its corporatist nature, the regime set up the first national labor legislation granting rights to urban organized workers while, at the same time, placing unions under the strict control of the federal government. These intricate political strategies provided the basis for the dissemination of a new pro-industrial outlook among relevant portions of political and economic elites, thus paving the way for the major industrial jump of the 1950s.

Given its historical relevance, the process of industrialization and its impact on the construction of a modern state apparatus has become one of the most relevant topics of study in the vast political literature on twentieth-century Brazil. Following either an economic or a sociological approach, classic examinations stress the role that the federal structures of government played in promoting the goal of fast industrialization, particularly after the 1930s.[10] Supplementary in-depth historical analyses alternatively identified the private, commercial, and even agricultural origins of the capital accumulation process supporting some of the first manufacturing units being created in the late nineteenth and early twentieth centuries.[11]

Political investigations on the state's participation in these complex historical events, particularly in the mid-twentieth century, have also been regularly advanced. From an early state-centered perspective, which emphasized the alleged autonomous capabilities held by the federal government, additional studies have shown the important role private agents played in the process.[12] How the central government may have influenced the course of development promotion in what have been defined as "late, late-comers" (i.e., peripheral economies that pursued fast-paced industrialization in the middle of the twentieth century, in contrast to what late-comers such as Germany, Russia, and Japan did at the end of the nineteenth century)[13] also merited attention from the specialized literature trying to make sense of the shortcomings of this delayed historical experience.[14]

As indicated above, in Brazil, deepening the path of substitutive industrialization in the 1950s was closely associated with the need to address persistent economic deficits.[15] Even the market-oriented administration of Eurico Dutra (1946–1951) was eventually forced to reintroduce government regulations in order to tackle the deteriorating economic conditions of the late 1940s. To be sure, starting in 1946, Dutra's market friendly economic advisors (who included the influential economics professor Eugênio Gudin) eliminated all war-time restrictions on imports assuming that the foreign reserves accumulated in the preceding years would be able to sustain a new period of liberal (market-based) economic growth. The administration believed that the promises for reorganizing the global economy along the lines of the liberal principles set out in the Bretton Woods Accords would be translated into effective economic assistance to developing nations such as Brazil. Market-friendly cabinet members had hoped that a flexible exchange rate approach would serve to attract needed foreign sources of capital and that the promised elimination of the limits on coffee prices paid in the U.S. market would be able to compensate for eventual losses caused by rising imports.

These initial optimistic expectations were quickly dashed in the second year of Dutra's presidential term, when he was forced to impose the first of a series of legal restrictions on imports in order to balance surging trade deficits. Foreign reserves had been depleted at a faster rate than anyone had expected and the assistance promised from the U.S., particularly in terms of public finance to support the goal of overhauling the infrastructure of the economy, never materialized.[16] As the confidence in the multilateral order set by the U.S. after 1945 rapidly faded, Brazil faced a growing balance-of-payments crisis. Given the heightened need to curb imports while also addressing the mounting problem of inflation rates, in lieu of devaluing an artificially high exchange rate of the Brazilian *Cruzeiro*, Dutra's administration instituted new regulations on the volume and type of imports. Though unintended, these measures helped foster the early stages of the path of industrialization consolidated in the 1950s, as sustaining an overvalued exchange rate and imposing growing legal restrictions on imported manufactured goods were key elements of the industrial policies pursued in the ensuing years.[17] Additional conceptual contributions during these early years of the postwar scenario to the goal of industrial promotion included the two investigative commissions created in a joint-effort between the governments of Brazil and the U.S. in order to find possible ways of improving Brazil's economic prospects.

The first examination was undertaken by the Joint Brazil-United States Technical Commission of 1948 (also commonly referred to as the Abbink Commission, after the leading U.S. representative chairing the work), which published a pessimistic report stating the urgent need for Brazil to find ways to attract private sources of foreign investment in order to enhance the economic competitiveness of the national economy.[18] In itself the report did not carry much weight among Brazilian authorities who were already looking for alternatives to conduct their own industrial plans. The study nonetheless represented one of the first explicit utterances of the notion that Latin American economic development was to be supported primarily on the basis of private sources of capital, a trend that was to become the main course of foreign policy of the Eisenhower administration towards the region—as will be examined in detail in Chapter Two. But as the official report from this earlier investigation had just become public, Brazilians authorities increasingly seemed to notice a positive shift in the American policies to the region in the so-called Point IV Program proposed by President Truman in his inaugural speech of January 1949, where he stated the importance of making technical and financial assistance available to developing economies.[19]

Inspired by this renewed commitment from Latin America's most powerful and influential neighbor to support developmental pursuits of impoverished nations, Brazilian and North American representatives decided to set up a much more ambitious joint commission. This time, the goal was not only to examine structural shortcomings of the national Brazilian economy but also to propose concrete solutions in the shape of viable projects for infrastructure investments that could potentially be financed by the two main funding agencies of the period: the U.S. Export-Import Bank and the International Bank for Reconstruction and Development (IRDB, later to be called the World Bank). The Joint Brazil-United States Economic Development Commission (JBUSDC) thus came to light in December 1950, with impacts being felt throughout the decade. Despite producing one of the best diagnoses of the Brazilian economy, the bold goals of the Joint-Commission (as it is commonly referred to) were only partially fulfilled considering that the U.S. only disbursed about half of all funds initially committed to support infrastructural investments in Brazil ($186 million out of a total of about $400 million).[20]

These important bilateral negotiations helped shape the so-called second Vargas administration (1951–1954), which was similarly plagued by balance-of-payment challenges.[21] Addressing the problem of depleting reserves in convertible currency required a coordinated effort by Vargas's long-time associate Oswaldo Aranha, who became minister of finance in 1953. Seeking to avert a looming crisis, the SUMOC (the federal agency in charge of regulating exchange rates in the absence of a proper central bank) issued its famous Normative Instruction #70, which established a complex five-tiered exchange rate system in which the government ranked imports according to their perceived importance (essentiality) for the country's economy. Once a base rate had been set for each category, the state-controlled Bank of Brazil auctioned available foreign reserves among importers who had to follow the legal requirement of depositing the corresponding dollar amounts needed to obtain specific import licenses. The high premium placed on the two non-essential items tiers became a major source of government revenues, indicated in the fact that between 1954 and 1960, profits from exchange auctions corresponded to about 15 percent of the entire federal budget.[22]

Back in power by a strong popular mandate, Vargas sought to accelerate the course of industrialization while being forced to deal with the deteriorating conditions of the national economy. These were challenging goals to reconcile and the administration counted on support from the JBUSDC, particularly in regards to financing needed infrastructural investments that could have provided headways on both fronts of action. In mid-year 1953, assistance from the U.S. seemed an ever-elusive goal as the new Republican administration imposed severe challenges to the Brazilian economy by abandoning the Point IV Program and abruptly terminating the activities of the Joint-Commission. Consistent with his own fiscally conservative views, Eisenhower promoted the notion that public financing to Latin American nations should primarily be provided by the IRDB rather than the U.S. Export-Import Bank (Eximbank), despite the major role the latter had played in supporting economic projects in the region in the preceding decade. Considering that the lending policies of the World Bank were based on more stringent conditions than those of the Eximbank, and that Latin America was not considered a priority area for investments from this global financial institution, Brazil faced growing difficulties for refinancing old loans and, especially, obtaining new ones throughout the 1950s.[23]

While strengthening the role of the central government in the national economy, Vargas also hoped to attract public and private capital from both domestic and foreign sources to support his industrial plans. These were not necessarily contradictory goals considering that the main objective of the administration was to unleash a renewed cycle of economic growth by means of industrial promotion. In fact, many of the president's closest associates were influential businessmen, including Horácio Lafer, his first minister of finance, and Euvaldo Lodi, the president of the National Industrial Confederation (CNI) who enjoyed open access to the presidential palace. Even Rômulo de Almeida, chief economist of the powerful Assessoria Econômica da Presidência—the Economic Advisory Committee of the Presidency—was himself a former adviser to Lodi at the CNI, which continued to pay his salary during the tenure at the assessoria.[24]

Along with the Council of Industrial Development (CDI)—an interministerial committee that tried to formulate industrial policies capable of enhancing joint efforts between the administration and private business groups—the assessoria provided important bureaucratic tools for the Brazilian government to implement its new agenda of development. Interviewed several years after his work at the agency had been completed, Almeida stressed the purported apolitical nature of the agency, which, according to him, was above all interested in promoting the rapid development of the national economy. In his view, foreign sources of capital, even private ones were always welcomed by the administration provided that investors agreed to play what he called a "constructive (productive rather than exploitative) role."[25] In addition to these two bureaucratic agencies, the National Bank of Economic Development (BNDE), which was also created by the second Vargas administration, quickly became the key institutional operator supporting the goal of industrialization throughout the entire decade, particularly during the implementation of the Targets Plan, as examined in Chapter Three.

Despite the divisive potential of such a course of action for a government coming to power on the basis of a nationalist platform of development, the former dictator consistently appealed to business sectors in order to gather support for his economic agenda. An indication of some of his success in fostering a new developmental approach among key economic agents was the Fifth Annual Meeting of the UN-sponsored Economic Commission for Latin America (ECLA) held in April 1953 in Petrópolis, in the state of Rio de Janeiro. Presided by Euvaldo Lodi, the event brought together key industrial associations, which had become increasingly disappointed with the continued protectionism sustained by industrialized countries and increasingly had come to see ECLA's state-led industrial approach as a promising alternative course of action capable of accelerating the pace of economic development of the country.[26]

Close relations with industrial interests notwithstanding, particularly in the powerful state of São Paulo, the second Vargas administration also sought to strengthen the role of the central government in the national economy, primarily by enlarging the number of publicly owned (i.e., government controlled) companies such as Petrobrás, created in 1953 on the basis of a plan produced by the assessoria. The original plan did not assign monopolistic rights nor provide majority ownership of the enterprise to the federal government, but because of the strong opposition Vargas faced in Congress and a well-run nationalist campaign supported by influential sectors of the military, the final approved legislative bill granted exclusive rights of oil exploration to the state-owned company.[27]

The main lines of the industrializing policies Vargas implemented in the 1950s harkened back to the Estado Novo period and thus, while no explicit objection to private sources of foreign capital existed, one could still see a clear preference for foreign public (governmental or inter-governmental) sources, considering that private investors had, in the administration's point of view, proven to be reluctant to assume the risk of investing in large infrastructural projects. Vargas himself and many of his closest advisors tended to see private foreign investors as excessively inclined to "exclusively seek a quick return on their investment and avoid areas of activity which required the largest amounts of capital."[28] By the same token, while many of the institutional tools used to pursue an accelerated path of industrialization were created in the first half of the 1950s, it was in its second half that the Brazilian developmentalist state assumed its most elaborate format. This was particularly true in the case of the unique partnership established between state and private economic agents during the JK Years.

In fact, whereas the second Vargas administration pursued a more nationalist and largely state-centered approach, under Kubitschek the association between governmental and non-government economic actors deepened and the pursuit of a market-centered and foreign investors-oriented course of action took historical prominence. It is worth noting, for instance, that the annualized foreign direct investment entering Brazil between 1947 and 1955 was less than U.S. $60 million, whereas from 1956 to 1961 these figures quickly climbed to over $140 million.[29] Along these historical lines, even though the federal government continued to play an important role, as the decade unfolded the role of both domestic and foreign *private* economic actors increased. At times, cooperation between state and private actors took the form of joint ventures in specific activities or, more commonly, involved different forms of financial support from the federal government to specific private industrial projects. The Brazilian government also acted as the provider of last resort for capital in the areas of energy supply and transportation networks.

The Kubitschek administration proved to be remarkably innovative and successful in its ability to provide state resources in support of private, including foreign, economic investors, on the condition that these investors advanced the administration's industrial goals. This was particularly true in the case of the automotive industry, which was funded by almost half of all foreign direct investments entering the country in the period.[30] In so doing, JK opened the way for a path of development promotion grounded on the basis of an alliance between governmental, domestic, and foreign private sources of capital, which was consolidated, ironically in the 1970s, during the military regime (1964–1985).[31] But although the association of state-domestic business groups was articulated as being in sync with the main lines of the nationalist ideologies propounded in the period, the role of foreign corporations was becoming a focal point of political division and ideological polarization throughout the 1950s, as will be demonstrated in upcoming chapters.

Considering that foreign investors were very influential in the remarkable industrial growth achieved during his administration, scholars have long posited that JK had relinquished control of national resources to private foreign interests, whereas Vargas is portrayed as having "stood his ground" in preventing such an outcome. In this sense, much of the historiography on the period characterizes the developmental paths followed in the early 1950s and the latter half of the decade under the Kubitschek administration as sharply divided on the issue of private foreign interests and national resources.[32]

The fact that Vargas committed suicide in August 1954, after having allegedly written his so-called testament letter blaming "obscure foreign interests" for his tragic death, has only served to sustain such views—even though many recent studies have shown a much more balanced view of Vargas's positions regarding foreign sources of capital.[33] Further complicating the matter is the fact that JK was consistently much more explicit in his pronouncements about the positive role foreign investors could play in the course of Brazilian industrial development. For instance, in his message to the National Congress (a similar document to the State of the Union address in the U.S.) in January 1957, JK stressed the point that "attracting foreign enterprises is a measure of importance for our government considering that their technology and capital can provide an immensely valuable contribution in the construction of our industrial base."[34]

Headed by a new national political figure inclined to accept and able to attract foreign investments in the country, ruling Brazilian elites became ever more interested in finding alternative ways of shifting the developmental course of their country from the horizontal industrial expansion of the 1940s to a vertical diversification of products, particularly in the area of intermediate goods. Such a path required more technologically sophisticated and capital-intensive know-how than the country could afford and, therefore, the Kubitschek administration engaged more assertively with foreign investors interested in expanding their activities in the country. As a direct result, Brazil's industrial production doubled and in key industries such as steel, mechanical, electrical, and transportation equipment, growth rates were even higher.[35] Furthermore, despite lacking any significant alteration in its traditionally exclusionary socio-economic structure, throughout the developmental decade, Brazil moved from being essentially a producer of agricultural commodities to becoming capable of supplying much of its domestic markets for intermediate and, in some cases, even durable goods.[36]

How politically sustainable this course of action was and how these events impacted Brazilian society in general is the guiding thread of this entire book. In order to continue setting the framework of analysis for the broad investigation at hand, in the next section, I examine how working segments have traditionally been characterized based on their responses to the many transformative historical experiences unfolding at the time.

POPULISM, WORKERS, AND THE PREDICAMENT OF POLITICAL INSTABILITY

The alleged existence of a national consensus in favor of economic growth associated with the deepening of the process of state-led industrialization is another central theme of the historiography on the mid-twentieth century in Brazil. It was during these years that a significant number of the industrial plants that eventually turned the country into a regional industrial powerhouse were established, a trend well illustrated in the fact that annual growth in the capital goods industry averaged around 25 percent between 1955 and 1961.[37] As briefly indicated in the introductory chapter to this work, several authors working on the period have argued that the notion of national development by means of rapid industrialization had become a consensual position among large sectors of the country's population.[38] Additional works have argued that the creation of technocratic managerial agencies within the structures of the executive branch was one of the main reasons for the many economic achievements of the period.[39]

Kubitschek himself has been repeatedly extolled for "uniting the nation" behind a course of development that promised that every social segment's share of the national economy would be enlarged by means of a process of fast economic growth, thus obtaining unparalleled social agreement and political support.[40] Along these lines, the many transformative events of the time have been often studied through the interpretive lens provided by the concept of populism, given that the political regime largely operated on the basis of corporatist-like power compromises established between the federal state and multiple socio-economic groups, including industrialists and important segments of the organized labor movement.[41]

Although populism has become a common heuristic tool present in the majority of the general descriptions of the 1950s in Brazil, the label clearly lacks analytical precision to account for the concrete events of the period. When the general characterizations of the JK Years are contrasted, for instance, with a detailed examination of the lived experiences of urban workers, one is easily impressed by the number of discrepancies that become evident. This is nowhere more apparent than in the disparity existing between the image of the immediate support provided by urban workers in favor of the developmental goals of the federal administration and the rising demands of organized labor. Independent union mobilization and the related growing political activism of workers were also on the rise during these years, a trend that fostered the creation of non-sanctioned inter-union associations that would increasingly act in leadership positions in the many cross-sectional, massive stoppages that helped shape the turbulent political context of the period.[42]

Given their historical relevance for the broad political dynamics of the time, labor mobilization became the focus of intense academic work. Classic studies on mid-century Brazilian labor have been linked to broader investigations dealing with the process of industrialization and urbanization taking place at the time. These works tried to ascertain how the rural origins of a significant portion of industrial workers, who had recently migrated in large numbers to the growing urban industrial centers located in the southeastern portion of the country, impacted union membership and the prospects for independent labor mobilization. The main argument therein advanced is that this burgeoning labor group manifested a conservative outlook regarding union organization and political activism.

Furthermore, this growing segment of the industrial labor force has also been portrayed as prone to judge the corporatist legal structure of the period as not only as an oppressive force but also as a potential ally in achieving economic gains, should one perform well at one's assigned duties.[43] Later examinations have alternatively advanced an image of the period as being defined by complex and challenging relationships between workers and industrialists, as well as between labor unions and the federal government. This claim was largely grounded on the perception that rising levels of independent organization and political activism on the part of workers occurred in tandem with the progressive deepening of the process of industrialization throughout those years.[44]

Certainly the developmentalist era of the 1950s offered new historical circumstances for labor mobilization in Brazil considering that, as the path of industrialization gained momentum, unions grew larger and ever more powerful. Likewise, as inflationary pressures further eroded wages, particularly beginning in 1957, workers felt increasingly compelled to carry out bolder paths of collective engagement. Several massive strikes were conducted, many of which involved workers of different union bases in non-sanctioned acts of mobilization, considering that cross-sectional (i.e., with workers from different professional groups) stoppages were proscribed by the corporatist labor legislation of the period. Especially relevant for the new forms of resistance it helped devise and for pressing new political themes into the national agenda of development, the struggle against deteriorating living conditions unfolding in the large urban centers of the country gradually changed the very nature of labor activism of the era. Traditional wage-based demands were displaced by more openly political mobilizations, and industrial workers became more actively engaged in debating and acting in response to the developmental policies pursued by the central government, as is examined in depth in Chapter Six.

But despite workers' growing interest in participating in the debates pertaining to which course the country should undertake, their concerns were consistently pushed aside by a federal administration that continued to pursue its own technocratic and essentially growth-oriented developmental vision. In the end, these divergent paths proved conducive to growing political dissonance and ideological polarization, which ultimately resulted in the demise of the democratic regime. These important events will be examined in detail in different sections of the book. First, in the next section, I present a general portrayal of the broad political context of the period, thus setting the stage for the more detailed examinations presented in the ensuing chapters.

THE EARLY 1950S AND THE EMERGENCE OF NATIONAL DEVELOPMENTALISM

On January 31, 1951, after having conducted what had been until then the most dynamic and geographically extensive presidential campaign in the history of Brazil, Getúlio Vargas was back in the presidential office ready to pursue an ambitious agenda of economic development and social reform.[45] The incoming president understood clearly that the growing urban working- and lower-class constituencies could prove useful in supporting his bold developmental goals. Such an understanding implied meeting at least some of the growing demands for social inclusion presented by an ever more active and autonomously organized labor segment.[46] The constitution of a politically active electorate in the second quarter of the twentieth century directly impacted these historical trends. Registered voters had grown from about 3.1 percentage points of the total population, in the final years of the so-called Old Republic (1889–1930), to approximately 19 percent by the 1950s; legal and practical restrictions preventing illiterates from voting notwithstanding. While general demographic growth in the decade was around 3 percent nationwide, in the urban environs this rate reached close to

6 percent; and whereas in 1950 the rate of urbanization was about 36 percent, ten years later the percentage of people living in cities reached the historic mark of 45 percent, leading to higher rates of urban political activism.[47]

Aiming at remaining in control of national politics amidst growing opposition and before being deposed in October 1945, Vargas created two of the most important political parties of Brazil during the so-called Populist Republic (1945–1964). The largest and electorally more successful one was called the Social Democratic Party (PSD), which, despite the name, had as key members political leaders who had supported the Estado Novo, particularly in the interior regions of the country. The second party was the Brazilian Labor Party (PTB) whose main supporters were found within sectors of the mostly urban, organized labor movement, which sustained close ties with the federal patronage disbursed by the corporatist union structure coordinated by the Ministry of Labor, Industry and Commerce. These two parties forged a loose political alliance for many of these years, a trend that allowed them considerable political strength to withstand a vocal and resourceful opposition. This opposition included not only much of the established media in the main urban centers, but also the National Democratic Union (UDN), a key opposition party of the time that was largely supported by wealthy and middle-class urban sectors who favored a free-market economic path.

Even with the existence of these formal political arrangements, it is important to point out that political parties were not able to harness support among the growing popular electorate on a consistent and reliable basis. In fact, patron-client political negotiations among the rural and even urban masses and strong political bosses—along the historical lines of the political logic functioning in Brazil since, at least, the dawn of the twentieth century—remained influential in the country despite the significant transformations the nation was undergoing.[48] These elements were largely behind Vargas's continued political significance in the 1950s, whose developmental agenda was based on the perception that the path of industrialization had to be strengthened. He similarly believed that the central state had to play a more direct and decisive role in the national economy so that the required economic growth demanded by a burgeoning urban population could be sustained. Trying to advance these very same positions in several of his many presidential campaign statements, the former dictator repeatedly made the case that "the ultimate goal of improving the national well-being of our people cannot be met unless we find a way to foster a more aggressive program of industrialization that is first and foremost focused on the primary industrial sectors that are the most essential and most promising in terms of returns."[49]

The belief that the country's traditional agrarian-based economy had to be replaced by an industrial one received an important conceptual boost from the different economic and political formulations originating from the new group of Latin American economists who coalesced in the final years of the 1940s with the formation of the Economic Commission for Latin America (ECLA). The agency had been created by the Economic and Social Council of the United Nations in 1948 and is one of the five UN regional economic agencies still in operation—in the present day under the acronym ECLAC, for Economic Commission for Latin America and the Caribbean. ECLA's propositions exerted an enormous intellectual influence in Brazil, particularly among key members of the political and intellectual elite, as well as among business leaders and labor associations, as will be demonstrated in this and upcoming chapters.

Since its inception, the organization's activities were largely influenced by the creative mind and entrepreneurial leadership provided by the Argentine economist Raul Prebisch. Serving as president of that nation's Central Bank in the early '40s, Prebisch sought to address the "peripheral" nature of the economic insertion of Latin American nations in the global economy. Along these conceptual lines, he consistently argued in favor of a process of fast-paced industrialization under the auspices of national governments of the region, which was seen as the most dynamic and effective way to redress the declining economic position faced by Latin American societies. These ideas assumed paramount relevance for those arguing in favor of fast-paced industrialization in Latin America in the 1950s, especially in Brazil.[50] In effect, even though World War II had initially impacted the Brazilian economy in a positive way, offering opportunities to increase the country's exports of food supplies, raw materials, and even textiles, once the period of reconstruction in Europe started taking place in the late 1940s, global sources of capital were primarily channeled to countries directly involved in battleground operations in Europe and Asia.

Inspired by these broad, challenging new economic and political circumstances and imbued with innovative regional intellectual propositions, a new paradigm for promoting national development in the region began to emerge. Largely based on the path of the Import Substitutive Industrialization (ISI) proposed by ECLA, different local governments began espousing in a more coordinated fashion the direct involvement of the national government in the economic activities of their countries. This was to be conducted in a variety of ways, including raising import tariffs on items to be produced domestically and artificially controlling exchange rates even at the cost of rising inflation and governmental deficits. Moreover, the domestic market was to be favored via subsidized credit to private industrial projects and direct public investments in the areas of infrastructure, i.e., energy production, transportation, and communication networks.[51]

In Brazil these new developmental efforts coalesced in the 1950s into an aggressive plan of industrial promotion. The project advocated governmental ownership of basic infrastructural industries and the overall coordination of the national economy by means of a range of different financial incentives. In its core propositions, these concerted policies are frequently described in the nationalist historiography on the period under the term "national developmentalism"—an economic agenda grounded on the notion that industrialization is a *sine qua non* condition for achieving national economic self-sufficiency and, along these lines, political autonomy.[52] This argument derived directly from Prebisch's theory of the "declining terms of trade," which argued that agriculture-based economies would remain in a state of underdevelopment unless a new set of economic policies, particularly pertaining to implementation of a national industrial program, could be implemented.[53] Brazil's national developmentalist agenda was also based on the formulations provided by the Joint Brazil-United States Economic Development Commission (JBUSDC), which had been set by the governments of both nations "to guide the inflow of investment, in its governmental and private (foreign and domestic) forms, as needed to promote the national economic development of the country."[54]

The institutional format of the Joint-Commission was not new and earlier bi-national committees of economic examinations between the U.S. and Brazil had already conducted detailed surveys of the Brazilian economy. The Cooke Commission of 1942, for instance, was an effective attempt at cooperation between these two countries towards the goal of assessing Brazil's economic prospects. Among its main conclusions, this earlier investigative work argued that the Brazilian economy was excessively dependent on commodity exports and that the national government should find ways to finance larger industrial projects. Similarly, the already mentioned Abbink Commission of 1948 restated the need for the Brazilian government to invest more substantially in industrial activities. The concluding reports of both of these earlier studies proved to be very important in providing key intellectual support to the goal of increasing governmental disbursements targeted at reforming the infrastructure of the Brazilian economy. Moreover, along the lines of the so-called Modernization theories, both analyses identified infrastructural bottlenecks as the main hindrances preventing an effective "economic takeoff' of the country. This problem was said to require active economic involvement on the part of the federal government, as no private investor would be able to come up with sufficient funds to redress the situation.[55]

Reiterating some of the conclusions of these earlier investigative works, in 1953 the JBUSDC published a meticulous examination of the Brazilian economy and similarly argued that the country could only pursue a sustainable course of economic growth if infrastructural bottlenecks were eliminated.[56] Considering the limited financial means the Brazilian government had at its disposal, undertaking such a program of investments and reforms represented a major challenge for the second Vargas administration. It was only with the creation of its national development bank that the country obtained the needed institutional means to redress the nation's historical structural lack of capital required to finance a plan of fast-paced industrialization. The National Bank of Economic Development (BNDE), which came into being through the direct action of the federal administration and the constitutional support of the Brazilian National Congress in June 1952, was to serve as the main funding agency for projects related to the areas of transportation networks and energy supply. But, as the decade unfolded, the bank's responsibilities and areas of activity were significantly expanded.[57] And, though created by Vargas after prolonged political negotiations between members of his own cabinet and the three main political parties in the National Congress, the BNDE did not completely fulfill its intended purpose of financing projects of industrial development until JK's presidential tenure, when "the Bank became the natural home for a group of economists who were convinced that economic development required various structural changes and needed to be firmly guided by the central state."[58]

Political continuity throughout the decade can be also found in the Plan of National Economic Rehabilitation and Industrialization attempted under Vargas (another outcome of the JBUSDC) and the developmental projects implemented by the Kubitschek administration under the auspices of the Targets Plan.[59] Equally important, in the concluding report of the Joint-Commission one finds the rationale underlying the projects and the goals that defined the plan itself. For example, the concluding report states that "the ultimate goal of the Joint Commission is to create conditions for, and eliminate obstacles to, increasing the flow of public and private investment, from both foreign and domestic sources, needed to promote and strengthen the economic development of Brazil."[60] Furthermore, though not as important in shaping the drafting of the plan, persistent infrastructural challenges that defined the economic and social scenarios of the 1950s—such as a shortage of energy supply, transportation networks lacking the ability to more efficiently provide food supplies to large urban centers, growing inflation rates, lack of domestic savings, and the growing need to find and attract new foreign sources of capital—were also core elements of the final report of the Joint-Commission.

The developmental projects outlined during Vargas' second presidential tenure and the so-called JK Years were thus inspired by, and sought to address, similar issues and concerns. This was clearly reflected in the list of economic priorities produced by the BNDE-ECLA Joint Study Group, established under Vargas, and the economic plans pursued in the Kubitschek period.[61] This additional study group carried out a series of meetings, from mid-1953 to mid-1955, under the coordination of the Brazilian economists Roberto Campos and Celso Furtado, members of the BNDE and ECLA, respectively, and its concluding reports provided additional elements guiding the constitution of the Targets Plan. Namely, the study group restated the need for attracting foreign sources of capital so that the traditional shortage of domestic savings could be addressed while, at the same time, trying to reduce the deficits in the balance-of-payments caused by the continued rise in the importation of capital goods, primarily by fostering a path of substitutive industrialization.[62]

These ideas exerted a profound influence on key bureaucrats working in governmental agencies that interfaced closely with core industrial associations, particularly the above-mentioned influential figures of Roberto Campos and Lucas Lopes. Campos was a career diplomat who served at the JBUSDC and later became a leading figure at the BNDE during the Kubitschek presidency. For his part, Lopes was a longtime political associate of JK and an experienced engineer and businessperson who had previously worked as energy secretary during JK's governorship in the state of Minas Gerais (1951–1955). Lopes played a leading role in defining major policies, including in the Targets Plan, when he served as president of the BNDE and secretary-general of the National Council of Development (CD)—the cabinet-level agency that coordinated the implementation of all developmental plans of the administration, especially those contained in the plan itself, to be further detailed in Chapter Three.[63]

Industrialists assembled at the National Industrial Confederation (CNI) and especially at the powerful Industrial Federation of the State of São Paulo (FIESP) were also very receptive to several notions underlining the economic policies referred to as national developmentalism. As examined in detail in Chapter Five, already in 1950 the CNI published a special issue of one of its main publications, the *Revista de Estudos Econômicos*, subscribing to the main developmental theses advanced by the Economic Commission for Latin America. The confederation also provided much of the funds needed to support the activities of the BNDE-ECLA Joint Study Group. Along this historical path, the goal of promoting accelerated national industrial development was to become a common conceptual currency present in almost all of the most relevant political, economic, intellectual, and cultural debates taking place in the 1950s in Brazil. Clearly not all parties involved shared similar notions on how to carry out this ambitious and broad objective, and different ideas were advanced by specific political and economic groups, as demonstrated in the different sections of this work.[64]

Thus, despite the ideological differences, it is clear that as the 1950s dawned in Brazil, the search for national development came to signify, at least to the country's leadership, an organized effort carried out by the federal government in the pursuit of fast-paced growth and industrialization. In the remaining pages here, I detail the key elements shaping the contours of the federal administration responsible for implementing Brazil's most coordinated governmental efforts toward achieving these same influential (yet persistently elusive) developmental goals.

THE KUBITSCHEK YEARS AND THE CONSOLIDATION OF NATIONAL DEVELOPMENTALISM

Juscelino Kubitschek de Oliveira was elected president of Brazil in October 1955 on the basis of an electoral platform centered on an ambitious agenda of national economic development. During his presidential campaign, he enumerated key areas of the national economy that should receive special treatment from the federal administration so that fast-paced growth could occur. Formulated by Lucas Lopes with the technical assistance of Roberto Campos, the *General Guidelines of a National Plan of Development* was inspired by the studies and reports produced by earlier examinations and became the basis for the drafting of the Targets Plan.[65] Soon after JK's inauguration on January 31, 1956, the candidate's original platform underwent multiple revisions until a detailed list of thirty targeted areas, distributed within five broad economic sectors, was released in mid-year. This initial list would eventually become known as the Targets Plan, though different versions of the proposal circulated in first months of the administration. Pieces detailing the implementation of each target of the plan were recurrently published throughout the JK Years as a way to update the general public on the achievements of each proposed goal.

The five core sectors of economic activity chosen in the five-year governmental plan for priority targeted investments are listed next. A more detailed and complete list of all of the targets is included in the Appendix, and an analysis of, on the one hand, the process of drafting and implementing key elements of the plan, and, on the other, its impacts across different sectors of the Brazilian society, is presented in Chapter Three:[66]

Energy: The main goal in this area was to double the supply from three million kilowatts within the five years of the administration. In the end, this sector received 42 percent of all (state and private) disbursements made in the period and in several areas the set targets were almost met. For instance, in the target of energy production, 95 percent of the set target for electricity was met, 73 percent in coal production, and 76 percent in oil production.

Transportation: The goals in this sector consisted primarily of reforming and expanding infrastructural transportation networks, which were extremely precarious at the time. This sector received about 30 percent of all investments and its achievements were unevenly distributed. In railroads construction the achievements were below target (less than 40 percent), while the expansion of naval networks reached 84 percent of its proposed goal, and the construction of highways surpassed the target of fifteen thousand kilometers by 24 percent.

Agriculture and Food Supply: Despite its importance in keeping food prices low, this sector received only 3 percent of all monies invested. With the exception of the goal of attracting foreign multinational companies to manufacture heavy agricultural machinery in the country (where the targets were met), the objective of doubling the national food supply of primary food staples achieved dismal results. Food production actually fell in the period, and the target of constructing food warehouses in a nationwide chain to regulate prices reached only 18 percent of the originally proposed target.

Basic Industries: This area involved a major expansion of the industrial sector and about 22 percent of all resources of the Targets Plan were directed to this growing and ever more important sector of the economy. The targets set in the area of steel and metallurgical productions were all surpassed, and special attention was given to the creation of a national auto-making industry, as will be examined in detail in Chapter Three.

Education and Technical Qualification of Labor: This sector involved the creation of a national system of technical schools and research institutes. With the exception of the creation of the Nuclear Energy Research Institute, this sector was largely ignored and under-funded, having received only about 3 percent of all investments.

Given the many accomplishments of the period, most analyses have recurrently characterized the Targets Plan as the most technically qualified and well-coordinated large-scale effort to implement a measurable program of governmental planning towards the goal of development promotion in the history of the country.[67] Some studies have even defined the plan as "the most consistent move towards the goal of industrialization in Brazilian history."[68] Without diminishing the historical innovations provided by the ways in which the plan was devised and deployed, it is important to point out that much of its focus and core elements were guided and indeed grounded on notions originally proposed in earlier documents, including the final report produced by the Joint-Commission in 1953 wherein the concept of structural "bottlenecks" and "germinative areas" of the economy (i.e., areas prone to foster growth in other productive sectors) were of foremost importance. Another important concept proposed in documents produced by earlier commissions and study groups, that of "economic linkages" proved very important in the production and implementation of the plan, particularly in the creation of a large-scale (mostly foreign-owned but with high rates of nationally produced parts) automotive industry, which rapidly became a cornerstone of Kubitschek's administration.

Despite having served as technical adviser of the Brazilian delegation at the JBUSDC, Lucas Lopes' own reading of these important documents was extremely selective. In fact, the examinations advanced by the Joint-Commission, as well as those published by the BNDE-ECLA Joint Study Group were very emphatic in their claims that while investments (including from foreign sources) were needed in order to address pressing infrastructural shortcomings, the country faced serious problems in other areas that merited special attention from state planners. Specifically, both studies conveyed a great deal of concern over the issue of regional economic imbalances between different geographic portions of the country, as well as over the rising and persistent problem of inflation, the lack of investment in public education, and the continued difficulties in managing growing trade deficits.

Revealing of this very idiosyncratic articulation of previous notions, these same points received little to no mention in either the General Guidelines or even in the many versions of the Targets Plan, and, at the end of JK's term in office, different social aspects of the country's economy and society were in worse shape than when the plan had been devised in its original form in 1955, thus perpetuating a reality of profound socio-economic inequality despite the many achievements of the period. These significant shortcomings notwithstanding, the Targets Plan directly impacted close to a quarter of all national economic activities. And while its formulators were quick to acknowledge that they never believed their actions could address all issues hindering the country's development, this was the first time when such a comprehensive list of economic sectors was included in the key priorities defining the policies of a federal Brazilian administration.[69]

Furthermore, though innovative, the underpinnings of the projects carried out by the Kubitschek administration were nonetheless well aligned with traditional economic values shaping the course of modern Brazilian economic history. It is indeed remarkable that when drafting the General Guidelines, Lucas Lopes made sure to explain that, though needed, "governmental intervention [in the economic realm] should not aim at suppressing private initiative but rather serve as the pioneering force coordinating all efforts aimed at economic development, not behaving like an all-absorbing Leviathan."[70] In the same fashion, this influential bureaucrat consistently argued that his approach to national development was, above all, a pragmatic one that did not suffer from what he called the critical "ideological orientation" manifest in the reflection produced at the ECLA.[71] The need to convey a moderate political stance seemed very important to Lucas Lopes, a position that could be extended to Kubitschek himself as he only agreed to publish the centerpiece document of his presidential campaign goals after he received the stamp of approval from Olympio Mourão Filho, one of the conservative military leaders behind the military coup of March 1964.[72] Another central figure in the formulation and implementation of the Targets Plan, the influential career diplomat Roberto Campos (who became even more influential during the military regime implemented in 1964) also defended targeted and limited public investment, rather than more structural reforms (e.g., land reform).[73]

Despite the reiterated defense of a traditional market-oriented approach to development advanced by its authors, the General Guidelines is a remarkable document for being so in sync with many of the ideas previously advanced in several ECLA publications. Especially relevant in showing the line of intellectual continuity between the theses propounded by the agency and those espoused by JK's closest advisers was the notion that the central government should play an ever more assertive and better coordinated role in the process of national development. This was said to be particularly important for economies transitioning from what was called a "semi-colonial state" toward one defined by a complete economic, and therefore political, emancipation.[74] This proposition was to become central to the intellectual reflection produced by a group of nationalist intellectuals working at the state-sponsored Higher Institute of Brazilian Studies (ISEB) in the final years of the decade, as is further examined in Chapter Four. Similar notions that also influenced the work of ISEB included the argument that only by fostering an accelerated expansion of substitutive industries (particularly in the area of durable goods, such as automobiles) would any underdeveloped nation be able to achieve a sustainable course of economic development.[75]

As seen, the rich literature on the JK Years has consistently claimed that Kubitschek's ability to implement his ambitious developmental plan was largely related to the creation of new, said-to-be politically insulated bureaucratic agencies placed under the president's direct personal control, so that the "give-and-take" logic of the Brazilian patrimonial political system could be kept in check. Buttressing this view is the fact that, on his first day in office (February 1, 1956), Kubitschek created the National Council of Development (CD), an autonomous bureaucratic agency devised to coordinate the implementation of all projects of his administration, especially those of the Targets Plan.[76] In pursing this technocratic approach, JK chose to rely on close, reliable advisers, such as Lucas Lopes and Roberto Campos, for the execution of his agenda of fast economic growth. Yet, as demonstrated in Chapter Three, despite the legal insularity of the Council of Development and in light of its alleged unique levels of bureaucratic efficiency, some of the main achievements of the Targets Plans seem to derive more from alternative variables than those normally advanced in the available literature. In fact, the very area normally described as quintessentially revealing JK's remarkable administrative technical efficiency—the creation of a national automobile industrial sector—was the focus of large debates encompassing most sectors of organized Brazilian society.

Conceptual and ideological differences on the developmental path the country should pursue and their role on both the achievements and shortcomings of the period notwithstanding, Kubitschek's economic agenda undoubtedly exerted a broad political appeal, particularly among members of the most influential socio-economic and political forces, including industrial elites and the urban middle and working classes.[77] A less polarizing political figure than the former dictator Vargas, JK was clearly much more able than his predecessor to neutralize the more conservative members of the civilian and military cadres. Similarly, as some of the most influential political examinations of the period have claimed, JK's ability to maintain stability while pressing for rapid industrialization derived from his "remarkable ability to find something for everyone, while avoiding direct conflict with his enemies."[78]

The main elements of the developmental course pursued in the JK Years were indeed defined by a conciliatory political arrangement among the most influential sectors of the national elites, including the traditional agrarian exporting sectors, as no intrinsic and unsolvable conflict existed between them and the influential industrial associations.[79] Also revealing of the restrained political tone and moderate course his administration pursued, Kubitschek saw national development as a "fundamental and unavoidable national objective [considering that] our fast-paced demographic growth demands that we become an industrialized economy, [and] our very sovereignty requires such an economic accomplishment capable of leading us beyond our still lingering colonial plantation status." By the same token, in the president's own words, "our own freedom and security depend on our successful economic development."[80]

Along these historical lines, JK adamantly defended the idea that promoting national development was an indispensable task in preventing social upheavals caused by widespread levels of poverty and the enormous inequality that characterized Brazil in the 1950s. In his view, "the social stability of our country can be sustained only by achieving fast economic progress" as only in such a new domestic scenario "the enemies of liberty would not be able to prosper in the substrata of poverty."[81] Moreover, as his administration faced growing international challenges in pursuing his goals, JK expanded his domestic focus to include the Latin American region in his quest for addressing what he called "the problems of poverty and underdevelopment"—as will be detailed in Chapter Two. For now, it should be stated that though certainly boldly pushing the boundaries of domestic and even inter-American relations, JK nonetheless shared elements of the conservative stance imbued in U.S. policies towards the region at the time.

This can clearly be seen, for instance, in Kubitschek's official pronouncement opening the parliamentary session of 1957, when he explicitly articulated the view that "strengthening our economic basis by means of attracting foreign sources of capital will prevent, once and for all, the dissemination of subversive ideas among our people."[82] Economic growth was, in this sense, defined as a means to achieving not only greater material (rather than social) well-being, but also to promote domestic order and political stability. Similarly, fast-paced national development, or rather fast-paced economic growth, as he and his close advisors at the Council of Development more commonly phrased the issue, was thus considered to be the only real assurance that what were defined as foreign, exotic ideologies (by which they primarily meant Communism) could be kept at bay. Similarly, in his first message to the National Congress in 1956, JK stated that "[d]evelopment is the key to the consolidation of a free and powerful nation capable of reciprocating in prosperity, justice, and security [. . .] [and] the struggle in defense of our Christian values, love of liberty and democracy."[83]

His conciliatory approach notwithstanding, Kubitschek consistently argued that nationalism and development were notions closely interrelated in an almost mutually interdependent fashion. As he objectively defined it, "our nationalism aims at placing our nation at an equal level with the other nations in the world. It is not a mere political, fanatic ploy, but a constructive effort towards specific objectives, multiple in appearance, but that are all fused together in the one and only goal, that of our development."[84] In the end, seen as the quintessential optimistic politician of the developmentalist era, JK's compromising political style, which relied heavily on the cooptation of any potential source of opposition—by means of monetary compensations or administrative sinecures dispensed to disgruntled economic sectors (e.g., coffee planters), politicians, and military officers—proved conducive to the consolidation of an ambitious developmental agenda amidst a conservative public opinion and political culture.[85]

Kubitschek's moderate course harkened back to his political trajectory in Minas Gerais, an important Brazilian state where—given its historical absence of a dominant political force and the need for constant political negotiations toward advancing any transformative governmental agenda—political moderation and the art of reaching a compromise has been valued as key to one's political success.[86] In fact, both during his tenure as mayor of the capital city of Belo Horizonte in the early 1940s and his governorship in the first half of the 1950s, JK learned that the role the government could play in pursuing any ambitious administrative goal (such as radical urban reforms, as well as the expansion of the state's energy supply) required the incorporation, approval, and support of private interests including contractors, powerful commercial and industrial business associations, and influential local politicians.[87]

This view reflects a very ingrained perspective on economic development shaping the recent history of Minas Gerais, where since the 1930s, echoing national trends taking place in the same time period, successive administrations had expanded the role of the government in the economic planning and execution of developmental policies. Most of these involved the input provided by local commercial associations, but, increasingly, foreign sources of private capital played an important part in the process of industrialization that local planners and decision-makers pursued.[88] Much of these earlier administrative experiences were later implemented at the national level, and considering Lucas Lopes's role as his secretary in key administrative positions in that state, JK's political pronouncements as governor already iterated the need for the government to play a decisive role in attacking structural deficiencies in the state's economy so that private investors were motivated to act as effective entrepreneurs.

It was also during his earlier experience as governor that Kubitschek rehearsed his dynamic and enthusiastic leadership style, including the very effective and exuberant communication skills that also marked his presidential term. To exemplify this last point, one could recall that in his final speech as governor on January 31, 1955, which was broadcasted on the radio to the entire state, JK stated that "if we had done a lot, we only did the indispensable for a state that can no longer afford to have an economy based on raw materials, which is the commerce of poverty. History urges us to open the doors for a new tomorrow."[89] Likewise, as president JK consistently impressed even members of the U.S. diplomatic corps with his "unusual talent for public relations and great ability to make, at the right time, the best gesture calculated to appeal to popular sentiment."[90]

Adding to his international appeal, Kubitschek was always very clear about the role of private sources of capital from other countries and, as president-elect, he travelled to several European countries and the U.S. to "show the world our potential as an economic partner."[91] Similarly, in his inaugural address to the first course aimed at training public servants of the Ministry of Finance, another outcome of the BNDE-ECLA Joint Study Group, JK was very clear in stating that:

> Foreign sources of capital are not only welcomed but highly needed. This can no longer be the focus of emotional debates, but needs to be treated exclusively as a technical matter. Attracting private investors from abroad in no way diminishes our nationalism given that the true nationalist is the one who tries to expedite the course of economic development of his nation, without which we will remain weak and poor.[92]

By the same token, when speaking to the first graduating class of the Graduate Program on Studies of Brazilian Problems taught at the ISEB, wherein heated debates concerning the role to be played by foreign investors in the promotion of development took place, JK reiterated the notion that

> we are nationalists not because we want to close the country to foreign influences but rather because we seek to place Brazil in close contact with current ideas shaping the world [. . .], and while we defend our own national traditions, we also defend the need to attract massive assistance from abroad, both in terms of technology and capital which are indispensable to our development.[93]

Thus, by consistently resorting to an optimism concerning the nation's future, Kubitschek paved the way for a moderate, market-oriented, and essentially pragmatic course of national development promotion, which implied fast-paced industrialization on the basis of a close association between state, domestic, and foreign private sources of capital.

Ironically, in tandem with the ideology of the very military regime initiated in 1964, particularly of its propounded "economic miracle" of the early 1970s, JK defined national development as a *moral* imperative given the security threat posed by continued poverty. Indicative of the many contradictions of the time, though pursued for nationalist reasons, the developmental path also appealed to foreign investors. Moreover, though innovative and bold, these policies did not seek to transform but rather to coexist with the traditional patrimonial logic of the Brazilian state. In effect, despite being very influential, this perspective on national development did not represent the broad range of views existing among different segments of Brazilian society, leading to serious consequences to the functioning of the political system, as will be demonstrated in upcoming chapters.

CONCLUDING REMARKS

The 1950s represented a new phase in the historical path of national development in Brazil. Throughout these transformative years public policies and intellectual debates assumed a developmental tone, and hindrances to rapid economic growth were increasingly judged through new interpretive lenses that associated the very concept of nationalism with the goal of fast-paced, state-led industrial promotion. The central notion supporting this new developmental perspective was that accelerated growth and industrialization would provide historic levels of socio-economic well-being to the entire nation—which was taken to be a homogenous whole, deep socio-economic cleavages notwithstanding—as well as associated political stability and diplomatic autonomy.

The literature on the so-called developmentalist decade has largely posited an image of ideological convergence structured on the basis of an interclass political compromise supporting rapid economic growth, as well as on the alleged consensual, optimistic ideological outlook disseminated by key national political leaders. As indicated above, this portrayal requires further examination given that no consensual definition of national development existed in the period and that different social segments were becoming mobilized in advancing their own development-related views and demands. Moreover, as will become evident in the course of this study, despite the unprecedented levels of political, ideational, and administrative coordination of the period, it is clear that the two most important elected leaders of the period, Getúlio Vargas and especially Juscelino Kubitschek held conformist political positions in regards to the reasons for promoting fast economic growth: namely preventing large-scale social upheavals caused by widespread domestic poverty.

Before the different positions on national development held by some of the most influential government officials, politically engaged public intellectuals, business associations, and segments of organized urban labor are examined (a task I undertake in Chapters Three, Four, Five, and Six, respectively), an analysis of the international context within which the Brazilian experiences of development promotion occurred is in order. This will help situate the concepts and projects formulated in Brazil within the broader context of related events taking place on a global scale during a time of growing international economic and political interdependence.

With this goal in mind, in the upcoming chapter I map out the reciprocal commonalities and influences of the trends and policies occurring at the international level and those proposed by Brazilian intellectuals and governmental authorities. Beyond this initial objective, a detailed analysis of the main diplomatic propositions undertaken by the Kubitschek administration is provided. The main objective in doing so is to demonstrate that the developmental drive of the 1950s was becoming so influential among governmental officials that the main elements of the international political behavior the country advanced in those years was also chiefly defined by the goal of fast-paced development promotion.

NOTES

1. One of the best analyses in English of this social stability structured on the basis of a corporatist-paternalistic legal and political order is Barbara Weinstein, *For Social Peace in Brazil: Industrialists and the Remaking of the Working Class in São Paulo, 1920–1964*, (Chapel Hill: University of North Carolina Press, 1996).
2. Marcelo de Paiva Abreu, "Crise, Crescimento e Modernização Autoritária: 1930–1945," in *A Ordem do Progresso: Cem Anos de Política Econômica Republicana, 1889–1989,* ed. Marcelo de Paiva Abreu (Rio de Janeiro: Campus, 1990), 73–104. For the general context of the period, see Bóris Fausto, *O Brasil Republicano: Economia e Cultura (1930–1964)*, Coleção História Geral da Civilização Brasileira (São Paulo: Difel, 1984).
3. For detailed numbers, see Presidência da República, *Relatório Geral de Exportações e Importações, 1947–1960.* (Rio de Janeiro, 1960).
4. Sérgio Besserman Vianna, "Duas Tentativas de Estabilização, 1951–1954," in *A Ordem do Progresso: Cem Anos de Política Econômica Republicana, 1889–1989*, ed. Marcelo de Paiva Abreu (Rio de Janeiro: Campus, 1990), 123–50.
5. See *Plano Cafeeiro para Safra 1957/1958* (Rio de Janeiro: Brazilian Coffee Institute, 1957), Fundo Lucas Lopes, LL bnde 1957.04.24, CPDOC Archive, Getúlio Vargas Foundation in Rio de Janeiro. For estimated expenditures on coffee price policies, see also Luiz Orenstein and Antonio Claudio Sochaczewski, "Democracia com Desenvolvimento: 1956–1961," in *A Ordem do Progresso: Cem Anos de Política Econômica Republicana, 1889–1989*, ed. Marcelo de Paiva Abreu (Rio de Janeiro: Campus, 1990), 191. For a comparative analysis of similar economic challenges faced by Mexico in these same years see Peter Evans and Gary Gereffi, "Foreign Investment and Dependent Development: Comparing Brazil and Mexico," in *Brazil and Mexico: Patterns in Late Development*, ed. Sylvia Ann Hewlett and Richard S. Weinert (Philadelphia: Institute for the Study of Human Issues, 1982), 116–68.
6. United Nations Economic Commission of Latin America, *Economic Bulletin for Latin America* 3, no. 2, (Santiago: October 1958), 6.
7. See repeated letters sent from coffee producers associations, such as Sociedade Rural Brasileira, addressed to Kubitschek himself or to Lucas Lopes when the latter served as finance minister. Fundo Lucas Lopes, LL mf 1958.06.24, CPDOC Archive.
8. Ministério do Planejamento e Coordenação Geral, *A Industrialização Brasileira: Diagnósticos e Perpectivas, Estudo Especial do Programa Estratégico de Desenvolvimento, 1968–1970.* (Brasília, 1969).
9. Some of the most important works by key ideologues of the Estado Novo who were responsible for many of its legal reforms include Francisco L. S. Campos, *O Estado Nacional: sua estructura e seu conteúdo ideológico* (Rio de Janeiro: José Olympo, 1940); and by Francisco de Oliveira Vianna, *História Social da*

Economia Capitalista no Brasil (Niteroi: Editora da UFF, 1988) and *Instituições Políticas Brasileiras* (Rio de Janeiro: José Olympo, 1949).

10. The most important works advancing an economic argument include Baer, *Industrialization and Economic Development*; Furtado, *Formação Econômica da América Latina*; Hirschman, *The Strategy of Economic Development*; Caio Prado, Jr., *História Econômica do Brasil* (São Paulo: Brasiliense, 1970); Roberto C. Simonsen, *A Evolução Industrial do Brasil e Outros Estudos* (São Paulo: Cia Editora Nacional, 1973); and Tavares, *Da Substituição de importações ao capitalismo financeiro*. Alternatively, works offering a sociological frame of analysis include Faoro, *Os Donos do Poder*; Fernandes, *A Revolução Burguesa no Brazil*; and Ianni, *Estado e Planejamento no Brasil*. Studies stressing the role played by the central government in promoting an incipient industrialization that occurred prior to the 1930s include Topik, *The Political Economy* and Versiani, "Cotton Textile Industry".
11. See Dean, *The Industrialization of São Paulo*; Thomas H. Holloway, *Immigrants on the Land: Coffee and Society in Brazil, 1886–1934* (Chapel Hill: University of North Carolina Press, 1980); Cardoso de Mello, *O Capitalismo Tardio*; Carlos Manuel Pelaez, *História da Industrialização Brasileira: crítica `a teoria estruturalista do Brasil* (Rio de Janeiro: APEC, 1972); Stanley J. Stein, *The Brazilian Cotton Manufacture: Textile Enterprise in an Underdeveloped Area, 1850–1950* (Cambridge; Harvard University Press, 1957); Suzigan, *Indústria Brasileira*; and Flávio Rabelo Versiani, *A Década de 20 na Industrialização Brasileira* (Rio de Janeiro: IPEA, 1987); and Emilia Viotti da Costa, *The Brazilian Empire: Myths and Histories* (Chicago: University of Chicago Press, 1985).
12. The first position has been argued in key works such as Benevides, *O governo Kubitschek*; Draibe, *Rumos e metamorfoses*; Peter Evans, *Embedded Autonomy: States and Industrial Transformation* (Princeton: Princeton University Press, 1995); Geddes, *Politician's Dilemma,* Lafer, *JK e o Programa de Metas*; Leff, *Economic Policy-Making;* Luciano Martins, *Pouvoir et Développement Economique: Formation et évolution des structures politiques au Brésil* (Paris: Éditions Anthropos, 1976). The second argument has been advanced in more recent studies, including by Caren Addis, "Cooperação e desenvolvimento no setor de autopeças," in *De JK a FHC: a reinvenção dos carros,* ed. Glauco Arbix and Mauro Zilbovicius (Sao Paulo: Scritta, 1997), 133–58 and *Taking the Wheel*; Boschi, *Elites Industriais*; Cardoso, *Empresário industrial*; Diniz, *Empresario, Estado e Capitalismo*; Leopoldi, *Política e Interesses*; Sonia Regina de Mendonça, *Estado e Economia no Brasil: Opções de Desenvolvimento* (Rio de Janeiro: Graal, 1988); Shapiro, *Engines of Growth*; and Loudes Sola, *Ideias Econômicas, Decisões Políticas: Desenvolvimento, Estabilidade, Populismo* (São Paulo: Edusp, 1998).
13. The concept of late, late-comers has been proposed by Hirschman as a counterpoint to Alexander Gerschenkron's notions of the late-comers of the end of the nineteenth century. For more, see Albert O. Hirschman, "The Political Economy of Import-Substituting Industrialization in Latin America," *Quarterly Journal of Economics* 82, no. 1, (Feb 1968), 1–32; and Gerschenkron, *Economic Backwardness*.
14. Caren Addis, "A Clash of Paradigms: Recent Interpretations of Brazilian Development," *Latin American Research Review* 32, no. 3 (1997), 123–39; Werner Baer, "Import Substitution Industrialization in Latin America: Experiences and Interpretations," *Latin American Research Review* 7, no. 1 (Spring 1972), 95–122; Luiz C. Bresser-Pereira and Marcia Van Dyke, "Six Interpretations of the Brazilian Social Formation," *Latin American Perspectives* 11, no. 11, Brazil in Crisis (Winter 1984), 35–72.

15. Further information on this can be found in Fassy, *JK*; Flavio Limoncic, "A Civilização do Automóvel: a instalação da indústria automobilística no Brasil e a via brasileira para uma improvável modernidade fordista, 1956–1961" (MA thesis, UFRJ, 1997); Pedro S. Malan, "Relações Econômicas Internacionais do Brasil, 1945–1964," in *O Brasil Republicano: Economia e Cultura (1930–1964)*, Coleção História Geral da Civilização Brasileira (São Paulo: Difel, 1984); Lúcio Meira, *A Industrialização e o Problema Agrícola no Brasil.* (Belo Horizonte: UFMG, 1960); and Mario Henrique Simonsen and Roberto Campos, *A Nova Economia Brasileira* (Rio de Janeiro: José Olympo, 1974).
16. Sérgio Besserman Vianna & AndréVillela, "O Pós-Guerra," in *Economia Brasileira Contemporânea (1945–2004)*, ed. Fábio Giambiagi, et al. (Rio de Janeiro: Campus, 2005), 21–44.
17. See Marcelo de Paiva Abreu, *The Brazilian Economy, 1945–1964,* Texto para Discussão no. 414, Departamento de Economia (Rio de Janeiro: Catholic University, 2000); and Fausto Saretta, "O Governo Dutra na Transição Capitalista no Brasil," in *História Econômica do Brasil Contemporâneo*, eds. Tamas Szmrecsanyi and Wilson Suzigan (São Paulo: Edusp, 2002), 99–120.
18. Institute of Inter-American Affairs, Foreign Operations Administration, *Report of the Joint Brazil-United States Technical Commission.* (Washington, D.C., 1949), 34–36.
19. Abreu, *The Brazilian Economy*, 9.
20. Institute of Inter-American Affairs, Foreign Operations Administration, *The Development of Brazil: Report of the Joint Brazil-United States Economic Development Commission* (Washington, D.C.: 1953).
21. Lessa, *Fifteen Years*, 159.
22. Leff, *Economic Policy-Making*, 16.
23. Vianna, "Duas Tentativas de Estabilização," 132–33. See also Sérgio Besserman Vianna, *A Politica Econômica no Segundo Governo Vargas (1951–1954)* (Rio de Janeiro: BNDE, 1987) and Maria Celina D'Araújo, *O Segundo Governo Vargas 1951–1954: democracia, partidos e crise política* (Rio de Janeiro: J. Zahar, 1982).
24. Maria Antonieta P. Leopoldi, "O difícil caminho do meio: Estado, burguesia e industrialização no segundo governo Vargas (1951–54)," in *Vargas e a Crise dos Anos 50*, ed. Angela de Castro Gomes (Rio de Janeiro: Relume Dumara, 1994), 164.
25. Banco de Desenvolvimento Econômico e Social, *Entrevista com Rômulo de Almeida. Projeto Memória Primeira Fase* (Rio de Janeiro: BNDE/Finame, 1982), 12.
26. Joseph L. Love, *A Construção do Terceiro Mundo: Teorias do Subdesenvolvimento na Romênia e no Brasil* (São Paulo: Paz e Terra, 1998).
27. The best narrative of these events is found in Skidmore, *Politics in Brazil*, especially in Chapter Three.
28. Getúlio Vargas, "Mensagem Presidencial ao Congresso Nacional na abertura da sessão legislativa de 1951," in Vargas, ed., *O Governo Trabalhista no Brasil* (Rio de Janeiro: José Oympio, 1952), 222.
29. Abreu, *The Brazilian Economy*, 25.
30. Superintendência da Moeda e do Crédito, *Relatório do Banco do Brasil* (Rio de Janeiro, 1964), 221.
31. See Peter Evans, *Dependent Development: The Alliance of Multinational, State, and Local Capital in Brazil* (Princeton: Princeton University Press, 1979); Rogério Proença Leite, *A Dupla Face do Nacionalismo: Ideologia, Discurso e Dominação em Kubitschek e Medici* (Recife: Editora da UFPE, 1995);

and Annibal Villela and Werner Baer, *O Setor Privado Nacional: Problemas e Políticas* (Rio de Janeiro: IPEA, 1980).

32. Carlos Lessa was one of the first to examine the economic accomplishments of the developmental decade and to highlight important differences between the developmental approach of the second Vargas administration and the one pursued under Kubitschek, but in his study the main difference is one of degree of governmental planning toward the goal of industrialization. The 1950s would therefore witness a gradual intensification of the search for state-led, fast-paced substitutive industrialization. See Lessa, *Fifteen Years of Economic Policy in Brazil*. See also Octavio Ianni, *Crisis in Brazil*. (New York: Columbia Univeristy Press, 1970).
33. The best description published in English of the events surrounding Vargas's suicide and the notion that his second tenure of power was not defined by an anti-foreign involvement attitude in his development agenda is still Skidmore's classic work, *Politics in Brazil*. See also Boschi, *Elites Industriais*; Diniz, *Empresário, Estado*; Pedro C. Dutra Fonseca, *Vargas e o Capitalismo em Construção, 1906–1954* (São Paulo: Brasiliense, 1989); and Leopoldi, *Política e Interesses*.
34. Juscelino Kubitschek de Oliveira, *Mensagem ao Congresso Nacional*. (Rio de Janeiro: Departamento de Imprensa Nacional, 1957), 246.
35. Evans and Gereffi, "Foreign Investment," 122.
36. Marshal C. Eakin, *Brazil: The Once and Future Country* (New York: St Martin's Griffin, 1998), 122.
37. Presidência da República, *Relatório Geral do Conselho do Desenvolvimento*, vol. 4:5.
38. See note # 3 in the introductory chapter of the book.
39. See Armijo, "Public Policymaking"; and Edson de Oliveira Nunes and Barbara Geddes. "Dilemmas of State-Led Modernization in Brazil," in *State and Society in Brazil*, ed. John Wirth, et al. (Boulder: Westview Press, 1987), 103–45.
40. Angela de Castro Gomes, ed., *O Brasil de JK* (Rio do Janeiro: FGV, 1991); Wander Melo Miranda, ed., *Anos JK: Margens da Modernidade* (São Paulo: Imprensa Oficial, 2002); Santos, *A classe média vai ao paraíso*. Praise-filled depictions of the period notwithstanding, it is important to recall that Kubitschek was elected president in October 1955, with only a small plurality (37 percent) of votes and that throughout his tenure, he had to resort to constant acts of negotiation in order to remain in power as well as to carry out his personal economic agenda, as will be detailed in upcoming chapters.
41. Tentative definitions have been provided by Michael Conniff in *Latin American Populism* and *Populism in Latin America*. (Tuscaloosa: University of Alabama Press, 1999).
42. These dynamics will be examined in detail in Chapter Six.
43. Erickson, *The Brazilian Corporative State*; Juarez Rubens Brandão Lopes, *Sociedade Industrial no Brasil* (São Paulo: Difel, 1964); José Albertino Rodrigues, *Sindicato e Desenvolvimento no Brasil* (São Paulo: Difel, 1968); Leôncio Martins Rodrigues, *Industrialização e Atitudes Operárias* (São Paulo: Brasiliense, 1970); and Azis Simão, *Sindicato e Estado no Brasil* (São Paulo: Dominus, 1966).
44. Ricardo Antunes, *Classe operária, sindicatos e partidos no Brasil* (São Paulo: Cortes Editora, 1982); Armando Boito Jr., *Sindicalismo de Estado no Brasil* (Campinas: Ed. Unicamp, 1991); Renato Colistete, *Labour Relations and Industrial Performance in Brazil: Greater São Paulo, 1945–1960* (New York: Palgrave, 2001); Paulo Fontes, *Trabalhadores e cidadãos: Nitro-Química,*

a fábrica e as lutas operárias nos anos 50 (São Paulo: Annablume, 1997); Timothy Fox Harding, *The Political History of Organized Labor in Brazil* (Palo Alto: Stanford University Press, 1973); John Humphrey, *Capitalist Control and Workers' Struggle in the Brazilian Auto Industry* (Princeton: Princeton University Press, 1982); Antonio Luigi Negro, *Linhas de Montagem—o industrialismo nacional-desenvolvimentista e a sindicalização dos trabalhadores* (São Paulo: Boitempo, 2004); Jose R. G. Ramalho, *Estado Patrão e luta operária: o caso FNM* (Rio de Janeiro: Paz e Terra, 1989); Salvador A. Sandoval, *Social Change and Labor Unrest in Brazil since 1945* (Boulder: Westview, 1993).

45. D'Araújo, *O Segundo Governo Vargas*; and Alzira Alves de Abreu and Israel Beloch, eds., *Dicionário Histórico-Biográfico Brasileiro Pós -30* (Rio de Janeiro: Editora da FGV, 2001).
46. Célia Maria Leite Costa, et al., *Impasse na Democracia Brasileira, 1951–1954: Coletânea de Documentos* (Rio de Janeiro: Editora da Fundacao Getulio Vargas, 1983); and Edson de Oliveira Nunes, *Dilemmas of State-Led Modernization in Brazil,* Serie Estudos, No. 39 (Rio de Janeiro: IUPERJ, 1985).
47. Ministério do Planejamento e Coordenação Geral, *Programa Estratégico de Desenvolvimento, 1968–1970* (Brasília, 1968), vol. 2: Chapter Fourteen.
48. See Victor Nunes Leal, *Coronelismo, Enxada e Voto* (Rio de Janeiro: Forense, 1948) and Maria Isaura Pereira de Queiroz, *O Mandonismo local na vida política brasileira* (São Paulo: Alfa e Ômega, 1976).
49. Getúlio Vargas, *A Campanha Presidencial* (Rio de Janeiro: José Olympio, 1951), 29.
50. For an overview of the commission's endeavors, see Celso Furtado, *A Fantasia Organizada* (Rio de Janeiro: Paz e Terra, 1985); Love, *A Construção do Terceiro Mundo*; and Octavio Rodrigues, *Teoria do Subdesenvolvimento da Cepal* (Rio de Janeiro: Forense Universitária, 1981).
51. One of the best descriptions of these events is found in Victor Bulmer-Thomas, *The Economic History of Latin America since Independence* (Cambridge: Cambridge University Press, 2003), particularly Chapter Nine.
52. Though repeatedly described as a set of economic policies, national-developmentalism also entailed a set of ideological propositions, which will be examined in detail in Chapter Four. It should also be noted that one of the most influential political narratives of these events alternatively labels this developmental agenda as "developmental nationalism"—see Skidmore, *Politics in Brazil.* I have alternatively decided to use "national developmentalism" here given its more common use in Brazil and in order to stress the developmental elements of the policies rather than the nationalist ones, which were indeed a topic of divisive debate in the period.
53. Raul Prebisch, *Interpretacion del proceso de desarollo latinoamericano* (Santiago: Comision Economica para America Latina, 1949).
54. Guido Mantega, *Desenvolvimento e Politica Econômica no Brasil: Os Anos 50*, Relatório de Pesquisa, no. 22 (São Paulo: Escola de Administração de Empresas de São Paulo, Fundação Getúlio Vargas, 1982), 14.
55. Details on this can be found in Alexander, *Juscelino Kubitscheck* and in Eduardo Campos Scaletsky, Dois projetos para o Brasil: 1945–1954: uma análise dos projetos da Missão Abbink, da Comissão Mista Brasil-Estados Unidos e do Grupo Misto BNDE-CEPAL" (MA thesis, UFRGS, 1988).
56. Fundo Roberto Campos, RC e ae 1951.06.06/ae, 1951–1953, CPDOC Archive.
57. Fundo Roberto Campos, RC e bnde 1952.10.30, folder 2, CPDOC Archive.
58. Hirschman, *Journeys Toward Progress*, 73.

59. Conselho do Desenvolvimento, *Documento de Trabalho. Número 1. Relatório Reservado.* (Rio de Janeiro: Presidência da República, 1956).
60. Institute of Inter-American Affairs, Foreign Operations Administration, *The Development of Brazil*, preface.
61. Lessa, "Fifteen Years of Economic Policy," 167–70.
62. Grupo Misto de Estudos BNDE-CEPAL, *Análise e Projeções do Desenvolvimento Econômico* (Rio de Janeiro: BNDE, 1957), 6–9.
63. Fundo Roberto Campos, RC e bnde 1952.09.29/e/bnde, CPDOC Archive.
64. For more on the different views and the political groups involved in the debates regarding the elaboration and implementation of projects of national development in the 1950s see Ricardo Bielchowsky, *O Pensamento Econômico Brasileiro: O Ciclo Ideológico do Desenvolvimentismo* (Rio de Janeiro: Contraponto, 2004).
65. Juscelino Kubitschek de Oliveira, *Diretrizes Gerais do Plano Nacional de Desenvolvimento* (Belo Horizonte: Livraria Oscar Nicolai, 1955), 32.
66. It is important to note that on the 1955 campaign trail, after being questioned by one member of the audience at one of his political rallies, Kubitschek decided to include in the Targets Plan (as the Thirty-First Target, called the Synthesis Target) the construction and the transference of the national capital from Rio de Janeiro to a newly constructed city in the heartlands of the country, which would be called Brasília.
67. See Celso Lafer, "O Planejamento no Brasil—Observações sobre o Plano de Metas (1956–1961)," in *Planejamento no Brasil,* ed. Betty Mindlin Lafer (São Paulo: Perspectiva, 1970), 29–50; Ricardo Fonseca Rabelo, "Plano de Metas e a consolidação do capitalismo industrial no Brasil," *E&G Economia e Gestão* 2&3, no. 4&5 (Dec 2002/Jul 2003), 44–55; and Alberto Teixeira, *Planejamento Público: de Getúlio a JK (1930–1960)* (Fortaleza: IPLANCE, 1997).
68. Lessa, "Fifteen Years," 167.
69. See Lopes' abridged memoir published by his son Rodrigo Lopes in *Sonho e Razão: Lucas Lopes, o Planejador de JK* (São Paulo: Arx. 2006).
70. Kubitschek, *Diretrizes Gerais*, 15.
71. Lopes, *Sonho e Razão*, 112.
72. Juscelino Kubitschek, *Notes of Draft of Diretrizes Gerais do Plano Nacional de Desenvolvimento Sent to Coronel Olympio Mourão Filho,* Fundo Lucas Lopes, LL pi ISEB 1955.00.00, CPDOC Archive.
73. Simonsen and Campos, *A Nova Economia Brasileira*, 53; and Furtado, *A Fantasia Organizada*, 158.
74. Kubitschek, *Diretrizes Gerais*, 15.
75. Ibid., 16–18.
76. See *Presidential Decree, number 38.744, of February 1, 1956.*
77. Alexander, *Juscelino Kubitschek*, 163.
78. Skidmore, *Politics in Brazil*, 167.
79. Lafer, *JK e o Programa de Metas*, 45.
80. Juscellino Kubitschek de Oliveira, *A Marcha do Amanhecer* (São Paulo: Best-sellers Livros, 1962), 112.
81. Ibid., 113.
82. Juscelino Kubitschek de Oliveira, *Mensagem ao Congresso Nacional* (Rio de Janeiro: Departamento de Imprensa Nacional, 1957), 79.
83. Juscelino Kubitschek de Oliveira, *Mensagem ao Congresso Nacional.* (Rio de Janeiro: Departamento de Imprensa Nacional, 1956), 47.
84. Kubitschek, *A Marcha do Amanhecer*, 199.
85. Sheldon Maram, "Juscelino Kubitschek and the Politics of Exuberance, 1956–1961," *Luso-Brazilian Review* 27, no. 1 (1990), 31–45.

86. For the historical roots of this alleged political culture, see Amilcar Vianna Martins Filho, *O Segredo de Minas: a origem do estilo mineiro de fazer política (1889–1930)* (Belo Horizonte: Crisálida, 2009). An additional work that demonstrates the historical tradition of the role the state government played in the development of Minas Gerais, and how the state's political and technocratic leadership were essential in this process is Angela de Castro Gomes, ed., *Minas e os Fundamentos do Brasil Moderno* (Belo Horizonte: Editora UFMG, 2005).
87. The process of industrialization in the city of Belo Horizonte required constant negotiations between political and economic groups. This frequently involved the work of extended family ties and connections, and in the end resulted in having the local state government play the leading role in the process. A fascinating analysis of these events can be found in Marshall C. Eakin, *Tropical Capitalism: The Industrialization of Belo Horizonte* (New York: Palgrave, 2002). A similar argument is advanced in Frances Hagopian, *Traditional Politics and Regime Change in Brazil* (Cambridge: Cambridge University Press, 1996).
88. Clélio Campolina Muniz, "Estado e Capital Estrangeiro na Industrialização Mineira" (MA thesis, University of Campinas, 1978); Governo do Estado de Minas Gerais, *Plano de Recuperação Econômia e Fomento da Produção* (Belo Horizonte, 1947); Alexandre Rios Marques, *Evolução Histórica do Planejamento Econômico no Brazil e em Minas Gerais—do Nacional-Desenvolvimentismo ao Neo-Liberalism* (Belo Horizonte: Fundação João Pinheiro, 2002).
89. Juscelino Kubitschek de Oliveira, *Quatro Anos no Governo de Minas Gerais (1951–1955): Síntese das Realizações do Governador Juscelino Kubitschek de Oliveira* (Rio de Janeiro: José Olympio Editora, 1959), 386.
90. "Political Situation of Kubitschek Administration, Foreign Service Dispatch from the U.S. Embassy in Rio de Janeiro to the State Department on May 7, 1956," in, *Records of the Department of State Relating to International Political and National Defense Affairs of Brazil, 1955–1959*, NARA Archives Microfilm Publications M1511Decimal File 732, Roll 1.
91. T. J. Watson, *O novo President to Brasil Visita aos Estados Unidos da América de Sua Excelência o Doutor Juscelino Kubitschek de Oliveira Presidente do Brasil* (New York: World Trade Corporation, 1956).
92. Juscelino Kubitschek de Oliveira, "Speech Pronounced at the Inaugural Lecture Opening the Training Session on Problems of Economic Development, Sponsored by the BNDE-ECLA Study Group at the Finance Ministry on September 18, 1956," in Juscelino Kubitschek de Oliveira, *Discursos proferidos no primeiro ano do mandato presidencial, 1956* (Rio de Janeiro: Presidência da República, 1956), 246.
93. Juscelino Kubitschek de Oliveira, "Speech Pronounced to Graduating Class of the First Course on Studies of Brazilian Problems at the Institute of Advanced Brazilian Studies, on December 19, 1956," in Juscelino Kubitschek de Oliveira, *Discursos proferidos no primeiro ano do mandato presidencial*, 390.

2 Development in a Global Perspective and Brazil's International Search for a New Historical Course

INTRODUCTORY NOTES

In the 1950s, Brazil witnessed rapid economic growth and many sectors of society experienced the sense that the country was about to embark upon a new historical path that would reshape the country's international presence.[1] Considering the high degree to which these transformative events impacted the general political, social, and cultural scenarios, much of the reflection on the period has associated its economic achievements to a generalized sense of optimism and ideational convergence among some of the country's most influential political actors, as already discussed. Though plentiful and still useful as a general political portrayal of the time, this important scholarly production is almost entirely silent, however, on how domestic events interfaced with related trends taking place elsewhere in the world. The dearth of comparative examinations is surprising considering that very similar socio-political and economic developmental dynamics were taking place at the time on a truly global scale.

As early as in the late 1940s, to be sure, prolific discussions on the topic of national development were noticeable in several countries undergoing the process of political decolonization. In 1947, for one, in New Delhi, India, and then again in 1954, in Colombo, Sri Lanka, representatives from several recently emancipated nations, including India, Pakistan, Ceylon, Indonesia, and Burma gathered to discuss the socio-economic challenges and prospects of their newly independent countries. These initiatives proved especially relevant in a rigidly divided and polarized world, and this budding cooperative endeavor only intensified in 1955 when representatives from twenty-eight newly independent nations met in Bandung, Indonesia, to advance an autonomous agenda of national development. During this turning-point conference, many of these same countries, which later would form the Non-Aligned Movement, decided to strengthen their collective search for an independent course that rejected the stringent constraints imposed by the dynamics of the Cold War.[2]

Considering the dynamic historical experiences involved in the ever more complex world order emerging in the aftermath of World War II, the events taking place in Brazil in the 1950s should no longer be examined exclusively from a purely domestic perspective. Thus, aimed at moving beyond the traditional nation-centered approach, the present chapter seeks to uncover how the prolific debates and policies formulated in Brazil in the 1950s were influenced by similar events taking place in the regional, hemispheric, as well as global realms. One the main arguments developed is that during the so-called "developmentalist decade" a new kind of interaction between the political projects and ideational propositions taking place in the domestic arena and associated dynamics occurring globally began taking shape. Likewise, by examining key elements of Operation Pan-America—the new foreign policy directive proposed by Kubitschek—I indicate the convergence between influential notions articulated by key domestic decision-makers and those of chief diplomatic initiatives of the time.

THE GLOBAL QUEST FOR NATIONAL DEVELOPMENT: A COMPARATIVE PERSPECTIVE

The promotion of projects of fast-paced national development was the focus of governmental planning in a multitude of countries from the late nineteenth century to the period of decolonization following the conclusion of World War II. Given the multiplicity of historical variations within which this phenomenon has taken place, authors have attempted to categorize the main dynamics involved in government-oriented development projects under key heuristic labels. One of the most influential accounts of the experiences of countries pursuing fast-paced industrial promotion in the late 1800s (such as Germany and Russia,) was produced by Alexander Gerschenkron in the 1960s. In this paradigmatic work, the author examined the challenges these same states faced when attempting to catch up with the already industrialized nations of Western Europe. He proposed the notions of "relative economic backwardness" and "late-comer states" to make sense of the specific elements involved in the successive economic and industrial surges taking place in the period. Moreover, Gerschenkron argued that the goal of industrializing via governmental planning was prominent in countries whose political leadership saw the economic state of "lagging behind" industrialized nations as a matter of national survival and a condition to overcome, if needed, by converting the central government into the most important agent of development promotion.[3]

The entrepreneurial role of the state as the risk-taker of last resort for economic activities not commonly funded by private capital, as well as the essential supplier of subsidies used to stimulate private investments is also a crucial feature in the influential work produced by prominent development economics professor Albert O. Hirschman. Examining what he alternatively called the *late, late-comers*, this influential author described the initially disruptive, but ultimately positive, role that fast-paced economic growth by means of targeted public investments can exert in developing economies pursuing the goal of fast-paced industrialization.[4] These ideas were corroborated by the examination of the Japanese developmental state formulated by Chalmers Johnson in the early 1980s. This author advanced the view that the rapid industrialization achieved by Japan in the aftermath of World War II derived from the ability of the Japanese state to act as an overarching surrogate agency inducing transformative investment decisions by means of protective tariffs on imports, subsidized financial resources granted to selected industrial sectors, and government-financed infrastructure improvements.[5]

This model of what came to be known as the "developmental state" was later applied to the experiences of other Asian economies such as those of South Korea and Taiwan, where central governmental planning "generat[ed] national economic plans, coordinate[ed] the efforts of individual business groups, target[ed] specific industrial projects, and resist[ed] political pressures from popular forces such as consumers and organized labor."[6] Analogous to the fragmented government capabilities said to exist in the Latin American developmental experiences with fast-paced, state-induced industrialization of the same period, these Asian nations faced initial hurdles in putting together an efficient developmental capability. But in a frequently advanced portrayal contrasting the lingering traces of Latin American patrimonial rule with those in East Asian nations, the latter cases are more often defined as having demonstrated a higher ability to remove traditional oligarchic interests and bureaucratic traditions from the decision-making process,[7] as well as having excluded, to a much higher degree, growing and ever more mobilized popular sectors from participating in the political process.[8]

The characterization of the Brazilian (usually along with either the Indian or Mexican) experiences with fast-paced industrialization in the 1950s and 1960s as an intermediate case within a range of successful and failed development promotion is by now an established truism in the literature of developmental studies, and more recent comparative works have reinforced such a view. Atul Kohli, for instance, has argued that South Korea's case represents the most successful experience, given that a vigorous export-oriented economy was erected from a primarily agrarian society within a period of thirty years, whereas Brazil, as well as India were only able to produce a mixed scorecard given their mediocre pace of industrialization and growth throughout similar periods.[9] In his view, the "historical tendency toward political fragmentation and multiclass politics limited the capacity of the Brazilian state to mobilize domestic resources for economic development" leading to a reality wherein the Brazilian government acted "in a pattern of intervention that produced industrial growth but did not create conditions for self-sustained national economic development."[10]

The alleged fragmented nature of the developmental experiences of Latin America is also advanced in still prominent political examinations focused on explaining the collapse of the populist democratic order in some of the most industrialized countries in the region (such as Brazil and Argentina) during the early 1960s. Based on the classic work of Samuel P. Huntington on fast-developing societies, which were defined as prone to political instability given the alleged excessive political activation of their newly mobilized socio-political actors, Guillermo O'Donnell defined the demise of democratic rule as deriving from the inability of the Latin American developmentalist state to deepen the pace of industrialization toward the production of capital goods.[11]

In addition to being overly simplistic and strictly linear—and the fact that more complex reasons for the collapse of the democratic institutions in these countries are found in specific political events such as those pertaining to the Brazilian experiences examined here—this scholarship advances a negative view of the ability of Latin American societies to become "development prone" (i.e., developmental) as those of East Asia. In fact, in his fascinating study on India's accelerated industrialization, Vivek Chibber, for instance, focuses on understanding the interaction between government and private economic actors within the experiences of Import Substitutive Industrialization (ISI). He contends that, in addition to the intrinsic cohesiveness of the state in formulating and implementing fast growth and industrial policies, the achievements (or lack thereof) of what would be better called quasi-developmental states (such as Brazil and India) are found in the inability of these regimes to discipline, resist the pressure from, and extract specific levels of performance from private firms in exchange for the subsidies doled out to them.[12]

Beyond the elements directly pertaining to the structures of the domestic government, wider structural economic and political factors should be taken into consideration when assessing the bold development projects taking place in agrarian economies in the second half of the century. In the 1950s, for instance, even after many trade barriers had been formally removed by the United Nation's 1947 sponsored General Agreement on Tariffs and Trade (GATT), most of the agreement's provisions were not applicable to the exports of developing nations, as agricultural products remained subject to differential and higher tariffs *vis-à-vis* those applied to exports manufactured in already industrialized nations. This taxing, clearly unbalanced, and obviously unfair state of affairs was denounced by several critics over the years, particularly those involved in campaigning for a new international economic order and who coalesced within the structures of the Non-Aligned Movement early in the 1960s.[13]

Though fundamentally shaped by a bipolar political logic, the 1950s represent a watershed moment in the dynamics of the Cold War. Initially shaped by a very turbulent beginning, when the world superpowers engaged in an open military conflict in the Korean peninsula, by its second half, the decade witnessed a marked shift from the uni-dimensional confrontational behavior between the two world superpowers towards more complex, and potentially cooperative forms, of inter-state relations. This represented the possibility that new political themes could enter the international agenda wherein economic demands, particularly on the part of underdeveloped countries, assumed a prominent place.

Yet, the formal commercial liberalization of the late 1940s notwithstanding, alongside new restrictions imposed by targeted protectionist tariffs, produce-exporting nations faced growing difficulties in obtaining international funds needed to support their incipient industrial projects. In fact, starting in 1954, non-industrialized economies received diminishing returns in their export transactions as commodity prices fell in the international market. This latter trend represented a sharp reversal in the agricultural price surge that had occurred during World War II, and though market deterioration was also caused by higher global commodity supplies, the entire situation was made worse by the economic slowdown in the U.S. economy that began taking place in 1956.[14]

Particularly grave for Latin American countries, the commercial restrictions imposed on primary products sold to the Common European Market, starting in 1957, represented an added challenge to balance trade and payment accounts in their still mostly agriculture-based economies. In a concerted reaction to the emerging global economic difficulties of the time, innovative regional debates and multilateral diplomatic projects began taking place in the non-industrialized world. These efforts also derived from the new political maneuverability allowed to non-industrialized peripheral states by the dynamics of a more peaceful co-existence established between the two world superpowers after the Suez Crisis of 1956. Similarly the acceleration of the process of decolonization—as well as the formulation of projects of economic autonomy in emerging states such as India, Pakistan, Indonesia, Sri Lanka, Vietnam, Algeria, and Ghana—helped create a new political mentality formalized at the various developmental multilateral conferences taking place in the period.[15]

Even if originally involving exclusively Asian and African nations, the Bandung Conference of 1955 truly marked the beginning of a prolific dialogue, as well as promising partnership, between non-industrialized nations across the globe on the topic of national development. Remarkably important and innovative, the event's twenty-eight delegations translated their individual plans and demands into a collective effort in favor of better international terms of trade for agricultural goods and global support for projects of industrial promotion in commodity-based economies.[16] The gathering helped foster the idea that the colonial (or even postcolonial) experience had to be surpassed considering that its underlying logic required that all sectors of the colonized society be oriented toward attending to the needs of the central industrialized countries.[17] Similarly, the Bandung conference's final communiqué proclaimed that industrialized countries held a historical responsibility to provide the support developing societies needed toward reaching the goal of national development. The communiqué's authors demanded that industrialized countries make better terms of trade available for primary produces in international markets, and offer economic developmental assistance to include the transfer of industrial technology so that industrialization could be promoted in agriculture-based nations.[18]

These demands intersected with additional claims being advanced by political leaders in recently emancipated (postcolonial) states, as well as by Brazilian nationalist intellectuals who coalesced at the Higher Institute of Brazilian Studies (Instituto Superior de Estudos Brasileiros, ISEB) in the second half of the 1950s, examined in detail in Chapter Four. Though no formal interaction ever existed between the leaders of the multilateral political engagements carried out in Asia and Africa (e.g., Nehru, Sukarno, Tito, etc.) and ISEB intellectuals, the arguments presented by Brazilian proponents of fast-paced industrialization were very much aligned with the discussions and projects undertaken by leaders of several recently independent Asian and African states. Kwame Nkrumah, the independence negotiator and first president of Ghana, for instance, declared in 1958 that "[i]ndependence in itself does not change the world. It only makes possible the existence of the political environment required for the real process of national regeneration. If independence is the first step, development must come soon after and no leader of any African or Asian country can escape this pressure."[19]

By the same token, some of the most important and influential Brazilian intellectuals of the period argued along very similar conceptual lines that only by pursuing an ambitious project of industrialization would their nations become effectively independent (i.e., economically self-sufficient).[20] Moreover, in tandem with influential formulations produced in the emerging newly independent world, Brazilian proponents of accelerated development posited that the main challenge that Brazil faced rested on the fact its national economy was structurally defined by the co-existence of pre-capitalist economic activities with few dynamic export-oriented sectors.[21] They also argued that underdeveloped economies were overly dependent on international commodity prices and demands prone to sharp fluctuations and contractions. Furthermore, developed economies were seen as responsible for the lack of economic alternatives available to underdeveloped (or developing) nations given their legacy of political or economic colonialism, which historically halted the emergence of a sense of national unity in the latter.[22]

Though essentially critical of the main elements structuring the global economy, Latin America's mid-century developmental views were nonetheless deeply committed to the goal of modernizing local capitalist modes of production along the lines of a nationalist rhetoric that assumed the national state to be a coherent entity promoting allegedly unified consensual goals. Likewise, each nation was conceived of as a cohesive homogenous whole in which the central government should lead the way towards higher levels of prosperity and political stability by means of modern economic practices. The theoretical insufficiencies, political misuses, and, above all, historical shortcomings of such a perspective are well documented.[23] This important critique should not prevent us, however, from seeing the originality of the frame of analysis pursued in several parts of the region in the transformative years of the 1950s. Thus, in the following section, I present a general account of how important regional scholars and policy-makers attempted to convert such diagnoses and ideational formulations into concrete projects aimed at overcoming the state of underdevelopment in the Latin American context.

DEVELOPMENT WITHIN A HEMISPHERIC PERSPECTIVE: LATIN AMERICA'S SEARCH FOR A NEW PATH

Though similarities existed between the goals and projects pursued by proponents of national development in Asian and Africa (as well as in portions of Southern Europe) and those pursued in Latin America in the aftermath of World War II, marked differences are also evident.[24] For one, the search for an autonomous route of national development carried out by countries like India, Indonesia, and Egypt eventually coalesced into a unified effort coordinated by the Non-Aligned Movement, which advanced an adamant anti-Cold War rhetoric that demanded demilitarization, economic assistance, and the transfer of technology.[25] Conversely, Latin American countries, and especially Brazil, traditionally accepted the dominant role of the U.S. in the Western Hemisphere and, accordingly, their developmental quests assumed, in most cases, a more moderate course.[26]

In fact, even Operation Pan-America (OPA), the new foreign policy directive that JK tried to implement, did not represent a radical departure from the alignment Brazil maintained with the U.S., but rather reflected a new attempt to direct the attention of the latter to Latin America's developmental needs. And despite the fact the diplomatic initiative did not amount to a radical departure from Brazil's key diplomatic principles (e.g., non-intervention, peaceful resolution of conflicts, etc.)—and that the Foreign Service establishment did not openly support the ideas proposed by the president himself—a reexamination of the traditional interpretations concerning Brazil's diplomatic history is still needed. This is particularly true considering that the canonic historiography on the period argues that it took the coming of a new, idiosyncratic presidential administration to power in 1961 for the country's foreign policy to assume a more autonomous, even developmental, inspiration: namely that of pursuing markets for Brazil's exports in non-capitalist countries.[27]

The developmental tone imbued in the many foreign policy initiatives conducted already in the second half of the 1950s indeed reflects a historical trend taking place broadly in Latin America, a move that received its initial conceptual articulation in the aftermath of World War II when local intellectuals began devising innovative ways to promote fast-paced economic growth in the region. At their core, these new political formulations posited that the very structure of international trade operated in ways constantly detrimental to produce-exporting economies, such as those in Latin America. This principal proposition was best formulated by scholars who began coalescing at the European Commission for Latin American (ECLA) in the late 1940s, whose main developmental argument posited that the global economy favored an unequal distribution of productivity gains between industrialized and non-industrialized countries. To remedy the situation, the agency would consistently urge governments in the agrarian-based economies of the region to design new policies favoring industrialization via deliberate state intervention. As already mentioned, in its foundational years, ECLA's main intellectual was the Argentine economist Raul Prebisch who authored a watershed study on the situation of the terms of trade for primary products in 1949. The following year this same scholar was appointed secretary-general of the same agency and his article was translated into English and published under the title *The Economic Development of Latin America and Its Principal Problems*.[28]

While indications that many of the core ideas advanced in the piece were articulated in some of his earlier works, it was in this definitive publication that Prebisch's defense of the need for fast-paced industrialization in Latin America would reach an international audience.[29] In his view, an economic center and peripheral economic regions were historically constituted and maintained by the very process of technological innovations taking place in the global economy. Technological advances were said to be easily integrated in the dynamic economic sectors of central industrialized states whereas in peripheral, commodity-exporting economies innovations tended to be almost exclusively absorbed in activities directly tied to export-related activities. Concretely, ECLA's secretary-general adamantly argued that, "while the reasoning behind the current international division of labor is theoretically sound, it is usually forgotten that this notion is based on an assumption which has been conclusively proved false by the facts [as] the benefits from increased productivity in the industrial countries have not reached the periphery in a comparable manner."[30] Along these innovative conceptual lines, the Argentine scholar claimed that regardless of how much their economic productivity improved, agriculture-based economies would never be able to match the technological advances occurring elsewhere. In his own words, a "manifest disequilibrium [exists] between these two global economic realities which could be reframed only if a profound process of industrialization were to take place in the developing world." Namely, the formulation of "declining terms of trade" for primary exported goods, first elaborated by Raul Prebisch in 1949, advocated industrialization as a necessary means towards durable national economic growth.[31]

To support his claims, Prebisch referred to an investigation conducted by the Economic and Social Council of the United Nations whose concluding report had been released earlier the same year. According to the report, between the last decade of the nineteenth century and the late 1940s, there had been a constant decline in the prices paid for primary products in the international market compared to the prices paid for manufactured goods.[32] Prebisch alternatively argued that non-industrialized economies had to embark on a path of rapid import substitutive industrialization in order to escape the trap of using their increasingly scarce export revenues to purchase goods manufactured in central economies. Toward such a goal, "a firm action by the national state in defense of domestic production is needed so that local investors and entrepreneurs are guided, stimulated, and protected."[33] Despite his staunch defense of industrialization in the region, it should be noted, Prebisch consistently warned against seeking an unbalanced process of industrialization where domestic food production would be removed from the list of governmental priorities.[34] He even argued that the production of food staples had to be sustained at its highest possible peak whilst industrialization deepened in order to assure that food prices in the large population centers be maintained at affordable prices for the growing masses of industrial workers and the general urban poor present in most Latin American cities.[35]

In Brazil, one of the main proponents of the ideas espoused by the Economic Commission for Latin America in the 1950s was the Brazilian economist Celso Furtado who worked with Prebisch in Santiago earlier in the decade. According to Furtado, Latin American economies had traditionally been organized on the basis of a structural co-existence of stagnated activities, such as subsistence agriculture, and modern, export-oriented ones. He alternatively posited that effective national development would not take hold unless efficient governmental planning in favor of a new sort of insertion in the global economy (i.e., one less dependent on primary-export revenues) occurred.[36] In his own words, he urgently claimed that:

> Our countries can no longer depend on the exporting of primary products to sustain their economies. The first task that we, as nations, must undertake is to reorient our investment policies towards the promotion of industrialization so that our commercial balance can be made even. Additionally, given that industrial promotion leads to gains of scale and technological innovation, promoting this goal should benefit our entire economies.[37]

An insightful, though regrettably mostly neglected element of Furtado's analysis of the efforts pursued in the Targets Plan demonstrated how the coordinated intervention of the central government toward industrial promotion had to be complemented by strong actions pertaining to food production destined for the domestic consumer markets. Furtado called this coordinated intervention: "the programming action of the state." Anticipating a concern that most ECLA's analyses addressed only later, Furtado argued that, "the current inefficiencies of our agricultural production are behind our current reality of price increases, in a trend that might become a major hindrance to our developmental aspirations."[38] Similarly, as one of the most successful experiences of import substitutive industrialization the country ever witnessed was being set in motion in the late 1950s, Furtado voiced misgivings about the developmental course of his beloved nation. In his view, the technology adopted tended to be too capital-intensive and the internal market too limited for industry to take full advantage of economies of scale. He also pointed out the inefficiency arising from the limited skills of both management and labor, even in cases where the modern technology was being employed, and expressed a deep concern about a possible "exhaustion" of the pace of industrialization due to the lack of diversification of exports and the continued dependence on the export of primary products to sustain the industrial course pursued.[39] Ironically, ECLA itself would eventually recognize these structural problems, stating in the 1970s that, "it was clear already in the early 1960s that regional economies lacked the necessary dynamics to maintain satisfactory rates of growth needed to remedy critical imbalances in their foreign trade [. . .], contain growing inflationary pressures, and provide sufficient levels of employment."[40]

Furtado's influence in Brazil can hardly be overstated; his role in promoting ECLA's developmental concepts proved very significant and many of the agency's proposals were turned into common currency among technocrats and decision-makers in the second half of the 1950s as many of them had been trained in courses on "development promotion" organized by the ECLA-BNDE Joint Study Group in the middle of the decade. Kubitschek himself proved instrumental in disseminating ECLA's propositions. In his very first presidential message to the National Congress in February 1956, for instance, he expressed his concurrence with the idea of a progressive deterioration in the international terms of trade for primary products and stressed the importance of cooperation among countries in the Latin American region.[41] Likewise, in his presidential campaign, JK more than once stated that

> the world today is divided between countries that are part of the industrial age and those that continue to be exporters of primary products and importers of industrial goods [and] [. . .] [g]iven that the prices of the former are increasingly lower than the prices of the latter, there is a persistent tendency towards unbalanced current accounts that can only be resolved by a steadfastness of action on the part of the federal state in promoting a national project of industrialization.[42]

Statements of this kind are good evidence of the shared belief that national development had to occur by means of government-sponsored programs of industrialization. Such a position asserted the view that any effective course of development depended on industrial activities that were a dynamic, catalytic, and vital sector of the economy. Industrialists assembled at the National Industrial Confederation (CNI) and at the Industrial Federation of the State of São Paulo (FIESP) proved particularly receptive to these ideas and, as early as 1950, the confederation published a special issue of its main publication, the *Revista de Estudos Econômicos* (*Journal of Economic Studies*), subscribing to the pro-industrial developmental theses proposed by the commission.[43]

Similar developmental propositions acquired a prominent place among members of the Brazilian federal administration, including those in the diplomatic realm. An example of how ECLA's ideas influenced Brazilian foreign officers can be found in the *Economic Study for Operation Pan-America*, produced by the Economic Division of the Brazilian Ministry of Foreign Affairs in 1958 to support the diplomatic efforts of the JK administration. The report was largely inspired by ideas advanced by ECLA, such as the argument that unless the country pursued a course of fast industrialization, it would remain not only poor but under the continued oppressive influence of industrialized economies.[44] Brazilian representatives participating in international conferences during those years were likewise proponents of related projects as those formulated by leaders of comparable developing nations. For instance, in a speech at the meeting of the Social and Economic Council of the United Nations in Geneva in August 1960, Vice President João Goulart proclaimed Brazil's unequivocal commitment to the cause of fast-paced industrial promotion. Similarly, in the views of this influential Brazilian politician, acting on behalf of the federal administration, the national pledge to the task of national development had to be matched by a similar undertaking on the part of the multilateral agencies and governments of the industrialized economies. In concrete terms, Brazil's vice president stated that

> in an increasingly interdependent world the fight against underdevelopment has to be fought not only domestically, but requires new levels of international cooperation so that the trend towards growing disparities between rich and poor nations can be broken. [. . .] [e]very nation has the fundamental right of development even if this right is halted by the lack of multilateral coordination among the countries. Promoting development has, therefore, to be seen essentially as a collective responsibility of the international community.[45]

Moreover, along similar conceptual lines, Goulart argued that national development had to be promoted simultaneously in the domestic and the international arenas given that formal (i.e., legal) independence had to be complemented by economic self-sufficiency. He even echoed the position expressed by President Nkrumah in 1958 (indicated above) by claiming that "[. . .] formal political independence [is] empty unless self-determination and economic self-sufficiency [can] be assured."[46]

An analogous defense of the existence of a global responsibility held by industrialized countries in promoting industrial projects in the developing world was advanced by Gustavo Capanema, a senior member of the Brazilian National Chamber of Representatives, in 1956. A former minister of education and health (during the Estado Novo), who served as the head delegate of the Brazilian diplomatic commission to the United Nations-sponsored Conference on Development, argued that

> despite the liberal promises of development promotion made at the end of World War II, world trade dynamics continue to be characterized by an increasing deterioration of the terms of exchange of underdeveloped countries in direct contrast to the undergoing fast growth of the industrialized nations.[47]

At another international conference in New Delhi the same year, Capanema further advanced the notion that Brazil had to strengthen ties with other developing countries as a way to promote the agenda of development on a world scale. He went as far as declaring that "as Prime Minister Nehru has claimed, the true division in the world today is not the one between East and West, but rather that between the developed and the underdeveloped nations."[48] Moreover, despite his traditional political moderation, this seasoned politician challenged all participating delegations in stating that

> if the prosperous nations of the world were effectively interested in promoting world peace, they should not raise objections to the creation of a global fund for promoting educational programs in favor of national development in poor countries.[49]

In a similar fashion, the former governor of Minas Gerais and then federal senator, Benedito Valadares, serving as head delegate of a Brazilian diplomatic mission—this time to the Eleventh Session of the United Nation General Assembly in 1956—criticized the difficulties that developing countries faced in obtaining the financial means necessary to promote their industrial goals. In his speech, the Brazilian senator stated that the inter-governmental (public) multilateral financial institutions (such as the World Bank) had yet to prove their genuine interest in supporting the legitimate goal of industrialization held by the nations of the emergent world. Expressing one of the more radical utterances of a Brazilian diplomatic representative on the topic, this conservative senator surprisingly argued that "the transition from a stagnant economy to that of sustained growth in our economies, a necessary condition to meet the growing demands of our populations, is currently halted by those who have already reached the industrial stage." This is why, "we strongly believe that industrialization is the only efficient solution to the old problem caused by the constant instability of prices and demands for primary exporting countries."[50] Furthermore, Valadares went on to advocate the ambitious proposition that

> only by undergoing the process of becoming an industrialized society can we expect to provide an efficient answer to the persisting and anguishing condition faced by our agriculture-based economies, which are always at the risk of sudden disruptions originating from price and demand variations on the part of the industrial powers. [. . .] It is based on such an understanding that we poignantly defend the right of becoming industrialized and the notion that the already industrialized countries are those primarily responsible for making this possible.[51]

These diplomatic pronouncements were consistently mirrored in several of the most influential intellectual formulations of the 1950s in Brazil, which similarly defended the need for promoting an autonomous (self-sustaining) path of national development. Nowhere was this logic more evident than in the works produced at the Higher Institute of Brazilian Studies (ISEB) where a new generation of self-proclaimed "concerned intellectuals" proposed the base of what they called an "ideology of national development." And while the specific propositions advanced at the institute will be examined in Chapter Four, it should be noted here that these constructions reflected analogous formulations proposed by internationally renowned intellectuals, such as George Balandier, Franz Fanon, and Jean-Paul Sartre.[52] Similarly, Cândido Mendes and Hélio Jaguaribe, some of ISEB's most prominent figures stressed the influence of the works of Karl Jaspers and José Ortega y Gasset in their own intellectual training.[53]

By the same token, one of the most important ideas proposed by Brazilian intellectuals—alongside their international counterparts—concerned the colonial or even the semi-colonial condition, i.e. the structural and systemic state of affairs (or a *fait social total*)[54] that continued to fundamentally shape underdeveloped societies even after they had achieved formal (legal) independence. According to this line of thought, despite being politically as well as legally independent, former colonial societies remained overwhelmingly defined by a persistent colonial "state of mind." Within this lingering condition, the self-identity of the populations of post-emancipated nations continued to be defined in contrast with the image they held of the industrialized world, which was perceived as superior and worthy of emulation. Considering that these so-called postcolonial nations were seen as heteronomous societies (i.e., defined from the outside), ISEB members correspondingly claimed that the only way for them to redefine their fates was by promoting an autonomous project of national development. Such a goal was assumed to mean the promotion of industrialization under the guidance of the national government, the only political agent capable of pursuing such a task. Moreover, it was argued, only by pursuing a new economic model—less dependent on the fluctuations and whims of the international markets—would the postcolonial (or semi-colonial) societies ever be able to overcome their underdeveloped condition.[55]

Given that these ambitious developmental concepts fostered the search for new, developmental diplomatic projects in the second half of the decade, in the next section I examine the central ideas underlining the most relevant foreign policy project carried out in Brazil during the Kubitschek administration: Operation Pan-America. I show that the program was clearly shaped by the overarching developmental goals of the administration and that these were not limited to the constraints of the domestic political sphere. Instead, the ambitious aim of national development in Brazil in the period translated into a new, multilateral, and economic-oriented direction for Brazilian diplomacy, at least in the Western Hemisphere.

DEVELOPMENT PROMOTION AND FOREIGN POLICY: THE PATH TO OPERATION PAN-AMERICA

The aftermath of World War II posed new challenges and opportunities for Latin America. The experiences of the Good Neighbor Policy that defined the 1930s and the war era had fostered a sense that more cooperative patterns of interaction with the "Colossus of the North" could be sustained. This hopeful scenario was quickly dashed, however, in the first months after the end of European hostilities. In fact, already at the Inter-American Conference of Chapultepec, in Mexico, in February and March of 1945 (thus before the formal end of the war), the U.S. indicated, to the great dismay of Latin American representatives, that its relations with the Western Hemisphere would be largely defined by security concerns and new global geopolitical commitments that would place Latin America, once again, in the backseat of the country's foreign policy priorities. The new guidelines for the U.S. treatment of Latin America were all but confirmed in the Rio and Bogota conferences of 1947 and 1948, respectively; and throughout the 1950s as a whole the U.S. did not offer much respite in this regard to the region.[56]

Early in 1953, to be precise, soon after General Dwight Eisenhower had begun his first presidential term, the U.S. seemed poised to modify the course of foreign policy the country had followed during the previous twenty years of Democratic rule. Pertaining to the Western Hemisphere, the new U.S. president hoped to close ranks with the nations of the region so that the "specter of Communism" could be kept at bay. Significant changes in the U.S. policies toward the nations of Latin America ensued. Foreign aid to the region was sharply reduced and loans from the U.S. Export-Import (Exim) Bank to regional governments were almost entirely curtailed. Namely, there was a reduction in disbursements from about $147 million in 1952 to only $7.6 million dispensed in 1953.[57] Conversely, in direct contrast to the stance held by the new American administration, most Latin American governments of the first half of the decade argued that their nation's primary need was not securing their country's borders from the threat of foreign ideological infiltration, but rather addressing widespread poverty and underdevelopment at home.

In Brazil, the abandonment of Truman's Point Four program of economic assistance directly affected the country's developmental plans. In fact, the very extinction of the Joint Brazil-U.S. Economic Commission (JBUSDC) in mid-1953 eliminated the most important financial source the country had at its disposal to finance projects of infrastructure reform. Attempting to curb the sense of frustration in Latin America, the Republican administration eventually agreed to hold discussions about the economic prospects of the region, and formal conversations began taking place at the Inter-American Conference held in Rio de Janeiro in 1954.[58] Having agreed to meet with regional leaders, U.S. ruling political elites nonetheless asserted that their role in the region was primarily that of facilitating international economic cooperation among private agents. As a fiscal conservative, Eisenhower had run a presidential campaign largely based on the platform of curbing public expenditure and he believed that private sources of capital should be favored in financing developmental programs in poor countries of the continent. This can be clearly seen in the letter the former general sent to his brother Milton Eisenhower, who served as his personal adviser for Latin America until 1956, where the U.S. president stated that foreign aid was only appropriate for those areas under direct assault from the "Communist menace." [. . .] [Conversely], Latin American governments should recognize that the bulk of the capital required for their economic development were best supplied by private enterprise and that their own self-interest requires the creation of a climate which will attract private investment.[59]

Despite the president's personal views on the matter, different members of the U.S. administration advanced divergent positions regarding how to support the development goals of countries in the region. Already in 1953, assistant secretary of state for Latin American Affairs, John M. Cabot, for instance, questioned whether foreign investment could resolve all of Latin American's economic problems. In his view, "[. . .] even in countries with favorable tax and investment laws, foreign investors stayed away because of an inadequate economic infrastructure and poor human resources."[60] Attempting to act on the matter, Cabot suggested that the Exim Bank assign $1 billion in public long-term loans to Latin America over the course of five years in order to support development projects in the area of infrastructure (i.e., transportation and communications networks). Cabot's position was largely based on the fact that Latin American nations had a favorable credit history with the U.S. Development Bank, and he believed that only by providing this type of overt material support, would the U.S.

> be able to convince our Latin American friends that our friendship is more than pious platitudes, that cooperation with us does benefit them and does raise their living standards, and that our democratic capitalism is far better for them than Communism with its rosy promises.[61]

Cabot's views ran against those held by the powerful U.S. Secretary of the Treasury George Humphrey, an industrialist and a fiscal conservative with close personal ties to the president. Moreover Secretary of State John Foster Dulles did not believe that economic matters should guide the policies the U.S. pursued in Latin America during a time of heightened High Politics. Thus, in the summer of 1954, Dulles named Cabot the U.S. ambassador to Sweden, and his successor, Henry Holland, sought to keep the U.S. policies in the region within the global Cold War commitments the U.S. espoused. Holland served as the head delegate of the American mission at the 1954 Rio Conference, where he defended the position that Latin America did not need state-funded development assistance. The conference produced few concrete results in terms of economic cooperation despite the high level of expectation surrounding the event—preparations for the gathering had begun already at the end of World War II.[62]

Another important international influence affecting domestic Brazilian politics in the first half of the 1950s originated in the interaction established with its historically most influential neighbor: Argentina. In 1951, the country had a richer and more industrialized economic base and a national leader poised to implement an even bolder nationalist development program. Juan Peron had come to power in 1946 on the grounds of an aggressive campaign of economic reforms favoring the working sectors and the nationalization of foreign-owned industries (e.g., the railroad system). Peron's plans for promoting national economic independence seemed more feasible than Vargas's considering that Argentina was self-sufficient in food and oil production, and its international alliances were less rigid that Brazil's. Argentina had remained neutral during most of World War II and, in its aftermath, had refused to join the Breton-Woods system of multilateral economic regulatory agencies. Moreover, the Argentine president relied more comfortably on the support of the organized labor sectors to implement his nationalistic agenda.[63]

Still, compared to Argentina, when Vargas returned to the presidency in 1951 Brazil was much less developed than his most important southern neighbor. The so-called "country of the future" had a highly inefficient infrastructure and lacked foreign sources of investment. In fact, "Brazil of the early 1950s fit quite perfectly into the diagnosis of the Economic Commission for Latin America which preached that only through a vigorous process of industrialization regional nations would break out of the long-time thralldom to the industrial powers which benefited from the long-term trend in the terms of international trade."[64] Complicating matters further, on May 4, 1954, Vargas's former minister of foreign affairs, João Neves da Fontoura, declared to the Rio de Janeiro-based conservative newspaper *A Tribuna da Imprensa* that both Brazil and Argentina (and potentially Chile) were considering the creation of a regional political alliance that threatened the traditional alignment Brazil held with the U.S.[65]

Having resigned a few weeks before the interview, the former chancellor argued that conversations between Brazilian and Argentine political representatives had been conducted since Vargas's presidential campaign in 1950. These negotiations, claimed Fontoura, represented a serious threat to the traditional hemispheric orientation (i.e., with the U.S.) carried out by the Brazilian diplomatic leadership since the turn of the century. The interview was followed by a series of official denials by both Brazil's and Argentina's foreign ministries, but the repercussion in the opposition press were sufficiently strong that a Congressional investigative commission was created by the National Chamber of Representatives in Rio de Janeiro. The commission supported a motion in favor of removing Vargas from office, but when the bill was brought to the floor of the House in June 1954 it was met with an overwhelming defeat.[66]

Speculation about a dangerous alignment between Vargas and Peron had been disseminated in Brazil since the time of Vargas's presidential campaign, mainly by influential opposition-leaning newspapers in Rio de Janeiro and São Paulo.[67] Contrary to such accusations, Vargas repeatedly declared that his administration would not embark on any radical political maneuvers, particularly none that could strain the traditional ties with the U.S. In Vargas's own words, "We are all Americans and should therefore form a single hemispheric bloc in order to face our common problems. Considering that the United States is the richest and most developed amongst us, we count on its involvement, support and good-will in fostering common development projects."[68]

Vargas's main foreign policy goal indeed consisted in attempting to improve Brazil's bargaining power *vis-à-vis* the U.S. so that he could obtain the funds he needed to implement his development plans. The Brazilian president believed that this general objective could be pursued by strengthening the scope of mutual projects between the two countries, particularly in the area of infrastructural reform. It is easy, therefore, to imagine the damaging effects that the U.S. government's unilateral decision to cancel any direct involvement in supporting economic development projects in Latin America—best exemplified in the closing of the JBUSDC in 1953—exerted over the Brazilian administration at the time. In concrete terms, it would take the coming of a new political administration to make possible the implementation of more constructive bilateral diplomatic relations between these two traditionally aligned nations.

Juscelino Kubitschek came to power in January 31, 1956, with a similarly ambitious developmental platform, which included a foreign policy also centered on the promotion of a more diversified and beneficial commercial relationship between Brazil and the international community, particularly with the Western Hemisphere. The new Brazilian president thus pursued the establishment of more favorable terms of international loans targeted to developing nations, and repeatedly stressed the urgent need that Brazil, along with all other Latin American countries, had to increase the pace of their economic growth. Kubitschek also argued that the U.S. had a "moral obligation" and a "historical debt" to provide the required resources to support the development ambitions of nations in the non-industrialized world.[69]

Contrary to the position upheld by the Eisenhower administration regarding the priority role private capital should play in supporting economic projects in the region, Brazilians had consistently argued for more favorable multilateral public (inter-governmental) sources of funds to finance their industrial goals. And in concrete terms, throughout 1951 the Brazilian government demanded that larger international public sources of funds be made available to promote long-term investments in countries where private capital was reluctant to invest. This goal received further support early in 1953, when the concluding report of the Joint Brazil-U.S. Economic Commission acknowledged the infrastructural hindrances that existed in the energy system and transportation networks of the Brazilian economy. Considering that that bilateral commission had been unilaterally terminated by the U.S. government, JK knew, early in his administration, that he would not be able to accomplish his campaign promises of economic development unless he introduced innovations in the course of the country's foreign policy toward its most important commercial partner and the hegemonic force in the Western Hemisphere: the U.S.[70]

It should be recalled that U.S. foreign policy toward Latin America in the aftermath of World War II was largely based on the goal of securing the region from foreign ideological infiltration, primarily by enhancing a welcoming domestic market-oriented environment for private investments. Accordingly, the second Vargas administration faced mounting difficulties when trying to make the case for public (governmental) support for its industrializing plans to the U.S. in the final years of the Truman administration.[71] These bilateral challenges became even more prevalent as the new Republican administration returned to the White House early in 1953, forcing the Kubitschek government to search for alternative routes in order to pursue his ambitious agenda of economic development. Some of the new diplomatic initiatives supporting the goal of development included the politically polarizing objective of strengthening commercial ties with the countries of Eastern Europe, promoting more favorable international prices for commodity exports, and espousing a course of action that would be more independent of the various multilateral agencies.[72]

The goal of economic and, thus the expected political, autonomy notwithstanding, at its core, JK's foreign policy ambitions were restricted to the inter-American realm and predominantly oriented at rearranging Brazil's traditional alliance with the U.S. along more favorable terms despite (or perhaps especially because of) the growing neglect from the latter towards the Latin American region.[73] In fact, attempting to promote a more autonomous developmental course to the country's traditional legalistic course of foreign policy, on his first day in office, February 1, 1956, in addition to creating the National Council of Development, Kubitschek spent most of his day in meetings with U.S. Vice President Richard Nixon in order to ensure that loans already approved by the Joint-Commission to support the expansion of Brazil's main steel mill would be disbursed. JK had similarly tried to persuade Eisenhower to support his ambitious developmental plans in a meeting in Key West in January 1956, during a pre-inaugural goodwill trip aimed at attracting private American investors and demonstrating to U.S. public authorities that the incoming Brazilian administration was, above all, aligned with U.S. concerns in the hemisphere. A second meeting between the two presidents occurred in Panama in July 1956, during the 130th anniversary celebration of the Congress of Panama held by Simon Bolivar in 1826. Though he continued to believe that the U.S. had a major role to play in Brazil's development, JK expressed disappointment that U.S. investors proved more reluctant to invest in Brazil than he had anticipated. In fact, the trip to Panama would only take place after the Department of State pressured the Brazilian embassy in Washington, D.C., on the importance of the meeting. And, in the end, Kubitschek conceded to attending the conference only after the Exim Bank released $152 million to support three projects previously approved by the JBUSDC.[74]

Trying to harness domestic support for his continued overtures to U.S. investors, and in line with his own market-oriented views on economic development, JK repeatedly communicated to Brazilian business elites his hopes for a higher role to be played by U.S. private capital in the projects of his administration. In January of 1957, for instance, when speaking to the commercial association of the city of Santos in the state of São Paulo, the Brazilian president was quite explicit in this regard. At the gathering he declared to be "very interested in convincing business groups of that great nation of the north that our national development is also in their own interest given our need for new sources of productive capital aimed at investing in our mutual future."[75] Along very similar lines, at the opening of the U.S.-controlled Willys Overland do Brasil automotive plant in São Bernardo do Campo in March 1959, JK stated that "We will continue to support private investors, particularly those from the United States, in creating a domestic climate favorable to their interests as long as they continue to be loyal in believing in and assisting our developmental capacities and the efforts of our government."[76]

These important presidential pronouncements notwithstanding, the continued need for inter-governmental assistance to finance the growing deficits in the country's balance-of-payments, as well as the persistently evasive position on the side of the U.S.—ever more elusive in regards to Latin America's demands for support in promoting Latin American plans for economic growth—made Kubitschek realize that he had to be creative in his dealings with the hegemonic force in the Western Hemisphere. Toward that end, the Brazilian president found a potential welcoming ground to purse a new bilateral and regional diplomatic approach in mid-year 1956. It was then that, after Henry Holland left the State Department, his immediate successor, Richard Rubottom, began directing the attention of the U.S. administration to the deteriorating economic conditions in Latin America. These calls were so vocal that he convinced Nixon to conduct a new diplomatic tour throughout the region. The trip was to coincide with the Argentine presidential inauguration of Arturo Frondizi in May, but the journey turned out to be a major political disaster as, after visiting Buenos Aires, Nixon was harassed by protesting students in Lima, and was nearly assaulted in Caracas by a mob that blamed the U.S. for Latin America's social ills.

No doubt the protesting students had grounds for their actions considering that the Eisenhower administration, which provided support for dictators in Guatemala and in the Dominican Republic, had not offered any substantial economic assistance to Latin America and had imposed new tariff barriers against the region's most important export item: coffee. In the end, however, Nixon's voyage proved important not only precisely for its embarrassing aspects, but especially for having provided the circumstance for the emergence of a new conversation on the topic of U.S.-Latin American relations. In a letter sent to President Eisenhower on May 28, 1958, conveying his personal solidarity and sympathy against the aggression that the American vice president had suffered during his trip to the region, Kubitschek declared:

> Time has come for our countries to revise the patterns within which our hemisphere has interacted and to proceed in the fullest sense towards our historical Pan-American ideals of cooperation. It is time to establish indestructible sentimental and practical connections amongst us. Your Excellency is in the position to lead this process as no one else, and you will understand promptly that the vague impression that we live in fraternity in the Americas needs to be substantiated by a unique sort of regional operation, which to be lasting, has to be capable of upholding the values of our Pan-American vision.[77]

JK strongly believed that his diplomatic efforts should focus on supporting his country's economic development, and his proposed foreign policy orientation for the hemisphere was embedded in such an understanding. In his presidential message to the National Congress of January of 1958, he stated that "the main new principle guiding our foreign policy is the promotion of a program of development through the intensification of international technical and financial assistance between the nations of the hemisphere."[78] Thus, in its moderate tone, the inspiration and foreign policy guidelines proposed at Operation Pan-America fit in nicely within similar negotiating techniques utilized by previous administrations. Like Vargas, Kubitschek had been elected to carry out an ambitious agenda of development and he was very conscious of the problems his predecessor faced when attempting to pursue similar goals. He sought therefore to formulate a more conciliatory, cooperative, and multilateral approach to obtain the needed foreign support to implement his plans.

By the same token, the very course of action the Brazilian president had selected proved to be quite strategic given that by sending Eisenhower a personal letter, Kubitschek approached his political counterpart on a direct, less ideologically marred, and ultimately effective basis.[79] In the document, JK not only proposed a revision of the traditional course of action that the U.S. conducted within the region but also expressed sympathy with the public embarrassment a senior American official had suffered during a trip abroad. In the end, this non-political approach proved instrumental in convincing Eisenhower of the need to send a personal envoy to Rio de Janeiro to hear from Kubitschek himself what his plans for the operation entailed. In a similar fashion, JK astutely chose not to mention, in his initial pronouncements on the topic, the institutional format the policy should assume. In fact, he purposefully decided to be sufficiently vague about his proposed program so that broad political support could be harnessed, especially from the market-driven, politically conservative American administration. Notably, in a speech given at a formal dinner offered to foreign delegations in Rio in June 1958, the Brazilian president declared that:

> Insofar as Operation Pan-America, our country only wishes to cooperate, in the limits of its own abilities, in creating a general process of understanding among our brotherly nations of the continent. [. . .] Brazil does not claim any specific role for itself beyond this purpose, and will not act unilaterally in any level. Among free nations, there is no place for unilateral control.[80]

The concern to convey restraint in presenting the country's new developmental foreign policy project was also expressed in an interview given to the *New York Times* in July 1958, when JK declared that the operation, "if seen only as a Brazilian initiative, is not a relevant political action, [. . .] [but] our project needs to be evaluated for its capacity to reshape the regional political and economic features of our continent considering that it expresses the interest and expectations of all countries in the region."[81] And, along similar lines aimed at gathering support for his new diplomatic agenda, in addition to contacting the U.S. administration, Kubitschek worked to obtain the support of other Latin American states. Thus, in a famous *aide-memoire* sent to every head of state in the continent in August the same year, the Brazilian leader proposed that hemispheric relations be guided by the goal of enhancing multilateral credit to foment industrial development in the region. The document also stated that such diplomatic initiatives should be seen as the most effective measure towards modifying the terms of trade that historically benefited the already industrialized nations. Particularly within the realm of inter-American affairs, the hope was that relations would move from ideologically driven positions to a new stance defined by the overarching goal of national development promotion.[82] The president's personal reflections about his foreign-policy initiative similarly indicate the ideational interconnections existing between the domestic needs of the country and the international policies that Brazil pursued in the 1950s. For instance, in one of his memoirs, JK claimed that

> My main intention with the letter to President Eisenhower was to urge him to act to rescue the strained state of inter-American relations before it was too late. The moment indeed required prompt measures, as the perception that the United States was to blame for our problems was becoming an accepted notion. The entire Pan-American system was being challenged on its effectiveness, beyond the formalistic juridical structures within which it found itself. The spirit of my letter could, in fact, be summarized in one coherent idea that guided my entire administration, that of sovereignty through development.[83]

Advancing a related reflection, Francisco Negrão de Lima, Brazil's foreign minister during the launching of the program declared that "Operation Pan-America is based on the principle that active participation in the international economy leads to higher political stability and that combating underdevelopment is the most efficient way to help defend our Western system of values."[84] Thus, by following this conciliatory course of action, the Kubitschek administration cleverly managed to promote a defense of national development that could be accepted in the United States by the hardline Republican administration in power. The Brazilian president personally believed that this was a time when it was essential to be seen as a trusted ally of the American anti-communist crusade.[85] Moreover, seeking domestic support, particularly among the ever more conservative and pro-U.S. armed forces, Kubitschek made sure to defend his new foreign policy initiative in front of officers of the three military branches before contacting the regional diplomatic corps. JK articulated this view as follows:

> While we do not seek to challenge our traditional ties with our neighbors, particularly with the United States, it is becoming increasingly clear that unless we address the spectrum of misery and hunger, our internal security we will be at stake. [. . .] The existence of underdevelopment at home is the same as having an internal enemy [. . .] which can only be combated in a continental cooperative effort aimed at assuring our own national security by addressing the roots or our underdevelopment.[86]

In a similar fashion, indicating a growing sense of urgency regarding the implementation of his innovative diplomatic project, when he addressed the leadership of the National War College (Escola Superior de Guerra) in November 1958, the Brazilian president stated that "whereas the Operation is a call against the inequality of economic conditions in our continent, it should be clear that we do not ask for favors but rather for cooperation. And though we do not challenge our commitment to the Western cause, we do demand loyalty from the industrialized nations of the continent in our fight against underdevelopment."[87] Much in the same way, in his annual Christmas pronouncement aired on all radios stations of the country, JK declared that "We have to be hopeful that, as Operation Pan-America continues to be debated by the legitimate leaders of the nations of the continent [. . .], our march against the anti-Christian reality of poverty that we continue to face may indeed be transformed." Similarly, he argued that "it is precisely our very Christian values that commit us to our fight against the evils of poverty and underdevelopment."[88]

Despite this personal presidential approach to U.S. political leaders, Brazil's partnership with the Western superpower did not imply a position of automatic ideological alignment. In fact, despite the initial positive reaction on the part of Eisenhower to Kubitschek's letter, when U.S. Secretary of State John Foster Dulles visited Rio de Janeiro in August 1958, and despite general pronouncements alluding to the historical strategic partnership between the two nations, some of the emerging differences between the two countries became even more evident. Even though the U.S. secretary pushed for the release of a mutual pronouncement exclusively focused on the need for combating communist infiltration in the hemisphere, the Brazilian president remained resolute on a formal recognition of the importance of his new diplomatic project. JK saw that the occasion required him to be firm and he refused to sign any document that did not make reference to his diplomatic program of development promotion in the Latin American region. Ultimately, this unyielding stance proved instrumental as many subsequent U.S. actions towards Latin America advanced the very same ideals giving rise to Operation Pan-America.[89]

In fact, even though the specific goals set out in the new Brazilian diplomatic initiative failed to gather momentum in the Committee of the Twenty-One American Republics—which had been set up in November 1958 under the auspices of the Organization of American States (OAS) to examine JK's initial proposal—Kubitschek's new diplomatic project did not completely die and, throughout much of 1959, the State Department repeatedly presented memos calling for a greater focus on development assistance in the region. Similarly, Brazil's regional quest for development promotion also reverberated in additional debates taking place at the OAS in Washington, D.C.[90] By the same token, while economic support to Latin America had been essentially focused on military aid and Latin America received only about 2 percent of the total global U.S. aid disbursements throughout the 1950s, pressured by State Department officials that had called attention to Latin American economic needs, in his final year in office Eisenhower came around in his positions regarding long-standing regional demands.[91]

In the end, JK's strategy for addressing the regional problem of underdevelopment introduced the concept of assertive regional cooperation in favor of development promotion within the realms of inter-American relations. Concretely, in a special meeting of the OAS in Buenos Aires, the long-pursued idea of creating a regional financing institution geared towards aiding the developmental needs of Latin American nations finally received the needed support from the U.S., which eventually led to the creation of the Inter-American Development Bank (IDB) in 1960. Furthermore, in the summer months of the same year, during a state visit to South America, which included stops in Brazil, Argentina, Chile, and Uruguay, Eisenhower was able to learn first-hand that even in the countries considered to be the most developed of the region, abysmal economic inequality persisted. Thus, upon his return to D.C., Eisenhower approved the creation of the Social Progress Trust Fund, a government economic assistance program focused on social policies to governments willing to pursue reformist policies.[92] This much-needed, though late-in-coming compliance by the U.S. with the creation of the IDB represented a major change in the country's traditional economic stance toward the region, and one that needs to be interpreted as resulting, at least in part, from the dissemination of development-oriented policies on the part of Brazilian political and diplomatic leaders.

Despite the increased relevance of development promotion as a legitimate topic of debate within the realm of the OAS, Brazil's ambassador to the U.S., João Carlos Muniz, remained pessimistic about how much the U.S. would actually commit to development promotion in the region. In a personal note to Foreign Minister Negrão de Lima, Muniz stated that U.S. authorities tended to consider the task of development promotion under a common label that included Africa and Asia, which, in his view, made it difficult to convince State Department officials of the specific needs of Latin America.[93] Along very similar lines, when examining the works of the Committee of 21, Roberto Campos, the ever influential Brazilian diplomat, who also became one of the most important conductors of the Targets Plans, expressed similar concerns regarding the prospects of the Brazilian propositions within the context of the debates regarding the implementation of Operation Pan-America. He even stated that

> While there are signs for optimism, given that the problem of underdevelopment and the economic inequalities between industrialized and underdeveloped countries is being debated more often in the United States, we also see disappointing elements since no one in the U.S. has a clear notion of how to treat the specific needs of Latin America nor have they been able to differentiate our claims from those of the African and Asian nations.[94]

Related worries were expressed by other Brazilian diplomats even after the U.S. had shown a much greater degree of commitment to the goal of development promotion in Latin America, namely by proposing and pursuing the implementation of what to this day is the country's most ambitious projects of economic assistance toward the region: the Alliance for Progress. In fact, at the very conference where this important new multilateral program was put in motion, in the Uruguayan coastal resort of Punta del Este in August 1961 the Brazilian delegation manifested a negative view stating that "the welcoming reception displayed by most Latin American nations to the proposed Operation Pan-America notwithstanding, it is regrettable to see that the U.S. has consistently refused setting measurable developmental goals in our continent."[95] U.S. observers of the period also seemed to notice the increasingly strained relationship between the two nations as the developmental decade was coming to a close, as secret reports from the U.S. embassy in Brazil readily pointed out. In their view, "the almost automatic harmony of interest between our countries has been subject to increasing strain [. . .] [A]n awakened sense of nationalism manifesting a growing discontent with the country's underdevelopment status which has been directed against the United States, which is popularly believed to have neglected Brazil [and] retard[ed] its emergence as a world power.[96]

Also symptomatic of the growing distance between Brazil and the U.S. in the period, an even more negative view of the latter's role in Latin America amidst the promises of the alliance was ironically held by one of the staunchest allies the U.S. had in Brazil, the diplomat Roberto Campos. Though very interested in distancing himself from the more left-leaning domestic policies carried by the Goulart administration (1961–1964), in a speech made in Chicago in the summer of 1963 while serving as Brazilian ambassador to the U.S., Campos argued that "[d]espite its rhetoric, there has not been to this day any transfer of real resources from the U.S. to Latin America. In fact, what our region has received in the way of financial resources via loans and grants is barely equivalent to the resources it has yielded to the American economy whose taxpayers and consumers enjoyed lower prices for raw materials and food products."[97]

This growing and generalized disappointment with the limitations imposed on innovative developmental cooperation imposed by the traditional diplomacy operating in the inter-American realm was gradually felt even by JK himself. His disappointment with the ideological commitments, security concerns, and economic orthodoxy of the Eisenhower administration inspired Brazilian authorities to pursue a multilateral agenda of economic development and support the creation of a Latin American Free Trade Association in 1960, as well as strengthening economic ties with countries of the Communist Bloc. Ever more disillusioned by the U.S.'s lukewarm support for this most treasured diplomatic initiative, JK stated that "while most have expressed support for the renewed and reinvigorated Pan-Americanism manifested in Operation Pan-America, it is becoming evident that unless urgent results can be achieved, our region runs the risk of losing the fight against the ills of underdevelopment."[98]

Kubitschek's personal frustration continued even after the U.S. had finally committed to financially support developmental programs in Latin

America. His own OAS-commissioned assessment on the Alliance for Progress expressed the former Brazilian president's disheartened perception that the expectations from the region, as well as the promises from the U.S. in Kennedy's speech of March 1961 to Latin American diplomats at the White House, were not being fulfilled. In fact, considering the U.S.' failure to concretely demonstrate an actual interest—the political will, resolve, and the needed administrative means to carry out the promised, and regionally well-received, program—JK was doubtful that much would ever be achieved.[99]

Looking back, it is certainly ironic that the critical historical *demarche* that Brazil pursued in the second half of the twentieth century from its traditional "special relationship" with the U.S. originated under the leadership of the moderate Kubitschek. Given the U.S.'s continued reluctance to partner with Brazil in its ever more influential pursuit of fast-paced economic growth, it is certainly not surprising however that these historical events took place when they did. The U.S. insisted throughout those years that all Brazil needed was to provide a "favorable climate" for private investment, a stance that consistently collided with Brazilians' continued defense of the view that unless infrastructural inefficiencies were addressed by means of inter-governmental assistance, foreign monies would continue to be scarce and reluctant in coming.[100]

In the end, taking everything into account, the ultimate influence of OPA is probably best found in the Charter of Punta del Este, which formalized regional support and institutionalized the means and goals of the alliance and which explicitly acknowledges the operation as its principal and most direct inspiration.[101] In this sense, although the peripatetic wanderings of the Castro brothers and their charming Argentine counterpart through the mountains of Cuba certainly exerted a more overt and pressing role in the final transition of U.S. policies towards Latin America, some of the most important roots of this significant historical shift are also found in the experiences surrounding the new, innovative, and ambitious, though still politically conservative, Brazilian diplomatic initiatives of the final years of the developmentalist decade.

CONCLUDING REMARKS

Throughout the 1950s the agenda of fast-paced national development became prominent among the political leadership in Brazil. This important new historical trend was not limited, however, by the constraints of political initiatives taking place within the domestic realm. In fact, this ambitious political push was eventually translated into innovative political and economic diplomatic initiatives carried out by Brazilian political authorities acting in an ever more interdependent international scenario. Even if one is to acknowledge that a more overtly autonomous developmental foreign diplomacy was to be undertaken by Brazilian authorities only in the first half of the 1960s, the evidence examined in this chapter indeed suggests that the intellectual and political grounds involved in such historical *demarche* were manifest in the second half of the 1950s. It should be evident that it is no longer analytically sound to continue to examine the historical events taking place in Brazil in the developmentalist decade as if exclusively circumscribed to the country's geographic boundaries.

Aimed at moving beyond this historiographical shortcoming, by placing the developmental dynamics of Brazil within the regional Latin American context, as well as tentatively within broad intellectual formulation taking place on a truly global scale, this chapter advanced a new and potentially fruitful direction for further comparative examinations. It is, in fact, clear that the main elements of the development policies being pursued by Brazilian authorities found resonance among similar groups elsewhere in the world. But while conceptual convergences existed between the propositions advanced by Brazilian and international intellectuals, particularly in regards to the search for overcoming what is commonly called the "colonial condition," the conservative nature of Brazil's approach to development should also be evident. This seems, first and foremost, to be the case when one compares the diplomatic projects carried out by Brazilian authorities in the period with those advocated by the political and intellectual leadership of countries that would eventually gather under the auspices of the Non-Aligned Movement.

The insurmountable differences between these two multilateral courses of foreign policy notwithstanding, Operation Pan-America—the most ambitious diplomatic project of the 1950s—proved successful in promoting Brazil's moderate developmental vision, initially in terms of enhancing Brazil's standing within the inter-American context, and subsequently by providing alternative overtures for the pursuit of more pragmatic developmental foreign policy projects. In this sense, this examination suggests that though derivative of perceived threats to its own national interests, the U.S.' historical change of course in Latin America early in the 1960s was, at least partially, motivated by new diplomatic initiatives emanating from the region, particularly Brazil.

Coherent with the historical course of the Brazilian diplomacy since early in the twentieth-century, the timid approach Brazil implemented in the 1950s—insofar as not openly challenging U.S. policies in the region—reflected the views held and projects pursued by key political, ideological, and bureaucratic operatives, particularly in the context of the federal Brazilian administration, which is the focus of the upcoming chapter. The piece provides a general characterization of the core features of the Brazilian (quasi-) developmental state and details how some of its core agencies unevenly interfaced with different socio-political actors during the transformative years of the 1950s.

NOTES

1. Throughout the 1950s the annualized GDP growth rate was around 7.5 percent, while in its second half this rate would reach over 8 percent. Detailed figures can be found in IBGE, *Estatísticas Históricas do Brasil: Séries Socio-Econômicas, Demográficas e Sociais, 1950–1988* (Rio de Janeiro: IBGE, 1990).
2. Odd Arne Westad, *The Global Cold War: Third World Interventions and the Making of the Our Times* (Cambridge: Cambridge University Press, 2005).
3. See Gerschenkron, *Economic Backwardness in Historical Perspective.*
4. Of special relevance, see Hirschman, *The Strategy of Economic Development* and *Journeys Toward Progress.*
5. See Johnson, *MITI and the Japanese Miracle.*
6. T.J. Pempel, "The Developmental Regime in a Changing World Economy," in *The Developmental State*, ed. Meredith Woo-Cumings (Ithaca: Cornell University Press, 1999), 139. See also Amsden, *Asia's Next Giant*; and Wade, *Governing the Market.*
7. Peter B. Evans, "Predatory, Developmental, and Other Apparatuses: A Comparative Political Economy Perspective on the Third World State," *Sociological Forum* 4, no.4, Comparative National Development Theory and Facts for the 1990s (Dec 1989), 561–87. Similar notions are advanced in Hagopian, *Traditional Politics*; and Fernando Henrique Cardoso, *Autoritarismo e Democratização.* (Rio de Janeiro: Paz e Terra, 1975). A less negative portrayal of the Brazilian experiences, which are therein portrayed as an intermediary case of developmental efficiency is found in Helen Shapiro, "State Intervention and Industrialization: The Origins of the Brazilian Automotive Industry" (PhD diss., Yale University, 1988); and Evans, *Embedded Autonomy.*
8. Ben Ross Schneider, "The Desarollista State in Brazil and Mexico," in *The Developmental State,* ed. Meredith Woo-Cumings (Ithaca: Cornell University Press), 299. Another important comparison between the experiences of Latin American nations, particularly Brazil and Mexico, with those pertaining to South Korea and Taiwan, but one more focused on the international economic context can be found in Haggard, *Pathways from the Periphery.*
9. Atul Kohli, *State-Directed Development: Political Power and Industrialization in the Global Periphery* (Cambridge: Cambridge University Press, 2004).
10. Ibid., 128 and 165. Kohli also argues that Latin American *fragmented* developmental states were also not as effective in creating a national ideology of development as East Asian nations had done, a notion that is partially challenged in the detailed analysis of the broad developmental political alliance that defined much of Brazil in the second half of the 1950s provided by Sikkink in *Ideas and Institutions.* That it was harder to promote a similar developmentalist agenda in Argentina due the almost irreconcilable differences between agrarian, industrial, and labor interests is advanced in Szusterman, *Frondizi and the Politics of Developmentalism*; and Sheahan, *Early Industrialization.* A similar argument is found in analyses focused on an even earlier period in the history of this important Southern Cone nation—see Piñeda, *Industrial Development.*
11. See Huntington, *Political Order in Changing Societies*; and O'Donnell, *Modernization and Bureaucratic-Authoritarianism.* Similar ideas are advanced in Evans, *Dependent Development*; and Fernando Henrique Cardoso, "Associated-Dependent Development: Theoretical and Practical Implications," in *Authoritarian Brazil,* ed. Alfred Stepan (New Haven: Yale University Press, 1973), 142–78.

12. Vivek Chibber, *Locked in Place: State-Building and Late Industrialization in India* (Princeton: Princeton University Press, 2003).
13. Yeonmi Ahn, "The Political Economy of Foreign Aid: The Nature of American Aid and Its Impact on the State-Business Relationship in South Korea, 1945–1972" (PhD diss., Yale University, 1992).
14. Phillipe Braillard and Mohammed-Reza Djalili, *The Third World and International Relations* (Boulder: Lynne Rienner Publishers, 1984).
15. See Mark P. Bradley, "Decolonization, the Global South, and the Cold War, 1919–1962," in *The Cambridge History of the Cold War*, eds. Melvyn P. Leffler and Odd Arne Westad (Cambridge: Cambridge University Press, 2010), vol. 1.
16. Pierre Queuille, *Histoire de l'afro-asiatisme jusqu'à Bandung* (Paris: Payot, 1965).
17. The argument that politically emancipated societies could be psychologically, as well as economically, dependent on other more developed countries (thus alienated from their own identities), had already advanced by the ISEB in Brazil in the 1950s. This concept is further conceptualized in Homi Bhabha, "Remembering Fanon: Self, Psyche, and the Colonial Condition," in *Colonial Discourse and Postcolonial Theory*, eds., Patrick Williams and Laura Chistman (New York: Columbia University Press, 1994), 112–23; and Ania Loomba, *Colonialism/Postcolonialism* (London: Routledge, 1998).
18. Royal Institute of International Affairs, "Final Communiqué of the Bandung Conference," in *Documents on International Affairs, 1955* (Oxford: Oxford University Press, 1958), 429–36.
19. Kwame Nkrumah, "African Prospects," *Foreign Affairs* 37, no. 1 (Aug 1958), 47.
20. An initial sample of works produced at the ISEB include Cândido Mendes de Almeida, *Nacionalismo e Desenvolvimento* (Rio de Janeiro: Instituto Brasileiro de Estudos Afro-Asiáticos, 1963); Alberto Guerreiro Ramos, *A Redução Sociológica* (Rio de Janeiro: ISEB, 1958); Hélio Jaguaribe, *Condições Institucionais do Desenvolvimento* (Rio de Janeiro: ISEB, 1958); Alvaro Vieira Pinto, *Ideologia e Desenvolvimento Nacional* (Rio de Janeiro: ISEB, 1960).
21. See "Plurality as Underdevelopment," Editorial Section, *The Indian Economic Journal* 6 (1958), 73–88, *vis-à-vis* the works in the preceding note.
22. For a critical analysis of these ideas, see George B. N. Ayittey, "The Failure of Development Planning in Africa," in *The Collapse of Development Planning*, ed. Peter J. Boettke (New York: New York University Press, 1994), 146–84.
23. On the former, see Arndt, *Economic Development*; Bergeron, *Fragments of Development*; Partha Chatterjee, *Nationalist Thought and the Colonial World: A Derivative Discourse* (Minneapolis: University of Minnesota, 1993); Albert Fishlow, *Some Reflections on Comparative Latin American Performance and Policy* (Helsinki: World Institute for Development Economics Research, 1987); Ian Roxborough, *Theories of Underdevelopment* (London: Macmillan, 1979); and Immanuel Wallerstein, "The Concept of National Development, 1917–1989: Elegy and Requiem," *American Behavioral Scientist* 35 (1992), 517–29.
24. Howard J. Wiarda called attention to the similarities between the experiences of national development promotion in the so-called Third World and Mediterranean countries such as Spain, Portugal, Greece, and even Italy. His argument is that both in Latin America and the Southern European countries a hierarchical, corporatist, patrimonial, and mercantilist traditional was in operation in the 1950s, when projects of fast economic growth were attempted. See his *Politics and Social Change in Latin America: Still a Distinct Tradition*

(Boulder: Westview Press, 1992). See also Claudio Veliz, *The Centralist Tradition in Latin America* (Boulder: Westview Press, 1981).
25. Michael Walker, *The Cold War and the Making of the Modern World* (London: Fourth State Press, 1993).
26. Ignacy Sachs, *Capitalismo de estado e subdesenvolvimento* (Petropolis: Vozes, 1969).
27. See Clodoaldo Bueno and Amado Cervo, *A Política Externa Brasileira, 1822–1985* (São Paulo: Ática, 1986); Ricardo W. Caldas, *A Política Externa do Governo Kubitscheck* (Brasilia: Thesaurus, 1996); Letícia Pinheiro, "Ação e omissão: a ambiguidade da política brasileira frente ao processo de descolonização africana, 1946–1960" (MA thesis, PUC-RJ, 1988); Alexandra Mello e Silva, "A Política Externa de JK: a Operação Pan-Americana" (MA thesis, PUC-RJ, 1992); and Paulo G.F. Vizentini, *As Relações Exteriores do Brasil: 1945–1964* (Petrópolis: Vozes, 2004).
28. Published under the auspices of the Economic Commission for Latin American. (New York: United Nations, Department of Economic Affairs, 1950).
29. Rodriguez, *Teoria do Subdesenvolvimento da Cepal*, 33. A very useful analysis of ECLA's influence in Latin American deveopmental thought in the 1950s can be found in Albert O. Hirschman, "Ideologies of Economic Development in Latin America," in *Latin American Issues, Essays, and Commnents*, ed. Albert O. Hirschman (New York: The Twentieth Century Fund, 1961), 3–42.
30. Prebisch, *The Economic Development of Latin America*, 1.
31. Raul Prebisch, "O desenvolvimento econômico da América Latina e seus principais problemas," *Revista Brasileira de Economia* vol. 3, no. 3 (Sept 1949), 48.
32. *Post War Price Relations in Trade Between Under-Developed and Industrialized Countries,* document E/CN.1/Sub.3/W.5, February 23, 1949, 115, cited in Prebisch, *O Desenvolvimento econômico da América Latina e seus principais problemas*, 49.
33. United Nations, *International Co-Operation in a Latin American Development Policy. Preliminary Report of the Secretariat of the United Nations Economic Commission for Latin America Prepared for the Meeting of Ministers of Finance at the Fourth Meeting of the Inter-American Economic and Social Council of the Organization of American States to be held in Rio de Janeiro, November 1954.* (New York: United Nations, 1954), 10.
34. Ironically, such would be the case of the industrial promotion carried out during the Kubitschek administration, as will be shown in Chapter Six.
35. Raul Prebisch, "Commercial Policy in the Underdeveloped Countries," *American Economic Review, Paper and Proceedings* XLIX, no. 2 (May 1959), 252. For more on the defense for balancing the process of industrialization with a modernization and intensification of agricultural activities see Celso Furtado, *A Economia Brasileira: uma contribuição à análise do seu desenvolvimento* (Rio de Janeiro: Editora A Noite, 1954); and Albert O. Hirschman, *A Bias for Hope: Essays on Development in Latin America* (New Haven: Yale University Press, 1971); and Raul Prebisch, *Dinâmica do Desenvolvimento Latino-Americano* (Rio de Janeiro: Fundo de Cultura, 1964).
36. For some of Furtado's main ideas, see *Formação Econômica do Brasil* and *Desenvolvimento e Subdesenvolvimento* (Rio de Janeiro: Fundo de Cultura, 1961).
37. Celso Furtado, *Manual of Programming and Economic Development Promotion* (Rio de Janeiro: Economic Commission of Latin American, 1956), 8. The notion that underdeveloped economies were structured along a dualistic fashion was not original to Furtado as it has been advanced earlier in the decade by W. Arthur Lewis, but Furtado's formulations proved particularly

influential in the Brazilian context. Additional information on Lewis's claims can be found in Escobar, *Encountering Development*, 78.

38. Celso Furtado, *Perspectiva da Economia Brasileira*, no. 15 (Rio de Janeiro: DASP, Ensaios de Administração, 1958), 19.
39. Celso Furtado, *Dialética do Desenvolvimento* (Rio de Janeiro: Fundo de Cultura, 1964), 101–17. A similar line of analysis can be found in Cristobal Kay, *Latin American Theories of Development and Underdevelopment* (London: Routledge, 1989).
40. United Nations Economic Commission for Latin America, *Development Problems in Latin America* (Austin: Institute of Latin American Studies, University of Texas Press, 1970), 81.
41. Kubitschek, *Mensagem ao Congresso Nacional* (1956), 14.
42. Kubitschek, *Diretrizes Gerais*, 32.
43. Love, *A Construção do Terceiro Mundo*, 363.
44. Fundo Roberto Campos, RC 58.09.23 d/md—Documentos relativos à Operação Panamericana, CPDOC Archive.
45. Fundo João Goulart, JG.vpr.1960.08.05, rolo 2, fot. 1221, CPDOC Archive.
46. Ibid., fot. 1227.
47. Gustavo Capanema, Discurso proferido pela delegação brasileira na segunda reunião preparatória para Conferência das Nações Unidas sobre Comércio e Desenvolvimento, em 21 de maio de 1956, Fundo Gustavo Capanema, GC L 1956.11.14, CPDOC Archive.
48. Gustavo Capanema, Opening Statement of the Head of the Brazilian Delegation at the New Delhi Conference on Education for Development of UNESCO, in November 1956, Fundo Gustavo Capanema, GC L 1956.05.23, p. 2, CPDOC Archive.
49. Ibid., 9.
50. Discours prononcé par le Sénateur Benedito Valadares, représentant du Brésil au Comité Economique et Social de la 11ieme Session de Assemblé Générale de l'ONU, sur le Problème de l'Assistance Technique aux Pais Sous-Développés. Speech made in New York, in November, 1956, Fundo Benedito Valadares, BVa cs 1956.10.17, p. 8, photogram 856, CPDOC Archive.
51. Ibid. A similar defense of the continued need of public (inter-governmental) funds to finance projects of national development in emerging countries was presented by one of Vargas' main advisers, Rômulo de Almeida, in a speech made at the United Nations annual conference in 1953. Detailed information can be found in Fundo Benedito Valadares, Bva.ig 1946.05.28, CPDOC Archive.
52. Some of the many important works that influenced the propositions advanced at ISEB are Georges Balandier, "Sociologie de la Dependance," *Cahiers Internationaux de Sociologie*, 12 (1952), 47–69; Franz Fanon, *Les Damnés de la Terre* (Paris: Galimard, 1961); and Jean Paul Sartre, "Le Colonialisme est un Systéme," *Les Temps Modernes*, no. 123 (1956), 1371–86.
53. This information was provided by the two members in informal interviews I conducted with them in March 2008.
54. According to Marcel Mauss in "Essai sur le don: Forme et raison de l'échangé dans les sociétés archaïques," in *Sociologie et Anthropologie* (Les Presses Universitaires de France, 1968), 4th edition, 149–279; which was reproduced in Balandier's, Fanon's, and Sartre's works, as well as in several works by members of the ISEB.
55. This was the definition advanced by Hélio Jaguaribe and Roland Corbisier to define the situation of countries like Brazil, which had acquired formal political independence early in the nineteenth century but that were still in a dependent (semi-colonial) state. Details on this will be presented in Chapter Four.

56. Margarita Lopez-Maya, "The Change in the Discourse of US-Latin American Relations from the End of the Second World War to the Beginning of the Cold War," *Review of International Political Economy* 2, no. 1 (Winter 1995), 135–49.
57. Export-Import Bank, *Semiannual Report* (Washington. D.C., 1953), 23.
58. United Nations, *International Cooperation in Latin America: A Development Policy. Preliminary Report of the Secretariat of the United Nations Economic Commission for Latin America Prepared for the Meeting of Ministers of Finance at the Fourth Meeting of the Inter-American Economic and Social Council of the Organization of American States to be held in Rio de Janeiro, November 1954.* (New York: Economic and Social Council 1954).
59. See Stephen G. Rabe, *Eisenhower and Latin America: The Foreign Policy of Anticommunism* (Chapel Hill: University of North Carolina Press, 1988), 65.
60. John M. Cabot, *Letter to Secretary Dulles, 28 March 1953* in Department of State Bulletin. (Washington, D.C.: Department of State, Agency for International Development, Overseas Loans and Grants, 1954), vol. 6:221.
61. Ibid., vol. 6:222.
62. Rabe, *Eisenhower and Latin America*, 69.
63. Thomas E. Skidmore, *A Case Study in Comparative Public Policy: The Economic Dimensions of Populism in Argentina and Brazil*, Working Paper no. 3 (Washington, D.C.: The Wilson Center, 1978).
64. Ibid., 9.
65. Leite Costa, et al., *Impasse na Democracia Brasileira*, 272.
66. Ibid., 278.
67. Monica Hirst, *Vargas-Peron y Las Relaciones Brasil-Argentina*, Série de Documentos e Informes de Investigacion no. 32 (Buenos Aires: FLACSO, 1985).
68. Getúlio Vargas, *Mensagem ao Congresso Nacional* (Rio de Janeiro: Departamento de Imprensa Nacional, 1951), 12.
69. See Robert J. Alexander, *Juscelino Kubitscheck and the Development of Brazil* and "Juscelino Kubitschek de Oliveira: Interview with *O Jornal do Brasil* of July 17, 1959," in *Artigos e Entrevistas Sobre a Operação Pan-Americana* (Rio de Janeiro: Ministério das Relações Exteriores, Seção de Publicações, 1960).
70. See Gordon Connell-Smith, *Los Estados Unidos y la America-Latina* (Mexico City: Fondo de Cultura Economica, 1977); and Gerald K. Haines, *The Americanization of Brazil: A Study of U.S. Cold War Diplomacy in the Third World 1945–1954* (Wilmington: SR Books, 1989).
71. Monica Hirst, "O Pragmatismo Impossivel: A Política Externa do Segundo Governo Vargas (1951–1954)," *Cena Internacional* 1, no. 3 (2003), 1–33.
72. Pio Penna Filho, "A Política Externa Brasileira do Governo Juscelino Kubitschek (1956–1961)," *Cena Internacional* 1. no. 1 (1999), 121–40.
73. Gerson Moura, "Avanços e Recuos: a política externa de JK," in *O Brasil de JK*, ed. Castro Gomes (Rio de Janeiro: FGV, 1991), 23–42.
74. Silva and Carneiro, *Os Presidentes*, 89.
75. Juscelino Kubitschek, *Discursos proferidos no segundo ano de mandato presidencial, 1957.* (Rio de Janeiro: Serviço de Documentação da Presidência da República, 1958), 33.
76. Juscelino Kubitschek, *Discursos proferidos no terceiro ano de mandato presidencial, 1958.* (Rio de Janeiro: Serviço de Documentação da Presidência da República, 1959), 155.
77. Juscelino Kubitschek, *Operación Pan Americana: Compilacion de Documentos–I* (Rio de Janeiro: Servicio de Documentación de la Presidencia de la Republica, 1958), vol. 1: 5.

78. Juscelino Kubitschek, *Mensagem ao Congresso Nacional.* (Rio de Janeiro: Presidência da Republica, 1958), 54.
79. Juscelino Kubitschek, "Letter to President of the United States Dwight Eisenhower, May 28 1958," in Silva and Carneiro, *Os Presidentes*, 112.
80. Juscelino Kubitschek, *Operación Pan Americana*, 1: 33.
81. Juscelino Kubitschek, Interview with the *New York Times*, July 6, 1958, Fundo Negrão de Lima, NL ad m 1958.05.28, CPDOC Archive.
82. Juscelino Kubitschek, *Aide-Memoire for the First Preparatory Meeting of Operation Pan-America,* Fundo Negrão de Lima, NL ad m 1958.05.28, CPDOC Archive.
83. Juscelino Kubitschek, *A Marcha do Amanhecer*, 117.
84. *Documentos a respeito da Operação Pan-Americana, lançada pelo presidente Juscelino e que objetivava renovar a expressão da solidariedade entre os países latino-americanos*, Fundo Negrão de Lima, NL ad m 1958.05.28, CPDOC Archive.
85. Ministério das Relações Exteriores, *Metodologia da Operação Pan-Americana.* Departamento Político e Cultural (Rio de Janeiro, Julho de 1958); and Documento Secreto do Ministro sobre a Gênese da Operação Pan-Americana, Fundo Negrão de Lima, NL ad m 1958.05.28, CPDOC Archive.
86. Juscelino Kubitschek, *Exposição da Operação Pan-Americana `as Forças Armadas no Palácio do Itamaraty, no dia 17 de julho de 1958* (Rio de Janeiro: Ministério das Relações Exteriores, Seção de Publicações, 1958), 10.
87. Kubitschek, "Discurso proferido na Escola Superior de Guerra em 26 de novembro de 1958," in *Discursos proferidos no terceiro ano de mandato presidencial, 1958*, 419.
88. Kubitschek, "Mensagem de Natal, proferida em 24 de dezembro de 1958," in *Discursos proferidos no terceiro ano de mandato presidencial, 1958*, 509.
89. Roteiro da declaração feita por Lucas Lopes ao Secretário de Estado John F. Dulles em reunião no Palácio do Itamaraty em agosto de 1958, Fundo Lucas Lopes, LL pi Lopes, L. 1958.08.06, CPDOC Archive.
90. Minutes of the Meeting of the General Council of the Organization of the American States Called to Discuss the Formulation of New Measures for Promoting Economic Cooperation in the Region, Fundo Ernani do Amaral Peixoto, EAP emb 1958.05.27, CPDOC Archive.
91. Jeffrey F. Taffet, *Foreign Aid as Foreign Policy: The Alliance for Progress in Latin America* (New York: Routledge, 2007), 19.
92. Rabe, *Eisenhower and Latin America*, 141–44.
93. Collection of Personal Documents on the Operation Pan-America, Fundo Roberto Campos, RC d.md.1959.01.02, CPDOC Archive.
94. Grupo de Trabalho do Comitê dos 21—Resumo do Relatório da Delegação do Brasil, apresentado em D.C. entre 15 e 30 de janeiro, de 1959, Fundo Roberto Campos, RC d.md.1959.01.02, CPDOC Archive. Related concerns, this time regarding the alleged excessive pressure placed by Brazilian negotiators on the American delegation at the same committee, were advanced by the U.S. diplomatic corps in Rio de Janeiro early in 1959. See "New Look in Brazil's Conduct of Inter-American Affairs, Foreign Service Dispatch from the U.S. Embassy in Rio de Janeiro to the State Department on January 30, 1959," in *NARA Archives Microfilm Publications M1511, Records of the Department of State Relating to International Political and National Defense Affairs of Brazil, 1955–1959*, Decimal File 732, Roll 1.
95. Relatório da Delegação do Brasil à Reunião Extraordinária do Conselho Interamericano Econômico e Social, em Punta del Este, agosto de 1961, Fundo Clemente Mariani Cma.mf.d.1956.11.28, CPDOC Archive.

96. Department of State, *Nationalism in Brazil.* Intelligence Report No. 8002 (Washington, D.C.: Bureau of Intelligence and Research, July 24, 1959), v.
97. Roberto Campos, Speech made at the National Conference on International Economic and Social Development at Palmer House, Chicago, July 19, 1962, Fundo Roberto Campos, RC d/emb 1961.10.19, folder 2, 8, CPDOC Archive.
98. Juscelino Kubitschek in Alexander, "Juscelino Kubitschek de Oliveira," 33–34.
99. Organization of American States, *Report on the Alliance for Progress: Presented by Senator Juscelino Kubitschek, former President of Brazil, on June 15, 1963*, Fundo Hermes Lima, HL pi Oliveira, JK. 1963.04.00, p. 13, CPDOC Archive.
100. See Stanley Hilton, "The United States, Brazil, and the Cold War, 1945–1960: End of the Special Relationship," *Journal of American History* 68, no. 3 (Dec 1981), 599–624 and W. Michael Weis, *Cold Warriors & Coups D'Etat: Brazilian-American Relations, 1945–1964* (Albuquerque: University of New Mexico, 1993).
101. See Committee on Foreign Relations of the United States Senate *Inter-American Relations Report: A Collection of Documents, Legislation, Descriptions of Inter-American Organization, and Other Material Pertaining to Inter-American Affairs* (Washington, D.C.: Government Printing Office, December 1988); and Lincoln Gordon, *A New Deal for Latin America: The Alliance for Progress* (Cambridge: Harvard University Press, 1963). It is important to point out that one recent study has corroborated the argument presented here that OPA played a more important role in defining the main lines of the Alliance for Progress than has been traditionally recognized in the literature. See Christopher Darnton, "Asymmetry and Agenda-Setting in U.S.-Latin American Relations: Rethinking the Origins of the Alliance for Progress," *Journal of Cold War Studies* 14, no. 4 (Fall 2012), 55–91.

3 The Targets Plan and the Council of Development

The Technocratic Path to Development Promotion

INTRODUCTORY NOTES

Considering its relevance in the developmental history of the country, the present chapter scrutinizes the process of formulation and implementation of the Targets Plan, the ambitious state-led program of fast-paced economic growth executed by the Kubitschek administration in the second half of the 1950s. While much of prevailing historiography on the JK government has argued that success in implementing key economic policies derived from the technocratic profile of key decision-making agencies, such as the Council of Development, this chapter demonstrates that this outcome was more often based on the close interaction established between members of the federal bureaucracy and large, influential, and private economic interests. Along this alternative analytical frame, the politically neutral portrayal of the developmental projects of the period is revised toward a more comprehensive characterization capable of accounting for the preferential treatment specific social segments received.

The piece begins by reviewing the events leading to the establishment of the National Bank of Economic Development (BNDE) early in the decade. This is followed by an analysis of the process of creation and the *modus operandi* of the Council of Development (CD), the main governmental agency in charge of implementing the developmental projects of the federal administration of the latter portion of the period. The central notion advanced in this section is that key agents acting on behalf of the Brazilian state were not evenly interested in responding to the many developmental demands originating from multiple segments of the nation's society, and were rather highly selective in pursuing economic policies that largely favored specific, well organized, and powerful economic actors. Indeed, indicative of the narrow focus and political priorities underlining the developmental projects implemented by the council, this course of action was followed despite the widespread interest and excitement about the federal administration's broad promises and goals seen among multiple social segments across the entire country. These historical dynamics and the established literature pertaining to them are critically scrutinized in the following section in light of these new historical findings. In closing the chapter, I examine a concrete case-study of the council's actions as a way to highlight the underlining logic of the Brazilian developmentalist state.

ADVISORY COMMITTEES, NORMATIVE INSTRUCTIONS, AND THE NATIONAL BANK OF ECONOMIC DEVELOPMENT: THE PATH TO A TECHNOCRATIC APPROACH TO DEVELOPMENT

In August 1955, Kubitschek presented to the national press a list of the main objectives his eventual administration would pursue toward the goal of accelerating the economic development of the country. Prepared by and published under the sponsorship of some of JK's closest friends and political associates, the suggestively titled *General Guidelines for a National Plan of Development* argued that "industrialization is the one essential goal for the economic development of any country, particularly one with a growing population, a large domestic market and adequate natural resources, such as ours."[1] With such an understanding of what the main task at hand for the upcoming years would be, after being elected in October and while preparing to undertake an international voyage to the U.S. and Western Europe to promote the economic potentialities of his country, the president-elect commanded the always loyal friend Lucas Lopes to expand on the list of governmental priorities included in the *Guidelines*.

This long-time political associate had already worked for JK when the latter served as governor of Minas Gerais between 1951 and 1955.[2] Lopes had also performed a technical advisory role at the Joint Brazil-U.S. Economic Commission (JBUSDC) where he worked alongside Roberto Campos, the career diplomat who would become another central figure in the implementation of the Targets Plan. Given this earlier experience of working together, Lopes asked Campos to join hands in putting together a more detailed version of what would later be referred to as the Targets Plan. By early December, a revised plan—substantially inspired by the concluding reports of the JBUSDC and by the work of the BNDE-ECLA Joint Study Group—was presented to the incoming president. The document specified economic sectorial growth goals and infrastructural investment targets to be pursued by the new administration in close association with private economic agents. The final list of targets to be accomplished was only concluded and published in early 1958 and many of these were constantly revised by bureaucrats placed in study or executive groups functioning within the structures of the Council of Development.[3] Finally, as seen in Chapter One, the specialized literature on the plan systematized the thirty investment goals to be achieved within the five-year period of the Kubitschek administration along five key economic areas (an expanded list of the thirty targets is included in the Appendix). It should be also pointed out that the project of constructing a new capital city in the central region of the country became a target in itself, called the Synthesis-Target, during JK's presidential campaign.[4]

Even though Kubitschek's bold new initiatives represented a better structured and certainly more ambitious and detailed plan of national development, such a course of action can be compared to analogous efforts undertaken by earlier federal administrations. Coalesced at the influential Assessoria Econômica during Vargas's second term in office (1951–1954), a new generation of technocrats had come to power with the goal of addressing the infrastructural shortcomings and limitations of the national economy. It was indeed under the pivotal leadership of Rômulo Almeida that the assessoria carried out broad economic examinations in close interface with the JBUSDC. A former technical consultant at the National Industrial Confederation (CNI), Almeida claims that the committee relied on secretarial work and logistical support provided by the Presidential Office despite Vargas's explicit instructions that the agency maintain a low profile considering the active presence the opposition exerted in the press at the time.[5] Operating thus in a very rudimentary fashion, the committee's work was nonetheless essential to set the stage for the role played by the National Council of Development (CD) during Kubitschek's presidential tenure.

Another key technocratic agency created by Vargas early in the decade was the Industrial Development Commission (CDI). Established in 1951, the CDI operated on the basis of study groups (called sub-commissions), and was staffed by high members of various existing governmental offices, such as the minister of finance, the director of the Council on Foreign Trade, the president of the state-owned Bank of Brazil, and two representatives from the Industrial Confederation. The most relevant industrial project formulated at the CDI (which was discontinued in 1954, a few weeks after Vargas's suicide) was produced by the Sub-Commission on Jeeps, Tractors, and Automobiles, coordinated by Admiral Lúcio Meira, who later served as minister of infrastructure and secretary-general of the Council of Development during JK's presidential tenure. Meira's initial report on the creation of an automotive sector in Brazil later served as the main inspiration for the automotive policies implemented during the Kubitschek administration—to be discussed in the final portion of this chapter.[6]

No other institution proved more important in providing the means to carry out key industrial initiatives, however, than the National Bank of Economic Development (BNDE), created in June 1952, to serve as the administrator of all projects of infrastructural construction and renovation, and to be partly financed by the Joint-Commission.[7] In exchange, the Brazilian government promised to allocate what corresponded at the time to U.S. $200 million, a sum to be collected by levying new taxes on revenues of large corporations that had to pay an additional 15 percent income tax on their annual net revenues for the subsequent five years. In 1957, a new law approved by Congress extended the duration of this corporate tax to an additional twenty-year period and established another tax targeted at individual income revenues.[8] It should be noted that the promised foreign funds were never delivered upon the termination of the JBUSDC in June 1953 as the mood of the U.S. government for funding projects of national development in Latin American had turned soured.

Despite these discouraging events, the Vargas administration decided to maintain the plans for creating a development bank in charge of managing the new Fund for Economic Restructuring, which has been set up to finance the Program of National Economic Restructuring, more commonly known as the Lafer Plan (after the finance minister who served between February 1951 and June 1953). Foreshadowing the format of the Targets Plan, this earlier plan listed priority areas of the national economic infrastructure to receive preferred (targeted) public and private investments. Additional funds came from a series of pre-existent funds, which were then redirected for the bank's discretionary use. These latter financial resources consisted of various sectorial taxes created on the basis of consumption of specific items allocated to pre-assigned budgetary expenses (e.g., fuel used to finance road construction). Not part of the budget-making political haggling taking place every fiscal year in the national Brazilian Congress, these additional funds guaranteed a significant portion of all budgetary needs used to finance the discretionary projects of the federal administration.[9]

Traditional studies of the historical role performed by the BNDE in accelerating economic growth in Brazil have consistently argued that the bank represented one of the most important and influential "pockets of efficiency" allegedly existing in the executive branch at least until the mid-1970s. A reason usually advanced to support this claim is the fact that Vargas appointed former participants of the Joint-Commission to serve as the BNDE's first directors. Additionally, scholars have argued that these technocrats proved very successful in insulating the bank from pressures originating in the traditional patrimonial logic of the Brazilian political system.[10] Even though BNDE symbolized a hallmark in the process of creating a professional bureaucracy in the country, it seems nonetheless clear, by the data examined below, that the bank was not immune to negotiations with and pressures from other political actors and business interests. In fact, despite being created in 1952, the bank fulfilled its assigned duties more completely only during the Kubitschek administration, when the president of the BNDE also served as the secretary-general of the Council of Development (CD), a key financial institution that provided close to 65 billion *cruzeiros* (U.S. $ 1.3 billion) for economic projects selected by the CD. The bank also frequently performed the all-important role of co-signer on foreign loans taken on by private Brazilian companies for projects of industrial expansion sponsored by the council, particularly in the auto-making industry.[11]

It is worth recalling that many of these important administrative innovations of the first half of the 1950s were aimed at responding to the difficulties faced by the Brazilian economy at a time when foreign trade revenues plunged more than 20 percent due to the overvaluation of the Brazilian currency (*cruzeiro*), international demand for cotton (about 25 percent of Brazil's export gains at this point in time) dwindled, and the national trade deficit worsened due to decreasing prices in the international coffee market.[12] These factors, combined with the curtailing of foreign loans on the part of the U.S. in mid-year 1953, fostered a growing interest on the part of Brazilian authorities in promoting a rapid plan of industrial conversion of the country's economy.

As briefly indicated in Chapter One, in June 1953, Vargas reshuffled his cabinet in order to curb growing inflationary pressures and appease the vocal political opposition in Congress and the growing dissatisfaction of the labor movement. His new finance minister was Oswaldo Aranha, a long-time political associate who had already served as Vargas's minister of foreign affairs between 1938 and 1944. A highly seasoned and pragmatic politician, Aranha quickly set out to address the economic problems of rising inflation by creatively restructuring the national commercial and monetary legislations in order to control the depletion of currency reserves. His main policy innovation was Normative Instruction (a legal economic regulation) Number 70 that came out of the SUMOC—the Monetary Superintendent's Office that, though formally a division of the Bank of Brazil, served as Brazil's central bank until such an institution was finally created after the coup of 1964. Normative Instruction Number 70 established that the monopoly on foreign trade be placed in the hands of the Bank of Brazil, and created five exchange rate categories, depending on the item being imported. Imports considered of national interest, particularly fuel, wheat, and print paper, were subsidized while other items were strongly discouraged by over-taxation.[13]

This surplus tax became a very important source of governmental revenues for the ambitious industrial plans of the Kubitschek administration, especially after Normative Instruction Number 70 was complemented by another normative instruction (Number 113), and together they served as the two most important pieces of commercial legislation supporting the import substitution industrialization policies of the period. This latter instruction was formulated in 1955 by economics Professor Eugênio Gudin while serving as finance minister of the brief Café Filho administration. Café Filho was Vargas's vice president and had only come to hold the presidential office when Vargas committed suicide in August 1954. President from September 1954 to November 1955, Café Filho was regularly out of sync with his political predecessor and supported the free-market policies pursued by his remarkably conservative cabinet.[14]

In concrete terms, Normative Instruction Number 113 granted special privileges to the industrial sector by eliminating the legal requirement of having to purchase importation licenses for industrial supplies at the Bank of Brazil. In this way, this latter legal provision played a particularly important role in stimulating the importation of industrial equipment in areas considered to be a national priority. Indeed, in light of the dearth of multilateral and inter-governmental loans available, Normative Instruction Number 113 proved to be the most effective instrument for attracting private foreign investments in the second half of the 1950s. In fact, close to 70 percent of all foreign private investments coming into Brazil in the period (estimated at about U.S. $ 500 million) indeed consisted of industrial materials imported under the rubric of suppliers' credit with low interest rates and with the approval and co-signing of the BNDE.[15]

Even though in the first half of the 1950s the industrial sector already represented the most dynamic segment of the Brazilian economy—growing at a faster pace than other economic sectors: 11 percent annual growth in the industrial sector compared to the 6 percent average national growth—the majority of industrial goods produced in Brazil consisted of non-durable items.[16] Likewise, despite his similarly ambitious industrial plans, Vargas's second presidential tenure (1951–54) was marred by political polarization taking place in the media and in the National Congress concerning the role to be played by foreign private capital in the implementation of infrastructural developmental plans. In fact, while Vargas's economic advisers believed that state-owned companies should be created and enlarged in order for industrial growth to take place, his opponents were adamant in defending free-market oriented economic views favoring low import tariffs and a more welcoming legislation aimed at attracting foreign private capital.

It would, in effect, take a new perspective that reconciled these two opposing views to consolidate industrialization in Brazil. This compromise was reached when a new developmental approach, which assigned roles to be played by both state-owned and private, national and foreign, business groups, came to occupy a leading position in the industrial pursuits of the Kubitschek era. It was during the latter years of the period that what is considered to be a second industrial revolution in Brazil indeed occurred. This new industrial push derived partially from the larger availability of private international capital, but was mostly caused by a purposeful effort on the part of the Brazilian federal government to implement a bold new plan of fast-paced industrial growth.[17]

THE TARGETS PLAN AND THE NATIONAL COUNCIL OF DEVELOPMENT: THE TECHNOCRATIC APPROACH REACHES NEW GROUNDS

In his main presidential campaign document, called General Guidelines for a National Plan of Development, Juscelino Kubitschek's closest advisors included six areas considered crucial for the so-called "taking off" of the Brazilian economy: energy production and transportation networks, basic industries (e.g., steel and chemical), agricultural production, labor conditions, the educational system, and regional economic inequalities.[18] Indicative of what the incoming president would actually pursue in office, when one of the first versions of Targets Plan was finally presented to the press (on the same day that the Council of Development was established, February 1, 1956), the topics pertaining to labor improvements and to geographic disparities had been suppressed and, in the end, the agricultural and educational sectors were those with the lowest rates of investment and improvements achieved.[19]

It should also be noted that no explicit mention of the expression "Targets Plan" exists in the documents presented in 1955 or early in 1956, and that it is hard to pinpoint exactly when the program received this shortened appellation. Despite these limitations, it is undeniable that these campaign documents were instrumental in advancing the position that "[t]o better focus our attention given the various dimensions of our plan, it would be more practical to set specific *targets* to be achieved within the five year-length of our administration."[20] Likewise, already in the first few months after the installation of the Council of Development, letters from various sectors of civil society (businesspeople, lawyers, teachers, etc.) praised the creation of such a coordinating agency, and referred to the president's plan as the Targets Plan.[21] In the end, this very designation would eventually become a common term utilized by the council's members themselves.

During its implementation, the Targets Plan mobilized close to 350 billion *cruzeiros* in public and private sources, a sum corresponding to about U.S. $7 billion, and close to 14 percent of the Brazilian gross national product.[22] The origins of these financial resources were primarily 1) sectorial funds (levies, about 55 percent); 2) private investors (30 percent, where 25 percent corresponded to foreign capital, mainly in the form of foreign industrial equipment brought into the country under the legal privileges granted by Instruction 113 or as suppliers credit, and 5 percent corresponded to domestic investors); and 3) state-owned banks (essentially the BNDE), as about 15 percent of all investments were granted as long-term loans directed to industrial and infrastructural projects.[23]

The institutional course chosen by JK to assure that his ambitious plan of development could be accomplished during his presidential tenure was largely defined by the goal of circumventing traditional arenas of political representation. Commenting on Kubitschek's inauguration, the already influential Hélio Jaguaribe argued that the incoming president had two administrative routes regarding the implementation of his developmental agenda. The first one required a profound restructuring of the entire bureaucratic apparatus of the federal government in order to ensure that the traditional patrimonial pressures would not undermine any reforming initiative, whereas the second path was to create what he called a "dynamic agency" within the traditional bureaucracy.[24] The second approach, later referred to by more recent scholars examining the period as "paralleled administration," was the one chosen by JK. In pursuing the latter course, JK created the Council of Development (CD) on suggestions made by Lucas Lopes and Roberto Campos.

Despite not being the first time that the executive branch had created specific bureaucratic agencies aimed at ensuring that the decision-making process pertaining to development promotion was more streamlined, the Council of Development was original in its supra-ministerial status and ability to conduct its own independently devised projects. Since its inception, the CD served as the main bureaucratic agency in charge of coordinating all governmental efforts pertaining to the implementation of the Targets Plan, and the very presidential decree creating the council (number 38,744) was explicit in stipulating that the agency should serve as the official, central, and all-encompassing governmental body put in charge of

> examining all potential measures and actions needed for the coordination of all policies related to the promotion of national development, such as: formulating plans and programs capable of increasing the efficiency of governmental efforts related to the goal of development, stimulating the private sector to become involved in the projects being deployed by the state, producing reports and analyses about the conditions and the evolution of the various sectors of the national economy, preparing bills, decrees and administrative resolutions that could foster economic growth and efficiency, as well as supervising the implementation of any legal measure approved by the Executive and Legislative branches.[25]

The council was headed by a secretary-general who also served as president of the BNDE even though this seemed to have been more a personal penchant of JK rather than a legal stipulation of the agency. Senior members of both civil and military sectors of the administration served in several roles on the council, as requested by the secretary-general, and daily operations were structured around working and executive groups, each one with its own mandate and member structure. Working groups primarily performed the functions of investigating specific economic areas selected as worthy of receiving priority action on the part of the administration and of putting together legal projects in support of these assigned sectors to be presented to the National Congress. These groups did not have any executive role and their decisions were not binding to any sector of the government beyond the council. Executive groups, on the other hand, were powerful inter-ministerial bodies, which could also include representatives of the business sectors, with the legal mandate to elaborate binding legal projects for specific sectors of the economy.[26]

To ensure that the early workings of the council would get off to a good start, Kubitschek appointed Lucas Lopes to serve as the agency's first secretary-general. He served in this position until August 1958, when he was put in charge of the Finance Ministry and replaced at the council and National Bank of Development by Roberto Campos. The career diplomat remained in this position until July 1959, when he was replaced by former

Vargas advisor at the assessoria, Admiral Lúcio Meira. Campos had decided to resign from any further direct involvement in the Kubitschek administration in solidarity with Lopes's forced resignation from the ministry in June 1959. Serving as czar of the economy at a time of rising inflation and international pressures for curbing growing governmental deficits, Lopes had been working for the approval of a plan of economic stabilization that would decrease public credit supply and thus reduce the rate of economic expansion. Constrained by such a dilemmatic choice, despite their long personal association, JK did not hesitate to choose in favor of his developmental goals in detriment to Lopes's recessive economic package supported by the International Monetary Fund. Similarly, after some initial ambivalence on what course of action to follow, JK eventually decided to suspend negotiations with the fund despite the unrelenting inflationary pressures of the period.[27] Meira had served as Kubitschek's minister of Infrastructure and Public Works since the beginning of the administration and, starting in 1959, also assumed the posts of secretary-general of the council and of BNDE's president. In these multiple roles, the admiral proved to be a decisive figure in the implementation of one of the council's greatest achievements: the creation of an auto-making industry in the country (further examined below).

The National Bank of Development functioned as the operational arm of the council and the latter operated at BNDE's headquarters. The bank also provided much of the administrative staff that the council needed to run its daily activities.[28] And while the council had been working since February 1956 on the basis of the mandate provided by decree number 38.744, on March 13, 1958 a new presidential decree (number 43,395) reformulated some of the council's prerogatives in order to better perform its assigned duties. Central to this modification was the goal of providing administrative flexibility to conduct detailed examinations of the implementation of the Targets Plan. Sectorial analyses were consequently undertaken from that point onward on a regular basis. Equally, the 1958 decree stipulated that every senior cabinet member of all agencies of the federal government had the obligation to provide any information requested by the council. One final provision of the decree of 1958 was the allocation of specific funds for the plan in the General Budget of the Federal government. Until then, most of the council's expenses had been paid by *ad hoc* requests made by the secretary-general to the finance minister and, at least based on the correspondence examined at the National Archive, had been granted in every case.[29] Finally, like many other agencies of the developmentalist era, the Council of Development was terminated by another presidential decree (number 53,14) on May 5, 1964, about a month after a military regime had been instated in Brazil. Ironically, this latter decree created the Ministry of Governmental Planning and Economic Coordination, an agency largely born out of the experiences of the CD in the late 1950s and early 1960s.

Despite the fact that the actions carried out by the council varied in scope and focus, they all had the common goal of increasing the levels of production in key areas of the Brazilian economy. Likewise, in addition to the projects related to governmental investments in government-owned or controlled companies, the Council of Development pursued the overarching goal of expanding the industrial sector by inducing foreign companies to come and set up shop in the country. By the end of the 1950s, this process would lead to the installation of advanced industrial technologies (such as auto-making companies), or so was the assumption held by the council's main decision-makers. This goal was pursued primarily with new economic incentives aimed at attracting multinational companies to Brazil. Foreign business groups received special privileges in the form of tax breaks and special exchange rate conditions to import industrial supplies intended for the domestic market. Pertaining to the automotive industry, however, these economic subsidies were granted and renewed on the condition that the multinational companies met a rigid calendar of converting their imported items into goods produced locally, as will be detailed later in this chapter.[30]

The technocratic, purportedly neutral, and, more importantly, consistently conservative (market-friendly) approach followed by the Brazilian developmental state in its search for an accelerated course of economic development in the latter years of the 1950s is well illustrated in many pronouncements made by some of the most important political actors, such as Lucas Lopes and even JK himself. In the opening meeting of the influential 1956 Course on Developmental Problems—a series of training sessions for elite members of the federal bureaucracy conducted at the BNDE by members of the Economic Commission for Latin America—Kubitschek stated, for instance, on the basis of another technical piece prepared by Lucas Lopes, that "[a]ccelerating our economic growth by means of enhancing our governmental capabilities towards a better economic environment for private agents, is the assured way we will be able to diffuse the dissatisfaction that currently gives rise to class struggle amongst our people."[31]

The Council of Development would serve as the main mechanism, along the National Bank of Economic Development, in implementing the most important state-led plan of national development in Brazil to date. This fact should not, however, lead anyone to believe that the council was a self-sufficient, neutral, and above-all, technical political agent, as portrayed in much of the historiography on the period. In fact, in key sectors of the economy the achievements of the plan derived directly from the close interface the council established with several non-government political actors. In addition, particularly in the case of the automobile industry, the new availability of international capital (particularly European) searching for new markets to invest in the second half of the 1950s must also be seen as a reason for this specific (allegedly positive) outcome.[32] A detailed account of the interactions between the federal bureaucracy and powerful, domestic and foreign, private economic agents is provided in the last section here.

Before this analysis can be presented, however, the following section scrutinizes the cultural and symbolic impacts of the Council of Development on the broader Brazilian society, beyond the realms of the federal bureaucracy. In following this new analytic line, I advance the view that the Council of Development interfaced directly or indirectly with a broad range of social sectors who consistently tried to influence the agency's daily activities. In fact, despite the positive reception found among multiple segments of Brazilian society, which persistently sought to have their own, more socially inspired views on national development taken into consideration by state planners, on the whole the council sustained its own strictly economic and, above-all, market-oriented developmental approach.

THE COUNCIL OF DEVELOPMENT IN THE CONTEXT OF THE BROADER BRAZILIAN SOCIETY

On September 20, 1957, Dorothy Del Ben Pedroso sent a letter to the Council of Development with the hope of obtaining information concerning the status of one of the objectives listed in the earlier publications pertaining to the Targets Plan, namely the goal of enhancing the level of mechanization of Brazilian agriculture. Given that receiving personal correspondence sent by Brazilians of all walks of life was routine for the agency, examining Ms. Pedroso's letter may help illuminate the impact the council exerted over broad segments of Brazilian society. To begin, some general elements of this missive need to be mentioned. First, the letter was addressed to the secretary-general in person and requested extreme urgency in dealing with her request. Despite this presumed anticipation in finding an expedited response, Ms. Pedroso's ability to make the council act quickly was probably minimal considering that she did not represent any specific lobbying sector that regularly contacted the council to advance their already higher political leverage over the operations of the Brazilian bureaucracy. Indeed, far from being a business leader, Ms. Pedroso was a student at the Cesário Almeida Public Middle School and a resident of the tiny farming town of Laranjal Paulista, and her half-page request for information from one of the most important bodies of the federal government was sought in order to complete a midterm paper on the state of Brazilian agricultural production, a topic presumably relevant for the rural community where she lived.[33]

The fact that such a young schoolgirl from the countryside would contact the most important developmental agency of the country seems to suggest, at least tentatively, that fast-paced development had become a relevant idea to Brazilians of all parts of the country and involved in all types of activities. Likewise, the paper trail Ms. Pedroso's missive created within the council also seems to illustrate the agency's *modus operandi*. To begin with, it should be noted that Dorothy's request seemed to have received the same formal treatment as any other correspondence arriving at the council. In fact, after being read by Secretary-General Lucas Lopes, the letter was examined by four different council executives who passed the letter down the hierarchical ladder along with their own instructions for how their respective subordinates should handle the matter. About three weeks after its arrival at the CD, the correspondence was sent to the Regional Office of the Ministry of Agriculture in charge of the portion of the state of São Paulo where the her city was located. Ironically, the local officer of the ministry's regional branch decided to resubmit the original letter back to the council in Rio de Janeiro, explaining that he could not answer the demands presented by the student given that his office did not have the information requested. The local officer of the Ministry of Agriculture similarly indicated that he had assumed that the council, of all governmental agencies operating at the time, should be the place where the information needed to answer Ms. Pedroso's request could be found and the council should therefore be the agency responding to the demand.[34]

No additional information could be located and we are therefore left to imagine what happened with Dorothy's original demand and, in the end, her school project. This limitation aside, it seems utterly suggestive of the impact the developmental plans and notions advanced by the council exerted over multiple social segments that such an important federal agency would spend some of its precious time and resources dealing with a letter sent by a middle-school student from a rural community. Similarly relevant is the fact that a young student like Dorothy would write to, and feel that she would receive a response from, an (allegedly) highly insulated decision-making agency of the federal government.

Taken at face value the majority of works on the Kubitschek period, particularly those dealing with the purported self-sufficient, centralized, and autonomous ways in which the council operated, one would have a hard time making sense of Dorothy's letter—unless it is considered as an exceptional or irrelevant case. When compared, however, with a long list of letters and requests sent by all types of individuals—ranging from people like Dorothy and elementary school teachers in fishing villages in the northeast, to mayors of small town in the Amazon region and business representatives of multinational corporations in the central, industrialized southeast region of the country—this young student's letter could be rather seen as potentially representative of, instead of a deviation from, the normal ways in which the council interfaced with the general Brazilian public.

As seen in Chapter two, much of the established literature on so-called late-developing countries stressed the essential role played by the central government in providing innovative institutions and practices that assured more efficient means, as well as the alleged insulation from, popular demands required to pursue the path of fast-paced growth. Pertaining directly to the case of the implementation of industrial projects in the mid-twentieth century, one classic characterization has claimed that "there was a small or nonexistent influence of Brazilian industrialists on policymaking and the government was able to 'turn a deaf ear' to the domestic equipment's petition for protection."[35]

Proponents of this line of interpretation have also argued that the targets set under direct supervision of the council (such as those pertaining to the creation of the automotive industry) had better results than those that remained under the traditional bureaucracy, such as the Ministry of Agriculture. Similarly, several of these works have also advanced the argument that the most important projects implemented during the JK Years were formulated and conducted by neutral technocrats who allegedly pursued nonpolitical goals in secluded bureaucratic agencies protected from the patrimonial politics of the time.[36] Additional studies have downplayed the exclusive role played by the central government in the developmental efforts carried out in the country, alternatively stressing the important ways in which business elites were also involved in the historical events, particularly in the 1930s and 1940s.[37]

Powerful economic groups undoubtedly maintained privileged levels of access to the Council of Development, but the agency equally interfaced with a vast number of additional socio-political actors. In fact, as demonstrated below, it was not due to the bureaucratic seclusion or protection from political pressure that some targets were more "effective" than others. Instead, different rates of completion among set targets of the plan seemed to derive more directly from the fact that some of these goals were implemented in closer association with private economic actors who constantly interacted with the Council of Development.

The rich thread of evidence of the flow of communication that took place between the Council of Development and a number of different members of Brazilian society is well demonstrated in the plentiful correspondence the agency received from all types of people in all types of places. Most of these missives consisted of requests for information about the council's work, structure, and projects, as well as for the receipt of the council's manifold publications. Complimentary notes and letters of support praising the creation of the council and the tasks it pursued were also numerous. And, as a whole, these pieces were overwhelmingly mailed not by business executives interested in establishing a good rapport with the agency, but rather originated from individual citizens whose main interest was to have their letters read by the agency's policymakers and to receive their responses.

The dynamic interaction between this governmental agency and the broader Brazilian society, or at least a significant portion of its literate population, seems to be thus indicative of the generalized interest that the creation of the council, its projects, and daily operations created on the Brazilian reading public. Starting soon after the council was created in March 1956 and following through to October 1960, hundreds of letters—commending the council's secretary-general for the extremely relevant and long-needed work performed by the organization and requesting copies of official publications—were constantly mailed by people and organizations from all over the country, including a diverse range of private citizens. Dozens of elementary school teachers, for instance, wrote to ask for updated publications on the stages of completion of the Targets Plan so that they could better teach their students about the various relevant projects presently under way in their nation.[38] Theodoro Fonseca, an elementary school instructor in the hamlet of Marquês de Valença, for instance, wrote to the council on March 16, 1958, stating:

> I was very excited to learn more about the activities of this esteemed organization when reading yesterday's paper. I believe that it would be extremely valuable for my students to have a better knowledge of the big problems our country currently faces and of the ways in which they are being attacked. I am therefore confident that you will promptly attend my request for several copies of your important publications pertaining to the state of the implementation of the Targets Plan.[39]

It should be noted that the council released a long list of published materials that included annual updates on the state of execution of the Targets Plan and pieces that assumed a definitive format in the multi-volume publication of December 1958. A related specialized report on the economic conditions of the country and execution of the plan published by the influential *Observador Econômico e Financeiro* was also published in 1958 and then again in 1959, presumably aimed at attracting private investors to specific economic sectors, such as mining and the manufacturing of heavy machinery. In addition, a special report on the activities of the council was published in December 1959 under the name of *Relatório Geral de Atividades do Conselho de Desenvolvimento*.[40]

A similarly instructive communication trail showing the interface of the council and diverse sectors of Brazilian society was established between the agency, small business groups, and small town politicians in the states of São Paulo and Minas Gerais early in 1956. This written dialogue had been inspired by the council's expressed interest in creating a new steel company in the country, a desire followed by intense negotiations between private domestic and foreign investors and the governments of these two economically important states. Given that viability studies were simultaneously underway in both regions, a vivid dispute for the council's support ensued between town representatives and businessmen of the municipalities where the mill installation would possibly take place (Cubatão in São Paulo and Ipatinga in Minas Gerais). Indicative of how specific developmental projects gave rise to widespread interest among several social segments beyond the scope of the Brazilian state and the most directly affected economic partners (such as companies and local governments), this dispute produced dozens of letters (addressing Kubitschek personally though mailed to the council) expressing what their authors (e.g., local chambers of commerce and Rotary Clubs) believed were sufficient reasons to decide in favor of their own municipality to the detriment of the one in the neighboring state.[41] In the end, JK, the ever conciliatory politician, followed a middle-ground course and presented a compromise decision that created two of the main steel holdings in Brazil by making the BNDE a key stockholder of Cosipa in São Paulo, with 55 percent of all stocks, and of Usiminas in Minas Gerais, with 45 percent of the company's stocks.[42]

Another common reason different organizations and people contacted the Council of Development was to submit unrequested socio-economic data on their cities or regions—such as from the cities of Crato, in the state of Ceará, Campina Grande in the state of Paraíba, and Juazeiro in the state of Bahia, as well as from the Industrial Federation of Vale do Itajaí, from the Association of the Cities of the Vale do Paraíba do Sul, and from the governor of Paraná—under the justification of "helping the Council devise its strategic plan of national economic development."[43] In most cases these materials were accompanied by a written appeal that the council consider investing in each specific region or city or that the council advise the city or region in promoting its own development. Demands for targeted investments were also submitted to the council by various agencies of the executive branch, such as from local representatives of the Ministry of Infrastructure and Public Works across the country. These requests normally received the same response given to the appeals made by mayors and business associations. As a standard procedure, the replies stated that the secretary-general was very appreciative of the interest the sender had shown in the works of the agency. Furthermore, the pieces explained that the council did not have the power, nor the resources, to authorize public investments (or even studies for that matter) in any geographical area or sector of activity beyond the strict scope of action defined within the limits of the implementation of the Targets Plan.[44]

Whereas it is clear from its numerous publications that the council wanted to make public its activities, it is also evocative of the council's serious institutional shortcomings—in direct contrast with the propagated image of administrative efficiency—that almost half of all requests for these published works included comments (many times by the council's directors) pointing out the impossibility of completing the request given that these same works were regularly out of print![45] One additional vivid demonstration that the council faced several types of difficulties in attempting to promote its plan of national development can be found when examining a long epistolary exchange between the secretary-general and the local phone company in Rio de Janeiro. The communication began when Lopes sent a formal request (using the presidency's letterhead, which was a recurrent habit of Lopes and demonstrated his proximity to Kubitschek) to the Companhia Telephônica Brasileira on August 14, 1956, asking for the installation of a phone line in the house of Gastão Ceccatto. The latter was Lopes's technical assistant at the council and the political liaison's officer between the agency and the National Brazilian Congress. Lopes's demand explained that the work that Mr. Ceccatto performed at the agency was extremely relevant for the country's future and that he expected a prompt response given that his assistant lived an Atlântica Avenue (one of the wealthiest addresses in Rio de Janeiro). Probably to the secretary-general's great dismay, the phone company responded, in a brief and dismissive note, that Lopes's request could not be met given that they did not have available lines in that region of the city at that point in time.[46]

In his instructive examination of the hundreds of letters sent by Brazilian workers to President Vargas in the late 1930s and early 1940s, Professor Jorge Ferreira demonstrated that the vast majority of these missives were aimed at obtaining some sort of personal favor, mostly in the form of employment or political appointment. The study also showed that this path of action was to be expected from individuals who tended to see the president as the caretaker of the poor—an image built by the regime's own propaganda machine.[47] Contrary to what was to be expected given the experiences under Vargas's Estado Novo, few letters sent to the Council of Development by private citizens included requests for personal employment or for any sort of economic assistance to be provided by the federal government, for that matter. Instead, even if presenting what could be considered personal appeals, these messages were filled with descriptions about the needs of a specific city or region, which, due to its underdeveloped and deplorable state (or so claimed their authors), deserved special attention from the council.[48]

Similarly, even when they included descriptions of personal economic difficulties—a typical discursive recourse utilized in the requests examined by Ferreira—the most recurrent element in these epistolary communications by common Brazilians of various regions and places was a demand that a more assertive role be played by the federal government in "controlling the rising prices that are hurting the poor and unprivileged amongst us."[49] A good example of the communication exchange between the Council of Development and private citizens who contacted the agency to present this type of generic developmental demand—instead of typical individual pleas that could be placed under the rubric of a patron-client political logic—took place in the first few months of 1956. In fact, in a handwritten letter, dated May 21, Estefânia Penido and Francisca Meireles, two self-identified *trabalhadoras* (female workers) from the town of Governador Valadares in the state of Minas Gerais, wrote to the council (while addressing the president directly, as most letters during Estado Novo did) asking the president's attention to their request for the creation of an industrial plant in their city. They also stated that they had been excitedly following the president's initiatives in favor of national development and hoped that the much promised economic transformation of the country would finally take place. Particularly relevant, the authors justified their claim not on the basis of personal gains, but rather by arguing that the president's developmental initiatives would benefit all workers in their town. Likewise, in closing their missive, the two women stated that they would be happy to meet in person with their national leader and invited JK to visit their city so that he would be able to see "with [his] own eyes how deserving of special developmental attention our city is."[50]

As indicated above, the correspondence exchanged between the Council of Development and multiple segments of Brazilian society was rich and diverse, though common discursive tropes were frequently used. Justifying one's plea for subsidized loans to open an industrial plant on the basis of "helping to promote progress in our community," for instance, was a very often-used narrative recourse. A vivid illustration of this procedure was offered by Mr. Antônio Alencar, a small businessman in the town of Crato (in the northeastern state of Ceará), who contacted the council on September 21, 1956, to present its "técnicos" a project to open a textile plant in his city so that he would be able to "[. . .] humbly support the developmental efforts of the government of President JK by helping promote progress in an impoverished backland region of our nation, from where hungry compatriots have fled to the main cities in the South, where they are a source of serious social problems."[51] Personally responding to the request, Lucas Lopes wrote back to Mr. Alencar denying his joint-venture business proposition that the BNDE become a partner in his industrial plans, stating that the bank "could not partake as shareholder in private business ventures."[52] Ironically, Lopes's strict bureaucratic reasoning, which might indeed be behind his denial to support Mr. Alencar's request, did not prevent his support for BNDE's economic involvement in the establishment of the large steel plants of COSIPA and USIMINAS.

Based on the multiple examples presented above, it should be clear that representatives of various walks of life constantly approached the Council of Development in order to further their own personal interests, as well as, interestingly, more often, to express their ideological support for the agency's plans. These facts should not detract us from seeing, however, that the most prolific web of interactions between state managers and private interests during the JK Years took place between the council's directors (particularly those running executives groups) and powerful business groups. In direct contrast to the findings revealing widespread interest and support for the agency's work from a diverse range of social segments, the close interaction between business executives and key figures at the Council of Development is not surprising. The council's inherent activities impacted private economic sectors in a direct manner and the agency's role in the national economy was a legal requirement that the organization had to follow. A clear illustration of the influence of the agency can be found in the fact that all economic incentives in the form of tax breaks, particularly in the case of tariff exemptions for importing industrial materials, had to be approved on an individual basis by the CD. This intricate bureaucratic proceeding forced most large business groups to contact the Council of Development (usually in the person of its secretary-general, who, in this sense, served a very clear political role) in order to obtain the agency's approval for any importation license needed to run their businesses.[53]

Furthermore, in addition to individual requests presented by specific industrial groups demanding tax exemptions privileges, the most common demand in this sort of correspondence was for the creation of a general law granting universal tariff protection for any company attempting to import industrial equipment.[54] Here it is important to explain that while very generous in its tax breaks and tariff privileges, Normative Instruction Number 113 specified that these benefits would be granted only to companies that had their industrial expansion projects approved by the council, which explains both the recurrent petitions industrial companies presented to the agency, as well as their continuous request for the sanctioning of a general tariff regulation. This general demand was finally met with the Tariffs Law of 1957 that simplified the existing exchange rate categories, and that needs to be seen as resulting, at least in part, from the pressures imposed by business groups on the government in favor of a specific legislation on foreign trade. Moreover, though streamlining legal provisions, the new bill nonetheless maintained the legal requirement that special duty privileges were to be granted on a case-by-case basis, thus maintaining the continued political need for constantly contacting the council for approval of industrial projects.[55]

These multiple approaches included requests ranging from import licenses to subsidized public credit, but they could also include appeals for legal revisions of trade quotas or of specific production targets. Once these cases had been presented, the council's secretary-general (normally with the support of in-house or externally hired consultants) examined each individual request. Should we believe the formal procedural regulations, any request could be turned down and, at least in theory, that would be end of it since there was no formal appeals process in place. The records at the National Archive abundantly indicate, however, that in these cases the sender, especially when this was an important business leader, regularly appealed directly to Kubitschek who, as a general rule, redirected the request to the secretary-general "for further consideration." Given JK's personal interest in each case, and in spite of the council's purportedly technical decision for denying the request, the council reexamined the request—this time around, presumably under a new light. It is not surprising to see that in most cases for which records are available these appeals would result in a reversal of earlier, unfavorable decisions.

In what could probably be seen as a reaction to the continued political interference from higher authorities, time delays to conduct a reevaluation of requests were a common device utilized by the council's *técnicos* to stall controversial approvals. This was done on the basis of the need for further technical examinations that demanded more time until a final decision could be made—usually leading to an ultimate negative deliberation, allegedly on purely technical grounds. Also, in many cases the council would not reach an agreement regarding the demands presented by one specific business sector given that different views were expressed by the multiple consultants examining the matter. When this occurred, unless the secretary-general intervened in favor of one specific position, the agency would not make any decision and the requests became "lost" in the bureaucratic maze.

On several occasions the request presented to the council came not from one individual company, but rather from influential industrial associations. Interestingly, in most of these cases the secretary-general presented a more detailed (and usually favorable) personal report to Kubitschek suggesting a sectorial adjustment in one specific legal provision, which would make the approval of the request possible. A good illustration of how these bureaucratic dynamics were concretely played out is found in the case of the communication from the Industrial Machinery Manufacture's Association of the state of São Paulo, on October 11, 1959, when the organization stated that "[g]iven the present difficulties in restructuring our production lines, we would like to request that Admiral Meira, secretary-general of the Council of Development put together a new importation legislation exempting all industrial equipment purchased abroad so that we may expand our facilities."[56] After examining the request for a few months, Secretary-General Meira contacted Kubitschek in a memo that explained that:

> Implementing an industrial complex composed of basic (heavy) industries is a *sine qua non* condition for our continued national development. It is therefore essential that Your Excellency's government provide a new legal framework that provides total importation exemption which the industry needs in order to expand its facilities. [. . .] Given that this provision needs to be crafted by the National Congress, I send attached for your perusal the drafted bill to be submitted to Congress. This bill will offer total tax exemption for all imported industrial equipment provided no similar products are currently being produced in the country.[57]

To further substantiate the notion that business groups were particularly able to influence the workings of the Council of Development, in the final section of the chapter I examine the negotiations taking place between the agency and some of the most important business groups directly involved in the implementation of an automotive industrial sector in Brazil. In detailing the intense interactions existing between policymakers and private corporations during the implementation of the Targets Plan, the examination refutes the prevailing notion that the Brazilian developmentalist state operated primarily on the basis of its bureaucratic imperviousness from political and economic pressures from the broader Brazilian society. The decision to center this analysis on the interplay between the federal bureaucracy and the private sector concerning the relationship the CD sustained with the budding auto-making sector is based on three main factors.

First, these historical experiences paradigmatically revealed the core developmental notion held and promoted by the most influential decision-makers of the period: namely that rapid industrialization, by means of an alliance between government and private business groups, was essential in order to promote national development. Secondly, the ways in which a large automotive complex was established in Brazil is the clearest expression of the industrialization model pursued by the Kubitschek administration. This approach combined what had until then been irreconcilable factors of production (i.e., foreign, national, and governmental capital), resulting in the creation of an industrial plant that placed Brazil among the largest auto producers in the world at the dawn of the 1960s. Thirdly, the implementation of this hybrid (and, at least in absolute numbers, successful) industrial project deepened broad, and in the long run ever more problematic, socioeconomic transformations. These included the expansion of the historically unregulated and unsupported process of urbanization, particularly in the center south of the country, which further expanded major economic disparities existing between different geographic regions of the country.

THE COUNCIL OF DEVELOPMENT AND THE BUSINESS SECTORS: REVIEWING THE BASIS FOR THE IMPLEMENTATION OF AN AUTOMOTIVE INDUSTRY IN BRAZIL IN THE 1950S

Even though consolidating the path of fast-paced industrialization was the foremost defining developmental motivation of the Kubitschek administration, additional reasons were repeatedly voiced by policymakers and interest groups involved in the creation of a Brazilian-based automotive industry. One of the most frequently advanced justifications pertained directly to the need to address growing economic difficulties derived from the ever larger commercial deficit caused by the rising importation of manufactured goods, wherein motorized vehicles represented the lion's share.[58] It is clear that, since at least 1953, the Brazilian trade balance was consistently in the red as a direct consequence of falling coffee prices in the international market and the continued need to finance imported goods with convertible currencies obtained abroad.[59] This situation was to become more challenging as the 1950s unfolded given the impact of imported automobiles in the commercial balance of the country.[60] In fact, already by the middle of the decade, Brazil needed to obtain about U.S. $300 million on an annual basis from lending international agencies just to balance its national current accounts.[61] Furthermore, despite Aranha's attempts at curbing the growing gap in the national balance-of-payment accounts by resorting to multiple exchange rates, when 1955 came to a close more than U.S. $143 million in "importation licenses" had been purchased at the Bank of Brazil to be used in buying foreign-manufactured vehicles.[62]

The continued need to stabilize persistent trade deficits thus played a decisive role in convincing the few remaining skeptics that the federal administration should steer the national economy toward higher levels of economic self-sufficiency.[63] Despite the interregnum caused by Vargas's suicide and the temporary presence in power of more conservative political forces, during the administration of Café Filho key sectors of the military establishment maintained, though in a more subtle fashion, their support for the goal of establishing an automotive industry in the country.[64] Having arrived in the presidential office amidst such a challenging economic and, consequently, political scenario, the Kubitschek administration was explicit about the fact that

> our balance-of-payment is overloaded by the burden created by the imports required to promote our process of development. This reality has inspired the government to begin examinations on the possibilities of stimulating the private sector to obtain alternative sources of financing industrial materials in the form of supplier's credits, particularly from Europe, to be applied in our automotive industries.[65]

This being the general context within which the new government had to operate, in April 1956, Kubitschek signed into law the Presidential Study Group of the Automobile Industry in order to examine the economic viability of creating a large automotive manufacturing sector in the country. The creation of this new investigative committee came in response to a request made by Kubitschek's minister of public works and transportation networks, Admiral Lúcio Meira. The study group included Roberto Campos among its main key officers and operated under the guidance of the admiral himself. Meira was an experienced bureaucrat who had conducted studies on the automobile industry since the late 1930s. In the end, the expedited concluding report produced by the group, presented to JK in May (largely on the basis of Meira's personal examinations on the topic written in 1954), suggested the creation of the first executive group of the Council of Development to be called the Executive Group of the Automotive Industry (GEIA), and set the original guidelines coordinating how an entirely new industrial sector was to be created.

Particularly relevant, the same report determined that its ambitious goal was to be pursued primarily on the basis of a strategic partnership to be established between the federal government and domestic and foreign private business groups.[66] GEIA's core task of reducing the need for the continued importation of finished motorized vehicles was consequently centered on finding creative new ways of attracting foreign auto-making companies to set up shop in the country. The hope was that these new locally based business groups would meet the target of producing 130,000 vehicles by the end of 1960.[67] Also important, and further indicative of the president's personal priorities, Kubitschek was quick in following through on the group's request and on June 16, 1956, he signed Presidential Decree number 39,412 creating the GEIA, which was to become one of the most powerful, and one of the most frequently praised, executive groups of the dozens created within the bureaucratic structures of the Council of Development.

Not surprisingly, Meira was assigned to serve as secretary-general of the GEIA, along with the superintendent director of the BNDE, Roberto Campos. This executive group held weekly meetings, either at the Ministry of Public Works or at the headquarters of the National Bank of Economic Development where government officials frequently met with representatives of various business groups and industrial associations. In addition to the important stewardship provided by these career bureaucrats, another key member of the GEIA was Ramiz Gattas, the official representative of the auto-parts industrial association, Sindipeças. In addition to his professional motivations, Gattas believed in the project on an intellectual level and he proved to be one of the main proponents of the implementation of a domestic-based automotive industry in the country in the 1950s due to the symbolic importance of such an endeavor. In his lengthy personal account of these historical events, a period he calls Brazil's "second industrial revolution," he indeed insisted—ironically paralleling ISEB's defense for a more assertive role for the federal government in the national economy, detailed in the next chapter—that what was at stake was not merely the economic solvency of the national trade balances, but rather the very viability and sense of pride of the country on the world stage.[68]

Suggestive of how ingenious were some of the new political arrangements set out by the JK administration in order to pursue its industrial goals, even though the policies implemented by the Executive Group of the Automotive Industry were primarily focused on having foreign-held industrial brands start production in the country, Brazilian auto-parts manufacturing groups would soon become central to the GEIA's focus, policies, and activities. A synergic business relationship between soon-to-arrive foreign auto-making firms and the already existing domestic auto-parts business sector was thus established.[69] Auto-parts companies had existed since the mid-1920s when Ford and General Motors began assembling vehicles locally by putting together parts brought into the country in separate lots, known as CKD (completely knocked down) components. In his early studies on the topic, Meira labeled the deepening of the symbiotic partnership, between local and foreign businesses under the auspices of the national government as "horizontal integration." This concept was central in Meira's report suggesting the establishment of the GEIA, and the perspective conveyed in this idea was to become central to the operations of the group itself.[70] Significantly, the process indeed represented the culmination of the approach already detailed in JK's presidential campaign when he defended that "the ideal course we should pursue [in implementing an automotive industry in the country] is to have domestic supply companies partner with foreign automaker companies, which would retain control over technology and patents."[71]

In addition to this market-oriented logic supporting the implementation of this key industrial sector, the documentation produced by the GEIA suggests that the Kubitschek administration consistently avoided the state-centered approach that had been attempted in the second Vargas administration, when the government-controlled Fábrica Nacional de Motores (FNM) was able to locally produce a very popular large truck in partnership with the Italian company Alfa Romeo. JK's personal advisors at the Council of Development staunchly considered its role to be essentially one of serving as an indirect promoter of industrial development by means of facilitating the operation of private companies.[72] In effect, and a clear demonstration of the new industrial course pursued in the second half of the decade, FNM was severely chastised in the very same document that proposed the creation of the GEIA.[73]

Meira himself left no room for doubt about this market-led approach when he later stated that "despite the strength of statist ideas still prevalent in the country at the time, what we tried to do at the GEIA, and which was the model for all executive groups, was to combat such a view and replace it with our market-centered approach."[74] GEIA officials indeed believed that the "implementation of an automobile industry in the county should be primarily dependent upon private enterprises," and that "currently state-owned automotive companies should be transferred to private hands."[75] And holding to this belief, these same technocrats advocated that the agency's main duties should be restricted to coordinating the creation of a vital new industry by means of targeted economic incentives, including favorable exchange rates, fiscal benefits, preferential credit terms, and market guarantees via tariff protection.[76]

In exchange for these many appealing incentives, the guidelines set out by the GEIA required incoming foreign companies setting up shop in the country to follow a timetable for "nationalizing" production (i.e., enhancing use of locally produced components). Despite this legal requirement, multinational corporations constantly lobbied both the executive group and the Council of Development in order to reduce the percentage rates or broaden the time frame for the process of nationalization, particularly in the case of passenger cars. And in one of these many episodes, GEIA's Executive Director Eros Orosco, who was widely considered to be one of the most qualified members of the agency, decided to resign from GEIA in June 1959, due to what he considered to be "undue political pressures" (which he did not specify) over the group's operations.[77]

Put together, the schedule for enhancing the use of locally produced industrial components (in terms of the percentage of the weight of each vehicle) was as follows:[78]

Table 3.1

Vehicle	12/31/1956	07/01/1957	07/01/1958	07/01/1959	07/01/1960
Truck	35%	40%	65%	75%	90%
Utility Vehicle	50%	60%	75%	85%	95%
Van	40%	50%	65%	75%	90%
Car	—	50%	65%	85%	95%

As indicated, the overarching goal was to have almost all the components used in each vehicle category be produced domestically by the end of the decade. This timetable was generally followed, and between 1956 and 1960 GEIA approved thirty projects for the installation or expansion of auto-making plants in Brazil. Twenty-seven of these were actually implemented, with the technology and capital from fourteen different companies from seven different countries (U.S., Germany, Italy, Sweden, France, England, and Japan). In addition to credit provided by the BNDE for the construction of industrial plants, the largest portion (64 percent) of all foreign investments arriving in the country in the period consisted of advanced credits in the form of industrial equipment. This was normally done under the legal category of supplier's credit provided by the headquarters of the foreign vehicle companies with the approval and co-signature of the BNDE.

The capital invested in creating the new industrial complex reached the sum of U.S. $414 million during the period, where about half (U.S. $214 million) of the total had come from abroad. Insofar as the concrete results were achieved, the initial target of 130,000 units was increased to the figure of 170,000 units by the end of 1958. And by the end of 1960, actual figures of locally-produced vehicles reached the impressive total of 220,000 units, with an average of 90 percent of the total parts or components being produced in Brazil. Furthermore, between 1957 and 1960, 483,000 units were assembled in Brazil, thus surpassing the original target of 377,000 units. If the country had continued importing similar figures of automobiles in the same period (rather than producing them locally), the GEIA estimated that the total cost involved in these operations would have been upwards of U.S. $ 560 million.[79]

It is clear, then, that private foreign and domestic economic agents performed a central role in creating an automotive industry in Brazil during the transformative JK Years. Without a doubt, already in the second Vargas administration, business representatives from the auto-parts sector steadily pushed their own vision on implementing a Brazilian-based automotive industry.[80] This approach was even translated into Meira's own position and plans when he defined the guidelines for the creation of the GEIA. This was particularly true in the case of the legal requirement, which forced foreign manufacturing companies to subcontract auto-parts services provided by the already existing domestic firms. Private business groups were especially favored and the privatization of the only Brazilian government-held automotive company was seen from the outset as a necessary step toward making the local market more appealing to foreign investors.[81]

In fact, given that the Fábrica Nacional de Motores had yet to be privatized (something that only occurred in 1968, during the height of the military regime), a new GEIA report was presented to Kubitschek in October 1957, proposing new guidelines for the successful implementation of the automotive industry in the country. Among its most important suggestions was the technical decision to reduce the size and weight of trucks allowed to be produced in Brazil. In practical terms, such a resolution hindered the continued production of the company's bestselling item, a hefty yet extremely popular truck.[82]

Beyond the legal, fiscal, and credit instruments benefiting private business groups that GEIA used to induce investments, the agency worked diligently to increase the availability of industrial workers serving this growing and ever more valued business sector. Early in 1958, GEIA established a legal agreement with the National Service of the Industry—SENAI, a division of the National Industrial Confederation charged with the training of industrial laborers in close partnership with the federal government since the 1940s—aimed at providing in-factory, short-term intensive preparatory courses for incoming rank-and-file workers. Technicians were to receive specialized classes set up at SENAI's own schools in the main urban industrial centers. In 1960, auto plants employed about 40,000 workers (while the auto-parts industry employed about 110,000 workers), and the GEIA was concerned about rising wages in the metropolitan region of São Paulo and thus sought creative ways to train additional industrial laborers.[83]

Later in the decade, GEIA established a new partnership with SENAI—as well as with the National Department for Combating Droughts (DNOCS) the federal agency in charge of providing public infrastructural work such as dams and reservoirs in the drought stricken region in the northeastern portion of the country—to recruit inexperienced workers in that poor and very populous region. The rationale behind setting up this program was to recruit new workers who would receive a crash course administered by SENAI instructors during twelve weeks in the warehouses of the DNOCS, particularly in the state of Ceará, and then be transported by truck to the metropolitan area of the city of São Paulo. The project was intended to attract around 15,000 northeastern workers on an annual basis in order to alleviate the inflationary pressure on industrial salaries in the auto sector. In the end, the planned joint initiatives of GEIA, SENAI, and the DNOCS were never fully implemented, and most workers from that portion of the country who eventually went to work in the auto-making industries, had done so on their own volition (and using their own funds), attracted by the rising salaries and large availability of jobs in the center-south portion of the country.[84]

It should be also noted that even though by mid-century the city of São Paulo had become the industrial hub of the country, by the end of Kubitschek administration most of the incoming foreign automotive companies either setting up shop or expanding their industrial activities in Brazil established their plants in the metropolitan region of the city of São Paulo known as the ABC region—a label that takes after the names of the suburban cities of Santo André, São Bernardo, and São Caetano. Despite the dearth of systematic information available, some of the most frequently suggested reasons for such a historical industrial concentration in this geographic area derived from the fact that, in addition to having one of the best-trained labor forces in the country, São Paulo-based industrial workers were becoming ever more mobilized. Moreover, cheaper and more readily available labor could be found in the ABC region, an area in close proximity to the burgeoning consumer market of the city of São Paulo, as well as the strategic port city of Santos. Finally, the region still had abundant and affordable land to be purchased by the incoming multinational corporations, and several municipal governments offered fiscal incentives, such as tax rebates to attract these companies to set up shop in the area.[85]

The importance attributed to business groups by the bureaucratic agencies of the Brazilian government can be also found in the ways the promotion of Target Number Seven (railroad construction) was conducted. Trains had a much longer presence than cars in Brazil, as the first trains had been implemented in Brazil in the mid-nineteenth century, but, by the mid-1950s, only about 25 percent of all passengers and cargo was transported by rail in the entire country. Initial studies produced by the Council of Development estimated that meeting the set goal of 1,500 kilometers of new tracks required approximately U.S. $150 million in terms of public disbursements, something seen as untenable by the council officials. The CD nonetheless hoped to repeat the successful business policies conducted by the GEIA in the railroad industry.[86] And therefore, early in 1959, the executive-director of the Council of Development, career bureaucrat Victor da Silva, prepared a questionnaire to gauge the interest of large private companies that utilized the rail system in joining with the federal government to purchase new trains and to build new tracks to renovate the existing network.

Copies of the survey were mailed to hundreds of companies but very few of them found their way back to the council, which, from the standpoint of private investors in the field, seemed to reflect their frustration with the fact that the agency had made them a low priority until that point in time. In the end, as a clear sign that relying on private hands was not going to be a panacea applicable to all infrastructural sectors, and that the instrumental part played by business groups in the automotive industry was not going to be easily replicated in the pursuit of all goals proposed at the Targets Plan, the few responses that made it back to da Silva's hands (about twenty-two) contained basically the same answer: "We have no interest in purchasing railroad equipment for the expansion of our business activities at the moment as we see no reason to believe in significant rates of growth in our industry in the upcoming years."[87]

CONCLUDING REMARKS

The official documentation examined in this chapter indicates how core domestic policies of the JK Years were fundamentally defined by the legal provisions and economic incentives provided by centralized governmental agencies in charge of development promotion. But although the administration devised a well-designed project of fast-paced economic growth via fast industrialization and targeted infrastructural "germinative" (catalytic) investments, it is also evident in the materials surveyed that the Council of Development did not hold demiurgic powers, nor was it immune to political influence. In fact, in what is considered to be one of its most noteworthy achievements, the completion of the previously set target of implementing an automotive industrial sector in the country was largely dependent on the prolific partnership established between the Council of Development and key private economic agents.

Similarly, the chapter also demonstrates how, even though national development mattered to multiple segments of Brazilian society, only specific socio-economic sectors were successful in making their own views and positions heard. In effect, the significant cultural and political impact of the dissemination of the Targets Plan over diverse and heterogeneous groups of Brazilians, and their repeated attempts to influence the course of actions pursued by the council notwithstanding, the agency sought promote its own, business-oriented developmental logic along a much narrower path than it would have needed to incorporate other development-related social demands and positions. Along these historical lines, the Council of Development's central industrial policies clearly favored large industrial projects, many of which were directly controlled by foreign corporations. Which other positions, views, and beliefs concerning national development existed among less politically and economically influential Brazilians, and how these alternative notions might have been articulated *vis-à-vis* the central Brazilian government at the time are key questions addressed in the following three chapters.

Specifically, Chapter Four scrutinizes the main ideological beliefs behind the debates pertaining to development promotion in the period. One of the main goals is to demonstrate the inherent contradictions of the Brazilian developmental state considering that while state-sponsored nationalistic intellectuals (along with most organized industrial workers) conceived of national development as a government-led and socially inclusive goal, the main intellectual formulators of the Targets Plan favored market-oriented industrial projects. Chapter Five transfers the cultural analysis of the previous chapters onto another two central actors: business and technocratic elites, whereas Chapter Six reviews the experiences of metalworkers of the country's most important urban and industrial centers.

In examining these three very important constituencies, I seek to demonstrate that alternative positions on national development were consistently advanced in order to help shape the main developmental policies of the period. While largely and, at least initially, supportive of core goals of the administration, these different social segments actively worked to advance their own developmental views and projects, thus fostering a rich and ideologically charged cultural milieu during the high years of the developmentalist era in Brazil.

NOTES

1. Kubitschek, *Diretrizes Gerais do Plano Nacional de Desenvolvimento*, 32.
2. A comprehensive analysis of Lopes' political trajectory can be found in Maria Letícia Corrêa, "Estado e desenvolvimento no Brasil: um estudo de caso sobre engenheiros e economistas (1956–1961)," *Revista Intellectus* 6, vol. I (2007), 1–15. A detailed analysis of the rise of an influential technocratic cadre in mid-century Brazil can be found in Maria Rita Loureiro, *Os Economistas no Governo: gestão econômica e democracia* (Rio de Janeiro: FGV, 1997).
3. A detailed list of the targets, with didactic charts and illustrations, aimed at the broad public, was finally published in 1959 under the name *As Metas do Governo: 50 anos em 5* (Rio de Janeiro: Presidência da República, 1959).
4. The new capital was built in approximately four years at a cost estimated to be about 3 percent of the national GDP. Details can be foun in Orenstein and Sochaczewski, "Democracia com Desenvolvimento," 179.
5. BNDE, *Projeto Memória: Entrevista com Rômulo de Almeida*. (Rio de Janeiro: BNDE, 1982), tape 11.
6. Ramiz Gattas, *A Indústria Automobilística e a Segunda Revolução Industrial no Brasil: Origens e Perspectivas* (São Paulo: Prelo, 1981).
7. It is important to note that the idea that state-owned lending institutions could play a central role in supporting economic development and industrial promotion was not unique to Brazil; other Latin American countries pursued similar plans. This was particularly important in the cases of Mexico and Chile. For detailed information see Maria Elena Cardero, "Estructura monetaria y financiera de Mexico: 1932–1940," *Revista Mexicana de Sociología* 41, no. 30 (Jul-Sep 1979), 729–68; Miguel D. Ramirez, "Public and Private Investment in Mexico, 1950–90: An Empirical Analysis," *Southern Economic Journal* 61, no. 1 (Jul 1994), 1–17; and Patricio Silva, "State, Public Technocracy and Politics in Chile, 1927–1941," *Bulletin of Latin American Research* 13, no. 3 (Sep 1994), 281–97.
8. BNDE, *Exposição sobre o Programa de Reaparelhamento Econômico: Exercício 1956* (Rio de Janeiro: BNDE, 1956).
9. As a good illustration of their importance, in 1957 these discretionary funds represented 24 percent of all financial resources of the national government, as well as 55 percent of all public investment made in the implementation of the Targets Plan that year. See Conselho do Desenvolvimento, *Relatório Geral para o Exercício 1960* (Rio de Janeiro: Presidência da República, 1961), 35.
10. See note 15 in the introductory chapter.
11. Foreign loans would bring to the Brazilian economy about the same amount of money that the BNDE had loaned to private companies in Brazil with its own resources in the period. For more, see BNDE, *Exposição sobre o Programa de Reaparelhamento Econômico. Exercício do ano 1959* (Rio de Janeiro: BNDE, 1959).
12. Malan, "Relações Econômicas Internacionais do Brasil," 68–74.
13. Vianna, "Duas Tentativas de Estabilização," 128–30.
14. It is important to point out that similar legislations based on multiple exchange rates existed in other developing countries at the time, particularly in South Korea, Hong Kong, and Taiwan, where these trade regulations proved to be similarly efficient instruments in promoting programs of import substitution industrialization. For more, see Gary Gereffi and Donald L. Wyman, *Manufacturing Miracles: Paths of Industrialization in Latin America and East Asia* (Princeton: Princeton University Press, 1990).
15. Conselho do Desenvolvimento, *Relatório Geral para o Exercício 1959* (Rio de Janeiro: Presidência da República, 1960).

16. Lessa, "Fifteen Years of Economic Policy in Brazil," 172–75.
17. Largely due to the economic assistance provided by the U.S. and the multilateral financial institutions set up after World War II, Western Europe and Japan were able to restructure their economies within the first ten years after the conflict, and by the second half of the 1950s were, once again, seeking investment opportunities in Asia, Europe, and Latin America.
18. Kubitschek de Oliveira, *Diretrizes Gerais*, 40–43.
19. This date corresponds to Kubitschek's first day in office. He opened the meeting at 7:00 a.m. by presenting the Targets Plan to his cabinet, submitting a copy to the press, and by creating the Council of Development in his first presidential decree.
20. Kubitschek de Oliveira, *Diretrizes Gerais*, 43; my emphasis.
21. See the series of statements in letters and documents available in Fundo Conselho do Desenvolvimento, 1Q, SDE, Box 3138, National Archive.
22. Lucas Lopes, The United States and Brazil Look Toward the Future: Commerce and Industry, speech given at the Conference on Brazil by the Brazilian Minister of the Economy at the Brazilian Institute at New York University on December 3, 1958, Fundo Lucas Lopes LL pi Lopes, L. 1958.12.01, p. 9, CPDOC Archive.
23. Conselho do Desenvolvimento, *Relatório Geral para o Exercício: 1960* and BNDE, *VI Exposição sobre o Programa de Reaparelhamento Econômico* (Rio de Janeiro, 1960).
24. Hélio Jaguaribe. "Sentido e Perspectivas do Governo Kubitschek," *Cadernos do Nosso Tempo* 1, no. 5 (Jan/Mar 1956), 1–18.
25. Presidential Decree number 38,744, of February 1, 1956, article 2, Fundo Conselho do Desenvolvimento, 1Q, SDE, Box 3130, National Archive.
26. See the series of documents available in Fundo Conselho do Desenvolvimento, 1Q, SDE, Box 3157, National Archive.
27. A good analysis of this process, highlighting the political cost involved in pursuing a deflationary course of action is presented in Sola, *Ideias Econômicas, Decisões Políticas*.
28. BNDE, *Lucas Lopes: 30 Anos do BNDES*. Projeto Memória: Primeira Fase. (Rio de Janeiro: BNDE, 1982), 22.
29. Presidential Decree number 43,395, of March 13th, 1958, Fundo Conselho do Desenvolvimento, 1Q, SDE, box 3130, National Archive.
30. Presidential Decrees numbers 39,412, 39,568, 39,569, 39,676-A, and 41,018, Fundo Conselho do Desenvolvimento, 1Q, SDE, box 3157, National Archive.
31. Juscelino Kubitschek, Opening Remarks Made at the Opening Event of the Training Course of Economic Development and Technical Programming, at the National Bank of Development in August 1956, Fundo Lucas Lopes LL pi Lopes, L., 1956/1958.00.00, p. 2, CPDOC Archive.
32. Helen Shapiro, "Determinants of Firm Industry Entry into the Brazilian Automobile Manufacturing Industry, 1956–1968," *Business History Review* 65, no. 4, The Automobile Industry (Winter 1991), 876–947.
33. Fundo Conselho do Desenvolvimento, 1Q, SDE, Box 3148, National Archive.
34. Ibid.
35. Leff, *Economic Policy-Making*, 208.
36. In addition to Geddes, *Politician's Dilemma and* Leff, *Economic Policy-Making*; see also Martins, *Industrialização, burguesia nacional e desenvolvimento*.
37. Boschi, *Elites Industriais e Democracia*; Diniz, *Empresário, Estado e Capitalismo no Brasil*; Cardoso de Mello, *O Capitalismo Tardio;* Leopoldi, *Política e Interesses na Industrialização*; and Limoncic, "A Civilização do Automóvel."
38. Fundo Conselho do Desenvolvimento, 1Q, SDE, Box 3138, 3139, 3140, and 3141, National Archive.
39. Ibid., Box 3141.

40. Ibid., Box 3139.
41. Fundo Conselho do Desenvolvimento,1Q, SDE, Box 3138, National Archive.
42. Detailed information can be found in Werner Baer, *The Development of the Brazilian Steel Industry.* (Nashville: Vanderbilt University Press, 1969).
43. Fundo Conselho do Desenvolvimento, 1Q, SDE, Box 3138, National Archive.
44. Ibid.
45. Only in 1958 did the Council of Development seek to distribute thirty thousand copies of the final version of the Targets Plan, which were published in a three volume series. See Letter from Gráfica Editora Jornal do Comércio to Lucas Lopes on May 9, 1958, Fundo Conselho do Desenvolvimento, 1Q, SDE, Box 3138, National Archive.
46. Letter to Council of Development, Fundo Conselho do Desenvolvimento, 1Q, SDE, Box 3141-A, National Archive.
47. See Jorge Ferreira, *Trabalhadores do Brasil: O Imaginário Popular* (Rio de Janeiro: Editora da FGV, 1997).
48. See the diverse materials available in Fundo Conselho do Desenvolvimento, 1Q, SDE, Box 3138 and 3139, National Archive.
49. Letter sent by Abel de Carvalho on June 26, 1956, addressed to Kubitschek but mailed to the Council of Development, Fundo Conselho do Desenvolvimento, 1Q, SDE, Box 3141, National Archive. Similar requests were consistently presented by labor unions throughout the entire JK Years, as will be examined in Chapter Six.
50. Fundo Conselho do Desenvolvimento, 1Q, SDE, Box 3138, National Archive.
51. Ibid., Box 3139.
52. Ibid., letter dated October 10, 1956, from Lucas Lopes addressed to Mr. Alencar, Box 3139.
53. Ibid., Boxes 3150, 3150, and 3153.
54. Ibid., Boxes 3149 to 3153.
55. Ibid., Box 3169.
56. Ibid., Box 3150.
57. Ibid., Box 3151. Unfortunately, the draft bill was not available at the National Archive in Rio de Janeiro.
58. See Baer, *Industrialization and Economic Development*; and Lincoln Gordon and Engelbert L. Grommers, *United States Manufacturing Investment in Brazil: The Impact of Brazilian Government Policies, 1946–1960* (Cambridge, MA: Harvard Graduate School of Business Administration, 1960).
59. Statements by Prof. Roberto de Oliviera Campos at the III Committee of the GATT in Washington D.C. on October 1, 1959, Fundo Roberto Campos, RC.d.md 1959.01.02, CPDOC Archive.
60. See multiple documents expressing Lopes's growing concern for the continued deterioration of coffee prices in the international market, as well as his frustration at not being able to convince additional coffee-producing countries to sign on with an international agreement on coffee production. Available in Fundo Lucas Lopes, FF mf 1958.06.24 and LL mf 1957.12.23, CPDOC Archive.
61. Donald Huddle, "Balanço de pagamentos e controle de câmbio no Brasil: diretrizes, políticas e história," *Revista Brasiliera de Economia* 18, no. 1 (Mar 1964), 5–40.
62. Conselho do Desenvolvimento, *Economic Cooperation between the United States and Brazil Document,* vol. 5 (Presidência da República, 1956).
63. Nícia Vilela Luz, *Aspectos do Nacionalismo Econômico Brasileiro: os esforços em prol da industrialização*, Volume XVI (São Paulo: Coleção Revista Brasileira de História, vol. XVI, 1959), 157.

64. Lúcio Flávio R. de Almeida, *A Ilusão de Desenvolvimento: Nacionalismo e Dominação Burguesa nos Anos JK* (Florianópolis: Editora da UFSC, 2006).
65. BNDE, *Exposição sobre o Programa de Reaparelhamento Econômico: Exercício 1957* (Rio de Janeiro: BNDE, 1957), 117.
66. Conselho do Desenvolvimento, "Relatório das atividades do GEIA," in *Plano de Desenvolvimento Econômico Industrial de Base* (Rio de Janeiro: Presidência da República, 1957), vol. 1, Indústria Automobilística.
67. Conselho de Desenvolvimento, Relatório sobre a Indústria Automobilística elaborado pelo Grupo de Estudos, Fundo Conselho do Desenvolvimento, 1Q, SDE, Box 3148, National Archive.
68. Gattas, *A Indústria Automobilística*, 113.
69. See "Ata de Fundação da Associação Profissional da Indústria de Autopeças para Automóveis e Similares do Estado de São Paulo, October 1 1951," in Gattas, *A Indústria Automobilística*. For a detailed discussion of the model, see Caren Addis, "Cooperação e desenvolvimento."
70. Anfavea, *Indústria Automobilística Brasileira: uma história de desafios* (São Paulo: DBA, 1994).
71. Kubitschek, *Diretrizes Gerais*, 147.
72. Benedito H. Nascimento, *Formação da Indústria Automobilística Brasilieira: Política de Desenvolvimento Industrial em uma Economia Dependente*, Série Teses e Monografias, Instituto de Geografia, no. 24 (São Paulo: Universidade de São Paulo, 1976).
73. Conselho do Desenvolvimento, "Relatório das atividades do GEIA."
74. Lúcio Meira, "A Industrialização," in *JK: O Estadista do Desenvolvimento*, ed. José Aparecido de Oliveira (Brasília: Memorial JK, 1991), 124.
75. *Relatório do Grupo de Trabalho sobre a Indústria Automobilística,* Document no. 6,Conselho do Desenvolvimento da Presidência da República (May 1956), 17–18, Fundo Roberto Campos, RC e/cd 1956.05.27, CPDOC Archive.
76. Conselho do Desenvolvimento, *Relatório sobre a Meta 27: Indústria Automobilística.* (Rio de Janeiro: Presidência da República, Serviço de Documentação, 1959), 22–26.
77. Detailed information can be found in Sydney A. Latini, *Suma Automobilística* (Rio de Janeiro: Editora Tama, 1984), vol. 1.
78. This chart is based on Conselho do Desenvolvimento, Relatório interno do GEIA, preparado para a elaboraçao da Mensagem Presidencial de Janeiro de 1960, Fundo Conselho do Desenvolvimento, 1Q, SDE, Box 3157, National Archive. A useful summary of these policies can be found in Confederação Nacional da Indústria, *Análise e Perspectivas da Indústria Automobilística* (Rio de Janeiro, 1960).
79. Conselho do Desenvolvimento, *Relatório sobre a Meta 27*, 26–29.
80. Associação Nacional da Indústria de Tratores, Caminhões, Automóveis e Veículos Similares, *A Indústria Brasileira de Automóveis Presta Esclarecimento ao Público.* (São Paulo, 1957), 7.
81. Conselho de Desenvolvimento, Relatório sobre a Indústria Automobilística elaborado pelo Grupo de Estudos, Fundo Conselho do Desenvolvimento, 1Q, SDE, Box 3148, National Archive.
82. Conselho do Desenvolvimento, *Relatório do GEIA sobre a Fixação de Normas Gerais a Serem Adotadas pela Indústria Automobilística, presented on October 23rd, 1957*, Fundo Conselho do Desenvolvimento, 1Q, SDE, Box 3148, National Archive.
83. Conselho de Desenvolvimento, Relatório sobre a Indústria Automobilística elaborado pelo Grupo de Estudos, Fundo Conselho do Desenvolvimento, 1Q, SDE, Box 3148, National Archive.

84. See CEPAL, *La creación de la industria automovilística brasileña analizada como un caso de programación sectorial*, Studios de Cepal (Santiago: Cepal, Juño 1961); and Martins, *Pouvoir et Développement Économique*.
85. For more see Luis Eduardo Simões de Souza, "Políticas Públicas em São Bernardo do Campo no Pós-Guerra: 1945–1964" (MA thesis, University of São Paulo, 2002).
86. Fundo Conselho do Desenvolvimento, 1Q, SDE, Boxes 3140 and 3148, National Archive.
87. Ibid., Boxes 3150, 3151, and 3152.

4 The Higher Institute of Brazilian Studies versus the Technocrats

Development as State-led Social Inclusion or as Market-based Policies

INTRODUCTORY NOTES

The intellectual reflection on national development taking place in mid-twentieth-century Brazil was generally structured around a binary reasoning juxtaposing agriculture-based versus industry-based economies, and export-led versus domestic-oriented activities, which were consistently seen as irreconcilable scenarios preventing the "true Brazilian nation" to emerge. This logic was paradigmatically displayed in key intellectual studies conducted at the time, particularly in the examinations produced by the group of prolific nationalist thinkers who gathered at the Higher Institute of Brazilian Studies (ISEB) in the second half of the 1950s.

Considering their role in advancing some of the most qualified and influential studies pertaining to the goal of national development, the present chapter examines how the work of these self-defined "concerned intellectuals" impacted the national debates on development promotion in the period. It should be already noted that individual analytical tools and ideological positions notwithstanding, the Higher Institute of Brazilian Studies defended a reasonably unified developmental position centered on the notion that the central government should act as the main promoter of socio-economic inclusion by means of industrial promotion and the enlargement of the domestic market aimed at achieving measurable levels of betterment for the majority of the country's population.

Given the sharp distinctions between these nationalist proposition and the most important policies and goals structuring the Targets Plan, the chapter also scrutinizes the ways in which the socially and politically driven concepts and projects espoused by the ISEB contrasted with the more market-oriented notions underlining the policies pursued by the Kubitschek administration. In fact, despite ISEB's growing influence in shaping the intellectual, cultural, and even political debates about national development in the second half of the 1950s, the Council of Development's technocratic course of action continued to reflect its lack of interest in incorporating alternative developmental positions, thus adding to the ideological polarization of the time.

THE HIGHER INSTITUTE OF BRAZILIAN STUDIES AND NATIONAL-DEVELOPMENTALISM: OVERCOMING THE UNDERDEVELOPED CONDITION

The origins of the Higher Institute of Brazilian Studies (commonly known in Brazil as ISEB and also referred to here simply as the institute) are found in the informal discussions taking place among a specific group of intellectuals from São Paulo and Rio de Janeiro in 1952. Throughout the year, a diverse set of politically interested journalists, lawyers, bureaucrats, and economists from the two largest and wealthiest Brazilian cities met every fourth weekend of each month at the Itatiaia National Park, a mountainous natural reserve located halfway between the two metropolitan areas, to discuss and propose solutions to what they saw as Brazil's most urgent problems. Coordinated from the outset by the charismatic figure of Hélio Jaguaribe and bringing together an ideologically heterogeneous group of individuals, later known as the "Itatiaia Group," these gatherings in this bucolic setting gave rise to a rich intellectual reflection pertaining to how best influence in shaping the country's future.[1]

The two most important practical outcomes of these meetings included the creation of the Brazilian Institute of Social and Political Studies (IBESP) and the launching of a periodical titled *Cadernos do Nosso Tempo* (Essays of Our Time), in 1953. Both the agency and magazine functioned only until mid-year 1955 and served as the main venues for publicizing the Itatiaia-based discussions. Mostly funded by their own members, both received some financial support from the Ministry of Education thanks to personal connections with key government officials. In addition to coordinating the activities of the IBESP, Jaguaribe served as editorial director of *Cadernos* as well as its main financial supporter.[2] These two earlier intellectual endeavors brought together the majority of the individuals later involved in key activities conducted at the ISEB in the second half of the decade, including, in more prominent roles, writers as important as Roland Corbisier, Cândido Mendes de Almeida, Guerreiro Ramos, Heitor Lima, and Nelson Werneck Sodré. Indicative of the historical significance of this rising generation of public intellectuals, during its two years of existence, some of the most important newspapers in Rio periodically reproduced *Cadernos*' articles, thus making future ISEB members' work well known to broader sectors of the still small but highly influential reading public located not only in the federal capital, but in several large cities across the country.[3]

A central figure in both the ISEB and in some of the most relevant political and economic debates unfolding in Brazil in the postwar era, Jaguaribe remained an active author well into the twenty-first century, always advancing very idiosyncratic, and usually controversial, political ideas, which, he claims, harken back to the humanistic legal training he received at the Catholic University in Rio de Janeiro in the 1940s.[4] He is the author of several books on the topic of national development wherein he consistently asserted that a "true" nationalist ideology had to be based on concrete concerns and focused on producing viable political solutions for the country.[5] In 1964, after a military coup brought a repressive regime to power in Brazil, thus forcefully ushering the closure of the institute, Jaguaribe was forced to leave the country. He went on to teach at prestigious universities such as Stanford, Harvard, and MIT until the early 1970s, at which time he returned to Brazil.

Contrasting with its privately funded predecessor, the Higher Institute of Brazilian Studies (ISEB) was a government-funded academic unit directly tied to the Ministry of Education, created in 1955 during the interim presidential administration of Café Filho to serve as an arena for producing a nationalist perspective on development promotion. The founding of an academic institution with such a profile during the market friendly administration of Café Filho can only be explained by taking into consideration the patrimonial political logic prevalent in Brazil in the period. Literary critic Cândido Mota Filho, a personal friend of Roland Corbisier, served as minister of education at the interim administration of Café Filho, and through this personal connection between the former two, Jaguaribe was introduced to Mota Filho in June 1955. ISEB's future central figure, Jaguaribe had prepared a document defending the creation of what he called a Higher Institute of Peace (in contrast to the already influential, Escola Superior de Guerra [National War College]), and at the official meeting with the minister, he defended the creation of such an investigative body to be placed in charge of finding ways to promote a self-sustaining path of development for the country. The proposal received Motta's support and early in July of 1955, probably unaware of the strong nationalistic direction that the institute would follow, Café Filho signed Presidential Decree number 37,608, which established the Higher Institute of Brazilian Studies "to provide a better understanding of the national reality and of the necessary tools for intervening in its economic and political realms [. . .] with a mandate to conduct higher-level [graduate] academic work in the fields of social sciences, philosophy, economics, and history."[6]

The institute's daily activities were coordinated by its executive director, a position that until 1960 was filled by Roland Corbisier, ISEB's only paid member of the agency, as all others were either employed by different sectors of the federal government bureaucracy, local academic institutions in Rio de Janeiro, or worked in private businesses. Additional original members with official appointments included the aforementioned Hélio Jaguaribe, who served as director of the Department of Political Science, Alberto Guerreiro Ramos, director of the Department of Sociology, Alvaro Vieira Pinto, director of the Department of Philosophy, Cândido Mendes de Almeida, director of the Department of History, and Ewaldo Correa Lima, director of the Department of Economics. The institute also had a board of trustees, which, despite the prominence of its members, exerted minimal influence on the routine operations of the organization. Some of the most important members of this board included Anísio Teixeira, director of the Program of Higher Academic Training of University Professors (CAPES) at the Ministry of Education, and Roberto Campos, the career diplomat who, alongside Lucas Lopes, played a key role in implementing Kubitschek's Targets Plan.[7]

During its nine-year existence, the ISEB published over thirty original works, mostly produced by its members, on a wide range of topics, as well as translations of various foreign titles. These later works included some of the main contemporary pieces written by influential European thinkers such as Karl Jaspers, Karl Manheim, and Gunnar Myrdal. The institute administered regular academic courses on a new field of research, called the Study of Brazilian Problems, and its most important official academic program consisted of a year-long post-graduate curriculum offered to senior civil and military members of the federal administration. At the end of the coursework phase, students were required to write a thesis on some "key problem" the country faced; and upon successful completion of their theses, their authors were awarded an MA degree in Brazilian Studies. ISEB intellectuals also regularly interacted closely with broader audiences beyond the academic setting. Especially relevant were multiple public speaking engagements, such as conferences and lectures, held by several members of the institute in cities across the country at the behest of universities, local governments, civic organizations, and a number of labor unions.[8]

Closely aligned with Jaguaribe's ideals, the intellectual production of the ISEB was essentially imbued with a clear, pragmatic orientation. Its main inspiration was the search for creative new ways to promote Brazil's socio-economic betterment, as well as the country's political and cultural modernization. While these notions can be easily derived from almost any work produced at the institute, they were also repeated by Hélio Jaguaribe and Cândido Mendes, the only living members of the ISEB, in individual interviews I conducted with them in February and March of 2008 in Rio de Janeiro. Both authors reinforced the social concern they consistently advanced in their works of the 1950s, and attributed such academic interest to the intellectual influence (noticeable in their writings) they received from the pragmatic philosophical tenets of the German Phenomenology of the 1940s, as well as French and Spanish Existentialism of the 1950s, especially from authors such as the already mentioned Jaspers and Manheim, as well as Ernest Cassirer, José Ortega y Gasset, and Jean-Paul Sartre.[9]

Despite important intellectual and personal idiosyncratic differences among its members, the intellectual production originating at ISEB demonstrates remarkable similarities and shared common ideological influences. One of the main features of the institute's legacy in the history of Brazilian socio-political thought is the idea that it was possible (and imperative) to formulate a unifying ideology of nationalism that would then instrumentally serve to support Brazil's quest for "emancipatory development." ISEB members insisted that creating a "national ideology of development" was vital for "galvaniz[ing] the disoriented, alienated masses into a project aimed at building national economic power and consolidating the political sovereignty of the nation."[10]

The search for an applicable knowledge capable of "redeeming the country" from its underdeveloped condition shaped the history of the institute from the start, and some of the main arguments consistently advanced in the extensive work produced by members of the agency were advanced in the pages of *Cadernos do Nosso Tempo*. Of special relevance, the articles written by Hélio Jaguaribe, particularly one titled "The Brazilian Crisis," published in the first volume of the journal in mid-year 1953, quintessentially defined what a so-called "ideology of national-developmentalism" was to promote. In the author's own words, the essay provided "a candid diagnosis" of the country's main challenges to sustained development and advanced a call for national unity so that what was defined as the socio-political, economic, and cultural crisis that the country faced could be overcome. No specific information is provided as to what this alluded to multidimensional predicament happened to be, but one can nonetheless reasonably infer that Jaguaribe considered this sort of information to be unnecessary given the widespread perception that Brazil faced dire economic difficulties deriving from growing trade deficits and rising inflation rates, as well as increasing political instability (e.g., cabinet reshuffling and congressional investigations) which culminated with Vargas's suicide in 1954.[11]

As a whole, the article examines what its author defined as "deep-rooted causes" of this alleged crisis and the focus of the piece is on presenting some possible solutions to these same problems. Pertaining to the economic dimension of the crisis, Jaguaribe argues that the main issue the country faced (namely diminishing foreign monetary reserves) derived from a continued deterioration of the terms of trade for agricultural products in the international market. In his view, the Brazilian economy had for far too long been tied to the exporting of primary goods, a situation made worse by the growing national consumption of ever more expensive manufactured imports. The nation also purportedly faced a national crisis deriving from a lack of awareness of its true needs and identity, something that was being aggravated by the refusal of the federal government to act as a proper agent of national development.

Building on the "diagnosis" provided, in the second part of the same essay, Jaguaribe argues that Brazil was essentially trapped in a "semi-colonial condition" given its inability to pursue a self-sustaining course of economic growth. This reasoning was largely grounded on the proposed opposition existing between the colonial condition and the state of being a fully independent nation; a heuristic recourse recurrent in several analyses produced at the institute that found resonance in similar propositions espoused by European authors of the time.[12] Considering, however, that the anti-colonial argument advanced by these latter authors was not applicable in its entirety to the reality of Latin American states—where political independence had been achieved 130 years earlier—ISEB intellectuals creatively devised the notion of the "semi-colonial condition" in order to make sense of the historical context of countries like Brazil in mid-century.

The latter concept was thus coined as a way to more aptly describe what these authors claimed to be heteronomously defined (from the outside) societies, which regardless of being legally sovereign states, could not fully exercise their national autonomy considering that their commodity-exporting economies were essentially organized on the basis of attending to foreign demands and interests. Along these conceptual lines, the semi-colonial condition was said to be a permanent state of underdevelopment characterized by large rates of unemployment or underemployment, low economic productivity, wages, and per capita income, as well as a lack of investment capital, and a deep social fragmentation between social groups involved in the dynamic exporting sector of the economy and those tied to subsistence agriculture.[13] ISEB's mid-century reflection on colonialism could therefore be seen as having advanced some of the first versions of theoretical formulations later proposed in the field of postcolonial studies. In fact, along with some of their influential contemporaries in Europe (e.g., Sartre, Balandier, and Fanon), in their extensive and creative studies of the semi-colonial condition Jaguaribe, Corbisier, and Mendes de Almeida, among others, argued that this was a state of being that was simultaneously legally independent yet economically (as well as politically and culturally) subordinate to others nations' needs, interests, wills, and values.[14]

As a way to remedy this challenging scenario, in the final section of *The Brazilian Crisis*, Jaguaribe urged the country to reshape its structures of government so that the central state could exert a "coordinating role in leading the nation in the direction of autonomous national development." He also called for the creation of a broad-based social movement in favor of economic efficiency inspired on a nationalist ideology of development and very concrete developmental goals promoted by an assertive central government "capable of defending the national interests at the international level and of offering hope for a common future to be reached by all social segments."[15] Jaguaribe believed that only by resorting to a developmental ideology capable of harnessing all sectors of Brazilian society interested in overcoming the condition of underdevelopment, would the country become a politically and economically viable and autonomous nation. Likewise, in his view, the formulation of such an ideology was the most important task that the nationalist intellectuals coalesced at the ISEB should perform. And he affirms to have coined the very expression that named the ideology the agency was to formulate in the period: national developmentalism.[16]

Further revealing the broad support these general ideas received, an analogous formulation can be found in an article written by Hermes Lima, published in *Cadernos do Nosso Tempo* in 1955. Lima served in the National Brazilian Congress during the 1940s, as minister of foreign relations in 1962, and as prime minister in 1963. In his more moderate political view, countries characterized by a non-autonomous economic system, such as Brazil, should formulate a nationalist sentiment in favor of fast-paced industrialization so that effective independence could be finally attained. Lima also believed that national development depended on understanding the country's concrete needs and potentialities and that the Brazilian government should assume its unavoidable developmental responsibilities toward meeting these same goals. Despite his poignant call for immediate action, Lima's nationalism was of a moderate strain, which he defined as "non-Jacobine," that saw a "positive role" to be played by foreign investors in the implementation of important economic undertakings that the country badly needed.[17] This position would later find support in Jaguaribe's own work, but it was by no means consensually shared by all members of the institute. In fact, revealing important changes occurring in his political positions throughout the 1950s, Jaguaribe moved from a passionate defense of a widespread process of nationalization of the means of production to a market-oriented stance that welcomed external sources of capital in the process of national development in Brazil, as will be further examined below.

Executive Director Roland Corbisier also supported the notion that national development had, above all, to attend to the needs of the majority of the country's population and stated that "any policy of development needs to be evaluated on its ability to improve the living conditions of the entire population and to reorient the economic structure of the country in ways that produce higher levels of consumption among the popular sectors."[18] An emblematic ISEB intellectual, Corbisier was similarly interested in producing works pragmatically tied to what he called the "problems of our time," and, like most other members of the institute, he was trained in law, but rather than practicing as a lawyer, he worked as a journalist for several newspapers in Rio de Janeiro and São Paulo in the first half of the decade. He served as the executive director of the ISEB until 1960, when he was elected to the state assembly of the recently created state of Guanabara (in the former capital city of Rio de Janeiro).[19]

Also in tandem with Jaguaribe's (and Lima's) use of a comparative frame of analysis about the colonial (or semi-colonial) condition, Corbisier's reflection is centered on what he defined as the "cultural dimension of colonialism." He claimed that even if different from the realities of the remaining colonial possessions, Brazil did not differ from them in lacking the means to exert its economic (and thus political) self-determination. Drawing many of his ideas from comparing the case of Brazil with those of other non-industrialized societies—more specifically with the situation of the European colonies of the African continent, which he saw as similarly culturally dependent societies—Corbisier also argued that a self-sustaining path of development was what effectively defined the achievement of national autonomy, rather than its mere formal (legal) aspects.[20] Accordingly, what above all was said to define the condition of colonialism and underdevelopment was the generalized sense of inferiority *vis-à-vis* the industrialized regions of the world, and while economic self-reliance seemed essential, such a reality did not seem possible unless cultural autonomy (i.e., a sentiment of national pride) existed. Moreover, in his view, there was no other option but "to invent our future by constructing our own culture as the guiding beacon of the new Brazil we want to create."[21]

The idea of the nation as a "common project" was central to ISEB authors, and Corbisier is explicit in stating that the main task at hand was the construction of a collective national project on the basis of an accurate understanding of the country's true identity. In the author's own words, "it is only on the basis of a true ideology of national development that we become aware of ourselves, of who we are and of whom we want to be, of our nation as a common task to be created."[22] With these categories in mind, Corbisier characterized underdevelopment as the condition of alienation concerning one's own potential, as well as the act of mimicking a foreign culture.[23] Ironically, in order to buttress his positions, the institute's executive director looked to works of European intellectuals who argued that the colonial reality was a deep-rooted and lasting system that penetrated the minds of the population in the colonized regions of the world, producing a situation of self-alienation.[24] As a solution to such a state of affairs, the agency's main focus should be that of formulating a concrete practical ideology, "a narrative of who we want to be as a nation, an image of a shared destiny which, in order to be viable, has to be defined by the very notion of development."[25]

Adding to the concern about the "national cause," one of the most enthusiastic defenses for the need for improving the lives of popular social segments came from one of the ISEB's most erudite thinkers, Alvaro Vieira Pinto. This prominent philosopher from the National University of Rio de Janeiro served as the institute's executive director between 1960 and 1964, and centered his research on the goal of inserting the needs of common people into the core of the philosophical reflection produced by the agency. Vieira Pinto's works at the ISEB were largely based on a Hegelian-Marxist inspiration and he would become one of the more radical intellectuals of the institute, who argued that national development had to attend primarily to the needs and interests of the working sectors as "without an effective ideology of national development interested in meeting the needs of the majority of the population, no real development can be ever achieved."[26]

Considering that being underdeveloped signified that a collectivity had no control over its own future, a nationalist project of development was the necessary means to achieving not only economic prosperity, but also political sovereignty. Likewise, without economic independence, said Vieira Pinto, "there is no possibility for the *real nation* to come to fruition, no possibility of being true to one's national essence."[27] Overcoming the reality of underdevelopment indeed required, in Vieira Pinto's view, eliminating global socio-economic divisions existing between industrialized and non-industrialized economies. This goal demanded that national development be pursued on a global scale in ways that harnessed the potentialities and the collective will of the populations in all poor nations in favor of an alternative path of economic insertion in the world economy.[28] In this sense, Vieira Pinto argued that given that underdeveloped states were at the mercy of the whims of rich nations, the formulation and promotion of an ideology capable of creating a global awareness in favor of development was one of the most important tasks to be conducted at the ISEB.[29]

For Alberto Guerreiro Ramos, ISEB's first director of the Sociology Department, pursuing a nationalist agenda of development also implied engaging in the global struggle to eliminate socio-economic disparities between developed and underdeveloped nations.[30] Like Jaguaribe, Guerreiro Ramos believed that the task of promoting national development required that all social segments interested in the goal of industrialization unite in a common front as "it is intrinsic to the colonial and semi-colonial condition to have the national society divided between national and anti-national poles."[31] This opposition, said to be inherent to the condition of not being fully developed as a nation, was to be the basis for a unified quest for development that, while taking place domestically was to be pursued on a truly global scale.[32] In line with Vieira Pinto's work, Guerreiro Ramos was also adamant that the intellectual reflection produced at the institute served the concrete needs of the larger national society. In his view, moving beyond the structural contradiction existing between national versus anti-national interests required the formulation of an engaged developmental ideology capable of motivating all so-called modern social segments along the "process of awakening, which really is the imperative task of Brazilian society today."[33] These notions were also shared by Werneck Sodré who believed that Brazil's main challenge resided in building a common front of all nationalists against "powerful obstacles placed by foreign economic interest and their domestic allies."[34]

The irreconcilable opposition between distinct social interests was best described by Jaguaribe with the concepts of "cosmopolitan" social forces, traditionally tied to produce-exporting activities and whose interests were opposed to those espoused by "nationalist" forces who favored national industrialization and the expansion of the domestic market. Ironically, in the very work where he defined these same terms (*O Nacionalismo na Atualidade Brasileira*), Jaguaribe defended a middle-ground position and argued that effective national development had to be based on a pragmatic stance rather than on impoverished versions of radicalized political stances. The latter formulation by someone who had earlier in the decade been one of the strongest defender of traditional nationalist positions, including a heightened role for the federal state in controlling key economic resources and industries, stirred a large controversy within the institute, leading to dramatic events.

Mostly deriving from the fact that Jaguaribe now advocated profoundly different positions from those traditionally said to represent the nationalist agenda (such as the refusal to accept foreign investors' involvements in infrastructural economic activities), the publication of *O Nacionalismo* in

1959 provoked a deep fracture among ISEB's members that resulted in the author's departure from the very institute he had almost single-handedly created. This internal strife was replicated in a larger scale between those arguing against all forms of foreign capital and those defending the position that unless foreign investors were welcomed into the country, no significant rate of economic growth could be reached. And despite the fact that what was essentially at stake in these debates was the very definition of a nationalist path of development, the group supporting the first position self-identified as the "true nationalists."[35] In fact, even though the Kubitschek administration favored industrial projects that included the participation of foreign private capital, most ISEB members were ever more adamantly opposed to such a developmental course; and, in direct contrast to Jaguaribe's late support for foreign sources of private investment, a more xenophobic nationalist position became prominent at the agency and beyond.

Articulating an anti-colonial ideology along these lines, this latter position vehemently repudiated foreign sources of capital *in toto* as manifestations of economic imperialism, which had to be rejected and replaced by a higher public (governmental) economic influence. In fact, even the otherwise moderate Cândido Mendes, Jaguaribe's close associate, passionately argued against enlarging the presence of foreign private capital in the country. In his view, foreign investors had historically played an essentially exploitative role and should, therefore, be rejected as reliable developmental agents.[36] In his own words, "Latin America share[d] a legacy of not being the subject of its own history and our alienation is, tragically, what we most have in common."[37] This negative assessment of the reality of non-industrialized societies notwithstanding, partaking in ISEB's existentialist *spirit de temps* and in Vieira Pinto's foreign policy propositions, Cândido Mendes believed that "the day to become owners of our own historical place has arrived," a reality that Brazil shared with the "nations committing to the Bandung agenda," all of which are now defined by having the "national idea intrinsically associated with the goal of promoting our own development."[38] Much in the same way, he argued that, "pursuing development as a deliberate policy towards the goal of self-determination" was the basis for establishing solidarity with other underdeveloped societies around the globe.[39]

After the controversy associated with the publication of *O Nacionalismo*, the more moderate members of ISEB left the organization, which was increasingly associated with the militant version of nationalism espoused in the National Congress by the Nationalist Parliamentary Front—a multi-party political alliance that supported higher levels of governmental involvement in the national economy.[40] The radicalization in the positions propounded by the institute in the late 1950s was closely attuned to similar trends taking place in broader political debates, especially in the discussions surrounding the negotiations being conducted between the federal government and the International Monetary Fund (IMF) throughout much of 1959. It was then that Brazil negotiated a stand-by loan with the international financial agency as a key element of the Plan of Economic Stabilization promoted by Lucas Lopes, who served as Kubitschek's finance minister.

After the agreement became a central focus of heated political debates in the national print media, the president refused to sign the terms of the international loan package given the stringent terms and credit restrictions demanded by the fund. JK made sure to utilize his decision to gather needed support among the so-called nationalists, but the decision was made to the detriment of his long association with the market-oriented Lopes and Lopes's close associate Roberto Campos and, in the end, also proved to be detrimental to the long-term solvency of the national economy.[41] Finally, it is important to point out that regardless of this specific politically motivated decision, the main points of the policies and projects implemented by the Council of Development were consistently aligned with these same two influential technocrats. Core elements of their developmental views are examined in the third section below. Before these elements can be studied, however, in the next section I assess ISEB's role in the long debate on development and modernization in Brazil.

ISEB'S PLACE IN THE INTELLECTUAL REFLECTION ON DEVELOPMENT IN BRAZIL

The role of the Higher Institute of Brazilian Studies in the national debates pertaining to the topics of development promotion and nationalism in Brazil has become the focus of various critical assessments in the last several decades, particularly from different Marxist perspectives.[42] A new interpretive lens can be advanced by moving beyond the influence of the institute's political formulations, activism, and its intellectual contributions, to the context of the broader social reflection of the first half of the twentieth century. In fact, though innovative in many of its specific propositions, the main inspiration underlining the examinations advanced at ISEB were analytical categories that had shaped the reflection on modernity present in Brazil since the turn of the century. Namely, beginning with the works of socially engaged journalists and social commentators, the notion that the country was characterized by a persistent contradiction between modern and premodern economic, political, and cultural realities was noticeable since when Euclydes da Cunha published the novel *Os Sertões* and Graça Aranha published the novel *Canaã* at the turn of the century. These works are considered precursors of the Modernist movement in Brazil and exerted a lasting influence in the national debates pertaining to the goal of redefining the country's national identity along the lines of a Western-style modern life. Similarly in the 1930s, after a centralized nationalist regime had been put in place at the federal level, the dichotomic reasoning opposing a traditional versus a modern Brazil resurged in the works of prominent authors such as Oliveira Viana and Sérgio Buarque de Hollanda.[43]

Particularly relevant for the analytical line presented here, trying to address contradictions purportedly existing between a social reality defined by amorphous social interests and institutions incapable of reconciling such a fragmented political arena, Oliveira Viana strongly defended a centralized tutoring role for the federal government in leading the national body toward a common project.[44] And even though Jaguaribe did not explicitly recognize his intellectual predecessors, his political views closely resemble the centralizing trend shaping the Brazilian state in the 1930s. Specifically, Oliveira Viana's critique of the existing liberal (bourgeois) political institutions designed after foreign models that did not correspond to the real needs of Brazilian society was echoed in much of Jaguaribe's own writings, and similar dualistic notions (i.e., real versus mimicked) became standard in emerging academic disciplines in the 1950s.[45]

Along with many others at the ISEB, Jaguaribe was also influenced by many dualistic developmental notions advanced at the Economic Commission for Latin America (ECLA), particularly those pertaining to the need to expand modern economic activities into traditionally stagnated sectors so that fast-paced growth and social betterment across different levels of society could be found.[46] A second important ECLA formulation with a profound influence over the ISEB argued that the increased technological gap between agriculture-based and industrialized economies required immediate action from governments across the region to stimulate an accelerated path of industrialization. Along these lines, given the enormity of the task at hand, as his political thoughts matured over the course of the 1950s, Jaguaribe argued ever more forcefully for a centralized form of government capable of overcoming the deleterious patrimonial logic of the legislative process; this line of thought is again consistent with Oliveira Viana's earlier claims. Jaguaribe was also very critical of the long Brazilian "tradition" of importing political models that did not respond to the country's actual needs, leaving the nation in a permanent state of alienation.[47]

As indicated in the previous section, the concept of alienation—which most members of the institute articulated in non-Marxist terms, i.e., without reference to the notion of unduly appropriate labor (plus-value)—was central for the reflection produced at the ISEB and even the otherwise conservative Roberto Campos believed that most of the economic challenges Brazil faced in the mid-century derived from domestic elites' misguided tendency of attempting to sustain foreign standards of consumption that did not correspond to the national capability and values.[48] Adding to this line of analysis, Roland Corbisier argued even more explicitly, though in more abstract ways that:

> The lack of critical consciousness in relation to our own selves is explained by the concept of alienation given that during our long colonial trajectory we were defined by what the old mother-countries stamped on us. [. . .] But even after that [experience of colonialism], we

> continue to produce only possibility, which others will take and transform into reality. [. . .] [In so doing], we produce only the *non-being*, while we continue to import the *being*, which is produced by others and which represents only them, not us.[49]

As described above, the condition of being alienated from one's true self was believed to be an all-encompassing reality that shaped every aspect of the semi-colonial condition defining underdeveloped societies. Thus, resorting to the concept of *total social phenomenon* (first articulated by Marcel Mauss but later applied to the study of colonialism by Sartre and Balandier), Corbisier argued that, "an economically dependent nation will necessarily also be culturally dependent," and that, "overcoming the colonial condition which still defines us will require that we embark upon a project that will, at the same time, provide us with economic and cultural autonomy."[50]

As to be expected in a pragmatically oriented academic institution, moving beyond this alienated social reality was also a topic that received a great deal of attention at ISEB. Most writers not only argued for the need for strategic, deliberate action on the part of the national government and its most prepared intellectual advisors, but consistently expressed optimism that this path of action was indeed taking place. Vieira Pinto, for instance, manifested his confidence that, "as we embark in our new stage of intense development, we are finally witnessing the possibility of building social thought that is authentically Brazilian."[51] Guerreiro Ramos also rejoiced in the fact that Brazilians were finally, "becoming aware of our true culture and national character" given the "recent transformations taking place in our economic system," which provided us with "a new way of positioning ourselves in the context of universal history."[52]

In articulating these many different formulations, ISEB intellectuals attempted to define what their own nation was, as well as more importantly, what it could become. In their views, the nation was an entity defined not by its current attributes, but rather by its prospective possibilities. Similarly, the national project of "allowing the true Brazilian nation to emerge" was a political proposition strategically deployed for achieving the fulfillment of the country's potentialities in the future. In this equally optimistic and militant reading of the national scenario—at least in the sense that despite the many present-day challenges, the country could trace a more promising future should the right corrective measures be taken—ISEB members assumed not only that something could be done in order to alter the country's prospects, but also that as engaged (organic) thinkers, they were uniquely equipped to understand the nation's essence and, consequently, guide it to the fulfillment of its potential. Along these creative interpretive lines, the reflection produced at the institute largely took for granted that Brazil's true identity could be known and that a new national narrative (ideology) could be constructed.

All things considered, the nationalist writers who gathered at the Higher Institute of Brazilian Studies believed that in pursuing a path of effective national development, the country's alienation from its own values, interests, and identity could finally be overcome. ISEB intellectuals also argued that in this very same historical process a prominent role was to be reserved for themselves as the emerging self-acclaimed national intelligentsia assigned to guide the actions of a more socially responsive national government. Their prolific intellectual production (more than thirty original books, hundreds of public lectures, and dozens of training courses involving several thousands of civil servants, military personnel, union members, and the general public) notwithstanding, the ISEB was never taken seriously by the most relevant academic institutions of the time. In fact, seeking to serve as organic intellectuals in the self-assigned role of producing applicable knowledge to assess and alter the historical trajectory of the country, the majority of the members of the ISEB were consistently derided by their contemporaries at the University of São Paulo, as well as at the University of Brazil in Rio de Janeiro, who saw this line of engaged examinations as a dangerous path detracting from the more serious pursuit of academic rigor and scientific investigative drive.[53]

Similar distrust of ISEB's intellectual mission was shared by some of the most important media outlets, as well as business associations across the country, particularly in the former capital city of Rio. Moreover, instead of the broad political support ISEB members expected, divergent developmental positions continued to exist within different realms of the federal administration. One view favored a higher role to be played by the government in economic promotion along with growing restrictions to be placed on foreign capital participation in what were considered to be strategic areas (e.g., mineral extraction, energy production, and public utilities distribution). This stance was largely advanced by lower-rank bureaucrats, but also found resonance among some leading decision-makers during the first half of the decade, such as Rômulo de Almeida. On the other ideological extreme, a much smaller but increasingly influential group of leading technocrats (such a Lopes and Campos) defended the higher involvement of private (foreign and domestic) investors and more strict control on public expenditures.[54]

Debates about national development were not restricted to government officials, but were rather replicated in various venues of the influential print media. Insofar as the ability the institute had to influence these discussions, it is worth noting that several of its members regularly published op-ed pieces in some of the most influential periodicals of the time (e.g., *Diário Carioca*, *Jornal do Comércio*, and *Revista do Clube Militar*). Much in the same way, starting in 1957, ISEB worked diligently to expand its reach outside of Rio as a way to influence a wider audience. One important way was by means of public lectures, such as those taking place in March in the city of São Paulo under the sponsorship of the powerful Industrial Federation of the State of São Paulo (FIESP). Similar initiatives occurred in several other major cities, such as Fortaleza and Porto Alegre, in 1959 and 1960, usually at the request of local labor unions. Ironically, in trying to expand its ability to reach larger numbers of different social segments, the institute became ever more visible, making it consequently more susceptible to criticism coming from growing numbers of conservative business and media groups.[55]

Taking everything into account, despite the broad and lasting impact of ISEB's formulations concerning the debate on national development in Brazil in the 1950s (and in subsequent decades), the institute never assumed an executive role in the Kubitschek administration, largely due to the fact that the developmental notions inspiring the actions of the Council of Development were essentially economic in nature and narrower in focus *vis-à-vis* the philosophically based and socially oriented views advanced at ISEB. As a way to highlight the growing divisions pertaining to the topic of development promotion in the period, the next section examines the complex at times, contradictory relationship established between the institute and key decision-makers in charge of executing the main developmental initiatives shaping the broad context of the second half of the 1950s.

DIFFUSE IDEOLOGICAL SUPPORT AND BALANCING ACTS OF NEGOTIATION: THE ISEB, THE KUBITSCHEK ADMINISTRATION, AND THE ROLE OF BUSINESS ELITES

Throughout the JK Years the executive branch of the federal administration maintained very contradictory patterns of interaction with the Higher Institute of Brazilian Studies. Whereas Minister of Education Clóvis Salgado consistently supported, financially and politically, the ISEB, members of the Council of Development and at the Military Council of the Presidency sustained a very different stance regarding the works of the institute. Despite being a conservative politician from Minas Gerais, Salgado repeatedly expressed public support for the agency, particularly when it had become the target of virulent attacks from the Industrial Federation of Rio de Janeiro in 1959 for being "dangerously associated" with the left-leaning Nationalist Parliamentary Front, something the federation saw as an unjustified detraction from the "purely academic role" the institute should perform.[56] Much in the same way, later the same year, General Nelson de Melo, chief minister of the Military Council of the Presidency (*Gabinete Militar*), presented Kubitschek with a disapproving Secret Intelligence Report on the ISEB produced by the Joint-Chiefs of Staff.

The investigation had been motivated by the fact that Navy Captain Aristides Campos Filho, a student enrolled in one of the regular courses in Studies on Brazilian Problems, had accused the institute of "disseminating communist-inspired ideas in its classes, lectures, and publications." The culmination of a two-year long investigation, the report stated that the agency's ideological positions were in direct conflict with the traditional Christian and Western values defining the "true Brazilian culture." Likewise, largely quoting Captain Campos Filho's own claims, the report indicated that most ISEB members regularly defended the formulation of a more independent course of foreign policy, which in the eyes of the military leadership represented a risky departure from the traditional alignment the country had historically maintained with the U.S. Moreover, this ideologically driven stance was considered a "dangerous flirtation with the irresponsible and fallacious neutral path currently espoused by newly independent countries like India and Indonesia."[57]

It should be recalled that the goal of forging a more autonomous foreign policy within the constraints of the Cold War was central to the reflections on national development advanced at ISEB. In concrete terms, Roland Corbisier, Cândido Mendes de Almeida, Guerreiro Ramos, and even the more moderate Hélio Jaguaribe had all argued that the Brazilian government should seek a more independent diplomatic orientation and that the country should subscribe to the principles enunciated at the Bandung Conference, such as non-intervention, equitable terms of trade, and multilateral support for the process of industrialization. According to leading sectors of the Brazilian military however, by espousing such a notion of political autonomy, the institute was going astray from its prescribed duties, thus becoming a subversive entity that paradoxically continued to receive institutional approval and logistical and financial support from an administration that prided itself on its "Christian ideals" and the defense of the inter-American family of nations. Making matters even more serious, the report stated that ISEB disseminated its subversive propositions among numerous subaltern ranks of the military and prominent union leaders who were "unprepared to differentiate between theoretical formulations of free-thinking intellectuals and the practical requirements of life."[58]

In his harsh personal remarks to the president, General Melo urged JK to replace the current members of the institute with non-subversive scholars who did not defend "in ultra-complex jargon the third position presently supported by Marxist elements," or better yet, to terminate the activities of the agency all together. No additional paper trail regarding the report could be traced. It seems nonetheless safe to assume that the military did not get its way given that ISEB continued its activities and no member of the organization was forced to resign by any decision coming from the president's office. But even though the institute never became the focus of severe retaliatory measures during the Kubitschek administration, it is clear that core members of the administration espoused very different ideological and political positions regarding nationalism and development promotion from those vocally propounded at ISEB. In fact, in sharp contrast from the institute's main propositions, the president himself consistently argued that the measure for attesting the existence of national development did not rest on higher levels of political autonomy, but rather on the governmental capabilities of preventing social disruption caused by poor economic growth. As a case in point, in a speech that he gave at the inaugural lecture opening the academic activities of ISEB in 1956, JK declared that:

> We are true nationalists not because we are xenophobic but because we search national solutions for our problems. We welcome and request

> support for our efforts from abroad, such as investment capital, equipment and technical assistance. [. . .] These are not the factors that will keep us in our underdeveloped state; rather it is precisely the absence of foreign productive investments [that is the cause of our current underdevelopment].[59]

Similarly, Roberto Campos, a leading figure in the formulation and implementation of the Targets Plan, believed that the reasons for the economic underdevelopment of the country rested mainly in the absence of investment capital and the low purchasing power of its population. Therefore, in his view, for economic development to occur what was most needed was the attraction of large sums of foreign investment to selected economic projects and that inflationary spending be kept at bay. Particularly during his tenures as director and president of the National Bank of Economic Development and executive director of the Council of Development, Campos consistently argued against the notion that the federal government should seek to attend to the basic social needs of the population by becoming the main promoter of economic development via excessive public expenditures.[60]

Conversely, given the insufficient rate of domestic savings, the main task the government should undertake, in his view, was to convince foreign investors to set up shop in the county so that higher rates of economic performance could be reached. The influential bureaucrat repeatedly argued that, "the option of development requires above all everyone's acceptance of the fact that fast economic growth, not socially oriented disbursement, is the main responsibility at hand and the only way to reduce social economic inequalities."[61] Moreover, even though he accepted the ECLA-espoused notion that industrialization was a preferred course toward improving per capita income in agriculture-based economies, Campos consistently warned that this goal should not be pursued at the cost of inflation, and that an industrial path would only be feasible if agricultural production and exports continued to be supported, including with more equitable terms of trade in the international commodity markets.[62] Persistent rates of inflation such as those seen in Brazil in the mid-1950s were seen as incompatible with a consistent and sustainable path of economic development as they "distort the possibility of governmental and business planning [. . .] [and] heighten social conflicts due to the erosion of living standards of waged workers [. . .] leading to an overall process of decreased productivity and stagnated growth."[63]

Interestingly, coming from someone who later would be consensually considered to be at the opposing end of the ideological spectrum, Celso Furtado, Campos's former associate at the ECLA-BNDE Joint-Group, had also called attention to the perils of assuming that effective social development would be a natural outcome of fast-paced industrialization, which, if left to its own devices, was more likely to result in increased regional and socio-economic disparities.[64] Campos and Furtado indeed espoused similar developmental agendas in the 1950s, but as the decade came to an end their political programs and affiliations gradually diverged, culminating in the different trajectories they followed under the military regime of the 1960s and 1970s. Whereas Campos would occupy key positions in the first authoritarian administration of Castelo Branco (1964–67), Furtado, who had become a key player during Goulart's disruptive years in power (1961–64), would be forced into a long exile. Differing personal paths notwithstanding, in examining closely their respective assessments of the policies pursued under Kubitschek, important convergences come to the foreground.

This seems to be particularly true in their examinations on matters as important as rising inflation rates, the role of foreign capital, and the social impact of economic growth. On the first point, both essentially agreed that much of the rising inflation derived from the over reliance on fast industrialization at the cost of a lack of modernization in the agricultural sector, which continued to be defined by either subsistence production or extensive but technologically dependent export activities. Interestingly, while these represent common points of their analyses, potential remedies were not as easily shared. In fact, whereas Campos came to defend the curtailment of the very developmental drive of the period, Furtado continued to support further developmental initiatives aimed at addressing some of the more structural problems of the national economy.[65] He nonetheless consistently warned that the chosen path of substitutive industrialization was essentially focused on what he called "less essential industries," which had been established on the basis of the excessive rates of mechanization of their production lines.[66]

Illustrating how much his intellectual positions evolved in the course of the recent developmental history of the country, along with most of the ISEB intellectuals, Campos initially held a moderate stance on the role of foreign capital; a position that was also largely shared by Furtado. Campos believed that while important in bringing the modern technology and the massive funds needed to activate costly and high-risk industries (e.g., mining), this source of funds should not be allowed to control strategic sectors of the national economy.[67] Furtado was more skeptical about any positive role that could be played by foreign capital given their history in the country and the Latin American region in general, but he did not argued for the total elimination of this source of funds, defending instead the creation of regulatory means to discipline them.[68]

Finally, on the third point of comparison, there seems to be a bit more dissonance between the two authors, as Campos was explicit about the importance of economic growth even if not addressing social inequalities. In his view, "the most important goal is development not economic justice given that only with economic growth will wealth be created, thus lessening the need for acrimonious competition for a stagnant production."[69] Furtado, on the other hand, was more concerned with how inequalities, especially geographical ones, could be—and frequently are—augmented in the process of fast-paced economic growth. This fear ultimately led him to work for reforms in the structure of land ownership and geographical economic inequalities between the industrialized center-south and the agrarian-base northeastern portions of the country.[70] Conversely, Campos's critical view of the course of industrialization pursued under the Kubitschek administration deepened as the decade unfolded, something that contrasted sharply with the optimism shared by most active members of ISEB. This can be seen clearly in one of the diplomat's most elaborate analyses of these historical events. In a speech given in 1960 at the University of Arizona, Campos stated that

> no one can contest the gains poor countries received from the process of industrialization. This is indeed a vital element of political stability in developing countries. Such a goal must be promoted even if protectionist measures have to be adopted. However, no one should believe that social upward mobility for all social segments can be a feasible and immediate outcome produced by pursuing this course of action, nor that inflationary growth can improve living conditions in the long run.[71]

This conservative economic position was also manifested in his analysis of what he defined as the ominous ideology of national development, which, in his view, was becoming dangerously prominent across Latin America in the late 1950s. Along these conceptual lines, this influential diplomat argued that this ideological construct was grounded on flawed reasoning structured on an intrinsic and irreconcilable asymmetry between the need for continued investment and the rising expectation to satisfy popular consumption. According to him, the ideology of national development disseminated in the period represented a mistaken variation of the valid traditional sense of nationalism that had historically served as a potent force of development, but which increasingly suffered from having become "an ambivalent force, whose negative effects are too often present in our regional landscape today [and that] [. . .] may even lead to irrational planning and prevent faster development by closing the doors to more productive enterprises, thus perpetuating local monopolistic positions."[72]

Lucas Lopes, the main formulator and key coordinator of the implementation of the Targets Plan until 1959, repeatedly uttered similar notions. For instance, in a speech given at a welcoming reception prepared for U.S. Secretary of State John Foster Dulles in 1958 (when Lopes served as minister of the economy), the Brazilian official declared that Brazil represented the best place for U.S. investments in the region. In Lopes's view, Brazil would be able to address its social ills, which represented a welcoming ground for foreign (Socialist) ideologies, only if private sources of capital were presented with an attractive legal framework. Making the case for higher levels of U.S. private investment in the country, Lopes nonetheless warned Dulles that unless substantial foreign aid was also provided, the opportunity for maintaining social stability would be wasted and social unrest could become a real threat. To support his claim, the Brazilian minister argued that since 1953 Brazil faced growing challenges in its balance of trade caused by the decreasing returns the country obtained internationally for its agriculture exports.[73]

In such a challenging scenario, Lopes elsewhere stated that "the easy call for state-centered demagogic nationalism could become an appealing motto in Brazil and throughout the entire continent."[74] Likewise, in a speech he gave at New York University on the topic of Brazil-U.S. relations, in 1958, Lopes stressed his support for a market-based path of development for his country. He nonetheless argued that controlling the rising material demands of the popular sectors was an urgent political task that threatened the entire set of developmental initiatives undertaken by his administration.[75] In the following year, in a speech given at the Inter-American Economic Conference of the Organization of American States, Lopes once again stressed the need for attracting foreign investments to Brazil, but interestingly also defended the notion that, "given the deterioration of the terms of our international trade, our process of development is running the risk of being halted as we can no longer finance the purchases of manufactured items necessary to support our economic growth."[76]

Revealing of the complexities involved in pursuing a path of fast-paced industrial growth in an essentially primary-based economy, as well as in the reflections proposed and positions held by key historical actors involved in this process, despite his market-centered economic positions, Lopes believed that promoting industrial projects of economic development—something he saw as a *sine qua non* measure for fast economic growth within an unstable international market for primary goods—could not be achieved without some measure of governmental involvement in the economic realm. In fact, in his view, the federal Brazilian government had to act through conscious fiscal and monetary policies aimed at creating an attractive environment for domestic and foreign investors.[77] Furthermore, in tune with similar propositions defended by Brazilian representatives in different international meetings (discussed in Chapter Two), Lopes argued for more favorable terms of international trade for developing countries considering that, in his own words, "[e]ven though the Regional Economic Commission of the United Nations [ECLA] has put together a well-argued doctrine of economic development, we still lack practical solutions for our insufficient rates of growth."[78]

It should be noted that even when arguing for a more favorable international environment for development promotion in the global periphery, Lopes still made sure not to partake in ISEB's defense that Brazil should establish strategic alliances with other developing countries. In fact, though he did acknowledge that the economic assistance coming from the industrialized world had proven to be insufficient, he vehemently expressed his conviction that center countries were becoming increasingly more receptive to the plight of developing nations. In his own words, "the selfish forces of colonialism are being destroyed and a more liberal spirit is becoming more noticeable in projects such as the Marshall Plan."[79]

Thus, along conceptual lines of thought that ironically did not have much support in real evidence, Lopes believed that Brazil should take advantage of a new historical trend, not by seeking to become a proponent of dangerous neutralist propositions such as those espoused by the recently emancipated colonial territories, but rather by focusing "our efforts on promoting our own economic development so that our present immature political culture, which could lead us into ridiculous projects capable of straining our relationships with traditional friends, can be overcome."[80] In this sense, Lopes's views on economic development promotion were clearly centered on creating an efficient governmental structure capable of targeting public investments to infrastructural priority areas and attracting private (domestic and foreign) investors to key industrial projects. His positions exerted a central influence on most of the industrial policies of the JK administration and also found strong support among some of the most important industrial associations of the period.

To be sure, in its main publication of the period, *Desenvolvimento & Conjuntura*, the National Industrial Confederation (CNI) espoused similar ideas, and in its first issue released in July 1957 the magazine published a cover article presenting a clear defense of moderate governmental intervention in the economic realm in countries described as "unable to promote industrialization based only on the laws of free market."[81] In the same way, on its editorial page, the periodical declared that "assertive promotion of industry in our country does not constitute a response only to the demands of the business sectors, but also answers the aspirations of our social masses, particularly those in impoverished regions," and that "expanding our productive forces, even by governmental intervention is not an end in itself, but a step in the direction of improving the human condition of our population."[82]

Despite these (at least at face value) resoundingly socially concerned statements, industrialists were very clear in stating that the most important role the national government should perform in its developmental quest was that of supporting private sources of capital, including foreign ones as, in the very words of the president of the CNI, "today, the entire nation claims close cooperation between private domestic and international capital in the promotion of our national task of development."[83] Likewise, despite the fact that, in a general sense, a constructive relationship was established between the federal government and industrial groups, at times, and depending on specific topics—such as the preferential importing rights granted to foreign-based corporations—industrialists made sure that the administration heard their complaints. The powerful Industrial Federation of São Paulo (FIESP), for instance, consistently voiced its own objections to the favored treatment dispensed to foreign investors, at times even by resorting to ISEB members who were invited to publish articles in its own official publication (*Boletim Informativo da FIESP*).[84]

Especially ironic, given the vocal defense for nationalizing key industries proposed by several members of the ISEB, connections between ideas proposed by these same intellectuals and those articulated by the most important industrial groups in the second half of the 1950s are also easily found in the pages of the *Boletim Informativo*. In its issue published in November 1955, for instance, we see that the FIESP advocated for "the entire nation to be brought together in the promotion of a common project capable of transporting the country into a new phase in its history, when the problems deriving from our underdeveloped condition would all be resolved."[85]

Its high praise for national unity notwithstanding, the very same publication left no room for doubt about how far FIESP would go insofar as sharing the gains of rapid economic growth among all parties involved in the task of overcoming the condition of underdevelopment. In fact, in the very same issue of the *Boletim*, for once, one finds the transcription of a speech of the federation's president Antônio Devisate at the Second Industrial Plenary Session in 1955, in which he states that "raising the living standards of our population must be sought by promoting higher levels of investment, not by wealth redistribution, which dangerously hinders our economic progress in the long run."[86] Similarly, FIESP's main leader declared that "no one should expect easy solutions nor wave the flag of social incorporation to our labor masses," who must be called, instead, "to serve in the difficult task of constructing a nation with sacrifices so that the future may reward those involved in the process with the fruits of progress."[87]

Reproaching domestic assessments of the nationalist propositions espoused by ISEB were corroborated by examinations produced by privileged outside observers. Namely, a classified report based on information provided by Brazil-based U.S. diplomats for the internal use of the State Department in 1959, detailed what, in the Americans' eyes, U.S. intelligence should know about the institute. Clearly critical of what were seen as "serious recent political developments in the history of nationalist ideologies in the country," the report ominously decried core ISEB propositions as "potentially disturbing the traditionally close and friendly cooperation between Brazil and the United States," which are "erroneously based on a sense of historical neglect unfortunately gaining ground among the general public."[88] The report also stated that even though not yet coalesced into a unified and electorally viable political movement, emerging radical nationalist positions "were endorsed by most if not all opinion-forming sectors of the Brazilian society, particularly among intellectuals and organized urban labor."[89]

Unintentionally presaging a central critique that Brazilian scholars studying ISEB would later make about the agency—particularly regarding its purportedly naïve optimistic views pertaining to the feasibility of forming a nationalist developmental front led by Brazilian industrialists—the report stated that while historically one of the core supporters of pro-industrial (protected) nationalism, industrial federations no longer subscribed to this path of development. This change of heart was said to be caused by the recent and promising industrial partnerships established between Brazilian and important U.S. industrial groups favored by the Kubitschek administration.[90] Unfortunately, claims the same piece, despite being the heralds of what was seen as a more rational stance on the relations between the two countries, industrialist had yet "to organize a positive political alternative amidst growing criticism of the United States [and a] decreasing willingness to wholeheartedly follow its regional leadership on the part of many Brazilians."[91]

Moreover, blamed for the "unjustified and adventurous historical trend" claimed to be unfolding in the country, ISEB's extensive intellectual activities were detailed in the same report. These included over seventy seminars in many different cities throughout the country and over three hundred public lectures dealing with "Brazilian Social Issues," which listed topics such as "Prospects in the Battle for National Development." Even more concerning, according to the piece, was the described tendency of many members of the institute to advocate an entire overhauling of the traditionally U.S.-friendly foreign policy supported by the country toward what was called a path of "greater independence" or, less positively, a "neutralist course," or, even worse, a "third position."[92]

In an attempt to countervail these damaging potential courses of actions, American diplomats advocated abetting Kubitschek's main foreign policy initiative: Operation Pan-America. Even though, as discussed in Chapter Two, U.S. support for the project was lukewarm at best, in this new report a more responsive approach was seen as needed in order to discredit more radical nationalist positions by showing the Brazilian public that Brazil-U.S. cooperation was not in itself an undesirable course.[93] But despite the fact that U.S. diplomats hoped that the ambitious economic and political autonomy proposed by ISEB intellectuals could be kept under control, it is clear that even for some of its more moderate members, such as Jaguaribe, leading Brazilian developmental elites should be ready to "pay the price" for pursuing a path of foreign policy that challenged the traditionally influential role the U.S. played in the region. And although such a course of action was not necessarily considered to be the most desirable one, it was nonetheless assumed to be unavoidable by many writers at the institute, who consistently advised strengthening political ties with countries with similar developmental trajectories, particularly in Latin America, in order to improve Brazil's bargaining position *vis-à-vis* the U.S.[94]

But were Brazilian business elites, particularly industrial groups, indeed ready to help lead the process of national development along the lines proposed and anticipated by the ISEB reflection and ironically shared by U.S. observers? This important question occupied not only much of the work produced at the institute, but also most of its critics, beginning in the final years of the agency itself.[95] One of the most eloquent and critical responses was produced soon after the military coup of 1964, by Fernando Henrique

Cardoso, one of the main proponents of the influential critique of the so-called Latin American developmentalist state formulated later in the decade under the paradigm known as dependency theory.[96] Still in the 1950s, however, the same author was more optimistic about the prospects of such a national developmental alliance between organized popular sectors and the national bourgeoisie.[97] In fact, despite their different intellectual influences and academic orientations, Cardoso's defense of the possibility of promoting national development was very much in line with core notions of the national-developmentalist formulations advanced at ISEB.[98]

The national focus of the ISEB formulations, which predicted that development was to be pursued primarily on a domestic basis, attracted additional forms of criticism later in the 1960s, including from people formerly supportive of the agency's endeavors, such as Cardoso himself who argued that the increased presence of foreign investors in local economies had made it impossible to pursue economic growth on a purely national basis.[99] Along similar analytical lines, and with the benefit of hindsight, Bresser-Pereira argued that ISEB's high hopes for the alliance between business leaders and organized labor proved harder than expected. More importantly, the view that fast-paced industrialization would be the highway to a developed condition was shattered as jobs in the industrial sectors were fewer than expected, leading to increased social exclusion in the cities—a trend aggravated by higher food prices given the continued ineffective agricultural production.[100]

It seems ironic to see that, exactly during one of the most dramatic experiences of the restructuring of the national economy by means of attracting foreign investors promoted by the Kubitschek administration, Brazil's official intellectual agency assertively propounded a developmental course centered on domestic ownership of industries and state-stimulated growth. This divergent historical course culminated, in the end, in a progressive radicalization of the positions held by the remaining, ever more nationalist thinkers at ISEB, as well as by the ever more assertive pro-market business associations, particularly in the city of Rio de Janeiro (examined in Chapter Five). Moreover, given the increasingly polarized political and ideological scenario of the closing years of the 1950s, the institute shifted its focus from trying to shape the developmental course of the country by influencing the policies devised within the main decision-making agencies of the federal government to disseminating its nationalist positions among broader segments of Brazilian society. This was particularly true in the main urban centers, and among sectors of organized labor, student unions, and the reading public at large.[101]

In addition to public lectures and training courses at the request of local entities of civil society, one of the main venues utilized by ISEB to promote its views was a series of publications collectively titled *Cadernos do Povo Brasileiro* (*Notebooks of the Brazilian People*). Conveying its propounded didactic ideological orientation, these pocket-sized, short pieces—primarily aimed at a broad audience so that the Brazilian *masses* could (hopefully) be reached—examined in schematic and unpretentious ways the controversial issues of the day. Published between 1962 and early 1964 under the editorial guidance of Vieira Pinto and the nationalist publisher Enio da Silveira, the twenty-eight known volumes delved into a varied list of topics, which were always introduced in a Q&A format in order to appeal to potential readers. These included: Who are the Brazilian people? Why don't the rich go on strike? Are salaries to be blamed for rising inflation? Who are the enemies of the people? What is land reform? What would a socialist Brazil be like? What does Yanquee imperialism do? How should we plan our development? Indicative of the level of interest in these sorts of matters of the general reading public, but also of the polarized positions present in large sectors of the Brazilian society, *Cadernos do Povo Brasileiro* was, contrary to all expectations, a huge editorial success, with over one million copies sold, collectively.[102]

The growing influence of the ever more radical political positions espoused by ISEB in the early 1960s led many to conclude that the institute played a major role in the political polarization leading to the collapse of the democratic regime early in 1964.[103] An assessment of this claim should start by noting that the institute did indeed exert a significant influence on the propagation of nationalist views of development in the period. And also that the many publications, training sessions, and public lectures the agency produced or conducted during the most intense years of national developmentalism in Brazil must have played a role in fostering a growing nationalist sentiment in many groups of the national society; a trend that was increasingly seen as dangerous by more conservative segments of the military and business elites of the time.

The historical impact of these intellectual initiatives notwithstanding, it is reasonable to assume that much of ISEB's influence derived from its consistent sense of optimism for the "national cause," something that could be articulated in different ways by social groups propounding very different political positions. In fact, contrary to the more retrograde, chauvinistic, or moralist versions of nationalism espoused by conservative forces in Brazil in the 1930s and 1960s, respectively, the Higher Institute of Brazilian Studies promoted a creatively-articulated (hybrid) ideational portrayal of the country, which helped advance a forward-looking sense of confidence in the viability of Brazilian society. Accordingly, despite the many specific projects formulated at ISEB, much of its popularity derived from its consistent articulation of the notion that Brazil's future was a promising one and that this future reality could be attained in a measurable frame of time. How specific segments of the mobilized civil society, particularly those of organized business and labor, interpreted these same propositions, as well as the projects and policies conducted by the federal administration, will be the focus of Chapters Five and Six, respectively.

Before we turn to these matters, it is worth reviewing how the only two remaining and most influential intellectuals of the original ISEB see the agency's role in shaping the national debates on development promotion from the perspective of today. First, both Jaguaribe and Cândido Mendes stress that much of the novelty imbued by ISEB's formulations is to be found in the fact that the agency had made it possible for a new intellectual generation to assert its place in the main political discussions of the time. Similarly, both emphasized the fact that their humanistic training, combined with the emerging critical perspectives produced by non-orthodox, as well as by non-Marxist, European contemporary thinkers was very instrumental in shaping their own heterodox intellectual propositions. Of special relevance, the idea of the "nation as a project" (inspired on the phenomenological and existentialist philosophies of the period), as well as that of colonialism as a "total social reality" (based on notions popularized by the emerging French Structuralism) were, in their views, the axes for articulating a prospective, engaging, and promising brand of nationalism, capable of exerting a broad, even if diffuse, ideological influence.[104]

More directly related to their own assessments of the work produced at the institute, Cândido Mendes is quick to acknowledge that the institute's intellectual reflection and, more importantly, its developmental propositions were excessively focused on the domestic context of the country, which precluded a more serious and constructive conceptual, as well as practical, political activism in tandem with similar events and discussions taking place around the world during those same years. He was similarly critical of the fact that, in his view, the Kubitschek administration did not seriously try to mobilize popular social segments for the cause of development, which, in the long run, was detrimental to the defense of the many achievements of the period.

Jaguaribe partakes in this line of reflection, highlighting that the work done at the institute successfully introduced a richer discussion about national development not only among other intellectual circles, but also within discussions taking place in labor unions and business associations alike. For this historic defender of the constitution of a truly Brazilian intelligentsia, the Higher Institute of Brazilian Studies played an unparalleled role in creating an essentially developmental imaginary (*imaginaire*) in Brazil. Considering that it would be almost impossible to make sense of present-day Brazil, as well as of its convoluted political, economic, cultural, and intellectual histories, without taking into account the ever elusive, but nonetheless constantly pursued goal of national development, Professor Jaguaribe's claims regarding the historical importance of ISEB seem truly warranted.

CONCLUDING REMARKS

In reviewing the positions on national development held by all of these different segments of the Brazilian intellectual elite, it becomes clear that the main lines of thought concerning the concept of national development held by the most important members of the Higher Institute of Brazilian Studies contrasted sharply with the positions held by the more influential decision-makers of the Kubitschek administration. In fact, the institute espoused a view on national development that implied the promotion of a plan of industrialization capable of enlarging the purchasing power of the country's population and the dissemination of new sense of pride and confidence in the country's national identity, economic potential, and place in the world. Similarly, these very goals were to be achieved by means of more a responsive and active central government, which, once purged of its semi-colonial legacy, would be able to act on behalf of most, if not all members of Brazilian society.

It has also become evident that the reasoning underlining most works produced by members of ISEB was largely based on the notion that under-development was a socio-economic, political, and cultural condition characterized by irreconcilable social divisions and by a lack of autonomous political will in pursuing one's national interests. Given such a reading of the national reality, these self-declared concerned social analysts increasingly believed that there was no alternative path of action for any government effectively interested in promoting consistent development than taking on the tasks of national political coordination and direct economic stewardship.

Despite being ever more influential in provoking prominent, prolific national debates regarding the future of the country, which were carried out in the national media and reached ever more segments of the broad urban society, the institute's core formulations would not be actively pursued by the central developmental agency of the Kubitschek administration. In fact, while continually providing institutional (logistic and financial) support for the institute, the federal government implemented economic projects structured along its own visions of development, which were based on a significantly narrower and essentially economic reading of the national reality.

This perspective was fundamentally defined by the notion that the main impediment for Brazil's economic successes derived from its historical lack of sources of capital, something that only would be resolved if the developmental course of the national government focused on finding new ways of attracting sources of foreign investment. Thus, in direct contrast with core ideas and propositions espoused at ISEB, the administration's technocratic conception of development equated the very term development with the goal of fast rates of economic growth under a logic that clearly meant the down-playing, if not the total elimination, of the very search for political autonomy that had been so forcefully argued for by most members of the institute.

Moreover, though ever more assertive and relevant for the discussions on development and nationalism of the late 1950s and early 1960s, and with significant levels of support among important social groups of the period, ISEB's positions were certainly not consensually shared by all political actors. How different influential segments of the broadly defined middle and upper economic sectors of Brazilian society perceived and engaged with these important discussions and, more specifically, the developmental projects and policies of the period, is the focus of the upcoming chapter.

NOTES

1. Detailed information on the structures of the ISEB is very scarce as its records were destroyed (or made unavailable) by the military forces following the coup of 1964. In fact, the institute was one of the first governmental agencies to be shut down by the military regime that was installed in the coup of March 31, 1964 (see Presidential Decree number 53.884 of April 13, 1964). However, a few works on the history, composition, and some of the main intellectual contributions of the institution do exist. Particularly relevant is Alzira Alves de Abreu, "Nationalism et Action Politique au Brésil: Une Étude sur L'ISEB" (PhD diss., Université René-Descartes, Paris V, 1975).
2. Alzira Alves de Abreu, "Os suplementos literários: os intelectuais e a imprensa nos anos 50," in *A Imprensa em Transição: O Jornalismo Brasileiro nos Anos 50*, ed. Alzira Alves Abreu (Rio de Janeiro: FGV, 1996), 13–60.
3. This claim is presented by Jaguaribe himself in an article aimed at summarizing his personal trajectory toward ISEB titled "ISEB e o Desenvolvimento Nacional," in *Intelectuais e política no Brasil: a experiência do ISEB*, ed. Caio Navarro de Toledo (São Paulo: Revan, 2005), 31–42. Alzira Alves de Abreu makes similar claims in "Os suplementos literários," 16. An analogous argument can be found in Angelica Lovatto, *A Utopia Nacionalista de Hélio Jaguaribe: os tempos do ISEB* (São Paulo: Arte Scritta, 2010), 20.
4. In March 2008, I had the opportunity to interview Professor Jaguaribe and Professor Cândido Mendes de Almeida, the only two still-living members of the original ISEB. This claim was made by Professor Jaguaribe and it highlights the main lines of thought of the political positions he sustained for much of his intellectual production.
5. His most influential works produced under the auspices of the ISEB were *Condições Institucionais do Desenvolvimento* and *O Nacionalismo na Atualidade Brasileira*. (Rio de Janeiro: ISEB, 1958).
6. Cândido Mota Filho, Exposição de Motivos, no. 627, presented in 07/13/1955 to President Café Filho, Fundo Castilho Cabral, CC c 0000.00.00/14, CPDOC Archive.
7. Ibid.
8. Hélio Jaguaribe expressed this point in an interview conducted in March 2008. The notion had already been advanced by Abreu in "Nationalism et Action Politique au Brésil," 179.
9. More on these interviews will be presented later.
10. Frank Bonilla, "A National Ideology of Development: Brazil," in *Expectant Peoples: Nationalism and Development,* ed. K.H. Silvert (New York: Random House, 1963), 244.
11. Hélio Jaguaribe, "A Crise Brasileira," *Cadernos do Nosso Tempo* 1, no. 1 (Oct/Dec 1953): 120–60.
12. See Balandier, "Sociologie de la Dépendance"; and Sartre, "Le Colonialisme est un Système."
13. In addition to the works by Jaguaribe already cited, see also Almeida, *Nacionalismo e Desenvolvimento*; Roland Corbisier, *Formação e Problema da Cultura Brasileira* (Rio de Janeiro: ISEB, 1959); Guerreiro Ramos, *A Redução Sociológica* and Vieira Pinto, *Ideologia e Desenvolvimento Nacional.*
14. Related formulations (e.g., hybridity) were later proposed by postcolonial scholars in order to account for the contradictory social realities of postcolonial nations. See Bhabha, "Remembering Fanon."; and Loomba, *Colonialism/Postcolonialism.*
15. Jaguaribe, "A Crise Brasileira," 144.

16. This claim was made in the interview I conducted with the author in March 2008 in Rio de Janeiro. For more on the need for creating a nationalistic ideology, see Jaguaribe, "Situação Política Brasileira," *Cadernos do Nosso Tempo* 2, no. 2 (1954): 101–22.
17. Hermes Lima, "Significação do Nacionalismo," *Cadernos do Nosso Tempo* 4, no. 3 (Apr/Aug 1955): 85–100.
18. Corbisier, *Formação e Problema*, 97.
19. "Guanabara" was the name given to the city-state created to replace the federal status that had historically defined the city of Rio de Janeiro after the capital of the country was transferred to the modernist-looking city of Brasília that same year.
20. Corbisier, *Formação e Problema*, 22. See also Roland Corbisier, *JK e a luta pela Presidência* (Rio de Janeiro: Duas Cidades, 1976), 155–57.
21. Corbisier, *Formação e Problema*, 50.
22. Ibid., 86.
23. Roland Corbisier, *Brasília e o Desenvolvimento Nacional* (Rio de Janeiro: ISEB, 1960), 68.
24. Of especial relevance are those works of Balandier and Sartre listed above.
25. Corbisier, *Speech Given at the Graduation Ceremony of the Graduating Class of the Regular Course on Brazilian Studies in December 1956* (Rio de Janeiro: ISEB, 1957).
26. Vieira Pinto, *Ideologia e Desenvolvimento Nacional*, 74.
27. Alvaro Vieira Pinto, *Consciência e Realidade Nacional* (Rio de Janeiro: ISEB, 1962), vol. 1: 497.
28. Vieira Pinto, *Consciência e Realidade Nacional*, vol. 2: 112.
29. Ibid., 129.
30. Alberto Guerreiro Ramos, *O Problema Nacional do Brasil* (Rio de Janeiro: Saga, 1960), 225.
31. Guerreiro Ramos, *A Redução Sociológica*, 33.
32. Ibid., 53.
33. Alberto Guerreiro Ramos, "A Problemática da Realidade Brasileira," in *Introdução aos Problemas do Brasil* (Rio de Janeiro: Instituto Superior de Estudos Brasilieros, 1956), 30.
34. Nelson Werneck Sodré, *Raízes Históricas do Nacionalismo Brasileiro* (Rio de Janeiro: ISEB, 1960), 30.
35. See Marcelo de Paiva Abreu, ed. *A Ordem do Progresso: Cem Anos de Política Econômica Republicana, 1889–1989* (São Paulo: Campus, 1990) and Bielchowsky, *O Pensamento Econômico Brasileiro*.
36. Almeida, *Nacionalismo e Desenvolvimento*, 244.
37. Cândido Mendes de Almeida, *Perspectiva Atual da América Latina* (Rio de Janeiro: ISEB, 1960), 19.
38. Ibid., 20 and 237.
39. Mendes de Almeida, *Nacionalismo e Desenvolvimento*, 272.
40. Lucília de Almeida Neves Delgado, "Nacionalismo como projeto de nação: a Frente Parlamentar Nacionalista (1956–1964)," in *Nacionalismo e Reformismo Radical (1945–1964)*, eds. Jorge Ferreira and Daniel Aarão Reis (Rio de Janeiro: Civilização Brasileira, 2007), vol. 2:358–76.
41. A detailed account of these events can be found in Sola, *Idéias Econômicas*.
42. In addition to Abreu, *Nationalisme et Action Politique*, see Bonilla, "A National Ideology of Development: Brazil"; Maria Sylvia Carvalho Franco, "O tempo das ilusões," in *Ideologia e Mobilização Popular*, ed. Marilena Chaui and Maria Sylvia Carvalho Franco (São Paulo: Paz e Terra/Cedec, 1978), 151–209; Donald R. Gaylord, "The Instituto Superior de Estudos Brasileiros

(ISEB) and Developmental Nationalism in Brazil, 1955–1964" (PhD diss., Tulane University, 1991); Bolivar Lamounier, "O ISEB: notas à margen de um debate," *Discurso*, no. 9 (Nov 1979): 153–58; Carlos Guilherme Mota, *Ideologia da cultura brasileira* (São Paulo: Ática, 1985); Renato Ortiz, *Cultura brasileira & Identidade nacional* (São Paulo: Brasiliense, 1985); Daniel Pecaut, *Os intelectuais e a política no Brasil* (São Paulo: Brasiliense, 1990); Simon Schwartzman, *O Pensamento Nacionalista e os Cadernos de Nosso Tempo* (Brasília: UnB, 1981); Nelson Werneck Sodré, *A verdade sobre o ISEB* (Rio de Janeiro: Avenir, 1978); and by Caio Navarro de Toledo, *ISEB: Fábrica de Ideologias* (São Paulo: Ática, 1977) and Toledo, ed., *Intelectuais e política no Brasil: a experiência do ISEB* (São Paulo: Revan, 2005).

43. It is important to note that while Oliveira Vianna argued in favor of a rapid pace of modernization, Buarque de Hollanda, on the other hand, valued several features of the traditional Brazil while acknowledging the inevitable fate of progress. See Francisco de Oliveira Vianna, *História Social da Economia Capitalista no Brasil* and *Instituições Políticas Brasileiras*; and Sérgio Buarque de Hollanda, *Raízes do Brasil* (São Paulo: Cia das Letras, 1995).
44. Among other works, these claims were first introduced in *O Idealismo da Constituição* in 1927, and later expanded in *Instituições Políticas Brasileiras* in 1949.
45. See Lucia Lippi de Oliveira, "A redescoberta do Brasil nos anos 1950: entre o projeto político e o rigor acadêmico," in *Descobertas do Brasil*, eds. Angélica Madeira and Mariza Veloso (Brasília: Editora da UnB, 2001), 139–61.
46. See Prebisch, *The Economic Development of Latin America.*
47. These claims were already present in Jaguaribe, *Condições Institucionais do Desenvolvimento*, and were expanded and articulated in better terms in Hélio Jaguaribe, *Desenvolvimento Econômico e Desenvolvimento Político* (Rio de Janeiro: Fundo de Cultura, 1962.
48. Campos, "Cultura e Desenvolvimento," in *Introdução aos Problemas do Brasil* (Rio de Janeiro: ISEB, 1956), 230.
49. Corbisier, *Formação e Problema da Cultura Brasileira*, 40 and 69.
50. Ibid., 32 and 68.
51. Vieira Pinto, *Consciência e Realidade Nacional*, vol. 2: 505.
52. Guerreiro Ramos, *O Problema Nacional do Brasil*, 242.
53. Caio Navarro de Toledo, "ISEB Intellectuals, the Left, and Marxism," *Latin American Perspectives* 1, no. 98 (Jan 1998): 109–35.
54. Additional positions and a detailed account of the many individuals involved can be found in Bielchowsky, *O Pensamento Econômico Brasileiro.*
55. Maria Emília Prado, "Os intelectuais e a eterna busca pela modernização do Brasil: o significado do projeto nacional-desenvolvimentista das décadas de 1950–60," *História Atual Online*, no. 15 (2008), 19–27.
56. See Clóvis Salgado's letter to *O Globo* (Dec 2, 1959), Fundo Castilho Cabral, CC c 0000.00.00/14, CPDOC Archive.
57. See Documento Secreto no. 003-B, Fundo Nelson Melo, NeM.vp. 1956.02.07, CPDOC Archive.
58. Ibid.
59. Juscelino Kubitschek, *Discursos Proferidos no ISEB no Ano de 1956* (Rio de Janeiro: ISEB, 1958), 48.
60. See Campos's letter to Lucas Lopes commenting on a draft version of the candidate's message that Lopes had put together in May 1955. Campos's comments were sent to Lopes on June 2, 1955, Fundo Roberto Campos, RC.e.ag.1955.05.02, CPDOC Archive.
61. Speech Pronounced at ISEB's Inaugural Lecture on December 21 1955, p. 51, Fundo Roberto Campos, RC.e.bnde.1955.06.30, CPDOC Archive.

62. Roberto Campos, *Economia, Planejamento e Nacionalismo* (Rio de Janeiro: APEC, 1963), 42.
63. Ibid., 158.
64. See Furtado, *Perspectiva da Economia Brasileira*. Furtado expanded on this critique after the military coup of 1964, when his ideas diverged from those of Campos. The fact that Furtado already foresaw the inherent risks of the process of industrialization in 1958 is remarkable, particularly considering that only in the early 1960s did the ECLA produce a similar critique of the excessive focus on industrialization *vis-à-vis* agriculture production in the path of import substitution industrialization (ISI) in Latin America.
65. See Campos, *Economia, Planejamento e Nacionalismo*, 61; and by Celso Furtado, *A Pré-Revolução Brasileira* (Rio de Janeiro: Fundo de Cultura, 1962), 43, and "O Desenvolvimento Econômico e suas Ilusões," *O Observador Econômico e Financeiro*, no. 256, (June 1957), 32–38.
66. Celso Furtado, "Political Obstacles to Economic Growth in Brazil," in *Obstacles to Change in Latin America*, ed. Claudio Veliz (Oxford: Oxford University Press, 1965), 145–61.
67. Roberto Campos, *Ensaios de História Econômica e Sociologia* (Rio de Janeiro: APEC, 1963), 113.
68. Celso Furtado, *The Diagnosis of the Brazilian Crisis* (Berkeley: University of California Press, 1965), 88.
69. Campos, *Ensaios de História Econômica*, 84.
70. Celso Furtado, *A Pré-Revolução Brasileira*, 51, and *A Fantasia Desfeita* (Rio de Janeiro: Paz e Terra, 1997), 173–80.
71. Roberto Campos, Lecture at the University of Arizona in 1960, Fundo Roberto Campos, RC.e.ag.1955.05.02, CPDOC Archive.
72. Ibid., 5.
73. Fundo Lucas Lopes, LL pi Lopes, L 1958.08.06, CPDOC Archive.
74. Lucas Lopes, Speech Pronounced at the Annual Meeting of the World Bank in May 1958, Fundo Lucas Lopes, LL pi Lopes, L 1958.00.00, CPDOC Archive.
75. Fundo Lucas Lopes, LL pi Lopes, L 1958.12.01., CPDOC Archive.
76. Fundo Lucas Lopes, LL pi Lopes, L. 0000.00.0012, CPDOC Archive.
77. Fundo Lucas Lopes, LL pi Lopes, L 1958.08.00, CPDOC Archive.
78. Ibid.
79. Fundo Lucas Lopes, LL pi Lopes, L. 1962.0000, CPDOC Archive.
80. Ibid.
81. National Industrial Confederation, *Desenvolvimento & Conjuntura*, no. 1 (Jul 1957), 43.
82. Ibid., 7.
83. National Industrial Confederation, *Desenvolvimento & Conjuntura*, no. 5 (Aug 1958), 203.
84. Leopoldi, *Política e Interesses*, 286.
85. Industrial Federation of the State of São Paulo, *Boletim Informativo da FIESP*, no. 319 (Nov 14, 1955), 32.
86. Ibid., 54.
87. Ibid., 58. This selective reading of the nationalist propositions formulated at ISEB on the part of business elites was also manifested in the ways that FIESP, in the first years of the decade, incorporated many of the theories formulated by ECLA. Details on this piecemealed absorption of the intellectuals' constructs proposed by this Santiago-based UN economic agency by São Paulo industrial elites early in the 1950s can be found in Renato P. Colistete, "A Força das Idéias: A Cepal e o Industrialismo no Brasil no Início dos Anos 50," in *História Econômica do Brasil Contemporâneo*, eds. Tamas Szmerecsanyi and Wilson Suzigan (São Paulo: Hucitec, 2002), 121–45.

88. Department of State, *Nationalism in Brazil*, Intelligence Report No. 8002 (Washington, D.C.: Bureau of Intelligence and Research, Jul 24, 1959), v.
89. Ibid., vi.
90. Ibid., vii.
91. Ibid., viii.
92. Ibid., 17–18.
93. Ibid., 68.
94. Jaguaribe, *O Nacionalismo na Atualidade Brasileira*, 244–51.
95. Some of the main criticisms were to be produced at the University of São Paulo in the 1970s, see Franco, *O tempo das ilusões* and Toledo, *ISEB: Fábrica de Ideologias*. Yet as early as the beginning of the 1960s, strong critiques were produced—some by internal members of the agency—which questioned whether an inter-class alliance was a viable long-term project and whether such an endeavor would benefit the popular sectors of the population. Of special importance are Wanderley Guilherme dos Santos, "Desenvolvimentismo: Ideologia Dominante," *Tempo Brasileiro* 2 (Dec 1962), 155–92; and Simon Schwartzman, "Desenvolvimento econômico e desenvolvimento político: do nacionalismo ao desenvolvimentismo," *Revista Brasileira de Ciências Sociais* 3, no. 1, Belo Horizonte (March 1963), 271–82.
96. See Cardoso, *Empresário industrial e desenvolvimento econômico*.
97. Fernando Henrique Cardoso, "Desenvolvimento Econômico e Nacionalismo," *Revista Brasiliense* 12 (Jul/Aug 1957), 88–99.
98. See Roland Corbisier, "Situação e Alternativas da Cultura Brasileira," in *Introdução aos Problemas do Brasil* (Rio de Janeiro: Instituto Superior de Estudos Brasilieros, 1956), 187–218 and Jaguaribe, *Nacionalismo na Atualidade Brasileira*, 99.
99. In addition to Cardoso, *Empresário industrial*, see also Fernando Henrique Cardoso and Enzo Faletto, *Dependencia y Desarrollo en America Latina* (Buenos Aires: Siglo XXI, 1969). See also Martins, *Industrialização*.
100. Luis Carlos Bresser-Pereira, "O Conceito do Desenvolvimento do ISEB Rediscutido," *Dados—Revista de Ciências Sociais* 47, no. 1 (2004), 49–84. See also by the same author "De la Cepal y el ISEB a Teoría de la Dependencia," *Desarrollo Económico* 46, no. 183 (Oct/Dec 2006), 419–39, and "From the National-Bourgeoisie to the Dependency Interpretation of Latin America," *Latin American Perspectives* 38, no. 3 (May 2011), 40–58.
101. Abreu, *Nationalisme et Action Politique au Brésil*, 257.
102. Ferreira, Jerusa, ed., *Editando o Editor - Ênio Silveira* (São Paulo: Edusp, 2002).
103. See E. Bradford Burns, *Nationalism in Brazil: A Historical Survey* (New York: Frederick A. Praeger, 1968); Octavio Ianni, *O Ciclo da Revolução Burguesa* (Petropolis: Vozes, 1984); and Skidmore, *Politics in Brazil*.
104. This information was obtained in individual interviews conducted with both thinkers in March 2008.

5 Economic Prosperity, Consumerism, and the Business World

Development as Market-Led Growth

INTRODUCTORY NOTES

In the aftermath of the World War II the U.S. emerged as the Western hegemonic superpower and its cultural influence on the region of Latin America grew proportionally. As the main driving force behind the multilateral efforts of postwar economic reconstruction and global political coordination, the U.S. projected an image of leadership and material exuberance that translated into an influential culture of mass consumption. In Brazil, the 1950s witnessed a correlated emergence of an incipient consumer-focused ideology based on the expansion of local manufacturing and the enlargement of the domestic market. Similarly, the dissemination of an enthusiastic discourse of consumerism was closely associated with the expansion of mass media, particularly in the areas of radio and photo-illustrated weekly publications. Business interests were closely involved in promoting these historical trends and frequently sponsored the production and broadcasting of popular radio programs, such as the daily news and soap operas that were later expanded to television programming when this new medium became more accessible at the end of the decade.[1] Likewise, the deployment of new advertising techniques focused on the cultural preeminence of the large urban environs helped consolidate the symbolism of the rising industrial centers as the locus where the promises of modernity, believed to be situated just around the corner, were to be realized.[2]

Most of the new products colorfully displayed in a growing number of ads published in illustrated magazines were still out of the reach of most Brazilians, to be sure, particularly in large portions of the countryside. The idealized lifestyle structured along new patterns of consumption nonetheless exerted an important role in shaping a diffuse yet effective collective perception (*imaginaire*) supporting the desire to rapidly transform the national society by means of fast-paced industrialization. And, as the developmental years of the 1950s unfolded, a redefined image of modern life was indeed taking shape. Brazil's future was believed to no longer depend on the cultural stewardship of the central government, which had restructured school curricula during the corporatist years of Estado Novo. Instead, if one was to believe the pages of the ever popular glossy magazines and the manifold cultural innovations taking place in the majority of artistic venues, the JK Years did seem to be fulfilling the historically repressed, unbounded potential of a heretofore elusive future. Although this expectant outlook helped define the general cultural milieu of the time, a more diverse and, many times, contradictory ideological scenario needs to be reconstructed so that a more accurate characterization of these important events can emerge. In fact, though supportive and particularly excited about the rise of a more sophisticated and influential consumer culture, members of the broadly defined middle and upper economic sectors firmly advanced critical positions regarding core development notions of the period.

Adding to the intellectual examination presented in previous sections, this chapter begins by scrutinizing key elements of the cultural and ideological milieus delineating the so-called golden years in Brazil. This is followed by a close review of the main ways in which key business and professional associations conceived of and responded to some of the main developmental trends and debates of the time. As a whole this chapter reveals that though initially supportive of the generic goal of rapid economic growth, corporate and technocratic elites steadily opposed more socially (what they called *politically motivated*) developmental propositions of the time. Alternatively, these self-described *conservative* or *productive forces* espoused a purportedly neutral (science-based), though essentially market-centered and strictly growth-oriented, developmental path, rather than any type of substantive alteration in the country's historical socio-economic structures.

CULTURAL TRANSFORMATIONS, THE RISE OF CONSUMERISM, AND DIFFUSE ACTS OF POLITICAL SUPPORT: REVISITING THE IDEATIONAL BASIS OF THE POPULIST COMPROMISE

The search for new forms of expression guided much of the most influential and creative cultural movements of the 1950s in areas as diverse as theater, music, cinema, literature, and the fine arts. Sometimes representing the culmination of artistic trends harkening back to earlier decades (such as in literature and architecture), other times leading to innovations that only reached full fruition in the early or mid-1960s (as in cinema), what all of these different endeavors had in common was the attempted *aggiornamento* (updating) of traditional cultural démarches by local forms of expression with global artistic movements.[3] In fact, in a typically Brazilian cultural tradition of trying to synchronize domestic cultural expressions with the latest international trends, the overarching goal of most artists involved in these many creative initiatives was, once again, to reshape the national culture by incorporating new foreign, at times disparate, cultural elements.[4] In effect, as the country rapidly transitioned toward a more urban, industrial society, the need to be innovative in the forms of cultural expression influenced cultural venues oriented toward mass consumption and industrial life (e.g., pop art and Neo-Concrete poetry), as well as more traditional venues (e.g., Regionalist literature). Furthermore, as the 1950s were coming to a close and the level of ideological polarization in the main urban centers reached unprecedented new grounds, many of these new cultural movements became deeply immersed in the intense politics of the period.

Notions of innovation, of practicality, and above all, of modernity (loosely conceived) shaped artistic creativity in the 1950s, largely along "the desire for change [. . .] and the search for new artistic forms of expression."[5] Radio broadcasting reached its apogee in terms of popularity and a domestic movie industry debuted despite continued challenges to its long-term economic sustainability. Especially important for defining the main ideology of local filmic production of the following two decades, a new movie style—politically engaged, and closely inspired by the Italian Neo-Realism of the postwar years—started being pursued in mid-decade, coming to full expression in the mid-1960s under the label of *Cinema Novo*. Similar trends were manifested in theater production, particularly in the experiences of the Arena and TBC theater houses. Poetry, sculpture, painting, and design were significantly impacted by the Concretist inspiration which sought to represent life in an ever more industry-oriented metropolis. Even popular music underwent one of its most important thematic, melodic, and, above all, harmonic transformations in many decades when urban audiences welcomed the advent of Bossa Nova in the final years of the decade.

All things considered, this cultural creative ebullience helped buttress the dissemination of a generalized sense of confidence in the ability allegedly shared by all Brazilians to construct a more promising future for their country.[6] This sentiment seemed to have reached a climax in mid-year 1958 when the mixed-race Brazilian soccer team won the World Cup for the first time against the much more monochromatic Swedish home team. Adding to this sense of optimism shared particularly among middle income urban sectors, Kubitschek himself proved to be an adroit leader in offering a grandiose vision of the future. This was something he had rehearsed in his tenure as governor of the state of Minas Gerais in the first half of the decade when his regular radio appearances updated *mineiros* on the promising implementation of his bold developmental agenda.[7]

As indicated in Chapter One, transplanted to the national stage, the annual messages to the National Congress are good indications of how successfully JK resorted to official pronouncements to advance his personal perspective on the future of the country. In addition to official speeches, Kubitschek was well versed in utilizing regular radio broadcasts and the printed media to build and sustain the image of an engaging, dynamic, moderate, and charismatic leader who consistently defended the view that a more promising future was within reach.[8] This was particularly well reflected in the level of support he was able to sustain throughout much of his term in the presidential office. For one, despite blaming the federal government for bearing the main responsibility for the continued price hikes, especially in food staples that particularly afflicted residents of large urban areas, most Brazilians were ready to give JK a stamp of approval when his first year in office had come to a close. Also indicative of this phenomenon, surveys done in the thirty largest metropolitan areas early in 1958 showed that over 50 percent of respondents approved of the federal administration, even though they also doubted that the national government was actually capable of putting an end to the constant increases in the cost of living. Significantly even higher rates of approval (above 60 percent) were found in the personal style of leadership displayed by the president.[9]

Deriving from a constructed, though nonetheless highly effective shared perception that the long-promised modernity and development were to be finally attained, this growing sense of confidence and optimism was also closely reflected in the printed media of the period, particularly in the weekly, photo-centered (styled after the U.S. *Life* magazine), *O Cruzeiro* and *Manchete*. Together the two publications reached a record number of close to one million issues being distributed on a weekly basis at the end of the 1950s, thus potentially reaching an estimated reading public of about four million out of a voting population of just over nine million literate Brazilians. Both the federal administration and, above all, Kubitschek himself, were regularly praised in the two publications, particularly for his ambitious goal of transforming the country from an agrarian-based economy with corresponding traditional cultural elements to a prosperous nation organized around industrialism, technological innovation, and a forward-looking, mass-consumption-driven modern national culture.[10]

The hopefulness that helped define the domestic cultural and political atmosphere of the JK Years was also shared, at least in a general sense, by foreigners increasingly interested in Brazil's growing consumer markets. Particularly in cases where Cold War driven ideological positions were not at the forefront of the interactions established between political and business representatives of the two countries, the market-oriented perspectives promoted by U.S. business executives portrayed Brazil's accelerated path to modernity in the light of the, allegedly benevolent, influence that higher exposure to U.S.-like items of mass consumption would exert. In fact, alongside important managerial and visual transformations redefining the role of print media in the country, substantial investments were made in the industry of advertising, particularly by foreign-controlled, mostly U.S.-based advertising agencies whose executives became influential agents of the dissemination of a U.S.-inspired consumer culture.[11]

Illustrative of these events, while conducting a business trip to several Latin American countries, influential advertising executive Shirley F. Woodell submitted a memo from São Paulo on July 23, 1955, to the J. Walter Thompson advertising company's headquarters in New York City, in which he expressed a great deal of optimism about the prospects of the Brazilian economy and the significant growth he expected for the local office in the upcoming years.[12] In a related letter, sent from Havana on August 29 that same year, Woodell reflected further on the Brazilian market as the most promising one in a region where the "business environment seem[ed] excellent and there [was] a well-established and thriving advertising industry." Adding to his instructions to the New York office, the writer stressed "the need to be clever in projecting an American positive image given that local middles classes seem more favorable to the French culture."[13] This sense of optimism seemed to have only deepened as the JK Years unfolded as, in mid-year 1960, R.F. Merrick, director of the J. Walter Thompson Company's São Paulo Office, reported back to the company's vice-president, Samuel W. Meek—a highly respected ad executive in the U.S. who would become increasingly involved in advising official U.S. cultural policies toward Latin America—sharing his own views on the state of the Brazilian economy. In his report, Merrick argued that:

> We are not alone in our optimistic view of the Brazilian economy and several American companies are expanding facilities here [and] (. . .) given the booming internal economy of Brazil in these last few years, I should like to give you our thinking with respect to the steps we must take if we are to keep pace with it.[14]

By the same token, responding to growing concerns expressed and widely voiced in the domestic media at the time about rising inflation, Merrick, a key representative of foreign investors, ironically counter-argued very much along the same lines as the national-developmentalists at ISEB saying that "the recent massive investments in industrialization, particularly in automobile plants and roads, will act as a stabilizing factor in the dollar expenditures with imports." Similarly indicative of how the actions of marketing agents of foreign business interests were permeated by domestic developmental ideational constructs of the period (at times, even very nationalist ones), several advertisements of the JK era explicitly articulated the notion that by strengthening its own economic resources, Brazil would finally develop into a modern society, thus becoming up-to-date with global trends and consumption patterns of the already industrialized world.[15]

The ideological ambiguity of some of these campaigns notwithstanding, and very revealing of the business logic imbued in much of the U.S. Cold War strategies of the time, in addition to being instrumental in promoting U.S. business interests in the country, J. Walter Thompson executives were repeatedly contacted by U.S. governmental officials asking for their advice on how to enhance the dissemination of a positive image for growing U.S. commercial influence in the region.[16] In effect, it should be noted that the market-based sense of confidence in the prospects of the national economy displayed in the advertisements of the Kubitschek era notwithstanding, as the 1960s dawned in Brazil, domestic political polarization reached new grounds, and optimism quickly turned into concern, for both Brazilian and U.S. marketing executives. Several letters from the Brazilian office of J. Walter

Thompson Company in São Paulo indeed reported back to the company's headquarters in New York City as early as in the summer of 1961 to make the case that regardless of the assurances given to international investors by the ever more market-friendly Quadros administration (January to August 1961), the company should seriously consider the path of legally turning its local operations into a separate Brazilian division given the general mood for new laws regulating foreign investments with strict limits on remittances and restricted tax benefits to foreign-owned companies.[17]

As perhaps was to be expected, advertising pieces of these same years clearly portrayed the image of modernity and development as essentially associated with the goal of economic prosperity and well-being. This reductionist, market-based notion of national development was consistent in advertisements showing how practical and convenient modern (city) life was being made by the items of consumption provided by the new and increasingly foreign industries operating in the country. The urban environ was invariably projected as the central location where this (said-to-be) fast-arriving progress and prosperity was to take place, and the industrial realm, along with its purportedly innovative "entrepreneurial spirit," was frequently characterized as performing a *de facto* "civilizing mission" of raising the standards of technical knowledge, integrating the country, and transforming the backward outlook of the general public.[18] Likewise, befitting the assigned role of not only becoming the new administrative center of a changing nation, but also of providing a vision and geographical and symbolic focus for a new path of modernity being pursued, Brasília was consistently featured in the pages of national magazines as the place where the future would arrive first. A future defined by the modern design of a city structured along large avenues indeed seemed the perfect setting for many advertisements praising the emerging domestic-based automobile industry. But despite its clear instrumentality for designing several marketing campaigns in the final years of the JK era, the transfer of the capital city from Rio to Brasília nonetheless not only provoked vibrant and acutely polarized debates involving some of the most important national newspapers based in Rio, but also sparked the creation of a multitude of new poems, songs, and, above all, sambas in defense of or against the project.[19]

Unquestionably, in building a new capital city, JK and his closest advisors involved in the process (including the world-renowned architect Oscar Niemeyer) hoped that such an move would serve to advance "an exemplar of progress for the rest of the nation [that would] propel the country as a whole into a planned future the city was said to embody;" they similarly hoped that the new capital "would stimulate leaps in the development process of the country itself."[20] Ironically, while trying to provide a new direction for the country, which was translated into a new futuristic capital-city, the very ways in which Brasília was built, i.e., by creating a geographical peripheral zone where former construction workers who refused to return to their homelands were forced to settle, the long-standing socio-economic exclusion that defined the history of Brazil was, once again, reproduced and physically perpetuated.[21]

While the dissemination of a material culture of progress shaped the period and important inroads on the path of industrialization were evident, Brazil nonetheless followed a very conservative path of modernization in mid-century. This quintessentially Brazilian contradiction is noticeable, for instance, in the contrast found between the optimism about the economic modernity shared by upper- and middle-income urban dwellers (well displayed in the first Salão do Automóvel of 1959), and in the fact that the growth of the period did not provide palpable betterment in the lives of the majority of those involved even in these very same important economic achievements. To be sure, while industrial output in the JK Years reached a remarkable average annual rate of 11 percent, industrial job creation amounted only to 3 percent annually.[22] And even in the much-showcased attainments of the automobile industry, which was constantly promoted as the main engine of the country's transformation toward a high modernity, wages lagged significantly *vis-à-vis* the productivity achieved, particularly in the plants held by foreign-owned multinational corporations.[23] Manufacturing automobiles was indeed said to represent the fastest and surest path toward industrial development, as well as the quintessential mid-century industry offering backward and forward economic linkages for the creation of supplementary business activities. Deploying a domestic automotive capability was also claimed to be the most instrumental ways of integrating the still vastly fragmented national territory.[24]

The widespread promise of a modern, bright, and soon-to-arrive future of limitless potentialities aside, many of the socio-economic, political, and cultural transformations taking place in the 1950s were seen by growing numbers of influential social segments as a generalized maelstrom caused by constant demographic upheavals, challenges to stable identities and established socio-economic (and racial) hierarchies, time-tested values, and deepening impersonal market-based relations.[25] In particular middle-income sectors, consisting primarily of liberal professional and middle-rank government bureaucrats, increasingly adopted a more conservative political outlook in the 1950s, a historical novelty sharply contrasting with the politically more liberal positions at least some in these same important social segments advanced in the 1920s, 1930s, or even the mid-1940s. This historical juncture seems to have derived from the fact that many of the core positions sponsored by the federal government were gradually incorporating a more popular component, particularly under the second Vargas administration in the first half of the 1950s, a historical trend that was often interpreted by members of the middle- and upper-income sectors as potentially threatening to their traditionally secure socio-economic and cultural standing.

Unquestionably, in the midst of a rapidly changing social landscape, middle-income sectors progressively thought of themselves in more explicit class, and even racial, terms. Their growing concern about a process of transformation believed to be "out of control" in the sense of upsetting traditional socio-economic (but also geographic, political, and even cultural) boundaries led many to believe that they, not the actual poor living in the ever more abundant urban shanties (let alone the destitute countryside), carried the heaviest burden of concretely felt economic difficulties (e.g., rising inflation) and challenges (e.g., growing competition for fewer-than-needed job opportunities). In turn, the largely influential middle sector grew ever more ideologically conservative, utilizing the "editorial voices of their white-collar organizations [. . .] to consistently recast deep-rooted aspects of social [racial and gender] hierarch[ies] in a new social context."[26]

The transformations caused by accelerated economic growth, industrialization, urbanization, geographical displacements, and innovative forms of political mobilization among traditionally excluded social segments (industrial workers, peasants, and even landless laborers) inspired traditional elites across the country to "re-entrench Brazil's patrimonial, authoritarian, and hierarchical roots," resorting at times to new forms of political mobilization, as will be further examined below.[27] Likewise, despite the promises of (and significant achievements in) rapid economic growth and industrial promotion, urban middle sectors were growing disappointed with the main political parties in power in the 1950s. Accordingly, in seeking to channel their sense of frustration into new collective engagement, the upper- and middle-income sectors tended to advance their own political views and positions in an allegedly non-political rhetoric, which espoused the value of hard work, technical expertise, traditional gender roles, personal educational improvements, and the de-politicization of politics. Correspondingly, as the country approached the beginning of the 1960s, the defense of a "technical" approach to politics found resonance in the gradual advancement of *técnicos* in higher levels of decision-making agencies. In the end, this historical trend was instrumental for the military regime emerging after 1964 as it provided the dictatorship with a much-valued justification for continuing to cleanse the political system of corrupt traditional politicians.

Between 1945 and 1964, Brazil had a multiparty system wherein three main parties competed for dominance. The most influential of these political organizations, in terms of their representation in the National Congress, were the Social Democratic Party (PSD, JK's own party), followed by the opposition party, the National Democratic Union (UDN, which sponsored a free-market stance on economic and political affairs), and closely followed by the Brazilian Labor Party (PTB), which still exerted a strong influence over officially sanctioned urban labor unions despite the growing strength of grass-roots independent mobilization). From a small presence, the PTB expanded its numbers significantly in the National Chamber, even surpassing the UDN delegation after the mid-term election of 1962. Together, these three parties controlled 81 percent of all seats in the federal legislature. More significantly, in direct contrast to the repeated notion that the main policies behind fast industrial growth had been essentially left up to politically insulated decision-making agencies, the fact of the matter is that the most consequential economic decisions regarding trade policy and taxes, as well as the most ambitious developmental projects of the period, all depended on legislative decisions made by the National Congress. As already discussed, examples of these developmental projects include the creation of new highly influential state-owned corporations (e.g., Petrobras), as well as the very creation and regular funding of the National Bank of Economic Development, and even the construction of the new capital city of Brasília.

The role the National Brazilian Congress played in supporting the programs of the federal government in the 1950s requires further explaining as it was precisely in the federal legislature that opposition forces could have acted to tame the developmental ambitions of the administration. First, it needs to be noted that the Kubitschek administration maintained unprecedentedly high levels of support in Congress for the promotion of its agenda. Examinations of the voting record of the National Chamber of Deputies in Brazil in the second half of the 1950s have indeed demonstrated that the executive branch of the federal government managed to get approval for its projects with a majority of votes in both houses of Congress even when submitting highly divisive bills, such as those pertaining to transferring the national capital.[28]

Wide legislative support for the projects pursued in the period indeed reveal, contrary to the experiences of other Latin American countries attempting to implement similar projects of development, that the behavior of the Brazilian Congress attested to the existence of an informal, unwritten compromise between the different economic interests therein represented. Powerful business sectors consistently managed to find compromise between core legislative differences, such as those pertaining to exchange rate policies. In fact, whereas agrarian forces pushed for lower rates in order to make their exports more competitive in the global markets, industrialists worked to maintain a stronger exchange rate beneficial for the importation of capital goods for their own activities.[29]

Although overvalued exchange rates were indeed maintained, coffee exports had to be continually supported at the cost of ever more expensive purchases of excess production so that price margins, in a declining international market, were sustained. Similarly, instead of a structural political weakness of the industrial sector, what was effectively experienced in political terms in mid-century Brazil was a very clever political resolution of a potentially highly damaging dispute between strong, entrenched interests in ways that allowed for a compromise favoring both sides, even though an industrialist path was ultimately pursued.[30] Exemplifying these historical trends, all bills funding core projects of the federal administration examined in the JK period received votes of over 72 percent of all of members of Congress, and there was no difference in the voting records of the four main parties.[31]

Moreover, a direct result of this costly political compromise was that even the powerful agricultural sectors tied to export production, particularly of coffee, cotton, and cacao—all of which were overrepresented in Congress due to the different electoral quotients held by different regions of the country—steadily supported the inward industrial path of the period as long as compensatory financial measures were put in place.[32] Along these political lines, both primary exporting and industrial sectors regularly benefitted from generous economic subsidies, but, whereas the former benefitted from across-the-board price guarantees, the latter tended to receive monetary disbursements on a case-by-case basis (i.e., at the level of the firm). In fact, whereas industrialists received generous support from the powerful National Bank of Economic Development (BNDE) for projects of industrial expansion, exporters of primary goods were able to sustain their economic well-being despite declining prices in global markets, leaving the general tax payers, particularly the poor, to bear the brunt of these same policies, which in some years exceed 10 percent of gross national product.[33]

This broad conservative (status quo-oriented) political arrangement aside, and even though more frequent than one would intuitively expect considering the underlining ideological divisions in Congress, parliamentary support was never assured and depended on the constant disbursement of political prizes (primarily in the form of public credit and tax incentives) aimed at appeasing different business interests, particularly in the state of São Paulo. This paradoxically democratic but also highly deleterious structural political logic was well-exposed in the final months of 1958 when a restrictive fiscal program was attempted (titled Monetary Stabilization Plan [PEM]) by the new minister of finance, Lucas Lopes. Business elites have been behind the course of governmental planning of the national economy since at least the mid-1940s, a historical trajectory that became ever more influential in the 1950s despite the continued opposition advanced at some of the most prestigious circles of economic reflection, such as the National Economic Council and the School of Economics at the Getúlio Vargas Foundation (FGV).[34]

Whereas almost all significant groups of the national elite agreed about the political primacy of industrial over agricultural growth, important arguments unfolded among relevant policymakers about the best ways in which to achieve this very same goal. Particularly relevant was the debate established in the mid-1940s between industrial tycoon and influential business leader Roberto Simonsen and the leading proponent of neo-classical economics in Brazil, Professor Eugênio Gudin.[35] These conceptual differences notwithstanding, Brazilian industrialists, especially those that coalesced in the powerful associations located in the city and state of São Paulo, articulated consistent though not automatic support for the main elements of the bold industrial drive implemented in the 1950s, which Kubitschek defined as "the very battle for our national survival."[36] The influential positions held by key industrial groups are examined next.

STATE-LED INDUSTRIAL PROMOTION THROUGH THE EYES OF INDUSTRIAL ASSOCIATIONS

In July of 1957, the National Industrial Confederation (CNI) launched a new publication that became very influential in promoting the general outlines of the developmental positions advocated by industrialists in the second half of the 1950s. Evocatively titled *Desenvolvimento & Conjuntura* (D&C), from its very first issue the magazine conveyed its appreciation for the "new generation of national leaders who have understood the strategic role that only the path of industrialization can play in economic development."[37] Surprisingly predicated on a quintessentially ECLA-inspired tenet pertaining to the stewardship function that the central government should exert in the national economy, D&C stated that in "peripheral countries, it is up to the national government, in partnership with the private sector, to pave the way to dynamic growth."[38]

This partnership naturally had to include public sources of credit for industrial projects and it was exactly the reduction in this source of funds, proposed in the Monetary Stabilization Plan (PEM) launched in October 1958, which caused the country's two most important industrial business associations, the National Industrial Confederation (CNI) and the powerful São Paulo Industrial Federation (FIESP) to rise up against Minister Lopes despite their alleged continued support for the administration and the president himself. In fact, despite the moderate approach of the PEM—given that it allowed for minimal salary increases and continued funding for the ambitious developmental projects of the federal government, while requiring these goals to be pursued at a slower pace—both industrial associations were adamant in rejecting the suggested restriction on public loans included in the bill submitted to Congress by Minister Lopes in the final months of year.[39] Alternatively, in the industrialists' perspective, the main reasons behind the economic challenges the country faced were found in the excessive public expenditures involved in constantly raising the wages of public servants and in the added economic demand created by these very policies. Ironically, this purportedly ominous trend required higher levels of public funds to be made available to private industrial initiatives, as well as a range of additional government policies, such as preferential exchange rates for capital goods imports and wage controls in the salaries of industrial workers.[40]

D & C centered its editorial attention on promoting another core position of the industrialists, which focused on a much-debated argument of the period, i.e., what role inflationary expansion played in promoting fast-paced economic and industrial growth. While most prominent economists of the time, particularly those teaching at the FGV, avowed a more monetarist stance and were critical of any positive role to be played by inflation, industrialists, particularly in São Paulo and among the leaders coalesced at the CNI, consistently argued that "differing from advanced industrial economies, we still need higher levels of investment and savings that can be best provided by reasonable rates of inflation that transfer funds from lower social classes, with their natural propensity for consumption, to the hands of the class with a higher ability to save."[41] Interestingly, this view was shared by Kubitschek himself, who continued to defend his developmental program at the end of his presidential term even in the face of mounting inflationary pressure. In his view, while presenting a summary of his accomplishments to the National Economic Council (CNE) in the final days of his presidency, JK explicitly stated that "the truth about Brazilian inflation is that it is fed by structural causes beyond monetary pressures, reflecting the socio-economic state of an underdeveloped country [. . .] undergoing strong demographic pressures leading to new consumption patterns not yet compatible with our productive capabilities."[42]

The fact that this administrative report conveying a structuralist-like analysis of the state of (under)development of the country was delivered at one of the most pro-market agencies of the federal government adds to the complexities, as well as the ironies, of the period. The CNE's core views on these same historical dynamics will be examined in detail in the next section of this chapter as part of a larger analysis of some of the most important critical, anti-nationalist developmental publications of the JK era. But first, it is worth returning to the positions sponsored by the more pro-national-developmentalist business groups, particularly those coalesced at the CNI and FIESP who consistently defended "the need for governmental stewardship in the process of national development so that the country fulfilled its 'reserved place in the world stage.' "[43] Much in the same way, the publication repeatedly argued that the "gap between developed and underdeveloped societies is only widening [. . .] [and] only by addressing this growing global inequality can countries that are still developing be allowed to follow the path of sustained economic development."[44] And that "the possibility of sustaining our growing needs for manufactured items on the basis of imports paid with revenues from our primary exports are dwindling [and only] [. . .] by expanding our domestic industrial base will we not only address these trade shortages, but also provide our agriculture with the technology to keep pace with the growing commodities supply of global markets."[45]

It is important to note that despite their reiterated usage of ECLA- and ISEB-related ideas, industrialists were undoubtedly not ideologues of national-developmentalist positions *in toto* and their take on these developmental concepts and projects was indeed highly selective.[46] In fact, while these two influential industrial associations consistently argued for a "productive partnership" to be established between a more active government and private companies, they thought that the focus of the projects of the central state should not include ambitious socially oriented goals (i.e., broad social betterment), but instead be primarily geared toward "interlinking private and public economic agents so that the needed path of accelerated economic expansion [could] be achieved."[47]

Not surprisingly, the National Industrial Confederation also argued that the model to be replicated, if possible, in all undertakings of the Brazilian government was the one established within the operations of the Executive Group of Automotive Industries (GEIA), where "the positive and clairvoyant action of the current administration in creating clear incentives for private businesses to lead the process of implementing a domestic-based automobile industry is the best example of how much the private sector can accomplish when well supported by the federal state."[48] Additional praise for the cooperation between public and private business interests can be found in the main publication of FIESP (*Boletim Informativo da FIESP*), which vocally urged "all Brazilians to support the alliance of efforts between the national government and private agents [given that] strengthening national industry is the most basic condition for strengthening our nation [. . .] [as] it is impossible to dissociate the interests of industries and those of the country, lest we risk sacrificing our entire future as a nation."[49]

Moving beyond their regular publications, industrialists were also very active in voicing their views in national and regional gatherings that attracted a great deal of media visibility to their agenda and causes. Even when taking place beyond the two main industrial centers of São Paulo and Rio de Janeiro, where FIESP and the CNI were respectively based, these meetings were traditionally led by these two same organizations due to their unparalleled economic means, personnel, and political clout. The main conferences that brought different business interests together in mid-century included the Primeira Conferência Nacional das Classes Produtoras (CONCLAP) in 1945 (which was followed by the Segunda Conferência das Classes Produtoras in 1949), and two national industrialist meetings, the Primeira Reunião Plenária da Indústria in 1953, and the Segunda Reunião Plenária da Indústria in 1955. In addition to naturally advancing their specifics demands, these meetings—particularly the first two—offered an opportunity for business associations to coalesce into a common pro-business political front.[50]

As these events unfolded, a move from the corporatist ideals that had defined much of the industrialists' outlook about labor relations in the 1940s was giving way to a more pro-market, critical stance on the current labor legislation of the period.[51] Indeed, the so-called "Letter of the Industry" (*Carta de Princípios da Indústria*), written in Porto Alegre in 1955 in between JK's controversial election in October 1955 and his taking of office in January 1956, clearly conveyed the conservative stance held by industrial associations about the social component of the developmental plans of the incoming administration. The piece states that "enhancing the minimum living standards of our people should be sought in measures that accelerate the pace of capital formation and increase the rate of productivity [, not in] redistributive policies that threaten our material progress by offering perceived advantages that cannot be sustained in the long run."[52]

Adding to this picture, business leaders from industrial confederations in different parts of the country who were interviewed by U.S. labor historian

Robert J. Alexander in the first few months of the JK administration expressed a hopeful view of the incoming government, but were quick to say that labor relations would improve only if negotiations between employers and employees were allowed to take place more freely, i.e., without the legally required government supervision operating through the tri-party system of corporatist labor legislation instituted in the early 1940s.[53] These informants similarly believed that the new, much praised developmental agenda proposed by Kubitschek could only take effect if a clear focus was placed on increasing economic productivity, rather than on socially oriented policies. In fact, in their views, workers would do best if they "learned, once and for all, to see the benefits of working harder [given that] everyone has to pull their fair share [and the country] requires sacrifices from everyone."[54] Given the still prevalent corporatist logic and legal framework within which capital-labor relations took place, these positions were usually justified by resorting to a paternalistic argument that stated that "employers know best what employees need given that they have established close and personal relations with them."[55] Furthermore, when Professor Alexander asked employers to comment on the so-called "problem of communism," most asserted that in their local context (be it in Recife, Salvador, or Porto Alegre) communist "infiltration" was not as big of a problem as in the center of the country (i.e., São Paulo and Rio de Janeiro).

Ironically, several business representatives claimed that the rank-and-file were, on an individual basis, truly receptive to the idea of partaking in direct negotiations with employers, but that this course of action was, unfortunately, not as prevalent as employers would have liked given the fact that union leaders were overly zealous in negotiating through the legal procedures specified in the labor laws.[56] This negative portrayal of labor legislation, particularly of the labor courts that were often said to be biased in favor of workers when supervising wage negotiations, was a constant in the 1950s. However, as labor unions in Rio de Janeiro and, especially, in São Paulo began engaging in massive collective (inter-union) mobilizations, starting in 1957 and again in 1959 and 1960, industrialists quickly supported the supervisory role of the labor courts, which, in fact, tended to rule along middle-ground lines, particularly regarding wage increases. A detailed analysis of these events, and especially of how labor creatively responded to them, will be offered in Chapter Six.

For now it is important to mention that, when trying to mobilize public opinion against a massive stoppage coordinated by an inter-union movement (something proscribed in the labor legislation of the period) taking place in São Paulo in mid-October 1957, FIESP President Antonio Devisate explicitly argued that "workers are trying to impose an extra-legal arrangement that disparages our judicial system, following a dangerous course of action that undermines public authorities and the very rule of law, thus opening the way to chaos and anarchy."[57] In contrast, FIESP adamantly argued that cooperative patterns of interaction between employers and workers, with minimal government interference if possible, were essential for a successful agenda of development. These opposing stances will become more evident in the upcoming chapter, where I examine the political polarization of the closing years of the Kubitschek era. At the same time, urban workers consistently demanded more engaged governmental involvement in settling not-always-reconcilable interests between themselves and their employers.[58]

Industrialists, for one, believed that the most important course of action to be pursued was one that required "everyone to perform one's duty to the nation." This claim is indicative of the deeply conservative position business groups were gradually assuming considering that, in spite of its grandiose nationalist tone, the statement reveals the belief that deeply deprived social segments (i.e., workers) could bear further economic sacrifices (namely wage freezes), as long as more privileged sectors also "joined in the struggle." This conservative type of nationalism was indeed held even by business groups placed at the forefront of the modernizing efforts of the Brazilian developmental age, and was well demonstrated in their efforts to promote "social peace" through training and educational programs targeted at industrial workers. In effect, aimed at promoting what was expected to be (or become) harmonious relations between capital and labor, SESI (Social Service of the Industry), the branch of the CNI in charge of educational programs to industrial workers, published different magazines, broadcasted a number of different radio shows, and held several performing arts, literary, and sports related activities in factory plants, union headquarters, and affiliated institutions across the country. These activities included organizing a host of literacy programs, and holding regular "Workers Olympiads," which were very popular and involved thousands of participants. Also popular were several SESI-produced radio broadcasts, which reached large audiences through over ten radio stations in the city of São Paulo.[59]

As the opening line of one these legal broadcasts stated (and which was reproduced in the printed version of *SESI Jornal*) the underlining goal was "to provide workers with basic knowledge of our labor legislation so that the rights of our working people can be preserved with no prejudice to the interests of employers, thus promoting the higher interests of our shared nation."[60] The fact that employers were promoting these specific educational initiatives is indeed reflective of the fact that they believed, despite the alleged bias of the labor courts, that the legislation pertaining to labor was safe enough for their own interests that a labor force better informed on the rights granted on the books would not pose a serious threat to business interests. Similarly, the very existence of so many literacy programs financed by industrial associations, which in the capital city of São Paulo alone involved more than two hundred teaching units and reached over twenty-two thousand workers, reflects the inability of the public school system to adequately teach basic reading skills to large enough numbers of people during a period of rapid economic growth and increasing industrial demand for a better-qualified labor force.[61] This was even revealed in events pertaining to one of JK's most praised developmental projects, the implementation of an automotive industrial park in the country, as auto business associations complained from the beginning to the end of his presidency about the shortage of skilled labor to fill the positions being rapidly created in their industry.[62]

Ironically, the few initiatives pertaining to education in the JK era were not targeted at enhancing basic training (such as effective reading skills, seen as the main challenge by employers), but were rather concentrated on scientific research (e.g., nuclear energy).[63] In fact, one of the more elaborate educational undertakings focused on elementary schooling during these years was indeed taken up, once again, by SESI. Though broadcasted on the state-owned Radio MEC, production, funding, and editorial content was placed under the auspices of the regional offices of the agency. Suggestively called "Sesinho no Rádio: a revista educativa semanal dedicada ao filho do trabalhador" (Sesinho in the Radio: A Weekly Educational Magazine Dedicated to the Workingman's Children) the program portrayed a little boy called Sesinho (little Sesi) who regularly posed a question to his wise uncle (Tio Graça) regarding a series of topics dealt with in each episode. This dependable storyline allowed the "benevolent uncle" to delve into long praises about the economic riches, geographical beauties, historical glories, and, above all, promising future of the rising Brazilian nation. In fact, in reviewing the two hundred, half-hour long programs transmitted during the JK Years available at the National Archive in Rio de Janeiro, one undoubtedly gets a small though eloquent glimpse of the sense of optimism and excitement about the county's prospects that the producers of the show consistently sought to convey. A good illustration of these events can be found in the broadcasts of mid-July and mid-September of 1958, when Sesinho learned from his all-knowing uncle that now that infrastructural investments were being made across the country, "the natural potential of our glorious nation, which has been provided by the grace of providence, will finally be fulfilled, leading us to reach our long-sought economic autonomy."[64]

Likewise, in the episode titled "Labor: Our Loyal Friend," Sesinho is praised by his uncle for having joined a local chapter of the Ants Club, the name of the elementary school SESI-sponsored children's associations set up across the country to discuss the radio broadcasts and accompanying comics magazine (also called *Sesinho*) mailed to member chapters. According to Tio Graça, this was the right course of action given that at his local club, Sesinho would learn about the importance of developing a work ethic, said to be "the only path towards progress." To stress his point, the uncle tells a story of a man who, tired of having to work so much, had asked God to not have to work any longer. Before his wish is fulfilled, however, the man had a dream that took him to a foreign land where no one had to work. To the man's greatest surprise, and so that the lesson of the story would be learned, soon after reaching this allegedly idyllic place, the man became bored and "realized that it is better to work every day even without being able to accumulate riches than having nothing to do."[65] Related praises to the importance of technological innovation were also a repeated theme in the "Sesinho no Rádio" shows, which stressed that modern industrial growth is "the key to the national economic liberation of our country as we will no longer depend on other nations, [thus] consolidating [by economic means] the political independence we obtained on September 7, 1822."[66]

Indicative of just how much this radio program was in tune with the official narrative of development, early the same year Kubitschek himself had proclaimed that, "we are changing the historical course of our nation by overcoming the condition of underdevelopment and placing our country in its due place among other peoples of the world."[67] Much in the same way, "Sesinho no Rádio" ventured to explain specific policies of the JK administration to its juvenile public. In an episode broadcasted in mid-year 1959, under the label of "Sesinho in the Wonderful World of Automobiles," for instance, the little boy tells his uncle that he had a dream in which he was driving Brazilian-made cars and asks rhetorically, "Uncle, do you think I would be driving foreign cars in my dream?" Pleased with the nationalism of his nephew, Tio Graça praises the boy for his sense of patriotism and explains to him that, "[t]hanks to the great work performed by GEIA, Brazil is on its way to becoming self-sufficient in automobile production." Finally, to effectively drive home the point, in the closing dialogue Sesinho states that, "all kids should become friends of Mrs. Geia, who is creating the basis of our national emancipation."[68]

An accompanying contemporary radio broadcast, also produced by SESI, but targeted to an adult audience, focused on "promoting a better civic culture." Simply called "Civic Education" and also aired on Rádio MEC, these short shows (ten minutes on average) were mostly aimed at "encouraging workers to vote correctly." The nationalistic tone of "Sesinho no Rádio" was likewise conveyed in this other radio program, which also dealt with topics "of national interest." In an episode of mid-year 1958, for instance, which was suggestively titled "Dangerous Age," youth behavior said to have become excessively influenced by foreign-based (mostly U.S.) consumption patterns was examined. According to the dialogue between two of the characters who are friends, "[t]he United States is a strong nation because they value their own national culture [. . .] and only by doing the same will we be able to become as strong an industrialized people as the Americans."[69] Similarly, in a show dealing with the topic of inflation, provocatively called "A Problem of Easy Resolution," producers urged Brazilians to "stop criticizing the federal administration [but rather to] engage the task of national development."[70]

The same case is made in the shows of mid-year 1960 as the country approached a very polarized presidential election. Reproaching those "who only criticize the inability of the federal government to lower prices," these episodes also admonished all who "did not realize that wages are also going up," alternatively advising that "only by supporting politicians committed to the developmental policies currently in place could prices be controlled, since our economic productivity would be increased."[71] The topic of inflation indeed shaped much of the political debate taking place in the final years of the 1950s. As will be demonstrated in Chapter Six, organized labor acquired an eloquent voice in very divisive arguments. These arguments involved representatives in prominent roles from technical professions, organized middle-income social segments, and different urban business associations beyond the scope of the industry. And though some overlap with core industrialists' demands for curbing governmental spending did exist, the positions espoused by these latter political actors (namely professional economists, commercial associations, and organized voices of government personnel) posited conservative and at times reactionary political views, which I examine next.

TECHNICAL PROFESSIONALS AND COMMERCIAL ASSOCIATIONS: MOUNTING CONSERVATIVE VOICES ON DEVELOPMENT PROMOTION

One of the main venues for advancing what was seen as a technical approach to development promotion was an influential monthly publication edited by the Brazilian Institute of Economics of the prestigious Getúlio Vargas Foundation (FGV) in Rio de Janeiro. Established in 1948, *Conjuntura Econômica* (*Economic Conjuncture*, *CE*) soon became one of the most important periodicals dedicated to economic matters in the country. Headed by prominent economist José Garrido Torres, *CE* advanced an academic-like editorial stance, even though the magazine circulated among business investors who quickly became its main subscribers. In general terms, *Conjuntura Econômica* endorsed a market-friendly, economically conservative frame of analysis, which was evident in the periodical's repeated calls for reducing federal deficits and supporting traditional commodity exports. One of the most frequent topics of the articles published in the magazine in the 1950s was the inattention and lack of support federal administrations—excessively focused on the goal of fast-paced industrialization—dispensed to the economically vital primary exporting sectors of the economy.

As the decade unfolded, industrial production and its domestic orientation assumed a higher relevance in the studies produced by the publication, but even then the traditional critical editorial stance was evident in the consistent iteration of a grave concern for how the structural shortcomings of the national economy imposed limits on the very goal of industrialization itself. As it was perhaps to be expected in a magazine published by an academic institution known for its Neo-Classical orientation, a significant portion of the analyses of *CE* pertained to the ever more present and widely discussed topic of inflation and its impacts on a sustainable course of growth. And, while early in the period, blame for inflation hikes had been placed on climatic conditions that had negatively impacted food production in certain regions of the country, as the 1950s unfolded the editorial thrust of the magazine focused on examining the impact of periodic wage increases (and, consequently, the rise in economic demand) on inflation rates. Thus, along with all the other published voices of the period examined here, including those from the organized labor movement, inflation was prominently dealt with in the pages of the magazine. The January 1953 issue, for instance, stressed the historical inability of the federal administration to control the rising prices of food staples, something that was seen as particularly problematic given that contracting export revenues impacted the ability of the national government to import items that structurally shaped inflation rates overall.[72]

Particularly grave in the large metropolitan areas of Rio de Janeiro and São Paulo, average price increases for *gêneros de primeira necessidade* (i.e., essentials such as food staples) throughout the year 1952 had amounted to almost 30 percentage points whereas in most other state capitals these figures had been kept to under a 20 percent margin.[73] This trend was not to subside during much of the decade, and in April the magazine published a grim description of the situation throughout the country. The piece stated that "the reality of food prices has only gotten worse in the last few years, particularly in larger urban centers, and the federal administration has yet to prove capable of resolving this grave matter which so negatively impacts our entire national economy."[74] Much attention was also given to the matter of shortages taking place with specific food items (e.g., beans, rice, meat, and particularly wheat, which was mostly imported) that occurred over and over again despite the efforts undertaken by COFAP (Federal Commission of Prices and Food Supply, the federal agency in charge of regulating food distribution and prices, particularly in large cities) to create regulatory supply warehouses in metropolitan areas, as well as in guaranteeing minimum prices for producers. In fact, as food shortages helped shape the general political context in metropolitan areas, CE went as far as to give credence to one of the major claims voiced repeatedly by industrial labor unions: that large food distributors were stocking specific items in order to raise prices; a claim consistently denied by important merchant associations, as will be detailed below.[75]

Also indicative of its critical perspective on the country's industrial prospects, two months before Vargas's tragic death, *Conjuntura Econômica* published a long article examining the state of the national economy in which the editors offered a grim forecast for the rest of the year. The main reasons for such a diagnosis, the piece argued, were that even though credit had become scarcer in both private and public financing institutions, inflation rates continued to rise, reflecting the structural shortcomings the country continued to face. Moreover, in line with the magazine's overall editorial ideology, the piece was also extremely critical of the 100 percent increase in the minimum wage granted by the federal government in the previous month of May. In addition to voicing the traditional argument that artificial rises in wages were conducive to price increases due to an "inflationary spiral," *CE* claimed that such politically motivated gestures only contributed to lowering business profits, thus reducing investment capabilities in key industries, and, ultimately diminishing employment opportunities for those who naively believed they had benefitted from excessive governmental interference in the economic realm.[76]

Not surprisingly, this same line of argument was repeatedly presented by several business associations and associated organized social sectors interested in promoting a technocratic approach to the needs of Brazilian society, as is further examined below. A related and consistently presented criticism pertained to what the editors of the publication saw as the excessive drive of industrial promotion on the part of the national government, particularly insofar as the excessive reliance of both the federal administration and private industrialists on public sources of subsidized credit to finance industrial projects. This line of reproach became ever more frequent in the pages of *CE* beginning in mid-year 1954 when coffee export revenues started facing a long and steady decline directly associated with increased supply and consequent falling prices taking place in the global commodity markets.[77]

Also in line with its conservative technical outlook, *Conjuntura Econômica* consistently defended the need for pursuing economic financial soundness in the realm of public expenditures, even if at the cost of incurring socially harmful recessive trends. Similarly, the magazine urged lower restrictions on foreign imports and investments, as well as halting public financing for industrial projects. Moreover, in keeping with what Professor Gudin had argued earlier in the decade, the editors of *CE* argued that if industrial projects were not competitive enough to sustain their undertakings on their own terms, they should not be the beneficiaries of support from the general public.[78] Much in the same way, and taking into consideration the ambitious electoral platform introduced to the nation during the presidential bid of 1955, *CE* did not see the prospects of the incoming administration of Juscelino Kubitschek in a positive light. In fact, in the month of his inauguration, the magazine found good reasons to assume that public spending was only to expand, leading to even higher federal deficits.[79]

An analogous pessimistic outlook was also echoed in the analyses the magazine conducted on wages in the city of Rio de Janeiro during the mid-months of 1956. As a general trend, the purchasing power of wage workers was found to be declining despite the so-called "overly generous raises" granted repeatedly by the federal government, considering that inflation systematically managed to keep up with periodic salary increases.[80] Interestingly, this negative diagnosis of urban workers' living standards was shared by the organized labor movement, particularly in the large cities, but whereas *CE* argued that regular improvements in the minimum wage were ultimately counterproductive and what was needed were effective measures to curb inflation, industrial unions repeatedly demanded higher and more systematic raises for the salaried population. Differences between the political positions espoused by the country's most articulate economic periodical and one of the better organized segments of Brazilian workers notwithstanding, *Conjuntura Econômica* was forced to acknowledge, early in 1957, that the economic landscape of the country was undergoing a rapid transformation wherein the industrial sector was becoming ever more relevant, and that, as a direct consequence of this new historical trend, the concrete living conditions of industrial workers had to be better understood and managed.[81]

Even if willing to accept the notion that Brazil could no longer be essentially defined as a primary-exporting economy since industrial production had presented a remarkable rate of growth in the preceding years, *CE* nonetheless insisted (and rightly so) that these events derived not from governmental assistance, but from higher levels of foreign investment moving into the country given its "higher production standards and superior technological know-how."[82] In addition, *CE* consistently expressed concern about "excessive governmental spending" even when used to improve the national infrastructure. In fact, in the editors' view, Brazil would do better if the administrative focus was placed on creating a more welcoming legal framework for foreign investors, who were seen as capable of promoting infrastructural investments in a more efficient manner—a claim in direct opposition to what nationalist ideologues at ISEB and labor leaders believed, but which found remarkable resonance in the positions held by business groups, particularly among commercial association held by middle-income social segments. Likewise, *Conjuntura Econômica* expressed growing alarm over the fact that half of all new industrial investments made in the state of São Paulo in previous years came from the central government's coffers, particularly through generous loans granted by the National Bank of Economic Development.[83] Additional admonitions were addressed at what the magazine called an "inflexible labor legislation," which, in its view, did not allow industrial plants to reduce the pace of production even in times of economic crisis given the excessive protection granted to workers who had acquired tenure (i.e., after ten years of continuous employment).[84]

Surprisingly, this aggressive critique of some of the few legal protections afforded industrial workers was presented in starker terms than related criticisms made in business publications (such as those associations examined here), and the contrast seems indicative of the professedly technical (i.e. scientific) perspective pursued by the magazine's editors. *CE*'s critical assessment of the Kubitschek era's economic policies, which was more commonly shared with the business community, pertained to the alleged lack of governmental attention paid to food-production agriculture. Measures to be taken in this regard were consistently seen as essential, as was the creation of new distribution centers focused on low-income social segments, with the hope that inflation could be brought under control.[85] Adding to the reality of constantly rising prices, the international crash in prices for coffee exports, starting in 1958 and persisting until the first years of the 1960s, was something that *CE* also considered to be of grave consequence for the Brazilian economy. Given the scale of the challenge, these events seemed to have inspired the editors of the publication to move beyond their traditional reproach of the Brazilian government's lack of support for export agriculture, thus paving the way to a defense of multilateral diplomatic initiatives (consistent with JK's foreign policies) aimed at stabilizing global commodity markets.[86]

Moving toward the end of the JK administration, the Plano de Estabilização Monetária (Monetary Stabilization Plan, PEM), presented to Congress in October 1958 by the new Finance Minister Lucas Lopes, was the focus of most pieces published in the final months of the year and the first months of 1959.[87] Not surprisingly, *Conjuntura Econômica* was highly supportive of the Monetary Stabilization Plan, portrayed as "perfectly compatible with the implementation of the Targets Plan,"[88] Oddly, even though the main line of criticism regarding the attempted goal of curbing public credit lines originated among industrial associations and the National Congress, which cited the threat of unemployment and economic slowdown, when urging public support for the economic stabilization program of 1958, *CE* centered its analysis on a harsh and highly condescending portrayal of the labor movement.[89] The magazine adamantly argued that labor unions were particularly at fault in preventing the deployment of needed economic adjustments in federal expenditures, and that they had to realize, once and for all, that wage increases aimed at keeping up with ever higher costs of living were, in the long run, detrimental to workers' interests. In specific terms, the publication argued that "governmental interventions in the wage market [as well as price controls] [were] inefficient instruments of public policy aimed at artificially stabilizing prices and raising living standards which can only be sustained on the basis of actual improvements in the productive capacity of the national economy." Moreover, it claimed that, "excessive increases in nominal rates of the minimum wage reduce investment capabilities of business sectors [. . .] negatively impacting labor productivity and real wages in the long run."[90]

As the main economic periodical of mid-century Brazil, whose market-friendly editorial ideology was quickly becoming out of sync with state-centered developmental notions popular among important organized segments of the general population, *Conjuntura Econômica*'s positions continued to be influential in shaping the national debates on development promotion of the 1950s. And while the recurrent criticism pertaining to the "problem of inflation," and of its associated alluded-to main causes (i.e., excessive public spending deriving from an overreaching, paternalistic-in-nature central government) is certainly well-taken—in the sense that even more socially concerned economists, such as Celso Furtado, agreed that governmental spending had to be brought under control—it is in the realm of the solutions suggested by *CE* that many of the disagreements of the final years of the JK era are to be found. In fact, even though the magazine regularly argued for modernizing the country toward the goal of economic efficiency (i.e., higher productivity), it is not clear how this overarching goal was to be reached if not by having the "investor of last resort" (i.e., the state) assume its role in leading the way. The case being made was for even higher levels of private investments, which, according to the same magazine, had to come from abroad.

Ironically, as indicated in previous chapters, and the divisive political nature of the matter notwithstanding, this was very much a course of action the Kubitschek administration was actively pursuing with significant rates of success, yet the magazine did not seem ready to grant JK's administration any credit. Similarly, even though consistently argued for, it is not clear in the pages of *CE*, how the editors believed that the political costs involved in pursuing a recessionary economic policy could be successfully managed at a time of heightened economic expectations and mobilization of multiple political forces. In fact, while it might be counterintuitive to expect that such a self-defined technical publication would engage in a direct fashion with specific and ever more polarized political debates, it seems nonetheless unfortunate that *CE* did not take into account relevant developmental demands that helped shape the transformative years of the 1950s in Brazil.

Another leading publication of the period advocating similar positions was the *Revista do Conselho Nacional de Economia* (*RCNE*), published by the National Economic Council, (CNE, Conselho Nacional de Economia). Founded in December 1949, the CNE, an official advisory board consisting of prominent economists appointed by the president, was in charge of providing regular and *ad hoc* assessments of the national economy, which were then presented to the National Congress and to the presidency. Its most important report was called the *Exposição Geral da Situação Econômica do País* (General Diagnosis of the National Economy). Produced in the final month of the each calendar year, it provided the most detailed sectorial examinations of the most important economic activities of the country, particularly before the institution of the annual reports on the state of the implementation of the Targets Plan, which started circulating in 1958. The CNE was a highly technical (allegedly non-political) agency without executive powers beyond that of requesting economic data from the different ministries, which it used to compile its annual reports; its creation marked a departure from the corporatist logic (that had allowed for more overt business influence in the decision-making process) that defined similar boards of Vargas's Estado Novo regime.[91]

Especially pertaining to labor and wage policies, as well as the need to more favorably support commodity exports, the *Revista do Conselho Nacional de Economia* was very much in line with the perspective promoted in the pages of the more widely distributed *Conjuntura Econômica*, and, at times, some of the nine members of the council happened to also be serving on *CE*'s editorial board or acting as additional prominent economics professors at the Getúlio Vargas Foundation. In this sense, the analyses produced by the CNE for the main centers of power in the nation's capital (namely the presidency and the National Senate) tended to be more market-oriented (insofar as consistently arguing for policies supporting free exchange rates, free unsupervised wage negotiations between employers and workers, and reduced subsidized credit for industrial projects) than those of business elites who were ready to support enduring elements of the corporatist structure of the Brazilian state if these were seen as beneficial to their own corporate interests.

In its first issue, published in mid-year 1952, *RCNE* clearly stated its defense that a technical orientation (rather than a politically motivated one) was what the country needed to adjust its economic profile to a new, challenging economic global context. Specifically, the magazine's editorial piece argued that "governmental action which has been focused on seeking to increase consumption patterns and living standards should be directed instead at achieving long-term gains in productivity."[92] This position was reinforced in another article in the same issue, which criticized the growing popular claim among industrialists that in developing economies public expenditures were acceptable given the economic stimulus these monies provided. The magazine overtly rebutted such a notion by alternatively arguing that "non-productive public spending tends to be detrimental to the economy given its harmful impact on public finances, which can be better served by conservative, even contractive policies."[93]

This minimalistic view of the role to be played by the central government was argued again and again in the pages of the *RCNE*. This indeed seemed to have been a core feature of the magazine's editorial ideology, which is particularly surprising given not only the ever more active presence of the federal government in the Brazilian economy, but especially the widespread acceptance among business elites of the positive influence this course of action provided. It is in fact remarkable that as Brazil experienced one of its most assertive experiences of state planning of the national economy, the periodical argued that "state economic intervention exerts an artificial and usually negative impact on the national course of economic forces."[94] This cautionary take on the developmental course shaping the main governmental policies of the 1950s preceded JK's ascendance to the presidency, and the CNE tried to warn him, even as he prepared to take office, that "the industrial drive expected to unfold in the upcoming years does not seem to be sustainable given the challenges presented not only by our declining export agriculture revenues, but also by our domestic food production."[95]

Ironically, this pessimistic assessment was produced under the supervision of one of JK's closest advisors and the co-author of one of the first versions of the Targets Plan, Roberto Campos. In effect, though certainly aware of the problems facing food production in the country, when trying to address these issues the focus of the Development Council was on promoting higher levels of mechanization and technical assistance rather than on more costly political initiatives (e.g., land reform) or expensive social investments aimed at maintaining rural working populations employed in agricultural production, rather than immigrating to the big cities for work (e.g., schools, health services, etc.).[96]

In addition to the pages of its monthly publication, the views and positions held by the National Economic Council were also well expressed in the main official document the agency produced annually, the *Exposição Geral da Situação Econômica do País*. These reports consistently criticized the corporatist labor legislation of the period, which was defined as "out of tune with the reality of a developing country that cannot afford to provide the generous [social] benefits that only a mature economy is able to offer."[97] Similar to the argument articulated in the pages of *Conjuntura Econômica*, the CNE also praised the efforts of the industry-led social organizations, Social Service of the Industry (SESI) and National Service of Industrial Learning (SENAI) for their "admirable job of training our labor force," and urged the federal administration to allow higher discrepancies in the wages paid to qualified and non-qualified industrial workers so that the latter would seek better training, resulting in higher economic productivity.[98]

The fact that the training courses provided by industrialists' associations only reached about 10 percent of the industrial labor force (acknowledged in the very piece produced by the CNE) did not seem to discourage the agency from its adamant defense of market-based wage negotiations. This position was indeed reiterated early in 1959, when the annual report went as far as to openly advance a hard criticism about the national minimum wage policy which, in the CNE's view, artificially created a medium salary for all workers regardless of their productive skills and the differences between the distinct regions of the country.[99] And consistent with some of its earlier claims, the final two reports published under the JK administration reiterated the position that better trained workers should be allowed to compete for higher wages in a more flexible (i.e., less regulated) labor market, while also making the case that the generous wage policies of the period should be revised, given the pressure they exerted in pushing prices upward. In the midst of increased labor mobilization in large urban centers, the January 1960 report urged "a profound revision allowing more flexibility in the legislation applicable to labor in order to neutralize its negative economic impacts."[100] Likewise, in tune with ideas presented in other publications of the period (such as *Conjuntura Econômica* and *Revista do Serviço Público*, examined below), the CNE espoused a technocratic vision for handling the national economy, which should be managed on technical terms in order to eliminate the "always tumultuous budget-making process that takes place in Congress [and] which regularly translates into major expenditures that have no economic purpose."[101]

Related criticisms were repeated in the biweekly magazine published by the Federation of Commercial Associations of Brazil, called *Revista da Associação Comercial* (*RAC*), which served as the main instrument for promoting (wholesale and retail) merchants' views and positions in the period.

Based in Rio de Janeiro, *RAC*'s editorial perspective was clearly influenced by the local chapter of the merchants association, the Associação Comercial do Rio de Janeiro, the country's oldest, most articulate, and most politically influential branch of all the commercial trade organizations. Rio-based merchants have traditionally espoused a market-oriented economic outlook and, at least since the 1930s, were closely associated with rising economically conservative (market-oriented) political forces. Closely aligned with the positions promoted in the pages of the aforementioned technical periodicals, *RAC* was nonetheless a more accessible and popular publication, which circulated largely among the general public beyond the membership of the federation. Regular topics of concern voiced in the pages of magazine included the "persistent problem of inflation" and its alleged main cause: the lack of investments in both export and domestic agriculture *vis-à-vis* industrial projects. Also in line with the other periodicals mentioned above, *RAC*'s articles were consistently critical of the labor legislation and the "excessive industrial focus" of the administrations of the time.

Indicative of the influence Rio-based merchants had over the magazine, *RAC* represented one of the most eloquent voices against the transferring of the national capital to the center of the country, a position that strengthened the ties between commercial groups and the congressional delegation of the conservative party UDN. More than any other matter, the publication's sharpest criticism against the federal administrations of the 1950s resided in their persistent attempt to enforce a policy of price controls, which by most standards had proven to be largely unsuccessful. In the merchants' view, the core problem of such an approach was not its ineffectiveness but rather the goal itself, which was seen as an unwelcoming intrusion on the "natural forces of the market." More importantly, the policy was said to foment a negative image of merchants. In a concrete sense, the director of the Associação Comercial do Rio de Janeiro, Manoel Jacinto Ferreira, explicitly asked "[w]hy do we insist on not facing reality and continue to impose price controls that are not only ineffective and detrimental to consumers since they create instability, but also give rise to an unjust negative image of the productive commercial classes."[102]

The magazine also proclaimed its strong disapproval of the federal administration's plans for deepening the process of industrialization in stating that "[u]nless our agricultural activities can be strengthened first, we will never be able to develop a sustainable industrial base."[103] Much in the same way, in 1952 Carlos Brandão de Oliveira, president of the Federation of Commercial Associations of Brazil went so far as to overtly criticize Vargas's end of the year address, which unveiled plans for strengthening domestic industrial plants by enlarging the role of the central government in infrastructural economic activities. Expressing concern about the purported overreach of the administration, Oliveira "refute[d] the argument that the federal government needed new laws to buttress its ability to intervene in the national economy." Instead, he stated that "[i]n our view, our development [. . .] depends on strengthening our productive forces, particularly in the area of agriculture."[104]

An analogous market-oriented position promoted by the federation relates to its staunch support for a "more welcoming legislation" pertaining to foreign investors. In the organization's point-of-view, such a legal framework would provide "a more realistic, intelligent, and rational policy [. . .] grounded on real world facts," rather than on the groundless conjectures of "radical nationalists."[105] Strengthening this alleged technically grounded economic perspective, the February 23, 1952, issue's editorial praised the federal administration's decision to submit the analysis on the union-supported profit-sharing bill under consideration in the National Congress to the CNE. Such a move by the Vargas government in essence halted the legal proceedings on the measure, thus saving the administration from having to take sides on such a divisive issue, which would not be taken to a vote in the period. In the words of the publication: "[T]he president's decision is praise-worthy given that it submits such a complex topic to the technical analysis of a non-political body which will examine the matter on a purely technical and scientific basis."[106]

Though the magazine, as well as merchants in general, sporadically offered support to the Vargas administration, more commonly the federation tended to be very critical of the industrial policies pursued by the federal government, assuming, at times, a confrontational position. This was clear in April, the same year, when the entity challenged the regime to stop giving credence to the negative image of merchants as "exploiters of the people," by continuing to impose price controls. Specifically, the magazine stated that "[t]he conservative classes do not demand prices increases, nor will we confront the administration or insult public authorities, [. . .] but we cannot accept the lies that continue to be made against us and which find support in the government's current course of action."[107] Similar outrage was expressed in mid-year after the Federal Commission of Prices and Food Supply (COFAP)announced it would expand its network of food staples distribution centers in large urban areas. The publication clearly stated that "this interventionist approach not only doesn't work, but it represents a clear affront to the commercial classes. [. . .] It doesn't matter how much the demagoguery tries to create new ways to make the market work, the law of supply and demand will prevail."[108]

These types of statements were constant during the Vargas presidency, with the only variation being the degree to which direct confrontation or attempted conciliatory moves were intercalated. The first half of 1953 was, in fact, very much defined by a rapprochement between the Commercial Federation and the federal administration, but commercial leaders maintained the position that governmental expenditures had to be curbed and that economic policies should be focused on promoting investment in the sectors of infrastructure and agriculture, preferably by means of attracting private capital including those of foreign origins.[109] By the end of the year, however, dialogue between the two sides had all but been broken down and *RAC*'s pages abounded in pieces directly accusing the Vargas administration of leading the national economy into chaos by insisting on its course of enforcing price controls and sustaining an active, interventionist role in the promotion of economic growth.[110] And, as the Kubitschek administration moved in and tried to implement its own developmental goals, the *Revista da Associação Comercial* sustained the main points of its critical stance *vis-à-vis* the federal government, but followed a less hostile course of action. In January 1957, for instance, the Commercial Federation hosted a "Plenary Session of the Productive Classes" in Rio, which also gathered representatives of the Rural Brazilian Confederation and the National Industrial Confederation, in the hopes of creating a common pro-business agenda, which was then presented to JK "in order to support his efforts of effectively rebuilding the path of national recovery."[111]

Undeniably, and in line with similar contradictions between the rhetoric and actual behavior of other business associations, though staunchly supportive of market-based initiatives for economic growth, *RAC* (along with industrialists and coffee growers) was very critical of the reductions in public credit proposed in the Monetary Stabilization Plan (PEM) of October 1958.[112] And, as the JK administration approached its end, the traditional fiscal line of attacks was supplemented by a strong opposition to transferring the national capital from Rio de Janeiro to the new city of Brasilia, as well as by an ever more passionate defense of export agriculture (a position that indirectly attacked the industrial achievements of the period), defined as "the foundation of our economic vibrancy" despite the neglect caused by the shortsighted and excessive reliance on "the dubious industrial pursuits" of the federal administration.[113]

Seeking a more coordinated and unified course of action, business groups of different sectors gathered in Rio de Janeiro in mid-year 1959, "in order to offer our productive classes the opportunity to create a common program aimed at preserving the foundations of our free-market economy."[114] Resembling a move that suggestively was also being pursued by labor unions in the final years of Kubitschek's presidency, the Conselho das Classes Produtoras (CONCLAP)—a label used to describe the leadership of the business associations behind the repeated attempts of coordinating their lobbying efforts—tried to foster a "unified front capable of better defending the common interests of the conservative classes outside of the traditional legal representative system, which has proven to be inadequate to that very same purpose."[115] Likewise, the Commercial Federation also sought to strengthen its ties with conservative forces in the National Congress as a way to legislatively advance its agenda, much in the same way that industrialists had been efficient in doing so for much of the decade. Raul de Goes, the magazine's editor, who also served as a representative of Rio de Janeiro's delegation in the National Chamber, gave an argument at the closing of the JK era that can serve as summary of the core positions promoted in the pages of the

Revista da Associação Comercial during those years. Specifically, the editor claimed that:

> No one can, at this point in our historical trajectory, reiterate the old adage stating that our economy is still essentially based on agricultural activities. At the same time, we cannot accept the idea that we should seek to become highly industrialized when this is being attempted to the detriment of our agricultural base and traditions. [. . .] Moreover, it is disheartening to see that needed resources to support our primary economic activities are questionably being spent in the construction of a still-unfinished sumptuous new capital.[116]

Equally or, at times, even more critical positions were consistently proposed by the official publication of the DASP (Departamento Administrativo do Serviço Público), the federal agency in charge of managing (i.e., hiring, allocating, promoting, etc.) public servants of the executive branch. As the formal voice of management of the federal bureaucracy, *Revista do Serviço Público* (*RSP*) did not necessarily convey the views of all government workers, nor was it representative of any sort of organizing efforts on the part of the federal labor force. In fact, in the conservative tone of its core ideas, *RSP* represents a surprisingly suggestive written source for understanding how the promotion of a professional cadre in the civil service was closely tied to, and thus indicative of, the defense of a technical, non-political public service—a project that ironically, but perhaps not surprisingly, helped promote an inherently elitist perspective of Brazilian society.

Most public servants living in the large urban centers, particularly in the administrative city of Rio de Janeiro, seemed to have managed to sustain a social status that placed them among middle-income earners despite the rising inflationary pressures of the period. And, as already indicated, at a time of rapid economic, cultural, and status-related economic transformations, these very same (still influential) social segments tended to support ever more conservative political positions. *Revista do Serviço Público* thus represented an effort to formalize the civil service, largely by promoting a technical and, at times, even academic-style defense of a "meritocratic" logic that should replace the patrimonial tradition of the Brazilian state. Considerable portions of the articles published in almost every single issue of the 1950s were translated pieces from foreign (consistently French, U.S., and British) kindred publications; even when Brazilian authors published in the magazine, their articles were rife with foreign-language quotes, expressions, and citations. Thus, though not necessarily indicative of the lives-as-lived of civil servants themselves, *RSP* offers a suggestive take into at least some of the key ideals and aspirations to which middle-income public workers could look to, and according to which they were being assessed by their peers. In this sense, though not offering actual perspectives from the average public servant, the periodical seems still useful for providing a glimpse into how the ideologues of public service in Brazil saw themselves and their role, and subsequently that of the federal bureaucracy itself in the promotion of a modern, economically developed society.[117]

Consistent with the publications scrutinized earlier, *RSP*'s general stance on economic affairs was a market-friendly one. Surprisingly for a magazine that "spoke" on behalf of the intellectual planners of the central government, the publication repeatedly defended the decentralization of the national government to a much higher degree than the business-sponsored periodical. The magazine's editors saw this decentralization as way to "better understand local realities," and even espoused the idea that the federal administration should play a secondary role in most development pursuits, since these pursuits were more likely to be successful if left "in the hands of private initiatives." And throughout the 1950s, the monthly proposed an ever more technocratic, managerial civil service as the most effective way to curb the much criticized (in the pages of the magazine, as well as in most of the regular printed press in the period), widespread corruption marring the federal government.

The argument in favor of a reduced role for the national administration was so patent in the editorial perspective espoused at the *RSP* that even the long-established governmental supervisory role held in salary negotiations was sharply criticized given that "curbing profits through excessive regulations and interventions in the economic realm only leads to inefficiencies [. . .] and given that the government mistakenly sees itself as responsible for the well-being of all, [it] is the greatest culprit."[118] Paradoxically for a magazine published by the agency in charge of managing public workers, this minimalistic view of the state was more vocally defended in the pages of the *RSP* than even in the business magazines examined above. This view was articulated very much along classical liberal (*laisser-faire*) economic lines, staunchly criticizing the "encroaching government" as ever more "reducing the personal freedoms of all those interested in entrepreneurial risks, which are truly the only real source of economic wealth."[119]

Similarly, the notion that the "national crisis" the country allegedly faced could be resolved "only by enhancing the technical expertise of public servants" was also repeatedly defended in the publication.[120] Consequently, in tandem with what the country's commercial leadership espoused, *RSP* steadily argued that inflation was primarily caused by "the central government's excessive artificial interventions in the national economy in ways detrimental to the good functioning of market forces."[121] The publication likewise concurred with the agenda promoted in the *Revista da Associação Comercial* regarding the need to better support agricultural activities, as well as with the criticism against price controls, which were seen as an inefficient means to address a problem (inflation) whose real causes were to be found in the excessive spending of the federal administration.[122]

These views did not subside even under the bold industrial push of the JK administration, but rather continued to be argued in the publication.

Particularly important was the regular defense of an exclusively "supportive role" to be played by the federal government in the promotion of economic development, as well as the corroboration of the notion that "excessive social concerns" (such as those granted in labor legislations) represented "an onerous burden on the activities of our productive forces," which allegedly "ultimately hurt[s] those whom these laws were said to protect."[123] Also indicative of the market-friendly perspective of the magazine, even the popularly cherished legislation pertaining to the minimum wage was extensively criticized in pages of the *RSP*, which alternatively argued that "no bureaucrat is able to regulate from above the local needs of workers" who should instead engage in factory-based wage negotiations with their own employers on an individual basis.[124] Furthermore, the conservative editorial ideology of the magazine went so far as to argue that Brazilian workers were to be primarily blamed for the low wages that they earned considering that this was a direct result of their own lack of professional skills, and "unless they see the need to enhance their productivity, higher wages cannot be disbursed."[125]

CONCLUDING REMARKS

As Brazil ventured into an incipient though rapidly rising culture of mass consumption, ideological differences between groups with better access to the promises of national development and those traditionally excluded became ever more evident. And although the promises of a national development largely structured along market lines received high praise in some of the most innovative cultural movements, most Brazilians witnessed these historical transformations with more immediate needs and concerns at hand.

Particularly relevant in shaping the ever more polarized political debates of the latter years of the developmental decade, some of the most influential business and technical professional publications steadfastly promoted a less state-centered, market-based, fiscally conservative, and even, at times, anti-labor vision for the development of the country. Granting that industrialists naturally supported the path of fast-paced industrial promotion, their support was consistently tamed by growing concerns about the financial solvency of several policies undertaken by the national government. Moreover, while, as a whole, the developmental path followed in the 1950s could be better seen as moderate reformism, organized workers did not believe that their needs were particularly relevant in shaping the projects and plans of the period and, particularly as the 1950s came to an end, affluent and ever more conservative socio-economic groups grew increasingly concerned about the developmental initiatives pursued.

In the end, the discrepancies between the views and positions held by business and professional leaders, government officials, and more popular social segments further deepened the ideational cacophony, ideological divergence, and political polarization that ironically defined the otherwise promising developmental dynamics of the closing years of the Kubitschek era. The alternative developmental course advocated by one of the best mobilized segments of the industrial labor force, which placed additional pressure on the fragile and inherently unstable political balance then at play, is examined next.

NOTES

1. Ricardo Ramos, *História da Propaganda no Brasil* (São Paulo: Edusp, 1972).
2. Lúcia Lippi de Oliveira, "Tempos de JK: a construção do futuro e a preservação do passado," in *Anos JK: Margens da Modernidade*, ed. Wander Melo Miranda (São Paulo: Imprensa Oficial, 2002), 31–44.
3. Detailed information on these historical trends can be found in Santuza Cambraia Neves, "Os novos experimentos culturais nos anos 1940–50: propostas de democratização da arte no Brasil," in *O Brasil Republicano: o tempo da experiência democrática, da democratização de 1945 ao golpe civil-militar de 1964*, eds. Jorge Ferreira and Lucilia de Almeida Neves Delgado (Rio de Janeiro Civilização Brasileira, 2003), vol. 3: 273–99.
4. The long trajectory of Brazilian artists who tried to revamp their own sense of national identity by means of incorporating and re-signifying foreign cultural influences is well examined in Christopher Dunn, *Brutality Garden: Tropicália and the Emergence of a Brazilian Counterculture* (Chapel Hill: University of North Carolina Press, 2001).
5. Marieta de Moraes Ferreira and Claudia Mesquita, "Os anos JK no acervo da Biblioteca Nacional," in *Biblioteca Nacional: 500 anos de Brasil na Biblioteca Nacional*, ed. Paulo Pereira (Rio de Janeiro: Fundação Biblioteca Nacional/ Nova Fronteira, 2001), 76–82.
6. Detailed analyses of how this shared optimism helped define the general perception of the future of the country, particularly among middle-income urban social segments, can be found in Maurício Parada, "A Fundação do Museu de Arte Moderna do Rio de Janeiro: a Elite Carioca e as Imagens da Modernidade no Brasil dos Anos 50" (MA thesis, PUC-RJ, 1993) and Simone Maria Andrade Pereira, "Os Anos Dourados: Copacabana e o Imaginário Urbano dos Anos 50" (MA thesis, UFRJ, 1991).
7. See by Juscelino Kubistchek de Oliveira, *Palestras Dirigidas ao Povo Mineiro pelo Rádio em 1951–1952* (Belo Horizonte: Imprensa Oficial, 1953); *Ao Povo Mineiro: palestra lida pelo rádio no transcurso da metade do mandato governamental* (Belo Horizonte: Imprensa Oficial, 1953); and *Realidades e Perspectivas: discursos dos 4 anos de governo em Minas Gerais, 1951–1955* (Belo Horizonte: Coleção Cultural, 1955).
8. For more on this, see Georgette Rodrigues, "Ideologia, propaganda e imaginação social na construção de Brasília (1956–1960)" (MA thesis, University of Brasilia, 1990).
9. Pesquisa de Opinião: Política, Pesquisas Especiais, 1958, Vol. 2:25, Pesqs. No. 04, 05, and 06. In Fundo IBOPE, Arquivo Edgar Leurenroth (AEL).
10. More on these ideas can be found in Santos, *A classe média vai ao paraíso*; and Ana Maria Andrade and José Cardoso, "Aconteceu, virou manchete," *Revista Brasileira de História* 21, no. 41 (2001): 243–64 and Adriana Hassin Silva, "A Modernidade em Alvorada: Brasília e a imagem do Brasil moderno no fotojornalismo d'O *Cruzeiro* e da *Manchete* (1956–1960)" (MA thesis, UFRJ, 2003).
11. Abreu, "Os suplementos literários," 13–60.

12. See Shirley F. Woodell Papers, 1943–1958, Office File and Correspondence, Box 3, c.1, in J. Walter Thompson Company Archives, David M. Rubenstein Rare Book and Manuscripts Library, Duke University. It should be noted that the U.S.-based J. Walter Thompson Company was one of Brazil's largest advertising agencies in the 1950s, and strongly competed for the top position with other U.S.-based agencies, such as McCann-Erickson. Detailed information can be found in *Profits on JWT-Brazil*, Edward G. Wilson Papers, International Offices, Brazil, São Paulo: Correspondence, vol. I, Jan 1961–Dec 1961, Folder 1, Box 2; and *International Organization of the J. Walter Thompson Company Report, 1955*, Information Center Records, Organization, Vertical Files, File 2, International 1930–1986, Box 17, c.1, both in J. Walter Thompson Company Archives.
13. Letter from Havana, p. 2, Shirley F. Woodell Papers, 1943–1958, Office File and Correspondence, J. Walter Thompson Company Archives.
14. Letter from R. F. Merrick, from Sao Paulo Office to Samuel W. Meek, vice-president of company in New York City, on August 26, 1960, Edward G. Wilson Papers: International Offices, Brazil, São Paulo, Sam Meeks Files, Oct. 1945–Dec. 1960, Folder 1, Box 2, J. Walter Thompson Company Archives.
15. Various marketing campaigns of the period explicitly reinforced this view in stating that by becoming a developed economy, a task achieved by resorting to enhancing national growth and industrialization, Brazilians would be able to reach the prosperity, consumption patterns, and habits of more advanced economies. Detailed documentation of many of these advertisements can be found in International Advertisement, Latin America, Brazil, Box LA4 c.1, J. Walter Thompson Company International Advertisement Collection, 1900–2004, J. Walter Thompson Company Archives. A good analysis of these historical events can also be found in Amara Souza Rocha, "Nas Ondas da Modernização: Uma História Social do Rádio e da Televisão no Brasil nos Anos 1950–1960" (PhD diss., UFRJ, 2004).
16. See Samuel W. Meek Papers, International Marketing, United States Information Agency, Correspondence, 1955–1961, Box 5, J. Walter Thompson Company Archives. The business logic behind U.S. economic, geopolitical, cultural, and, at times, military presence in Latin America during the Cold War is well examined by Thomas O'Brien in *The Making of the Americas: The United States and Latin America from the Age of Revolutions to the Era of Globalization* (Albuquerque: University of New Mexico Press, 2007), and *The Century of U.S. Capitalism in Latin America* (Albuquerque: University of New Mexico Press, 1999).
17. See Correspondence, São Paulo Office, May 1961–1962, Edward G. Wilson Papers, Box 1, J. Walter Thompson Company Archives.
18. Ana Cristina Camargo Moraes Figueiredo, *Liberdade é uma calça velha, azul e desbotada: Publicidade, cultura de consumo, comportamento político no Brasil, 1954–1964* (São Paulo: Hucitec, 1998).
19. Alessandra Ciambarella, "A tradição abre as portas à modernidade: o Rio de Janeiro e a transferência da Capital Federal (1956–1960)," in *O Rio de Janeiro nos Jornais: ideologia, culturas políticas e conflitos sociais (1945–1964)*, ed. Jorge Ferreira (Rio de Janeiro: 7 Letras, 2011), 136–53.
20. James Holston, *The Modernist City: An Anthropological Critique of Brasília*. (Chicago, The University of Chicago Press, 1989), 4.
21. James Holston, "Autoconstruction in Working-Class Class," *Cultural Anthropology* 6, no.4, (Nov 1991), 447–65.
22. Marcelo de Paiva Abreu and Dionísio Dias Carneiro, "1944–1994: 50 anos de política econômica no Brasil," in *50 anos de Brasil, 50 anos da Fundação Getúlio Vargas*, eds. Bolivar Lamounier, et al. (Rio de Janeiro: FGV, 1994), 113–80.

23. Renato P. Colistete, "Productivity, Wages, and Labor Politics in Brazil, 1945–1962" *Journal of Economic History* 67, no. 1 (Mar 2007), 93–127.
24. This is one of those areas where the contrast between the JK administration and that of his developmental predecessor, Vargas is clearest. In fact, while Kubitschek was keen on promoting the physical integration of the country by means of massive, intense, and impressive construction and paving of highways connecting distant geographic regions, Vargas favored regional economic projects that tried to promote (with little success) the economic viability of poorer economic areas (e.g., the Amazon and the mid-west). An insightful recent work on Vargas's regional developmental policies is João Marcelo Ehlert Maia, *Estado, território, e imaginação espacial. O caso da Fundação Brasil Central* (Rio de Janeiro: FGV, 2012).
25. Brian P. Owensby, *Intimate Ironies: Modernity and the Making of Middle-Class Lives in Brazil* (Stanford: Stanford University Press, 1999).
26. Ibid., 50.
27. Regina Horta Duarte, " 'It Does Not Even Seem Like We Are in Brazil': Country Clubs and Gated Communities in Belo Horizonte, Brazil, 1951–1964," *Journal of Latin American Studies* 44, no. 3, (Aug 2012), 438.
28. See Luanda Pereira Antunes, "Legislativo e Desenvolvimento no Governo JK" (MA thesis, IUPERJ, 2002) and Maria Isabel Valladão de Carvalho, "A Colaboração do Legislativo para o Desempenho do Executivo durante o Governo JK" (MA thesis, IUPERJ, 1977).
29. An unresolved dispute between agrarian and industrial elites proved to be particularly damaging to the developmental policies pursued in Argentina in the 1950s. Detailed information on this can be found in Sikkink, *Ideas and Institutions*; and Szusterman, *Frondizi and the Politics of Developmentalism.*
30. The first argument is advanced, for instance, in Haggard, *Pathways from the Periphery*. See also Luciano Martins, "Formação do empresariado industrial no Brasil," *Revista do Instituto de Ciências Sociais* 3, no. 1 (1966), 91–138; and Francisco C. Weffort, "Classes populares e política: contribuição ao estudo do populismo" (PhD diss., University of the São Paulo, 1968).
31. Carvalho, *A Colaboração do Legislativo*, 51.
32. The electoral weight of each region is well examined in Phillipe C. Schmitter, *Interest Conflict and Political Change in Brazil* (Stanford: Stanford University Press, 1971).
33. Donald Huddle, "O Sistema Brasileiro de Taxas Cambiais Flutuantes: Sua Equidade Distributiva, Suas Relações com a Inflação e Sua Eficiência," *Revista Brasileira de Economia* 24, no. 4 (1972): 149–68.; and Pedro Malan, et al., *Política econômica externa e industrialização no Brasil, 1939–52* (Rio de Janeiro: IPEA/INPES, 1977). Beyond the economic costs, this conservative political arrangement also exerted a damaging, long-term political effect that is insightfully examined in José Luis Fiori, *O Vôo da Coruja: uma leitura não-liberal da crise do Estado Desenvolvimentista* (Rio de Janeiro: EdUERJ, 1995).
34. See CONCLAP, *Carta Econômica de Teresópolis, Documento da Conferência das Classes Produtoras do Brasil* (Rio de Janeiro, 1945), 3–4.
35. The debate which unfolded in different publications and official venues is reproduced in IPEA, *A Controvérsia do Planejamento da Economia Brasileira* (Rio de Janeiro: IPEA/INPES, 1977).
36. Juscelino Kubitschek, *Industrialização: batalha pela própria sobrevivência da nacionalidade*, speech given at the graduation ceremony of the School of Industrial Engineering of the Industrial Federation of São Paulo, May 1958 (São Paulo: FIESP/CIESP, Serviço de Publicações, 1958), 9.

37. *Desenvolvimento & Conjuntura* I, no. 1 (Jul 1957), 84.
38. Ibid., 43.
39. "Editorial," *Desenvolvimento & Conjuntura* II, no. 10 (Oct 1958).
40. "Editorial," *Desenvolvimento & Conjuntura* II, no. 12 (Dec 1958).
41. Ibid., 28.
42. Juscelino Kubitschek de Oliveira, *O Avanço do Brasil: o governo e os problemas do desenvolvimento econômico brasileiro*, speech given at the National Economic Council, January 16, 1961. (Rio de Janeiro: Departamento de Imprensa Nacional, 1961), 28.
43. "Bases para uma Política para o Desenvolvimento," *Desenvolvimento & Conjuntura* I, no. 1 (Jul 1957), 6.
44. Ibid., 7.
45. Ibid., 9 and 12.
46. The selective reading of ECLA's economic policies on the part of CNI and FIESP has been examined by Colistete in "A Força das Idéias."
47. "Editorial," *Desenvolvimento & Conjuntura* (Oct 1958, Vol. 2:10), and issue of Feb. 1958, Vol. 2: 2, 171.
48. Ibid., 192.
49. "Editorial," *Boletim Informativo da FIESP* (Oct 1955).
50. On the common policies that industrialist and agrarian groups were able to agree upon, particularly during the meetings occurring in the 1940s, see FIESP, *Revista Industrial de São Paulo* (May 1945), 1–8 and Maria J. Trevisan, *50 anos em cinco: a Fiesp e o desenvolvimentismo* (Rio de Janeiro: Vozes, 1986).
51. The industrialists' corporatist ideology in the São Paulo of the 1940s is well explained in Weinstein, *For Social Peace in Brazil*. Additional information can be found in Walmer Jacintho Soares, *Os Interesses Industriais na Consolidação do Nacional-Desenvolvimentismo* (Rio de Janeiro: IUPERJ/PUC, 1994).
52. "Carta de Princípios da Indústria: Documento da II Reunião Plenária da Indústria," *Boletim Informativo da FIESP* (Dec 26, 1955), Vol. 6, 23.
53. Papers of Robert J. Alexander, Interview Collection, Box 5, Folder 15, Brazil, Series Employers/Sindicatos, Federations and Confederations, 1956.
54. Interview with Ernesto Street, senior adviser at the CNI, on March 6, 1956, Papers of Robert J. Alexander, Interview Collection, Box 5, Folder 15, Brazil, Series Employers/Sindicatos, Federations and Confederations, 1956.
55. Interview with Eugênio Lobato, secretary of Industrial Federation of Rio Grande do Sul, on April 30, 1956, Papers of Robert J. Alexander, Interview Collection.
56. Interview with J.M. Moreira de Moraes, secretary of the Textile Industrial Federation of São Paulo, on April 1956, Papers of Robert J. Alexander, Interview Collection.
57. Antônio Devisate, "Manifesto aos Trabalhadores e à Opinião Pública de São Paulo," *Boletim Informativo da FIESP* (Oct 28, 1957), No. 421, 7.
58. For FIESP's central developmental claims in the period see *Boletim Informativo da FIESP* No. 345 (May 1956). For important labor counterpoints of the period, see Rafael R. Ioris, "*Fifty Years in Five* and What Is in It for Us? Development Promotion, Populism, Industrial Workers and the Case of *Carestia* in 1950s Brazil," *Journal of Latin American Studies* 44, no. 2 (May 2012), 261–84.
59. *Sesi Jornal: Publicação do SESI*, CNI, Departamento Regional de SP, Divisão de Educação Social para Empresas, Clubes, Círculos e Sindicatos Associados (Apr 1950), 8.
60. *Sesi Jornal* (Mar 1951), cover page.
61. *Sesi Jornal* (May 1955), 3.

62. "O Problema da Mão-de-Obra para a Indústria Automobilística," *Revista da Indústria Automobilística* (Dec 1958), 20–22.
63. The main sectors of the national economy to receive special treatment from the federal government under the rubric of the Targets Plan are listed in Chapter One.
64. "O Rio São Francisco," broadcast September 1958, Fundo Fonográfico do Sesi, Programa Sesinho no Rádio, Radio MEC & Sesi, 1950–1960, AN:Sesi, T3FC4 in National Archive,. Similar notions were argued for in the episode "Milagres do Trabalho," of mid-July the same year, Fundo Fonográfico do Sesi, Programa Sesinho no Rádio, AN: Sesi, T3FC42 in National Archive.
65. "Trabalho: o Amigo Fiel,"broadcast May 1960, Programa Sesinho no Rádio, AN, Sesi, T3FC27 in National Archive.
66. "A Fabulosa Cidade do Aço," broadcastJune 1960, Fundo Fonográfico do Sesi, AN, Sesi, T3FC12 in National Archive.
67. Juscelino Kubitschek de Oliveira, "Mensagem Presidencial XXVIII," in *Discursos* (Rio de Janeiro: Imprensa Nacional, 1960), 26.
68. "Sesinho no Mundo dos Automóveis," broadcast mid-year 1959, Fundo Fonográfico do Sesi, AN, Sesi, T3FC11 in National Archive.
69. "A Idade Perigosa," broadcast mid-year 1958, Fundo Fonográfico do Sesi, Programa Educação Cívica. Rádio MEC & Sesi, 1950–1960, AN, Sesi, FC34 in National Archive.
70. "Um Problema de Fácil Solução," Fundo Fonográfico do Sesi, Programa Educação Cívica," AN, Sesi, FC46 in National Archive.
71. See episodes "Isto Acontece todos os Dias" and "Votar para Baixar os Preços," both broadcast mid-year 1960, Fundo Fonográfico do Sesi, Programa Educação Cívica," FC58 and FC59, respectively, in National Archive.
72. *Conjuntura Econômica* (Jan 1953), 2–3.
73. Ibid., 101.
74. *Conjuntura Econômica* (Apr 1953), 10.
75. *Conjuntura Econômica* (Jan 1954 and Mar 1955), 130, and 63–69, respectively.
76. *Conjuntura Econômica* (Jun, 1954), 1–11, and (Jan 1955), 33 and 160.
77. *Conjuntura Econômica* (Sep 1954), 1–9.
78. *Conjuntura Econômica* (Mar 1955 and May 1955).
79. *Conjuntura Econômica* (Jan 1956), 4–5.
80. *Conjuntura Econômica* (Jun 1956), 41–45.
81. *Conjuntura Econômica* (Feb 1957).
82. Ibid., 38.
83. Ibid., 84–86.
84. *Conjuntura Econômica* (Nov 1957), 9.
85. *Conjuntura Econômica* (Feb 1958), 1–3, and 109–203, and (Aug 1958), 3 and 45. Interestingly, these specific policy recommendations were also present in the main list of demands promoted by the organized industrial labor movement in the larger cities of the country in the final years of the Kubitschek era (to be detailed in Chapter Six).
86. *Conjuntura Econômica* (Nov 1958), 40.
87. These measures were aimed at curbing the spiraling inflation and growing public deficits of the period by imposing restrictions on the ability of the federal government to lend and to expand the means of payment of the national economy. Similarly, revisions on wage policies (including limits associated with future salary increases and the gradual elimination of price controls) were also to be put in place. Detailed information can be found in Ministério da Fazenda, *Programa de Estabilização Monetária para o Terceiro Quadrimestre de 1958 e Ano de 1959*, Vol. I, (Rio de Janeiro, 1958).
88. *Conjuntura Econômica* (Nov 1958), 42–45.

89. A detailed account of these events can be found in Sola, *Idéias Econômicas*.
90. *Conjuntura Econômica* (Nov 1958), 59–60.
91. The National Economic Council formally replaced the Conselho Federal de Comércio Exterior, created by Vargas in 1934 and provided business elites direct access to the presidency. The CNE was terminated in 1967 when the military regime that came to power in March 1964 introduced a new, highly centralized constitution to the country.
92. "Editorial," *Revista do Conselho Nacional de Economia* I, no. 1 (1952).
93. Ibid., 64.
94. "Os Ciclos Econômicos e a Ação do Estado," *Revista do Conselho Nacional de Economia* 9, no. 1 (1959), 164–65. The piece was written by Luiz Souza Gomes, director general of the Economic Department of the National Economic Council and thus certainly someone who represented some of the core positions of the agency.
95. BNDE, "Sumário das Conclusões," in *Situação Atual e Perspectivas Imediatas da Economia Brasileira*, (Dec 1955), p. ii.
96. Conselho do Desenvolvimento, *Documento Agricultura e Alimentação*, (Rio de Janeiro: Presidência da República, 1957), vol. 1.
97. Conselho Nacional de Economia, *Exposição Geral da Situação Econômica do País* (Rio de Janeiro: Presidência da República, 1956), 56.
98. Ibid., 57–58.
99. Conselho Nacional de Economia, *Exposição Geral da Situação Econômica do País* (Rio de Janeiro: Presidência da República, 1959), 75.
100. *Exposição Geral da Situação Econômica do País*, Rio de Janeiro, 1960, 59.
101. Conselho Nacional de Economia, *Exposição Geral da Situação Econômica do País* (Rio de Janeiro: Presidência da República, 1961), 43.
102. "Editorial," *Revista da Associação Comercial* XVII, no. 715 (Jan 10, 1952).
103. Ibid., 33.
104. Ibid., 35.
105. "Editorial," *Revista da Associação Comercial* XVII, no. 717 (Feb 10, 1952).
106. *Revista da Associação Comercial* XVII, No. 718, 4 (Feb, 1952).
107. "Editorial," *Revista da Associação Comercial* XVII, no. 721 (Apr 10, 1952).
108. *Revista da Associação Comercial* XVII, no. 728 (Jul 25, 1952), 39.
109. See *Memorial da Reunião Plenária da Federação*, presented to President Vargas by the Commercial Federation on March 2, 1953, published in *Revista da Associação Comercial* XVIII, no. 743 (Mar 10, 1953), 2–5.
110. See various pieces published in *Revista da Associação Comercial* XVIII, no. 762 (Dec 25, 1953).
111. "Editorial," *Revista da Associação Comercial* XX, no. 836 (Jan 10, 1957).
112. See multiple *RAC* issues of later 1958 and early 1959.
113. These positions were eloquently voiced in almost all issues published in the final two years of the JK administration. Of particular relevance, see *RAC* issues of March, April, September, and November 1959, as well as those of May, August, and December 1960.
114. *Revista da Associação Comercial* XXII, no. 879 (Aug 15, 1959), 23.
115. Ibid., 24. The non-sanctioned cross-sectorial labor mobilization of the period will be examined in Chapter Six. For now, it is worth noting that the very same legislation preventing labor unions from acting in a coordinated fashion across sectors of activity also prohibited business representatives from different industries from acting together.
116. *Revista da Associação Comercial* XXIII, no. 919 (Dec 1960), 2.
117. The best demonstration of the instrumental role for accessing the conservative outlook of middle-income groups in Brazil provided by the *RSP* is found in Owensby, *Intimate Ironies*.

118. *Revista do Serviço do Público* (Jan 1951), 28.
119. *Revista do Serviço do Público* (Sep 1951), 25.
120. *Revista do Serviço do Público* (Apr 1952), 43–47.
121. *Revista do Serviço do Público* (Feb 1953), 75–76.
122. Of special relevance for demonstrating this argument are *Revista do Serviço do Público*, issues of June and July 1953, and of May 1954.
123. *Revista do Serviço do Público* (Feb 1957), 85–86.
124. *Revista do Serviço do Público* (Jun 1956), 463–72.
125. *Revista do Serviço do Público* (Jul 1956, 46).

6 National Development and Industrial Labor

Metalworkers, *Carestia*, and the Basis for a Popular Path of Development

INTRODUCTORY NOTES

In May 1956, a few days after the first Labor Day of the Kubitschek Presidency,[1] *A Voz do Metalúgico* (*The Voice of the Metalworker*) published a cover-page article reproaching the president's behavior during the workers' main celebration of the year.[2] Written by Eurypedes Ayres de Castro, president of the Federation of Metalworkers of the State of Rio de Janeiro,[3] the piece stressed the disappointment metalworkers felt with JK's cold reaction to the list of demands presented at the same event by the National Confederation of Industrial Workers' (CNTI) president,[4] Dioclesiano de Hollanda Cavalcanti.[5] In a general sense, the article expressed some of the most important elements consistently present in labor publications of the period, particularly in periodicals published by industrial unions in São Paulo and Rio de Janeiro, Brazil's largest industrial centers. Castro's sharp criticism was centered on the fact that:

> The president's speech did not respond to our needs nor did it suggest a single thread of hope to us, the poor. [. . .] As producers of the wealth of our nation, we expected to hear a serious plan of governmental actions from President Kubitschek, not a candidate's platform. [. . .] There is still time, Mr. President, to mend your deplorable Labor Day performance. Not much time, though. The sharks[6] are always ready to oppress the poor by maintaining the situation of *carestia*,[7] and unless your government is ready to stand by our side, they will dash our hopes, leading to uncontrollable and desperate actions on the part of the working peoples. [. . .] Mr. President, beware![8]

Carestia was a core expression displayed in most labor pronouncements of the 1950s to make reference to the rising costs of living and related decreasing living standards of workers. Examining this type of labor documentation seems, therefore, a useful approach to assessing workers' views on national development in the period. In fact, though directly targeted by the developmentalist rhetoric and policies of the period, industrial workers nonetheless grew increasingly disillusioned with the ways in which development promotion was being carried out. Thus, more than simply an illustration of how a specific labor leader perceived the Kubitschek administration, the above vignette richly describes the broader context of urban labor in the developmentalist decade. As previously demonstrated, in the 1950s Brazil experienced impressive rates of growth along a historical path that transformed the country into Latin America's largest industrial economy by the end of the decade. And even though the economic gains of the time provided the basis for accommodating industrial working-class and business interests, considering that wages did not keep up with productivity and that the gap between industrial wages and profits widened, the heyday of the developmentalist experiment in the Brazil rapidly, and largely unexpectedly, witnessed a rising confrontational pattern of labor relations.[9]

The present chapter examines these influential historical dynamics. Specifically, it demonstrates that throughout the 1950s Brazilian industrial workers challenged traditional structures of labor control by resorting to creative and increasingly autonomous forms of mobilization. In so doing, this progressively active social segment demanded politically responsive and economically interventionist actions from the state in lieu of the rapid, but socially excluding policies the federal administration was implementing.

ASSESSING INDUSTRIAL LABOR IN THE POPULIST ERA: THE ROLE OF METALWORKERS

Initial investigations of urban labor in Brazil have emphasized the difficulties that most unions faced when attempting to mobilize their specific constituencies in the context of the early years after World War II. The situation was largely explained on the grounds of the backward political outlook allegedly held by industrial workers who, in the 1950s, predominantly consisted of recently arrived rural migrants who valued their geographical dislocation as an expression of upward social mobility to be sustained at all cost. Likewise, consistent with ideas espoused by regional versions of the so-called Modernization Paradigm,[10] analysts of the prestigious University of São Paulo argued that the national economy was undergoing a profound transition from an agrarian base economy to an industrial one, resulting in a situation where, facing difficulties in adjusting to the urban reality, the majority of industrial workers mistrusted the recruitment efforts made by union officials. Workers were thus assumed to have been essentially co-opted into a subordinate political role by the charming appeals dispensed by populist leaders acting within the logic of a corporatist labor structure.[11] Labor's autonomy was correspondingly described as being essentially curtailed by the existence of an entire set of labor legislations and a series of economic benefits (in the forms of public employment and union contributions administrated by the Labor Ministry) granted to obedient state-sponsored union leaders.[12]

Setting the stage for almost all subsequent examinations of Brazilian industrial labor, these initial studies, mostly produced in the 1960s by labor sociologists, were complemented in the 1970s by new assessments of the "political consciousness" of workers. Indeed, about ten years after the 1964 military coup had taken place—and after a wave of social mobilizations had occurred in the metropolitan areas of Belo Horizonte and São Paulo[13]—analysts, such as Francisco Weffort and Octavio Ianni, sought to explain why organized labor did not act more assertively in 1964 in defense of the so-called populist system that preceded the military regime and that (allegedly) benefited popular social segments.[14] In advancing a possible explanation, a new line of interpretation came to the foreground under the label of the Populist Collapse paradigm. Overall, this influential line of thought essentially argued that so-called populist unions performed a functional (but passive) role in maintaining the populist regime, a reality considered to be inherently precarious, given that their subsidiary importance "reduced [unions'] potential for effective resistance when needed."[15]

Another important idea advanced concerned the assumed differences in organization and levels of political involvement said to exist between workers of traditional versus modern industrial sectors. The core of the argument was that unions organized in traditional industrial plants (e.g., food processing and textiles) tended to focus their demands on making the federal administration grant regular wage increases, whereas workers in modern industrial units (e.g., metalworkers) centered their mobilization on direct salary negotiations with employers and tended to be less inclined to partake in broad, politically motivated mobilizations that were becoming increasingly important in large urban centers in the late 1950s.[16]

While this classic literature provided a good overview of some of the most important political elements shaping the years when Brazil witnessed high rates of economic growth and accelerated industrialization, it nonetheless construed a stereotypical and mostly reductionist description of urban labor dynamics. In fact, as advanced by a second wave of works on the populist experiences in Brazil, this transformative period in the history of the country was also characterized by a growing and ever more independent, active, and assertive labor movement.[17] Furthermore, throughout these same years, growing numbers of Brazilian workers engaged in a series of autonomous labor negotiations in order to have their own specific developmental needs and demands taken into consideration by the national government.[18] In short, while traditional, concept-driven studies have overemphasized workers' subordinate position within the spheres of the populist political arrangement, a later wave of empirically grounded examinations has cogently shown that "workers' ability to act independently of the State [in order to] resist capitalist domination and advance [alternative] ideals of democratic citizenship" defined much of the populist experiences in the country.[19]

Far from automatic supporters of the government and its developmental policies, metalworkers in the two most important industrial centers of the country consistently engaged in collective acts aimed at influencing the path of development that would be pursued. The centrality of the experiences of metalworkers for the general labor dynamics of the period cannot be overemphasized given their close involvement in the main developmental policies implemented in the second half of the 1950s. In fact, one of the areas of the Targets Plan with some of the highest rates of completion pertained to the goal of increasing industrial output in the metalworking sector.[20] Metalworkers' historical significance also derives from the fact that they were one of the most active labor segments at a time when Brazil was deepening its process of import substitution industrialization.

Critical of the main developmental policies of the time, metalworkers persistently mobilized, along with other industrial professional labor groups to advance their own developmental agenda and demands. In particular, they conducted a wide range of activities aimed at addressing what they saw as one of the most pressing issues affecting their lives: the rising costs of living for the urban poor, which ironically existed amidst high rates of economic growth and the dissemination of a more intense consumer culture. Metalworkers were at the center of the industrial efforts of the federal administration,[21] and have been said to represent a "pragmatic," i.e., non-political path of labor mobilization in the latter part of the 1950s.[22] As will be shown below, this characterization is inaccurate and does not do justice to the complex historical dynamics of the period. Moreover, though essentially centered on one key union segment, the experiences examined below are representative of broader historical dynamics defining mid-century Brazilian labor, political, and cultural scenarios.

METALWORKERS OF SÃO PAULO AND RIO DE JANEIRO AND THE CASE OF *CARESTIA*

Legally bound to organize with workers of related industrial activities, metalworkers officially coalesced under the label Sindicato dos Trabalhadores das Indústrias Metalúrgica, Mecânica e de Material Elétrico do Rio de Janeiro (Union of Workers in the Metal, Mechanical, and Electrical Material Industries, STIMMMERJ). For the sake of brevity, the generic label of "metalworkers," used at the time by workers in all of these areas themselves, will be utilized here to make reference to the entire labor segment.[23] Likewise, the suffix RJ (SindMet/RJ) is applied to the metalworkers union of the city of Rio de Janeiro, and SP (SindMet/SP) for the metalworkers union of the city of São Paulo. The metalworkers' union of the city of Rio de Janeiro (SindMet/RJ) was established in 1917, whereas its counterpart in the city of São Paulo (SindMet/SP) was founded more than a decade later in 1932.

In the mid-1950s there were close to twenty-six thousand workers formally affiliated with the SindMet/RJ out of a group of about sixty thousand workers in the metropolitan area of the city. A significant effort to enlarge the active membership base of the organization was launched in 1957,[24] and a good indication of the success of these very efforts, a new union headquarter building (called the Metalworker's Palace), largely funded by the fees paid by new members, was inaugurated in the neighborhood of São Cristovão, in downtown Rio, late in 1959.[25] In São Paulo, the metalworkers' union estimated in mid-decade the existence of one hundred thousand potential members, out of which about forty-eight thousand were formally registered as union members in 1956 and, consistent with events taking place in Rio, throughout the decade these numbers grew significantly.[26]

In a trend that was taking place across the country in the late 1940s, the SindMet/RJ was placed under the strict control of the Ministry of Labor, and it was only in 1953 that Brazilian unions were once again able to select their own leaders. It was then that the political commentator who authored the piece that opened this chapter, Eurypedes Ayres de Castro, a long-time member of the SindMet/RJ, was elected president of the organization, along with Benedito Cerqueira (a rising figure in the local and national labor movement), who was elected the union's secretary-general.[27] In May 1955 Cerqueira was himself elected president of the SindMet/RJ, a position he held until 1962 when he became a representative at the National Chamber on the Brazilian Worker's Party (PTB) ticket.[28]

The main demands advanced by the SindMet/RJ during Cerqueira's tenure were made public in his successful electoral platform in the middle of the decade. Those meriting a special note include the call for reducing the cost of living through direct governmental intervention in the national economy and the implementation of a massive program of industrialization.[29] Cerqueira received unanimous support with union members, thus managing to bring together the two most important political forces competing for control within the organization. One group was led by influential long-time members and former associates of the Brazilian Communist Party (PCB), which continued to exert significant influence over labor unions in the 1950s despite the fact that the party itself had been outlawed by the Dutra administration in 1947. The most prominent members of this faction included Izaltino Pereira and Heraclides Santos, both of whom will receive more attention below. The second ideological group was primarily represented by Cerqueira and close supporters who tended to be more inclined to back more moderate positions defended by the party of Vice-President João Goulart (PTB), which held sway by means of sinecures within the large bureaucratic machinery of the Ministry of Labor.[30]

Pertaining to the experiences of metalworkers in the city of São Paulo, both presidents of SindMet/SP in the second half of the 1950s were of moderate political inclination, namely Fortunato Martinelly, from 1955 to 1958, and Remo Forli, a former member of Martinelly's administration, between 1958 and 1962. Another important member of the São Paulo-based union was Aldo Lombardi who served as the SindMet/SP's secretary-general during the entire period. He exerted large influence over the association through the publication of well-written articles and editorials dealing with the broader socio-political context of the country regularly included in the union's official periodical called *O Metalúrgico* (*The Metalworker*). The publication, which had been established in 1942, was distributed for free to all regular members and, after an interruption during the military regime, continues in circulation today.

The SindMet/RJ also published its own periodical, edited by members of the union but delivered by paid subscription (one issue cost as much as one loaf of bread in 1955, i.e., 1 *cruzeiro*). The journal was called *A Voz do Metalúrgico* (*The Voice of the Metalworker*) and it was first published in May 1953. The editors included Izaltino Pereira and Heraclides Santos. The latter also served as secretary-general of the union during Cerqueira's term in office, and, under their leadership, the Rio-based newspaper served as an important instrument in disseminating their views, and reporting on events pertaining more broadly to the reality of urban labor. *A Voz do Metalúrgico* was similarly suppressed by the military forces that had come to power in the coup of March 1964, but was never brought back into circulation even after a new democratic political order was reinstated in Brazil in the mid-1980s.[31]

Both publications were primarily geared to their respective union bases, but it was common to see that workers of other unions were also among the reading public of each newspaper.[32] Particularly relevant in the case of metalworkers in the city of Rio de Janeiro, it is clear that *A Voz do Metalúrgico* exerted at least some level of influence over unions nationwide as well as over the national printed press published in Rio.[33] This was probably due to the fact that this periodical circulated in the (then) federal administrative capital (which was transferred to Brasília early in 1960) and included articles reporting on union delegations from the entire country that had come to town to present their demands to the national government. The two newspapers were published every month but sometimes an issue was halted for a month or two, most likely due to lack of funds. Most pieces normally ran on an average of twelve pages in length, but it was common to have special issues reporting on regional and national conferences of metalworkers as well as other industrial labor sectors. Small advertisements of items being sold by union members were occasionally published in these newspapers, particularly in the case of the São Paulo-based paper.

In addition to regular articles and columns commenting on the national (and occasionally international) political context—where the most often repeated topic was that of the rising cost of living, as will be shown below—both periodicals also published general interest articles and announcements on a regular basis which included: poetry (in most cases written by members of the unions), reports on athletic activities, news on upcoming social events (such as the union's annual ball), announcements of upcoming birthdays, the christenings of family members, and the passing of union members or of their family members.[34] In fact, both unions offered a wide range of membership services and each organization had a Social, Athletic, and even a Women's Department, and, in the case of Rio de Janeiro, there were also sewing and flower-arranging divisions within the structure of the union. Both entities also had an active drama club that performed in the various annual celebrations, and they ran a permanent small library for use by members and their families. Additionally, both unions provided medical and dental services and organized vacations trips and sport events. Moreover, it is important to note that, insofar as the services provided, women merited special attention in both entities even though no women served in the board of directors of either labor representative body during the entire period examined.

Indicative of the wide audience of both newspapers and their impact on the rank and file worker, it was common to find mailed-in articles written by union members (who had their registration numbers published under their names in the articles) commenting on the growing economic difficulties faced by workers amidst an enthusiastic nationalist rhetoric that defined the period. These pieces included poems, such as one written by Alcebíades Silva, published in the June 1955 issue under the title of the very operative inspirational word of the main demands advanced in the period: "A Carestia." In the piece, Silva described in a joking rhyme the dire situation of salaried workers who had to make ends meet amidst constant rising prices.[35] In March 1956 (the second month of the Kubitschek administration) the same topic was prominently displayed on the front page of both unions' newspapers. The cover story of *A Voz do Metalúrgico* claimed that the price of a loaf of bread had gone up twofold in the previous six months, a historical trend said to represent "an aggression to the popular economy," which was blamed on "those who controlled the means of production and distribution of goods and who did not behave like true patriots."[36]

Much in the same way, in the editorial column of the same issue, Izaltino Pereira argued for a strong mobilization on the part of workers in favor of salary increases, both in the official minimum wage and the basic salary paid in the metalworking sector.[37] Pereira claimed that such an action should be pursued on the basis of a broad inter-union movement in favor of an effective freeze (*congelamento*) on prices charged for items of popular consumption, such as food staples. The article made use of a reasoning manifested in several other labor pieces in the period, which argued that unless prices were frozen and placed under strict control of governmental authorities, the "sharks" (powerful economic groups who controlled the production and distribution of food staples) would simply transfer the wage gains of salary increases to the prices of items they produced or distributed.[38] Consistent with the agenda of metalworkers in Rio de Janeiro, the reality of the rising cost of living was similarly discussed at the national level. A good illustration of the importance the topic assumed in the period was the call for the first National Conference of Workers in the Metal, Electrical, and Mechanical Industries, published in *A Voz do Metalúrgico* in December 1955. Even if only an announcement of an event still in the works, the piece quintessentially revealed how metalworkers would interpret the broad national context of the JK Years. The piece reads as follows:

> No one today can deny the fact that our county needs and deserves a more assertive national policy of industrialization. It is important, as the new administration gets ready to take office, that we, workers of Brazil, make our own views clear. [. . .] As our nation becomes industrialized, those who contribute more see their share in the national economy and their own rights as citizens become a dead letter. To correct this situation, we summon our National Conference to state our position in unity and in defense of our rights.[39]

The conference was held in Volta Redonda, an industrial city in the state of Rio de Janeiro, in April of the following year with the participation of eighty-two delegates of nine Brazilian states who gathered to formulate a common agenda for future negotiation with both employers and the federal administration. The president of the National Conference of Metalworkers was Benedito Cerqueira, and in the special issue on the conference published in *O Metalúrgico*, we find a long list of resolutions deliberated during the event.[40] Those meriting special consideration included appeals for: strengthening metalworker's unified struggle for better pay and safer working conditions, asserting higher levels of independence *vis-à-vis* the Ministry of Labor, promoting an ambitious program of land reform, and defending and protecting domestic industries by providing governmental subsidies to nationally owned companies, as well as by expropriating foreign-owned companies holding monopoly positions in the area of infrastructure.[41]

Equally suggestive of how workers in São Paulo were concerned about the situation of *carestia* in 1955, the September issue of *O Metalúrgico* reported on an inter-union roundtable held earlier the same month among more than a dozen unions in the city to discuss the situation of rising prices. In the article, influential union member Remo Forli described "an unbearable situation where our families are starving, our children go to school hungry, and we get up and go to work, day after day having eaten only beans for supper."[42] In the December issue of the same year, one month before Kubitschek's inauguration, the editorial column stated that despite the many difficulties they faced, metalworkers of São Paulo believed that the upcoming administration deserved a "cautious vote of confidence." Urging union members to support the new president, the editor nonetheless concluded by stating that the incoming president should "remember us, humble workers, who make sacrifices every day to meet our commitments in favor of national development."[43]

A related note of political reservation about the new administration was expressed in *A Voz do Metalúrgico*'s editorial column of March 1957. In the piece Heraclides Santos, who regularly wrote about general political aspects of the country, evaluated in negative terms JK's first year in office, stating that "the high number of promises made during the presidential campaign made workers supportive of the current administration [. . .] [but] we don't see reasons to celebrate now as several unions continue to be harassed and the cost of living has grown to unprecedented levels."[44] Demonstrating a similar lack of trust in the political projects upheld by the new administration, the editorial column of the August 1958 issue criticized Kubitschek's most important diplomatic project: Operation Pan-America. The goals of such a foreign policy program were actually supported in the article, which nonetheless expressed disbelief that such an initiative could achieve any significant results given its alleged excessive reliance on the "good will" of the U.S. The editorialist defined the project as naïve considering that "there are sufficient cases to deny any confidence that the State Department will support our just claims." Still, according to the author, the country should "once and for all pursue an autonomous path of development [rather than] continue to be trusting of the political branch of the plutocracy of Wall Street."[45]

Additional articles published in the same periodical dealing with the domestic economic policies of the period expressed a similarly critical tone. This seems to have been the case particularly in editorials and political columns examining the policies carried out by Lucas Lopes, the deviser of the Targets Plan who was one of the main figures in the Council of Development and who also served as Minister of Finance from mid-1958 to mid-1959. These writings repeatedly stressed the difficult situation faced by workers in the urban centers, and they regularly tended to be construed around the notion of *carestia*. Thus, along with the recurrent recourse of describing in emphatic terms the desperate conditions workers faced, these pieces normally included the arguments for what was to be done to resolve, or at least minimize, the very situation. For heuristic purposes, proposed solutions to the stated "problem of *carestia*" could be placed under two general categories: immediate and structural actions. In the first group one could place the requests for salary increases and price controls, whereas more profound reforms normally included those such as land reform and the strengthening of the domestic industry, demands which became increasingly relevant for all workers regardless of industry or profession, as the decade unfolded.[46]

Metalworkers in Rio de Janeiro and São Paulo (as well as in the rest of the country) consistently argued that a more socially inclusive and autonomous national economy could be achieved under the guidance of an economically interventionist and socially responsive central government.[47] The reasoning behind this latter claim reflected several elements of propositions similarly advanced by nationalist intellectuals and politicians, as indicated in Chapter Four. This ideological reading posited that attaining a more efficient (economically) and independent (politically) modern nation required a national government that directly owned the most important industrial units and promoted direct investments in the areas of infrastructure and land reform. By the same token, a constant theme present in labor publications, the argument for a government that intervened more directly in the economy and for an administration that was more responsive to the social needs of workers was central to the notion of national development urban workers espoused in the period.

In fact, in the editorial pieces, political columns, and general labor articles of the period one sees that Brazilian society was assumed to be divided into a majority representing the effective interests of the nation and a powerful minority segment who defended anti-national (foreign) positions favoring multinational corporations and their associates. State-owned companies, such as the Fábrica Nacional de Motores (examined in Chapter Three), were consistently portrayed as representative of the path that the federal administration should also undertake in other sectors, such as that of food production and distribution where multinational companies were highly influential. Much in the same way, reporting on the events pertaining to the Second National Congress of Metalworkers, the editorialist of the April 1959 issue of *A Voz do Metalúrgico* strongly criticized several projects carried out by the Council of Development, especially those related to the implementation of an automotive industry in the country. The article stated that the ways in which this industrial project was being carried out would lead to "transferring ownership of our national industry to foreign agents."[48]

The claim was reiterated in bold terms in the October issue of the same year in a cover article arguing that foreign investments were not needed for development promotion given that, "though much has been said in defense of foreign capital to promote our development, it is clear that we are becoming industrialized in spite of foreign capital and not because of it as these companies are not relevant to improving our production levels."[49] Taken together, the pieces reveal key notions defining the general conception of national development held by (at least the leadership of) the two most important metalworkers' unions of the country. Namely, this increasingly influential labor segment reproached foreign sources of capital at the very time when foreign-owned companies were creating large numbers of jobs in the industrial sector. Conversely, core demands presented by metalworkers in the period were centered on actions largely dependent on the direct involvement of the national government to be successful. These included regulating private (national and mainly foreign) interests and promoting a state-led developmental path that, as inflation grew sharply in the latter years of the JK era, had to comprise price controls.

A clear indication of the increasing demands for a responsive government in support of the purchasing power of working groups is found in the documents pertaining to the Second National Conference of Labor Unions taking place in November 1959. At the gathering, union workers acknowledged that the country was undergoing a positive experience of economic prosperity but stressed their apprehension that, "Thus far this level of progress has not translated into better living standards for our working people." Organized labor also claimed that "[i]t is deeply disheartening to see that the federal government has yet to act decisively to support our interests despite its commitment to do so which was manifested so many times in similar events in the past."[50]

Pertaining to future courses of action, one of the main deliberations taken at the same meeting was to "call on all workers to demand a more stringent action on the part of the Federal government regarding the 'problem of carestia.'" Moreover, the conference reiterated the notion (previously advanced in the First Congress of Metalworkers and in the "Economic Letter of the CNTI," detailed next) that national development promotion could only achieve tangible results for all workers if such a goal were promoted on clear nationalistic bases. The core element of a nationalistic path of development was defined by having the federal government act as the main agent of economic promotion and as the main defender of the interests of the "majority of the population."[51]

The National Confederation of Industrial Workers (CNTI) published its own periodical called *Tribuna Sindical* (*Union Tribune*). Its first issue came out in March 1955 and the periodical was mailed for free to every affiliated union nationwide. Throughout the JK Years, the confederation was headed by unionists known as *pelegos*, or those who provided almost immediate support to the governmental labor policies in exchange for favors dispensed in the national or regional branches of the overextended bureaucratic structure of the Ministry of Labor. The main directors of the CNTI in the period were Diocleciano de Hollanda Cavalcanti and Ari Campista, long-time, pro-government members of the organization. In effect, the organization spent a good deal of time in balancing acts aimed at sustaining its influence over unions, which were becoming increasingly more autonomous of governmental influence. Moreover, on several occasions the CNTI's leadership had to defend its actions as its leaders were becoming the focus of accusation of misdemeanors in the handling of workers' pecuniary contributions provided by the Labor Ministry.

Like the other union-based papers examined, *Tribuna Sindical* regularly published articles on the topic of *carestia* but normally its tone was less critical of the federal administration given that, as one of its articles stated, "no one can deny the sincere interest of the administration in attending to the just demands of our working classes, who should not succumb to the siren song of striking against a supportive and attentive government."[52] There were also regular pieces on the experiences of the so-called free unions of Western Europe where workers (described as having understood the need to cooperate with the business classes) were moving ahead in promoting their economic betterment. In most cases, these articles connected an international focus with the experiences of Brazilian industrial workers who should learn that support for the government was needed so that "social peace" could be attained.[53]

The notion that workers had to be supervised in the industrial environ by the structures of a paternalistic corporate legal structure created late in the Estado Novo lingered into the 1950s. But although this paternalism, well expressed in the Consolidation of Labor Laws (CLT) of 1942, defined the general contours of labor relations at the time, it was also then that workers managed to voice their growing resentment for the general provisions of the system. While workers certainly did find reasons to support core elements sanctioned by the CLT, the legal limitation to cross-sectional autonomous mobilization began outweighing the protection provided by the existing legislation. This was particularly true in the case of former members of the communist party who exerted a great deal of influence in grassroots movements. Much of this new outlook derived from the experiences involved in mass strikes that proved to be instrumental in allowing a convergence in the activities of communists and laborists (PTB), as will be demonstrated below.[54]

Revealing of these transformative historical trends, *Tribuna Sindical*, which had traditionally been against the idea of mass stoppages, was forced to support this recourse when a historic strike brought industrial production to a halt in São Paulo for almost a month in 1957.[55] It was only then that the paper disingenuously claimed that the confederation had supported the movement all along and, more importantly, that this historic stoppage had not targeted the administration, but rather greedy employers who could not see that without workers' monetary gains their goods could not be purchased.[56] Though shifting a bit its editorial perspective toward a more critical stance, *Tribuna Sindical* nonetheless continued to espouse a more moderate tone than the one assumed in the publications of the metalworkers' unions herein studied. But given the unprecedented levels of the autonomous, largely grassroots based and led mobilization of the "400 thousand-workers strike," the paper then urged the federal administration to "pay more attention to the fact that the important wage increases consented generously to industrial workers were rapidly depleted by the rising prices for basic consumption items, particularly in the large urban centers."[57]

Further evidence that the topic of *carestia* harnessed the sentiments of industrial workers in a very vibrant fashion—thus leading them to act in innovative and increasingly overtly critical ways—is noticeable in the level of importance that the theme received in a key document industrial workers handed to Kubitschek at the Catete Palace (the presidential administrative office in Rio de Janeiro from the 1890s to 1960) in November 1956. The "Economic Letter of the CNTI" had been prepared to celebrate the tenth anniversary of the organization and was said to express industrial workers' views about the socio-economic context of the country.[58] Meant to convey positions of a diverse labor population, the letter claimed that all Brazilian workers found themselves under a "general sense of despair and economic insecurity deriving from the continued price increases that our families face. This situation defines our spirits, which are increasingly filled with images of famine, unrest and chaos."[59]

As previously indicated, metalworkers consistently argued that resolving such a bleak situation (i.e., "fighting against the desperate situation of *carestia*") required very concrete measures. These included intervening in foreign-owned meat-packing companies, establishing producer-run open markets in all neighborhoods of large urban centers (so that prices could be kept at production costs), arresting food distributors (mostly tied to foreign companies) who did not respect price freezes to be imposed by the national government, and incorporating autonomous labor union representatives in the existing official bodies in charge of regulating food distribution in the most important cities.[60] It is worth noting that, starting in 1951, a federal agency (the Federal Commission of Prices and Food Supply, known as COFAP), structured within the Ministry of Labor and with state (COAPs) and municipal (COMAPs) branches, had been set up by the national government to regulate the distribution of food staples in the main urban centers—primarily via seasonal warehouse stock pilings.

COFAP was organized by a hierarchical logic where local commissions mainly performed the role of providing statistical reports on price increases in each large city to local, state, and federal divisions of the agency. Local (city-based) commissions were composed of five representatives from food processing industries and, beginning in October 1956, also of five representatives from labor unions indicated by the Labor Ministry which also assigned the head of the commission. But increasingly, as food prices rose sharply from 1957 onwards, industrial unions in general became ever more vocal in demanding that the agency play a more assertive role in controlling prices and providing alternative forms of food distribution in the urban centers.[61]

Growing union-based pressures for concrete action from the federal administration resulted in the National Plan of Food Supply produced by the Food Supply Coordinating Council (CCA), in January 1958. The council had been created by the Vargas administration in February 1954 to set the guidelines for the activities of the COFAP, but would only become fully operational in the JK era, presumably because of the magnitude the topic of *carestia* assumed in these years and the associated mobilization of labor and broad segments of the general population (detailed in the next section). The Plan of Food Supply listed suggestions for improving government oversight over food production and distribution. These encompassed several propositions regularly advanced in the demands promoted by labor unions, such as the need to expand the network of warehouses used to regulate food stocks, as well as revamping transportation channels connecting the different regions of the vast interior of the country.[62] Finally having something to show, a report on the plan published in January 1960 praised the creation of four new "popular markets" (*mercados populares*) in the capital city of

Rio de Janeiro, where food prices were said to be 30 percent cheaper on average than retail. This course of action was naively (or perhaps hypocritically) seen as so successful that the same report states that a legislative bill was to be submitted to the National Congress so that similar markets could be set up across the entire nation.[63] In the end, it is clear that the approach followed did not aim at addressing any structural feature of the process of food production in the country, something that would have required, as consistently articulated by labor unions publications, the political will to promote a profound program of land reform as well as revisiting the virtual monopoly of food processing plants then overwhelmingly in the hands of multinational corporations.

Further indicative of how much the Kubitschek administration unsuccessfully tried to follow a non-political approach to such a highly politicized topic, its main policies aimed at increasing food production were derivative of the industrial focus of the Targets Plan and primarily centered on the goal of mechanizing agricultural activities—i.e., making agricultural machinery available to producers who, given the high costs of these tools, not surprisingly happened to be prosperous land owners—rather than attempting to overhaul the country's historically highly unequal land tenure structure. Understandably the latter course of action would entail an enormous political cost that JK did not seem willing to take on. Surprisingly though, his government did not seek to implement even less controversial measures proposed by the CCA, such as making subsidized credit for food producers more easily accessible and setting minimum prices for food staples.[64] Corroborating the existence of different views on how to effectively tackle the matter of *carestia* within the administration, the CCA vented its frustrations about how the issue had thus far been handled by saying, very much in line with the labor publications examined, that "the current approach to addressing the problem of constantly rising prices for items of popular consumption is clearly not working since it does not deal with the structural inefficiencies on the production side, resulting in growing popular discontent."[65]

The low priority ascribed to non-export oriented agricultural sectors was thus evident throughout the 1950s and, as the 1960s dawned in Latin America's largest country, repeated bureaucratic attempts to find technical solutions to a problem that clearly entailed political decisions persisted. In 1961, for instance, the CCA published another National Plan of Food Supply that reaffirmed the need to "expand the deficient transportation and warehousing networks, which disturb the regular flow of goods from producing units to the larger urban centers."[66] Moreover, the Triennial Plan of Economic and Social Development submitted to the National Congress by Special Minister of Planning Celso Furtado in 1963, once again stressed the need to increase food production by means of subsidized public credit so that the persistent rates of inflation could subside.[67] Not surprisingly, his market-oriented counterpart, Roberto Campos, who would be the future planning minister of the military regime that would be installed in 1964, continued to argue in favor of export agriculture as the most efficient way to finance the industrial course that defined all other political goals of the period.[68]

The demand for a higher degree of governmental involvement in addressing the problem of rising food prices and food shortages in large urban areas, involved broader social segments beyond organized labor. Hundreds of request from all parts of the country were indeed regularly mailed by a multitude of different individuals and groups (such as the National Association of Housewives) to the presidential palace in Rio de Janeiro, addressed to Kubitschek himself in the latter years of his term in office, asking the president to get personally involved in resolving the many problems regular people faced in "simply trying to resupply the pantry." Many times these letters came from local city councils that claimed to be acting on behalf of their residents in order to have "abusive price hikes be brought under control by the president." Likewise, numerous requests from rural cooperatives of small food producers, particularly in the southern states of Rio Grande do Sul, Santa Catarina, and Paraná, were regularly addressed to JK seeking political support for already denied loan applications for subsidized credit submitted to the National Bank of Economic Development.

Together these many missives claimed that their credit requests were aimed at the construction of food processing units and that the Development Bank's reasons for denying their plans were political rather than technical.[69] Though no paper trail of any response from the presidential office could be found, it seems reasonable to assume that perhaps no action was ever taken by the palace's chief of staff, Minister Sette Câmara, to address these latter contacts. Moreover, considering the industrial focus of the administration as a whole and the fact that food processing was highly concentrated in the hands of a few powerful business groups, it is plausible indeed that these small food producers never actually got a response from the president, notwithstanding the relevance of their cause for addressing the "persistent problem of *carestia*."

Concerning the roles the federal Brazilian government played in the national economy, it should also be pointed out that in addition to the salary negotiations that each union (organized by each specific sector or activity) periodically held with their respective employer's association (so that their respective sectorial basic salary could be stipulated and ratified by the Labor Ministry), the federal government granted regular increases in minimum wage indices. Raises were determined according to the geographic location as the country had been divided into fifty-four broad national areas depending on the cost of living of the region. The metropolitan cities of Rio de Janeiro and São Paulo represented one specific area each, wherein a Minimum Wage Commission, composed by representatives from workers and employers and headed by a representative of the Ministry of Labor, was put in place to serve in the role of examining local costs of living. Commissions provided the statistical branch of the Labor Ministry (Serviço de

Estatística da Previdência e Trabalho, SEPT) with their conclusions regarding the regional living indices so that the ministry could advise the national president on the value of the raise needed in that region.[70]

How often these raises occurred also depended on the economic and political situation of the country at any given time. Salary increases, their dates, and the value of the minimum wage throughout the 1950s are indicated below. Also shown in the tables are the inflation rates for the JK Years and the equivalent real (not nominal) value of the minimum wage based on whether there was a respective loss or gain in the purchasing power in each year.[71]

Considering the steady deterioration in the living standards of most urban workers in the period, it is not surprising to see that industrial labor consistently and assertively mobilized to counteract this state of affairs. What was not to be expected however, if one is to believe the more established literature in the field, was the degree to which this mobilization by workers included non-wage-related, well-defined, broad and highly politicized topics in their list of demands, wherein the goal of national development was prominently displayed. Moreover, in what seems to be one of the most relevant aspects of the historical path of increased labor activism in mid-century Brazil, industrial workers proved to be highly autonomous, resourceful, and creative in establishing new forms to advance their ever more ambitious social agenda—as will be further demonstrated below.

Table 6.1 Dates of raises in the legal minimum wage in the 1950s and their nominal value in Rio.

Date of raise	Nominal value of minimum wage (in the capital city of Rio in *cruzeiros*)
January 1, 1952	1,200.00
July 4, 1954	2,400.00
August 1, 1956	3,800.00
January 1, 1959	6,000.00
October 18, 1960	9,600.00

Table 6.2 Inflation rates and their impact on purchasing power in Rio.

Year	Annual national inflation rate	Minimum wage loss/ increase
1956	21%	-2%
1957	16%	-10%
1958	14%	-9%
1959	39.2%	-13%
1960	29.5%	+19.4%
1961	33%	-14.7%

INDUSTRIAL WORKERS AND THE RISE OF AUTONOMOUS LABOR ACTIVISM

In addition to publishing vocal pieces decrying "the desperate situation of *carestia*" and demanding more assertive actions on the part of the federal administration in controlling prices and providing alternatives sources of access to basic food staples, metalworkers consistently engaged in a variety of acts of protest throughout the 1950s. At times, this course of action required legally banned inter-union alliances, which buttressed the bargaining position of unions vis-à-vis that of employers and governmental officials. In concrete terms, labor mobilization included ever more frequent massive stoppages, walk-outs, and large public events organized in cooperation with several organizations from the broader civil society which had the common goal of "fighting the plight of *carestia*." Likewise, throughout the JK Years, industrial workers exhibited a new and increasingly strong sense of confidence in their own organizational skills, a trend that became manifest in the creation of the workers-run Inter-Union Department of Socio-Economic and Statistical Studies (DIEESE), in December 1955 in the city of São Paulo.

The creation of DIEESE marked the culmination of a process that had begun in March 1953, when the Inter-Union Unity Pact (PUI) was initially formed by labor representatives of various industrial sectors in the midst of a general strike that stopped several industrial plants in São Paulo. The department was primarily funded by contributions from its nineteen original member unions, which in pursuing this course of action were trying to devise a technical agency dedicated to examining the constantly rising costs of living for urban workers in the city so that their upcoming salary negotiations could be carried out on a "level playing field." In fact, the main inspiration behind the creation of this research entity was being able to gather alternative statistical data on price increases, thus preparing unions to better negotiate wages as, until that point in time, all figures used to calculate salary losses had been provided by the Ministry of Labor, the São Paulo prefecture, or industrialist associations in the city.[72]

A founding member of DIEESE, the SindMet/SP considered the establishment of the agency to be a major achievement on behalf of industrial workers in the city and in its first issue of 1956, *O Metalúrgico* published a one-page article reporting on the creation of the department. The relevance of such an initiative is stressed in the piece, which claimed that the new research body represented a much-needed capability for participating unions to "find out real inflation rates in the city of São Paulo [. . .] a move that will empower all workers to advance their continued claims for better wages and living conditions."[73] The piece similarly stated that the new union-run organization had finally placed workers on an "equal footing" for all upcoming wage agreements given that the new institution would "end the uncomfortable situation of going into a negotiation with the supporting data being provided only by one side."[74] Moreover, the article claimed that the work of DIEESE would have to be respected by employers and governmental authorities considering that its investigative work was coordinated by the reputable economics professor of the prestigious University of São Paulo, José Albertino Rodrigues—who coordinated the Technical Division of the agency between 1956 and 1962, and played a very influential role in defining the initial contours of most labor investigations produced in the 1960s.

In tandem with the new momentum of inter-union collaboration that began with the creation of the department, in June 1956, twenty-four labor unions in the city of São Paulo reaffirmed their commitment to act together in all future wage negotiations, as well as in the "fight against *carestia*." The decision, which represented a tactical maneuver that was a *de facto* recreation of the Inter-Union Pact (PUI) of 1953, had taken place in a large gathering of workers held at the SindMet/SP headquarters, in downtown São Paulo, from which a large march originated upon the meeting's conclusion and proceeded all the way to the state of São Paulo legislative assembly, in front of which a "massive demonstration against *carestia*" was held.[75]

In specific, the revived inter-union pact defended the position that combating the "desperate situation of *carestia*" required: 1) expanding public credit availability to small farmers who were "the real producers of our food supplies," 2) improving transportation networks so that the delivery of food staples in the large urban centers could take place at a lower cost, and 3) enforcing governmental controls over food distribution networks so that prices could be reduced, primarily by curtailing the "excessive and nefarious influence exerted by private speculators"—who were also described as "sharks" and as "enemies of the popular will."[76]

This extended list of demands became very popular and was regularly reiterated in most labor-related political events of the period. In fact, as living conditions further deteriorated in the final years of the decade, industrial workers were increasingly aware that their problems were caused by factors situated beyond their own places of work. Thus, as will be detailed below, a gradual realization that addressing such complex economic matters required structural transformations in the national economy is apparent in most labor activities of the JK Years. In effect, industrial workers, in general, and metalworkers, in particular, became involved in broader, increasingly political collective mobilizations demanding structural measures, which included the matters of land reform and the nationalization of food processing and distribution companies.

The topic of the nationalization of foreign-held companies, particularly those in food-related industries demarcated, along with the issue of land reform, much of the debate pertaining to the structural economic transformation the country was said to require in order to develop. Much of the discussion on these matters was defined by a conceptual division that placed at one end conservatives who upheld the notion that foreign investment was what the national economy lacked, and, at the other extreme, those who favored higher governmental involvement (even ownership) of what they called key economic activities. Given the importance of U.S. investments in Brazil and Latin America in the period, as well as the associated ever more assertive U.S. efforts to reshape labor relations in the region during the Cold War, the underlying ideology of and some of the strategic courses of action pursued toward implementation are spelled out below.

First, it is worth recalling that the cornerstones of the' growing involvement of the U.S. in Brazil's labor dynamics in the 1950s were set already in the closing months of World War II. It was then that U.S. labor operatives more actively sought to isolate communist ideologies and their alleged local representatives from labor unions in order to reshape Brazilian labor along the lines of the so-called "free trade-union movement" of the U.S. The creation of a unified Brazil labor federation resembling the American Federation of Labor was an important objective pursued by U.S. labor attachés in mid-century. American-sponsored local branches of regional labor organizations (especially the Inter-American Regional Organization of Workers, ORIT) thus set out to promote a higher degree of "freedom" in labor-employer negotiations beyond what was allowed in the Brazilian corporatist legislation.[77] Likewise, the official publication of ORIT's office in Brazil, called *Boletim Sindicalista do Brasil* (*Brazilian Union Bulletin*) continued to make the case, even amidst the deepening experience of *carestia* and associated increased grassroots mobilization of industrial workers, that "though salaries are low, it is clear that repeated salary increases without a correlated increase in the levels of productivity can only result in higher costs of living."[78]

ORIT opened its local office in Rio de Janeiro in 1953, which was headed by conservative Brazilian unionist Joviano de Araújo, and based at CNTI's own headquarters in downtown Rio. Since its opening in 1953, ORIT's Brazilian branch vetoed any sort of interaction or joint programs with unions seen as "infiltrated by dangerous communist elements" (as was allegedly the case of the SindMet/RJ). It also should be noted that, presumably to U.S. representatives' greatest dismay, in the long run, this overly ideological approach proved to be counterproductive to the regional labor organization's own goals of exerting higher levels of influence on Brazilian industrial workers as it denied the ever more present broad political alliances and inter-union cooperation taking place on the ground.[79]

Ironically, though the Brazilian government approved a higher degree of involvement from U.S. official (governmental) and sponsored (AFL) labor agencies in the country (both the Dutra and Vargas administration encouraged Brazilian labor federations, chiefly the CNTI to become a member of ORIT), the aims of these same initiatives were proscribed in the labor legislation of the period and seen as a questionable course of action by important members of the higher echelons of organized labor. In fact, throughout the 1950s, Diocleciano Cavalcanti, president of the CNTI until 1962, systematically objected to important ideas espoused by the different U.S. labor attachés serving in Brazil, as well as by the local leadership of the Brazilian office of the regional labor branch. He consistently claimed to be supportive of ORIT's ideals, goals, and programs but justified his inaction on pursuing them by stating: "it is very difficult to do so given that our average industrial worker is quite ignorant and has little consciousness of how independent trade unions need to be run."[80]

U.S. labor officials increasingly saw more independent unions as "dangerously politicized" and supported strengthening strategic alliances with the pro-government unionists. Complicating matters further, it was among more autonomous labor organizations (such as metalworkers in São Paulo and Rio) that many of the notions and goals espoused by U.S. representatives were seen as a valuable means to strengthen workers' independence from governmental oversight. Interviewed by Professor Alexander in August 1959, *A Voz do Metalúrgico*'s editorial director, Izaltino Pereira, indeed claimed that metalworkers approved of and were in fact seeking to establish direct negotiations with employers as a way to advance a broader agenda beyond wage increases.[81]

Thus, in a not very promising historical trend, labor relations in Brazil in the developmentalist years of the 1950s were indeed defined by contradictory ideological alignments that did not bode well for the interests of the U.S. Concretely, Brazilian partners of U.S.-condoned (and financed) labor agencies (e.g., ORIT) tended to be conservative unionists rapidly losing legitimacy among workers. Conversely, segments of labor more aligned with the autonomist tenets espoused by U.S. agents consisted of rank-and-file supported organizations that ironically were also willing to work with perceived-to-be communist activists. In fact, Aldo Lombardi, secretary-general of the SindMet/SP, argued early in the JK era that *paulista* (São Paulo-based) workers were becoming ever mobilized and freer from ministerial control, thus able "to demand changes in the price control agencies that have been traditionally staffed by military men who don't know the least thing about the problems of inflation, let alone of workers." He also expressed labor's growing independence and assertiveness by stating that "now that we have established the DIESSE, we will be better prepared to confront both employers and government officials in all upcoming wage negotiations."[82]

Considering these complex historical dynamics, it should not be surprising to see that, as Brazil ventured into the 1960s and the ideological polarization of the political system reached new grounds, the U.S. would rapidly replace many of its ambitious labor-related initiatives by conservative, pro-market, business-focused partnerships and programs that later proved essential in providing ideological legitimation for the violent, reactionary military events surrounding the military coup of 1964. Paradoxically, their pro "free union" rhetoric notwithstanding, in the eyes of U.S. officials, the heightened independence of unions *vis-à-vis* the attempted government control defining the period (as elected union leaders no longer had to be approved by the Labor Ministry in order to take office), was seen as a challenging precedent that demanded the close scrutiny of North American representatives, as the threat of "communist infiltration" was said to be growing among more autonomous union organizations. In fact, though trusting the Brazilian government to continue to monitor labor unions as a way to prevent the "misuse of their social base," U.S. diplomatic officers were nonetheless critical of the federal administration for not being able to successfully address the problems deriving from the persistent food shortage in large urban areas, which are "being used to foster growing social discontentment and unrest among workers and the urban poor."[83]

The notion that the rank and file would become politically radicalized by indoctrination promoted by "communist agitators" was shared by government officials in the Brazilian Ministry of Labor, business elites, and U.S. members of the diplomatic corps in those years. It was therefore increasingly difficult for these many different influential political actors to make sense of the fact that labor mobilization, which included massive numbers of union members and broad sectors of civil society in general, was on the rise despite the fact that no dramatic increases in the presence of communist unionists could be perceived—Irving Salert, U.S. labor attaché for much of the decade, had actually denied, when speaking to Professor Alexander, the claim that communists were controlling unions across the country.[84]

More complex than the oppositional stereotype construed by conservative groups and large segments of the print media, the official communist political platform in the 1950s could not be reduced to any one single issue, and the official party line guiding the actions of most affiliated activists underwent different phases and inclinations in the period. Examining the party's most influential publications is thus relevant as a way of reaching a more complete portrayal of labor relations at the time. Though proscribed from participating in competitive electoral bids for most of its existence, the Brazilian Communist Party (PCB) maintained a series of official (as well as, at different times, semi-official) periodicals in its long and active history as a small, but very active and influential party in terms of disseminating its political ideas.

Early in the 1950s, PCB's official periodical was called *Voz Operária* (*Worker's Voice*), which, along with another influential paper (which was not directly headed by party leaders), called *Imprensa Popular* (*Popular Press*), circulated pieces on several important and highly debated topics, such as the role of foreign capital in development promotion, land reform, and labor rights. As Kubitschek's term in office began, and after the mid-decade publication of the "Khrushchev Report" on Stalin's massive atrocities, both papers challenged the direction of the party by publishing a series of op-ed pieces debating the very report. This action would eventually become unacceptable to the party's leadership and in May 1957 both papers were terminated.[85]

In March 1958, PCB revisited its own positions and began espousing a reformist agenda supporting the establishment of a "nationalist front" of progressive social segments, including members of the national bourgeoisie (very much along the lines of what the ISEB intellectuals were also arguing for) as the best way to confront the encroaching threat posed by "global imperialism" and its "domestic allies." In fact, starting with Vargas's suicide in August 1954, and the associated realization that conservative forces were better organized than earlier assumed, and followed by the Twentieth Congress of the Soviet Union's Communist Party in 1956, PCB ventured into a renewal phase culminating in the "March 1958 Declaration," which proclaimed that the main challenges the country faced were overcoming its lingering semi-feudal rural structure as well as the growing threat of imperialism.[86] Facing these powerful challenges required a "united front" of nationalist forces organized under the leadership of the urban proletariat so that a nationalist and popular government could pursue a developmental path grounded on industrial growth structured on the domestic ownership of industries, freedom of organization for labor unions, and independent foreign policy projects.[87]

The adoption of this more moderate political stance on the part of PCB's directors represented a historic opportunity for the deployment of new means of mobilization, alliances, and dialogue between party members and other socio-political actors, including intellectuals, industrialists, and the labor movement in general. Formal associations with *Trabalhistas* (members or supporters of the pro-government Brazilian Labor Party, PTB) were then approved and even encouraged, particularly in the context of industrial unions. New cooperative patterns of interaction between communist labor organizers and those aligned with the PTB seem to have helped shape workers mobilization in the late 1950s and early 1960s toward more autonomous, stronger, and better organized actions, which included a clear political element. Moreover, it is essential to note that much of this new historical course was led by the grassroots rather than the party leadership.[88]

Closely aligned with this new position, a new periodical, suggestively called *Novos Rumos* (*New Directions*), was launched in January 1959, soon becoming the quasi-official voice of the party in these crucial years of the developmentalist experiences in Brazil. *Novos Rumos* was a reasonably well-known and influential publication with a regular circulation of about sixty thousand issues despite the fact that the main articles were written by party members along very dualistic lines of thought stressing the glories of the Socialist Bloc *vis-à-vis* the travails of life under capitalism, something probably not well fitting for a journal aimed at expanding the readership of PCB-related periodicals. Even its non-political articles, such as those reviewing the latest movie and book releases, were also marked by a highly intellectual tone that clearly reflected the editors' own interests and positions (Mario Alves, a long-time intellectual member of the party, served as the paper's editor during its brief five-year existence). It seems plausible, therefore, to assume that perhaps *Novos Rumos* intended to reach middle-income and better educated social segments rather than a union-based audience. In this sense, while the journal's successes cannot be entirely assessed, the publication indeed seems to have helped shape the debates on national development of the final years of the 1950s and early 1960s as references to its articles are found in several labor publications in the period.

The paper's treatment of the Kubitschek government was more critical than one would expect given the new "united front" guideline, and even during Goulart's brief term in office (1961–1964), the weekly sustained its line of criticisms despite the disingenuous and patently hyperbolic recurrent accusations of the mainstream, conservative media, as well as the investigative police apparatus (particularly the State Departments of Public and Social Order, DEOPS), which frequently claimed that communists were massively infiltrated in almost every corner of the federal government. This autonomist approach *vis-à-vis* the national state was evident in the consistent defense for a combative labor movement, and significant portions of the articles printed in the paper reported on the "brave work" being done by ever stronger, larger, more unified, and better organized workers. Equally, along with all the union-based periodicals examined here, *Novos Rumos* was also very critical of the governmental handling (mismanagement, to be more in tune with the paper's positions) of the "situation of *carestia*." Furthermore, in the paper's editorial view, COFAP had become "a machine to approve price hikes demanded by the sharks," rather than an agency working to protect people's interests.

To reverse course, *Novos Rumos* reported in February 1959 that "more than 300 labor unions and over 350 neighborhood associations of the city of São Paulo, along with student organizations and women's groups met last week to formulate a common plan of action to fight more successfully the desperately high cost of living we all face."[89] Likewise, in the following March, the periodical claimed that "while industrialists are happily prospering, workers continue to live at the margins of society [and unless] workers pressure the still remaining nationalists in the federal administration to act more responsively toward the people's demands," little hope remained.[90] Wage issues were also regularly commented on in the paper, including in headlines expressing a clear hint of poetic license and irony, such as one in the April 17 issue of the same year, which stated that "salaries for workers grow like a horse's tail." Similarly, the topic of land reform was frequently mentioned in the pages of *Novos Rumos*, including in long interviews with experts in the field, such as Josué de Castro (author of the classic work *The Geography of Hunger* and first secretary-general of the United Nations-associated Food and Agriculture Organization) who argued that unless land reform was implemented, problems of food scarcity, including its related high prices, could not be properly addressed.[91]

Much in the same way, along with conceptual articles on the history of global communism, the paper published a series of articles (between May and July 1959) observing the ambiguous role that the national bourgeoisie would play in the promotion of the "Brazilian Revolution" (at this point said to be essentially a nationalist movement). As a whole, the pieces argued that this was an important socio-political segment with whom the constitution of a "nationalist front" had to be pursued. At the same time, the articles' author(s) cautioned that the remaining conservative elements of the domestic business elites would only act with the nation's general interest at heart if workers pressured them to do so.[92] What's more, as the end of the year approached and the general state of rising inflation and lagging wages persisted, the paper's demands for action on wages and price hikes assumed a more radical tone, and *Novos Rumos* published various cover page pieces in the third and fourth quarter of 1959 stating, among other things, that by not acting, the federal "[g]overnment is making people die of hunger," and that "JK is the main person responsible for the social disquiet pervading the country."[93]

Consistently publishing articles on labor, particularly on the case of industrial workers, *Novos Rumos* stated in its first issue of 1960 that the previous year had been one of the most intense periods of struggle for Brazilian industrial workers, but also a time of increased unity and mobilization for the labor movement in general. The article also argued that the very "fight against *carestia*" had broadened the base of appeal of workers' demands to additional sectors of organized civil society in the country, thus helping in the construction of a "common front of action."[94] Despite this enthusiastic appraisal of the general labor scenario, at least in the main urban centers, the paper's editors continued to believe that union mobilization had to try to move beyond the legal limitations imposed by the CLT, particularly regarding the formal impossibility of creating a unified national labor federation across multiple union sectors. It is interesting to note that, in another ironic turn of events pertaining to the policy position of coalescing the mobilization under a unified national labor federation, both communists and U.S. associated or supported labor activists, such as those working at the local ORIT office in Brazil, were very much in agreement, as earlier indicated.[95]

It is clear, therefore, that throughout all of the transformative experiences that helped to define the 1950s in Brazil, industrial workers were well aware that the developmental process undertaken by the federal government disproportionally benefitted business groups and interests—a perception that was increasingly corroborated by technical measurements produced by labor organizations themselves. DIEESE, for instance, reported in the end of period, that despite the fact that "industrial growth between 1956 and 1959 [had been] close to 80 percent in terms of total production, and levels of productivity in most industries [grew] around 40 percent, average wages for industrial workers has decreased by about 10 percent last year alone." Adding to this dreary portrayal, the agency also pronounced what could be seen as a general assessment of labor dynamics in the period as a whole: "The logic behind the current process of economic growth focused on accelerated industrialization depends excessively on inflationary spending and is exclusively targeted at rewarding capital owners, the privileged sectors of our development."[96]

Empowered by this type of data and ever more poised to counteract the reality they faced on the ground, metalworkers of the city São Paulo proved to be one of the most politically active segments of industrial labor in the final years of the developmentalist decade. This was clearly demonstrated in July 1957 when the SindMet/SP held a general assembly to discuss "the alarming rates of increase in the rapidly growing cost of living." In effect, according to the figures provided by DIEESE, living costs had gone up by 43 percent in the previous thirteen months.[97] And, in reviewing the pages of *O Metalúrgico* in the following months, one clearly notices that the tone of the publication was increasingly critical of the federal administration. In the August issue, for instance, the SindMet/SP warned that it was becoming harder to dissuade the base from the desire to strike and urged the federal government to act soon.[98]

However, since no positive changes occurred, in mid-November the publication was almost exclusively dedicated to reporting the events pertaining to a major strike that had taken place in the previous month. This mass stoppage which involved about four hundred thousand industrial workers from eight different fields of activities, was led by the SindMet/SP and the Textiles Workers' Union of São Paulo, and virtually halted all industrial production in the city of São Paulo for twenty-eight days. The strike had been coordinated by the new Inter-Union Pact (PUI) and the (then created) Inter-Union Alliance for Salary Increases and Against Carestia. Strikers demanded a 25 percent wage increase for all participating unions and their initial walk-out proved successful in forcing employers to accept their pecuniary demand. In the end, however, after having managed to bring workers back to the assembly lines, local industrialist associations appealed to the Federal Labor Court (Tribunal Superior do Trabalho) which reduced the raise to 18 percent for all labor segments.[99]

The so-called "400 thousand-workers strike," proved to be a landmark experience for industrial workers who had become ever more critically mobilized in the latter years of the JK era. Commenting on the events of October, *O Metalúrgico* stressed that despite the final blow they had received from governmental authorities, workers should be proud of their level of unprecedented mobilization as the strike represented a new experience in the "march of unity of industrial workers in the city." Furthermore, probably concerned about sustaining a good public image with other social segments with whom the union needed to establish or maintain partnerships (and also an indication of the paper's broad reading audience), the periodical went on for about three more pages trying to make the case that "responsible industrial workers of São Paulo had been forced" to come to such a radical course of action given the intransigent position held by employers who had "pushed moderate and responsible workers into a situation of despair."[100]

Another event that similarly reflected how industrial workers were becoming increasingly mobilized, assertive, and politically inclined during the JK Years was the first National Congress of Metalworkers that took place in Porto Alegre in November 1957, where metalworkers decided that the following themes should be included in all future salary negotiations: inclusion of workers in all committees of the COFAP, restriction of public subsidized credit to foreign-owned companies, and a wide program of land reform aimed at increasing levels of food production.[101] Similarly, the Second National Congress of Metalworkers, in Itanhaém (in the state of São Paulo) reiterated a similar list of demands in 1959, namely the strengthening of their mobilization in favor of price controls and periodic wage revisions, the elimination of the influence of private speculators involved in the process of food distribution, and the creation of a nationalist program of industrialization, particularly in the auto-making sector, so that domestic companies would be able to compete on equal grounds with foreign-owned ones.[102]

Frequently displayed in most of their published materials, throughout the 1950s and ever more present in its second half, metalworkers consistently demanded that national development had to take place on "autonomous grounds" and be primarily aimed at achieving higher "economic independence" rather than higher economic entanglements with global economic agents and interests. The argument in favor of nationally (state) owned industries was repeated both in the publications of the SindMet/SP and the SindMet/RJ. This was particularly true after 1957, when their editorials began expressing adamant denunciations of the "desperate situation of *carestia*" pervading both urban contexts. These columns demanded a more rigorous involvement of governmental authorities in controlling prices and in increasing production of consumer goods by means of government-run companies. In its January/February 1959 issue, for instance, *O Metalúrgico* described how what were expected to be frozen prices had in fact gone successively up from the previous month of November through the first five weeks of the following year. The cover article then claimed that such a situation revealed in actual numbers the disconcerting lack of interest and political incompetence of the COMAP of the city of São Paulo to defend the rights and interests of workers. Moreover, it argued that the administration should act more promptly and responsively or its alleged commitment to workers would be "questioned on the streets."[103]

As all these events seem to indicate, industrial workers' demands were becoming guided by a strong sense of political nationalism, which favored a state-centered approach to the social problems for which unions were so obstinately interested in finding solutions. Of special importance, almost all labor publications that were examined consistently made the case that the persistent "problem of *carestia*" required not only immediate actions on the part of the federal government but also structural reforms to the national economy. Alongside the continually voiced demand for price controls, *carioca* (Rio-based) and *paulista* metalworkers also repeatedly argued that food production and distribution be placed under more strict public supervision so that the will of the majority of the country's populations (in their words, the "national interest") could be protected. A related criticism was utilized to assess the general industrial policies pursued in the period. Interestingly, despite their ever more evident role in the creation of industrial jobs, particularly in the automotive industry, foreign investors were repeatedly criticized in almost all metal workers' documents scrutinized here. And, at least in the eyes of union leaders, the nation's interests would be better protected if the state or, at a minimum, domestic business groups controlled the most important industrial plants in the country, and "foreign investors operated on the basis of a strict legislation that defended the real interests of the nation."[104]

In addition to revealing a high degree of political awareness, the mobilization of industrial workers during the latter part of the 1950s reflects an acute sense of solidarity for their fellow working brethren, particularly in the case of the demand for land reform, which was seen as a structural measure that not only addressed the problem of food shortage, but also improved the living conditions of the rural and urban working poor. In fact, this ever more active and politically influential segment of industrial labor regularly argued that "without an effective program of land reform, which includes subsidized credit to small landholders and bans foreign investors from the production of food staples is implemented, the developmental policies of Mr. Kubitschek will be nothing more than a giant with clay feet."[105]

This sense of shared interests and goals across professional segments was also evident in the experiences involved in all cross-sectional strikes and subsequent wage negotiations, as well as in all "marches against *carestia*" conducted throughout the decade. In addition, it is important to note that, as the JK Years were coming to a close, critical commentary on the administration was progressively directed at the president himself who was increasingly perceived as someone who could do more to alleviate the predicament faced by workers, if only he were truly concerned about the suffering of the working poor.[106] Thus, amidst this growing sense of frustration deriving from the lack of an effective resolution to their plight, industrial workers organized a new wave of inter-union meetings to plan the course of actions needed to redress the problem of price hikes that marked much of 1959. These gatherings were aimed at better organizing the so-called "fight against *carestia*" and were regularly held at the headquarters of the metalworkers' union in São Paulo.

A turning-point in all of these events, the idea of conducting a massive "March on Catete" (the presidential palace in Rio) to show Kubitschek the miserable living conditions of workers was debated in a meeting held between unions leaders from São Paulo and Rio de Janeiro early in March of that same year. The plan occupied unionists of both cities for most of the following month, until the minister of labor, Fernando Nóbrega, decided to open negotiations with a committee of workers led by Benedito Cerqueira and Aldo Lombardi, key leaders of the metalworkers' movement. As the march continued to be planned, various articles were being published in *Novos Rumos* (along with several other union-based papers) through which one can get a glimpse of the potential magnitude of the event; it was said that more than "800 representatives of 7 workers' federations, 194 unions, 300 popular civic organization, and 135 students' unions the state of São Paulo alone plan to descend upon the presidential palace on the 19th to present their list of demands to JK."[107]

By mid-April, the month when the rally was to occur, Minister Nóbrega told union leaders that the march would not be allowed to take place and that all possible measures to forestall the event would be pursued.[108] In the end, given the president's final refusal to meet in the public eye, unionists decided to send a small negotiating committee to meet with and hand him a letter describing the "desperate situation of *carestia*" workers faced and demand more efficient measures to control the problem of price increases.[109] Union leaders also took up a multi-targeted approach, organizing local "demonstrations against *carestia*" and conducting a massive mailing effort to publicize these very events to different sectors of the local media, state legislatures, and even to the National Congress in Rio de Janeiro.[110]

In addition, several large "acts against *carestia*" were seen in the months following the failed march, including a three-day vigil at Sé Square in the heart of downtown São Paulo.[111] The event had been organized by the Jornada Against Carestia (Campaign Against Carestia), a broad-based movement that included an expanded version of PUI, which by then included more than 118 unions in the city, numerous student associations from different local universities, and various neighborhood-based associations that were similarly becoming ever more assertive in demanding better living conditions in the final years of the JK era.[112] Also starting in 1959, one sees a proliferation of labor publications signaling an ever more radical political tone to their growing demands and overall sense of frustration among urban workers in general.[113] Continuously functioning as a key herald to the industrial labor movement in São Paulo, *O Metalúrgico*, for instance, reported that more than three hundred strikes had taken place in the city throughout the year, and that a similar number of "marches against *carestia*" had also occurred.[114] In the case of Rio de Janeiro, as inflation rates grew even faster in 1959, a new local inter-union pact, led by SindMet/RJ's President Benedito Cerqueira, was established: the Permanent Commission of Labor Union Organization (CPOS), an alliance that would play a central role in the labor activities taking place in Rio de Janeiro in the first years of the 1960s.[115]

Thus increasingly mobilized and ever more vocal in their demands, metalworkers of São Paulo and Rio de Janeiro served in a clearer and ever emboldened fashion in the role of harnessing the diffuse but real sentiments and demands of industrial labor in the latter part of the JK Years. Unfortunately, the federal government was too slow in seeking to understand and respond to these rapidly changing events pertaining to industrial labor, thus further alienating workers from the important developmental experiences and projects that the county experienced in the period. In response, in February 1960, two months before the new capital city of Brasília was to be inaugurated, *A Voz do Metalúrgico* published in its editorial page an assessment of the federal administration, which also helped to position the paper in face of the upcoming presidential election of October 1960.[116]

The paper urged that the new president would do more to defend the real interests of workers as "in spite of the high economic growth achieved, workers continued to live in miserable conditions." Similarly, the article argued that, "the union movement advocates and supports the development of our country but we have consistently demanded that this be achieved to the benefit of our general population rather than the interests of foreign investors." What is more, as a closing assessment of the JK Years in general, the editorialist concluded by saying that "Mr. Juscelino's Targets Plan has in reality placed our country at a dead-end since our economy has grown while our people remain poor."[117]

CONCLUDING REMARKS

By the mid-twentieth century, labor dynamics in Brazil were clearly more complex than has generally been described in the traditional historiography on the period. Particularly regarding the case of industrial labor throughout the JK Years, one finds a remarkable process wherein this growing segment of Brazilian workers progressively manifested more autonomous levels of mobilization. As the industrial sector expanded, particularly in the southeastern portion of the country (where the cities of São Paulo and Rio de Janeiro are located), industrial labor became increasingly more active, vocal, and engaged in some of the most important socio-economic transformations taking place at the time. In this sense, as the 1950s unfolded, growing numbers of industrial workers would come together to press the national political leadership to become more attentive to their needs.

As one of the labor segments most positively affected by the ambitious industrial goals of the period, metalworkers not only struggled to defend their own most immediate interests and needs, but also prolifically acted to articulate and advance their own views on national development. Exerting a prominent organizational role in this historical process, these workers held regular meetings and conferences to debate the case of wage decreases, published articles demanding more frequent and better enforced price freezes, and engaged in inter-union strikes and large civic demonstrations against the high costs of living. In so doing, metalworkers specifically, and industrial labor in general, became increasingly aware that solutions to the persistent "situation of *carestia*" required broader and more fundamental political and economic reforms than periodic salary raises would be able to provide.

Along these new historical dynamics, workers mobilized in increasingly stronger, better funded, and more responsive ways to their own constituent organizations, along a path of mobilization progressively performed by ever more autonomous and creatively devised inter-union pacts and alliances—a course of action that continued to be proscribed by the labor legislations of the period. Within these rich and transformative experiences, labor demands and conceptions on national development acquired a wider scope and the very search for structural solutions to the "problem of *carestia*" involved ever larger and more assertive acts of mobilization.

These promising new trends notwithstanding, as the 1950s were coming to a close, workers also became increasingly skeptical of the prospect that their positions would ever successfully influence official developmental policies and thus lead to a more "popular path" of national development. Consequently, the latter part of the JK Years, as well as the following years, were shaped by growing political polarization, rather than by the ideological consensus and political compromise expected by those directly involved in defining the main economic policies pursued, as well as the very political logic of the developmentalist era. As can be easily imagined, in the mid-term, this proved to be a very concerning evolution, which exerted long-lasting, deeply negative consequences for the country as a whole.

NOTES

1. Labor Day is celebrated on May 1 in Brazil.
2. *A Voz do Metalúrgico* was a monthly published by the Metalworkers' Union of the city of Rio de Janeiro.
3. Since the 1940s, the structure of labor (and business) organizations in Brazil follows a pyramidal logic wherein each labor sector is allowed to organize into only one union at the local (city) level. Unions of every state are then combined into a federation and at the national level one single national confederation is formed. The underlining rationale of the system is corporatist in nature as on the side of employers a similar structure is followed. Every union has to be registered at the Ministry of Labor in order to be allowed to function and labor unions are involved in every aspect of any employed person's professional life, from hiring to firing, regardless of whether the person is affiliated or an active member of his or her specific sector-based union.
4. The National Confederation of Industrial Workers (CNTI) was created in 1946 as part of the hierarchical system of labor representation that is still in operation in Brazil. The organization was a member of the International Confederation of Free Trade Unions (ICFTU) and of its regional branch in Latin America, the Inter-American Regional Organization of Workers (ORIT), vocal opponents of the alleged "communist infiltration" in the labor movement.
5. Cavalcanti was a long-time unionist known to be supportive of the government, who served in this position throughout the Kubitschek administration. A detailed analysis of the behavior of the CNTI is presented later in this chapter.
6. In the 1950s and early 1960s, shark (*tubarão*) was a very popular term for the wealthy. Normally the word was used as a generic label to criticize those whose interests were allegedly opposed to the interests of the poor.
7. *Carestia* refers to deteriorating living standards among the urban poor and throughout the 1950s the term was articulated in most labor pronouncements to make reference to the rising cost of living and related suffering of workers.

The reasons for the rising inflation throughout the decade are complex and the object of much debate in Brazil, as shown in the different views advanced by various political actors in the preceding chapters. Among the main elements of any explanation of the phenomenon is the fact that the period witnessed a massive migration from the countryside to the urban centers, particularly in the center southern region, where Rio de Janeiro and São Paulo are located.

8. "Ecos do Primeiro de Maio," *A Voz do Metalúrgico* (May 1956), cover page and 3.
9. Details on the growing income disparity of the period can be found in Colistete, "Productivity, Wages, and Labor Politics in Brazil."
10. This sociological paradigm was initially advanced in Latin America by Argentine sociologists Torquato Di Tella and Gino Germani in their now classic works, respectively, *Para uma política latino-americana* (Rio de Janeiro: Paz e Terra, 1969), and *Política y sociedad en una epoca de transicion: de la sociedad tradicional a la sociedad de masas* (Buenos Aires: Paidos, 1962).
11. See Lopes, *Sociedade Industrial no Brasil*; Rodrigues, *Sindicato e Desenvolvimento no Brasil*; Leôncio Martins Rodrigues, *Industrialização e Atitudes Operárias*, and *Conflito Industrial e Sindicalismo no Brasil* (São Paulo: Difel, 1966); and Simão, *Sindicato e Estado no Brasil.* Similarly, see Michael Lowy and Sarah Chucid, "Opiniões e atitudes de líderes sindicais metalúrgicos," *Revista Brasileira de Estudos Politicos* 1, no. 13 (1962), 132–69.; Alan Touraine, "Industrialisation et conscience ouvriere à São Paulo," *Sociologie du Travail* III, no. 4 (1961), 77–95; and Alan Touraine and David Pecaut, "Working-Class Consciousness and Economic Development in Latin America," in *Masses in Latin America*, ed. Irving Louis Horowitz (New York: Oxford University Press, 1970), 59–93.
12. The most important piece of labor legislation, which is still in effect today, are the Consolidated Labor Laws (CLT), which were granted by the authoritarian Estado Novo in 1943 and wherein rights and obligations of organized labor are clearly stipulated.
13. In contrast to what had been said about worker mobilization in the 1950s, the events taking place in Contagem and Guarulhos, and later in the ABC region in the late 1970s, were seen as representatives of a new type of syndicalism, defined as more autonomous and democratic than its predecessor of the time, the so-called Populist Republic. See Marco Aurélio Santana, "Entre a Ruptura e a Continuidade: Visões da Histórica do Movimento Sindical Brasileiro," *Revista Brasileira de Ciências Sociais* 14, no. 41 (1999), 103–20.
14. See Ianni, *Industrialização e desenvolvimento social*, and *O Colapso do Populismo no Brasil* (Rio de Janeiro: Civilização Brasileira, 1978); and by Weffort, *O Populismo na política brasileira.*
15. Weffort, *Origens do Sindicalismo Populista no Brasil*, 12.
16. See Robert J. Alexander, *A History of Organized Labor in Brazil* (Westport: Praeger, 2003); Erickson, *The Brazilian Corporative State*; Humphrey, *Capitalist Control and Workers' Struggle*; and Weffort, "Democracia e movimento operário: algumas questões para a história do período 1945–1964," *Revista de Cultura Contemporânea*, no. 1 (1978), 3–11.
17. Of special relevance are Colistete, *Labour Relations and Industrial Performance in Brazil*; Jorge Ferreira, ed., *O populismo e sua história* (Rio de Janeiro: Civilização Brasileira, 2001), and *O Imaginário Trabalhista: getulismo, PTB e cultural política popular, 1945–1964* (Rio de Janeiro: Civilização Brasileira, 2005); John French, *The Brazilian Workers' ABC. Class Conflict and Alliances in Modern São Paulo* (Chapel Hill: University of North Carolina Press, 1992); Angela de Castro Gomes, ed., *Burguesia e Trabalho. Política e Legislação Social no Brasil, 1917–1937* (Rio de Janeiro: Campus, 1979), and *A Invenção do Trabalhismo* (Rio de Janeiro: FGV 1994); Harding, *The Political History of Organized*

Labor; Ricardo Maranhão, *Sindicatos e Democratização. Brasil, 1945–1950* (São Paulo: Brasiliense, 1979).

18. Hélio da Costa, *Em busca da memória* (São Paulo: Scritta, 1995); Fontes, *Trabalhadores e cidadãos*; Alexandre Fortes, et al. *Na Luta por Direitos: Estudos Recentes em História Social do Trabalho* (Campinas: Editora da Unicamp, 1999); Negro, *Linhas de Montagem*; Ramalho, *Estado Patrão e luta operária*; Marco Aurélio Santana, *Homens partidos: comunistas e sindicatos no Brasil* (Rio de Janeiro: Boitempo, 2001); Fernando Teixeira da Silva, *A carga e a culpa: Os operários das Docas de Santos: Direitos e Cultura de Solidariedade, 1937–1968* (São Paulo: Hucitec, 1995); and Joel Wolfe, *Working Women, Working Men: São Paulo and the Rise of Brazil's Working Class, 1900–1955* (Durham: Duke University Press, 1993).
19. Oliver J. Dinius, *Brazil's Steel City: Developmentalism, Strategic Power, and Industrial Relations in Volta Redonda, 1941–1964* (Stanford: Stanford University Press, 2011), 7.
20. Faro and Silva, "A Década de 50 e o Programa de Metas," 61; and Thomas M. Jordan, "Contesting the Terms of Incorporation: Labour and the State in Rio de Janeiro, 1930–1964" (PhD diss., University of Illinois Urbana-Champaign, 2000), 193. For detailed figures on the remarkable rise of the metal-working industry in the 1950s, see Baer, *Industrialization and Economic Development*, 75.
21. Throughout the 1950s industrial production grew from 21 percent to 34 percent of GDP, and while the overall annual industrial growth in the five years of the Targets Plan was 12 percent, in the metalworking sector this rate was 15.7 percent. For details, see IBGE, *Estatísticas Históricas do Brasil.*
22. See Humphrey, *Capitalist Control and Workers' Struggle*; Weffort, *Democracia e movimento operário*; and Jordan Young, *Brasil: 1954–1964, o fim de um ciclo civil* (Rio de Janeiro: Nova Fronteira, 1973).
23. Alternative ways to refer to this labor union are presented in the following works: Jordan, *Contesting the Terms of Incorporation*; Carmen Lúcia E. Lopes, "A Organização Sindical dos Metalúrgicos de São Paulo" (PhD diss., University of São Paulo, 1992); Marco Aurélio Santana, "Partido e militância sindical: a atuação comunista no Sindicato dos Metalúrgicos do Rio de Janeiro STIMMMERJ, 1947–1964" (MA thesis, UFRJ, 1992); Lisa Stuart, "A atuação dos conselhos sindicais na indústria metalúrgica do Rio de Janeiro, de 1953 a 1964" (MA thesis, Universidade Federal Fluminense, 1992).
24. *A Voz do Metalúrgico* IV, No. 43 (Oct 1956), cover page.
25. See the list of Minutes of Meetings of the SindMet/RJ between 1947 and 1957, transcribed and collected by Marco Aurélio Santana and maintained at the Center for Research on Labor and Society at the Federal University of the City of Rio de Janeiro, and the newspaper collection *A Voz do Metalúrgico* at Arquivo de Memória Operária do Rio de Janeiro (AMORJ).
26. Papers of Robert J. Alexander Collection, Reel 3, Series Interview, 1947–1994, Box 5, Folder 14, Interview with Aldo Lombardi, Secretary General of Sindicato dos Metalúrgicos de São Paulo in April 1956. See also *O Metalúgico*, periodical owned and published by the SindMet/SP and Minutes of Meetings of the SindMet/SP from 1955 to 1960 available at the SindMet/SP.
27. See Minutes of Meetings of SindMet/RJ.
28. Two months after Cerqueira's election, Eurypedes Ayres de Castro was elected president of the state-based Federation of Metalworkers Unions of the State of Rio de Janeiro. See Minutes of Meetings of SindMet/RJ.
29. See *Programa da Chapa Renovação* published in *A Voz do Metalúrgico* (May 1955), p. 3.

30. See Santana, *Homens Partidos*.
31. See newspaper collection of *A Voz do Metalúrgico* at AMORJ/UFRJ in Rio de Janeiro.
32. This can be demonstrated by the fact that articles published in both periodicals were regularly mentioned in similar periodicals of other union sectors, such as those of textiles, railroad, and carpentry workers. See labor publications available at Fundo Roberto Morena in the ASMOB Collection, available at the Center for Documentation and Memory (CEDEM).
33. This can be attested when reviewing newspapers from Rio de Janeiro published during the second half of the 1950s, wherein recurrent mentions of the metalworkers' publications of that city can be found. See the newspaper collection available at the Public Archive of the State of Rio de Janeiro, Fundo DPS, Série: Dossiês, Notação 30070.
34. See newspaper collection of *A Voz do Metalúrgico* at AMORJ/UFRJ and newspaper collection of *O Metalúgico* available at the SindMet/SP in São Paulo.
35. Alcebíades Silva, "A Carestia," *O Metalúrgico* (Jun 1955), 7.
36. "O Preço do Pão," *A Voz do Metalúrgico* (Mar 1956), cover page.
37. While the minimum wage had set the standard for salaries nationwide since early in the 1940s, it was common to see sectorial salary rates among urban labor being associated with those of factory workers.
38. Izaltino Pereira, "Editorial Notes," *A Voz do Metalúrgico* (Mar 1956), cover page.
39. "Manifesto de Convocação da Conferência Nacional dos Trabalhadores nas Indústrias Metalúrgicas, Mecânicas e de Material Elétrico," *A Voz do Metalúrgico* (Dec 1955).
40. *O Metalúrgico*, Special Issue on the National Conference of Metalworkers of Brazil (May 1956).
41. Ibid., 6–8.
42. "Mesa Redonda dos Sindicatos Paulistas," *O Metalúrgico* (Sep 1955), 3.
43. "Apelo ao Novo Governo," *O Metalúrgico* (Dec 1955), editorial column, p. 2.
44. Heraclides dos Santos, "Atentado às Liberdades Democráticas," *A Voz do Metalúrgico* (Mar 1957), 3.
45. "A Operação Pan-Americana," *A Voz do Metalúrgico* (Aug 1958), editorial column, p. 3.
46. Heraclides dos Santos, "O Congelamento de Preços de JK," *A Voz do Metalúrgico* (Feb 1958), 3.
47. See the deliberations and minutes of the Metalworkers' National Congresses that took place in 1957 and 1959 in Porto Alegre and Itanhaém, respectively, as will be indicated below.
48. "Desnacionalização da Indústria Automobilística," *A Voz do Metalúrgico* (Apr 1959), 6.
49. "Não são fundamentais as empresas estrangeiras para o Brasil,"*A Voz do Metalúrgico* (Oct 1959), cover page.
50. *Relatório Final da Segunda Conferência Sindical Nacional* in Fundo ASMOB, A1, 41 (4), CEDEM.
52. Ibid.
53. "A situação da carestia," *Tribuna Sindical* (Aug 1956), cover page.
54. See *Tribuna Sindical*, issues of September and October 1956, and February and April 1958.
55. See Heloísa de Souza Martins, *O Estado e a Burocratização do Sindicato no Brasil* (São Paulo: Hucitec, 1979) and Antonio Luigi Negro and Fernando Teixeira da Silva, "Trabalhadores, sindicatos e politica (1945–1964)," in

O Brasil Republicano: o tempo da experiência democrática, da democratização de 1945 ao golpe civil-militar de 1964, eds. Jorge Ferreira and Lucilia de Almeida Neves Delgado (Rio de Janeiro: Civilização Brasileira), 47–96.
56. See *Tribuna Sindical*, issues of July and August 1957.
57. "Grande Movimento Grevista dos Trabalhadores Paulistas," *Tribuna Sindical* (Oct 1957), cover page.
58. Ibid.
59. "Comemoração de 10 anos da CNTI com presença de JK," *Tribuna Sindical* (Nov 1956), cover page.
60. "Carta Econômica da CNTI," *Tribuna Sindical* (Nov 1956), 2.
61. *A Voz do Metalúrgico* (Dec 1959), 3–5.
62. Presidential Decree number 1,522 of December 26, 1951.
63. Relatório das Atividades do Conselho Coordenador do Abastecimento e Apresentação do Plano Nacional de Abastecimento, Fundo Conselho Coordenador do Abastecimento, CODES, Caixa 2, National Archive.
64. Relatório de Estudos sobre o Plano Nacional de Abastecimento of January 1960, Fundo Conselho Coordenador do Abastecimento, CODES, Caixa 2, National Archive.
65. Minuta da Situação da Agricultura, of January 1959, Fundo Conselho Coordenador do Abastecimento, CODES, Caixa 2, National Archive.
66. *Programa de Contenção de Preços dos Alimentos: Relatório Oficial do Conselho Coordenador do Abastecimento* (February 1959), Fundo Conselho Coordenador do Abastecimento, CODES, Caixa 2, National Archive.
67. *Plano Nacional de Abastecimento: Análise de Conjuntura do Abastecimento*, Fundo Roberto Campos, RC e/ed 1958.12/00, CPDOC Archive.
68. See Presidência da República, *Plano Trienal de Desenvolvimento Econômico e Social, 1963–65* (Rio de Janeiro, 1962).
69. Roberto Campos, *Cinco Verdades sobre a Economia Brasileira*, Fundo Roberto Campo, LL pi Campos, R. 1958.00.00, CPDOC Archive.
70. Fundo Conselho Coordenador do Abastecimento, CODES, Caixa 7, National Archive.
71. See *Nova Lei do Salário Mínimo, Decreto Presidencial no. 39,604-A, of July 14, 1956*, Fundo Roberto Morena, ASMOB Collection atCEDEM.
72. Both tables are based on data available in IGBE, *Estatísticas Históricas do Brasil.* Detailed information can be also found in Lessa, "Fifteen Years of Economic Policy in Brazil."
73. For more on these developments, see Harding, *The Political History of Organized Labor in Brazil.*
74. "Criado o Departamento Inter-Sindical de Estatística," *O Metalúrgico* (Feb 1956), 5.
75. Ibid.
76. "Refundado o Pacto de Unidade Inter-Sindical," *O Metalúrgico* (Jul 1956), cover page.
77. Ibid.
78. Detailed information on these events can be found in Cliff Welch, "Labor Internationalism: U.S. Involvement in Brazilian Unions, 1945–1965," *Latin American Research Review* 30, no. 2 (1995), 61–89.
79. "Editorial," *Boletim Sindicalista do Brasil* V, no. 41 (Aug 1959).
80. Anthony Carew, "Towards a Free Trade Union Centre: The International Confederation of Free Trade Unions (1949–1972)," in *The International Confederation of Free Trade Unions*, ed. Marcel van der Linden (Bern: Peter Lang, 2000), 287–339.
81. Papers of Robert J. Alexander Collection, Reel 3, Series Interview, 1947–1994, Box 5, Folder, 14, Interview with Diocleciano de Holanda Cavalcanti in March 1956.

82. Papers of Robert J. Alexander Collection, Reel 3, Series Interview, 1947–1994, Box 5, Folder, 14, Interview with Izaltino Pereira in August 1959.
83. Papers of Robert J. Alexander Collection, Reel 3, Series Interview, 1947–1994, Box 5, Folder, 14, Interview with Aldo Lombardi, Secretary General of Sindicato dos Metalúrgicos de São Paulo in April 1956.
84. Papers of Robert J. Alexander Collection, Reel 3, Series Interview, 1947–1994, Box 5, Folder, 14, Interview with John Fishburn, U.S. Labor Attaché in August 1959.
85. Papers of Robert J. Alexander Collection, Reel 3, Series Interview, 1947–1994, Box 5, Folder 14 Interview with Irving Salert, U.S. Labor Attaché in March 1956.
86. Jorge Ferreira, *Prisioneiros do Mito. Cultura e imaginário político dos comunistas no Brasil (1930–1956)* (Rio de Janeiro/Niteroi: Eduff/Mauad, 2002).
87. Moises Vinhas, *O Partidão: a luta por um partido de massas, 1922–1974* (São Paulo: Hucitec, 1982).
88. José Antonio Segatto, *Reforma ou revolução: as vicissitudes políticas do PCB, 1945–1964* (Rio de Janeiro: Civilização Brasileira, 1995), 33.
89. Of special relevance for this argument, see Marco Aurélio Santana, "Bravos companheiros: a aliança comunista-trabalhista no sindicalismo brasileiro (1945–1964)," in *Nacionalismo e reformismo radical*, eds. Jorge Ferreira and Daniel A. Reis (Rio de Janeiro: Civilização Brasileira, 2007), vol. 2: 238–77. How this historic trend impacted the metalworkers' union in Rio de Janeiro is well-described in Marco Aurélio Santana, "Trabalhadores e militância sindical: a relação partido/sindicato/classe no Sindicato dos Metalúrgicos do Rio de Janeiro, 1947–1964," in *Trabalho e Tradição Sindical no Rio de Janeiro a Trajetória dos Metalúrgicos*, eds. José Ricardo Ramalho and Marco Aurélio Santana (Rio de Janeiro: DP&A, 2001), 165–212.
90. *Novos Rumos* (Feb 28, 1959), 4.
91. *Novos Rumos* (Apr 3, 1959), 5 and 7.
92. *Novos Rumos* (May 29, 1959), 6.
93. *Novos Rumos* (Jun 19, 1959), 3.
94. *Novos Rumos*, (Sep 17, 1959), 10; and (Nov 19, 1959), 8.
95. *Novos Rumos* (Jan 1, 1960), 5.
96. *Novos Rumos* (Sep 24, 1959), 3.
97. *Boletim DIEESE*, *Participação da mão-de-obra no desenvolvimento industrial do Brasil* 7, nos. 1, 5, and 7 (1960).
98. "Batalha de Reajustamento de Salários," *O Metalúrgico* (Jul 1957), cover page.
99. "Metalúrgicos Decidem: 45 Por Cento de Aumento," *O Metalúrgico* (Aug 1957), cover page.
100. Details can be found in Fontes, "Centenas de estopins acesos ao mesmo tempo—a greve dos 400 mil, piquetes e a organização dos trabalhadores em São Paulo (1957)," in *Na Luta por Direitos: Estudos Recentes em História Social do Trabalho*, Alexandre Fortes et al. (Campinas, 1999) 145–72; and Colistete, *Labour Relations and Industrial Performance in Brazil.*
101. "Vitória da Unidade dos Trabalhadores," *O Metalúrgico* (Nov–Dec 1957), 1–5.
102. "Resoluções do Primeiro Congresso Nacional dos Trabalhadores nas Indústrias Metalúrgicas, Mecânicas e de Material Elétrico do Brasil," *O Metalúrgico* (Jan 1958), 4–6.
103. "Resoluções do Segundo Congresso Nacional dos Trabalhadores na Indústrias, Metalúrgicas, Mecânicas e de Material Elétrico do Brasil," *O Metalúrgico* (May 1959), 4 and 5. See also "Publicações do Segundo Congresso Nacional dos Metalúrgicos," Fundo Roberto Morena: Archivo Storico del Movimento Operario Brasiliano, Cod. OS-0145, Public Archive of the State of São Paulo.

104. *O Metalúrgico* (Jan–Feb 1959), 2–4.
105. "Salve o III Congresso Sindical Nacional dos Trabalhadores," *A Voz do Metalúrgico* (Aug 1960), 12.
106. "As Próximas Eleições," *A Voz do Metalúrgico* (Feb 1960), editorial page, p. 3.
107. "Todos Poderes Contra o Presidente," *O Metalúrgico* (Jan/Feb 1959), 3.
108. *Novos Rumos* (Mar 12, 1959), 1.
109. *O Metalúrgico*, issues of March, April, and May 1959.
110. The general press of São Paulo and Rio de Janeiro also published several articles on the negotiations between unionists and representatives of the Labor Ministry as a way to preempt the political costs that these public gathering would entail for the administration. For a sample of these pieces, see *A Notícia* (Apr 4, 1959); *O Dia* (Apr 5, 1959); and *Última Hora* (Mar 24, 1959), Fundo DPS, Série: Dossiês, #30070, Public Archive of the State of Rio de Janeiro.
111. See *Diário de Notícias* (Mar 15, 1959); and *Gazeta de Notícias* (Mar 20, 1959), Fundo DPS, Série: Dossiês #30074, Public Archive of the State of Rio de Janeiro.
112. See *Ultima Hora* (Aug 26 and Sep 2, 1959); *O Dia* (Sep 2, 1959); and *Jornal do Brasil* (Sep 9, 1959), Fundo DPS, Série: Dossiês #30069, Public Archive of the State of Rio de Janeiro.
113. "Protesto Geral dos Trabalhadores de São Paulo," *O Metalúrgico* (Sep 1959), cover page. See also "Manifesto ao Povo de São Paulo," Dossiê DEOPS, Cod. OS-0145, Public Archive of the State of São Paulo.
114. Fundo DPS, Série: Dossiês, Notação 30074, Public Archive of the State of Rio de Janeiro.
115. See *O Metalúrgico*, issues of June, July, and August 1960.
116. Fundo Roberto Morena, Archivo Storico del Movimento Operario Brasiliano, Cod. OS-0145, Public Archive of the State of São Paulo.
117. This political selection divided, once again, the national political spectrum into one candidate supported by the Social Democracy Party (PSD) and the Brazilian Workers Party (PTB), and another candidate supported by the National Democratic Union (UDN).
118. "As Próximas Eleições," *A Voz do Metalúrgico* (Feb 1960), editorial page, p. 3.

Conclusion

In the final hours of March 1964, a military coup ushered an authoritarian regime into power in Brazil, thus bringing to an end not only democratic rule, but also the developmentalist experiment of the 1950s. Similarly, these events abruptly and violently halted the creative intellectual and cultural innovations involved in, as well as the growing empowerment of popular social segments deriving from the developmentalist experiments of the first decades after World War II. Even though the coup was supported by key former players of the JK administration, including industrialists and politicians closely aligned with the president—and even Kubitschek, in the end, would agree with the removal of the enfeebled administration headed by Vargas's former protégé and JK's own pivotal vice-president, João Goulart—the twenty-one long years of political violence, censorship, and exclusionary economic policies Brazilian society subsequently endured were a direct consequence of the gradual political radicalization that defined much of the postwar era. But how was it possible that such a tragic outcome would mark the closing of one of the country's most promising political and economic periods?

The early 1960s were certainly defined by growing economic difficulties (e.g., rising inflation and stalled economic growth) and, especially, political and ideological polarization. It is also clear, though, that beyond these ominous trends that helped shape the rising social turbulence of the time, much of the support the right-wing coup plotters received from the national media, key political figures, and significant portions of the public opinion, was also grounded on the growing and widespread disappointment with the very developmental path pursued in the preceding years. The developmentalist era certainly represented one of Brazil's most auspicious opportunities for pursuing fast-paced economic transformations within a democratic regime. It was indeed then that the goal of industrialization assumed political prominence for growing members of a diverse set of social segments. But, as demonstrated in the previous sections, no univocal position about the developmental path the country should undertake ever emerged, and as the policies of the federal administration gradually took hold ideological differences assumed predominance in the political debates and associated divergent courses of action of the period.

Inspired by these key historical findings and aimed at advancing a more comprehensive and critical review of these transformative historical events, the analysis presented here centered on the prolific ideational reflection surrounding the topic of national development taking place in Brazil in the postwar years. Similarly, in order to showcase in vivid terms the many different developmental conceptions that helped defined the most influential discussions and political trends of the period, the investigation largely focused on the experiences of the JK Years, when an ambitious agenda of economic reform was implemented. The study tried to reconstruct, as much as possible, the historical context in which these events occurred, while also advancing a much-needed general assessment of the legacies of these foundational developmental experiences.

By the same token, closely grounded in the rich historiography on the mid-twentieth century in Brazil, as well as on both the important traditional and the more recent literature of development studies, particularly that which looked at fast-industrializing societies, this book detailed the many facets of the rapid evolution large segments of Brazilian society experienced in the postwar era. In addition to reviewing how broad sectors of the better-articulated political forces would all converge in support, at least initially, of the goal of fast-paced industrialization, the work detailed how key public negotiators perceived and interfaced with broader, regional, and global socio-economic and political dynamics of the period. Much in the same way, the study provided an in-depth examination of the developmental agenda and associated political behavior held by key, and ever more vocal and influential, non-state actors.

Central to understanding how the post-1964 military regime gathered political support, it is important to note that, as demonstrated above, while the federal administration actively sought to raise the productivity of the Brazilian economy by deepening structural linkages between domestic industrial production lines and the rapidly expanding international capitalist economy, key business and professional associations (who espoused purely economically oriented views, similar to those held by key policy operators at the Council of Development) were becoming increasingly skeptical about the pace, as well as the specific means (state-led) used to promote fast industrial growth.

Conversely, and thus further deepening the political divide that marked the closing years of the flourishing democratic regime of the postwar period, nationalist intellectuals argued ever more vocally that promoting true national development required decreasing the interconnections between the Brazilian economy and foreign economic interest while alternatively strengthening the role of the national government in order to attend to the needs of an ever more industrialized nation. Moreover, at the forefront of the labor mobilization of the period, industrial workers demanded, ever more independently and assertively, that the country's main centers of power become more responsive, by means of more economically inclusive initiatives, to the *real* needs of the majority of the country's population.

As similarly indicated, the policies the Brazilian developmental state sought to implement in mid-century were largely inspired by the idea that the central government should focus its attention on creating the infrastructural, financial, and legal conditions needed to attract and support different forms of investment capital so that the overall competitiveness of the Brazilian economy could be improved. Consistent with this very perspective, key institutional, political, ideological, and even cultural elements for deepening the path of industrialization—which was increasingly considered to be a *sine qua non* requirement toward the goal of becoming a fully developed society—were instrumentally coalesced through a variety of historical events shaping the developmentalist policies of the 1950s. Notably, the Brazilian economy faced the growing challenge deriving from declining revenues for its agriculture commodity exports, all the while the country's political and intellectual leaders witnessed the emergence of a regional body of policies for import substitutive industrialization, a growing labor segment ready to be mobilized for nationalistic economic reforms became ever more visible, and a set of similar trends unfolded across the globe.

Despite becoming more and more directly or indirectly involved in the developmental experiences of the period, the Brazilian state was not monolithic in its views, nor did it operate under one single political directive beyond that of fast economic growth. Similarly, in contrast to much of the historiography on the period, while substantial enthusiasm for the guiding projects of the economic transformation being implemented did exist, this reality did not reflect the existence of any formal type of broad political compromise, but rather the fact that the goal of national development had risen to the top position in the agenda of some of the most influential sociopolitical actors of the period.

Growing disagreements about the definition of national development reflected not only conceptual ideological divergences, but also the different commitments of the federal structures of power. Disputes over how to best promote national development, therefore, reveal the politicized nature of state intervention, and the very controversies and hesitations that characterized the period provided key opportunities for stronger interest groups to capture the functioning of public agencies according to their specific demands—as was best displayed in the experiences surrounding the implementation of an auto-making industry in the country.

Building upon the goals and reforms implemented by Vargas early in the decade, Kubitschek shrewdly innovated in the purview of the executive branch over the industrial plans of the federal administration. The national government then became the ultimate and essential provider of both the regulatory framework as well as much of the funds needed to sustain a growing market for locally produced industrial goods, whereas multinational corporations committed to meeting the industrial goals set out by federal decision makers, and national industrialists agreed to act as junior partners in the implementation of ambitious industrial projects seen as quintessential symbols of a modern society. Along these lines, moving beyond Vargas's accomplishments and learning from his mistakes—by setting a course of planned rapid industrial promotion, which reconciled conservative political groups with increasingly influential new socio-political actors, including national industrialists and growing active sectors of organized labor—JK proved vastly more effective in implementing an ambitious, though eminently conservative developmental agenda in both its domestic and international elements.

Ironically (if not tragically), it was this very administration, one of the best institutionally equipped and politically supported for setting a course for long-term sustained economic growth with significant levels of social inclusion, that ultimately remained trapped within the short-term logic of the so-called populist political regime. In fact, the reluctance to respond in any significant fashion to the many pertinent and ever more vocal developmental views and demands advanced by actively mobilized social groups—including key sectors of the national intelligentsia, business and professional associations, and organized labor, as examined above—would rapidly drain this otherwise promising political coalition of much needed legitimacy. What is more, despite the ambitious goals set out in the Targets Plan, the widespread sense of optimism about the country's economic potential and viability, the significant economic growth achieved, and the many important industrial projects implemented, by the end of the decade, most Brazilians beyond the high- and middle-income urban sectors saw few positive benefits of the developmental efforts of the 1950s, and the majority of urban dwellers were negatively affected by the rising cost of living brought on by these very developmental efforts.

The collapse of the democratic regime in March 1964 undeniably derived in many ways from the process of economic deterioration and ideological polarization that defined the intervening years of the politically weak Goulart administration (1961–1964), as well as from the growing new Cold War global commitments of the U.S., which once again proved less willing to accept social experimentation in Latin America than its benign rhetoric of progress would have indicated. It is important to note, however, as demonstrated here, that the very origins of these turbulent historical events are found in the transformative and purportedly harmonious developmental experiences of the 1950s. It is therefore warranted to assume that what provoked the final destabilization of the democratic political system in operation in Brazil in mid-century was not that popular demands were rising at an exceedingly fast rate, but rather the fact that the wider social conceptions and expectations related to national development were flattened (when not totally shut out) into a top-down plan centered exclusively on fostering fast rates of absolute economic growth.

In the end, even though much was realized—as the industrial base of country was radically transformed and even a new capital city was created from the ground up—the very industrial path chosen by Brazilian authorities ultimately favored foreign capital and labor-saving technology, which did not fulfill the promises and expectations of job creation. Even in the said-to-be successful cases, the new industrial activities (e.g., auto-making) were only able to take hold in the country due to its highly protected domestic market—an industrial course that proved, in the long run, to be less beneficial to raising living standards than the export-led policies implemented in Southeast Asian countries in the same period. Rising demands for better-paying jobs and new consumption patterns indeed proved difficult to achieve within the fragile political alliances of the period, leading to long-term economic difficulties and persistent social inequalities.

In this sense, despite the fact that the idea of promoting fast-paced industrialization on the basis of direct or indirect government action, prominently inserted into the political agenda of Latin America in the aftermath of World War II, represented a major and promising historical innovation, the actual process by which these projects were implemented tended to homogenize the needs and interests of each country's population in ways that deepened social tensions and ideological polarization. In fact, though instrumental in positioning Latin America within the global debates pertaining to the so-called underdeveloped condition, the developmental projects devised in the 1950s in Brazil reduced multiples narratives of the nation into a political project that, above all, helped perpetuate the country's historically unfair socio-economic structure. Equally relevant, considering that national development was largely pursued in ways that did not harness support from the majority of traditional and emerging politically assertive social groups—as the national government flattened down a complex "debate" on national development into a uni-dimensional project of fast economic growth, almost exclusively focused on rapid industrial promotion by means of foreign investment and technology—political instability and its harsh authoritarian-associated response came to the fore only a few years after the implementation of the highly praised and widely supported Targets Plan.

The recent experience of high rates of economic growth with initial levels of more meaningful social inclusion has motivated a renewed discussion about the long-term direction of national development and the different mechanisms of state intervention in Brazil's economy and society. And although the country has been increasingly perceived as an emergent nation with a domestic market of more than 140 million consumers, serious challenges towards the consolidation of a politically sustainable and socially equitable insertion into the globalized economy remain. Increasingly dissatisfied with the poor quality of public services amidst growing numbers of users, the perceived rising levels of political corruption, and the escalating costs of living, particularly for the urban poor, millions of Brazilians took to the streets in June 2013 to demand more democratic and attentive responses from all levels of government. Challenging the very institutions of political power, protesters forcefully pushed their own agenda into what seemed to be an era of economic prosperity and optimism related to upcoming global sporting events, such as the soccer World Cup scheduled to take place in June 2014.

Were Brazilians to revisit the experiences of the mid-twentieth century, valuable lessons would be certain to emerge. Indeed, taking into account the prospects and challenges of the rapid but only partially socially-responsive and sustainable economic growth Brazil experienced in the last decade, this book critically revisited the paradigmatic phase of fast-paced industrialization and socio-economic reforms that defined Brazilian society in the 1950s. The investigation challenged customary interpretations of the phenomenon of populism in Latin America, as well as much of the still prevailing political and economic reflection on the topic of development promotion in the second half of the twentieth century.

As seen, the experiences involved in the process of fast-paced, state-led development promotion in the 1950s in Brazil were influenced by a wide range of mobilized social segments, all of which sought to advance their own views, conceptions, political positions, and projects of national development. And despite the heretofore unprecedented levels of growth delivered and the initial changes in the main lines of the socio-economic landscape, the very logic of the populist regime then in place ultimately hindered higher levels of social and political inclusion, leading to rapidly growing social frustration and associated political polarization.

In the end, in lieu of confirming the teleological tone present in studies describing the unstable nature of political institutions in fast-changing societies, this investigation revealed the complex but also undetermined course of historical events. Indeed, should a more inclusive approach to national development been pursued, alternative scenarios could have been envisioned. Future studies may certainly offer an even richer characterization of the multidimensional dynamics involved in the debates and concrete initiatives unfolding in the country in the turbulent context of the mid-twentieth century. It is my hope, however, that this examination may contribute towards a more profound understanding of how political, cultural, and even ideational negotiations may indeed impact socio-cultural, economic, and political realities undergoing fast-paced transformations, such as those occurring in Brazil during its most important and fascinating developmentalist experience.

Bibliography

UNPUBLISHED PRIMARY SOURCES

The reading of unpublished primary sources was conducted in the following archives and collections:

Archive of the Center for Research and Documentation on Contemporary Brazilian History (CPDOC) of the Getúlio Vargas Foundation (FGV) in Rio de Janeiro [CPDOC Archive]:

Fundo Benedito Valadares
Fundo Castilho Cabral
Fundo Edmundo Macedo Soares
Fundo Ernani do Amaral Peixoto
Fundo Getúlio Vargas
Fundo Gustavo Capanema
Fundo Hermes Lima
Fundo João Goulart
Fundo Juscelino Kubitschek de Oliveira
Fundo Lucas Lopes
Fundo Negrão de Lima
Fundo Nelson Melo
Fundo Roberto Campos

National Archive (AN) in Rio de Janeiro:

Fundo Conselho do Desenvolvimento
Fundo Fonográfico do Sesi
Fundo Presidência da República
Fundo Conselho Coordenador do Abastecimento

Archive of the National Bank of Economic and Social Development (BNDES) in Rio de Janeiro:

Projeto Memória

Center of Research on Labor and Society at the Federal University of the City of Rio de Janeiro (NETS):

Minutes of internal meetings of the Metalworkers' Union of the city of Rio de Janeiro

Public Archive of the State of Rio de Janeiro (ArqP/RJ):

Fundo Divisão de Política Pública e Social (DPS)

Center of Documentation and Memory (CEDEM) of the State University of São Paulo:

Fundo Roberto Morena
ASMOB Collection

Archive of the Metalworkers' Union of the city of São Paulo (SindMet/SP):

Minutes of internal meetings

Public Archive of the State of São Paulo (ArqP/SP):

Fundo Roberto Morena

David M. Rubenstein Rare Books and Manuscripts Library at Duke University:

J. Walter Thompson Company Archives

PUBLISHED PRIMARY DOCUMENTS

The reading of published primary materials took place in the institutions listed below:

Anfavea Archive
Biblioteca Pública Estadual Luis de Bessa
Biblioteca da Fundação João Pinheiro
Biblioteca Histórica do Ministério da Fazenda
Central Library of the Catholic University of Rio de Janeiro (PUC-RJ)
Edgard Leuronth Archive (AEL) at the State University of Campinas
Mario Henrique Simonsen Library at the Getúlio Vargas Foundation
National Archive
Octávio Ianni Library at the State University of Campinas
Regional Library of the Economic Institute of Applied Economics (IPEA)
Research Center of the Brazilian Institute of Geography and Statistics (IBGE)

The list of the most important published primary documents examined is presented below:

Associação Nacional da Indústria de Tratores, Caminhões, Automóveis e Veículos Similares. *A Indústria Brasileira de Automóveis Presta Esclarecimento ao Público*. São Paulo, 1957.
BNDE. *Situação Atual e Perspectivas Imediatas da Economia Brasileira*. Dec 1955.
———. *Exposição sobre o Programa de Reaparelhamento Econômico: Exercício 1956*. Rio de Janeiro, 1956.
———. *Exposição sobre o Programa de Reaparelhamento Econômico: Exercício 1957*. Rio de Janeiro, 1957.
———. *Exposição sobre o Programa de Reaparelhamento Econômico. Exercício do ano 1959*. Rio de Janeiro, 1959.

———. *VI Exposição sobre o Programa de Reaparelhamento Econômico.* Rio de Janeiro, 1960.
———. *Lucas Lopes: 30 Anos do BNDES.* Projeto Memória: Primeira Fase. Rio de Janeiro, 1982.
———. *Entrevista com Rômulo de Almeida.* Projeto Memória Primeira Fase. Rio de Janeiro, 1982.
Committee on Foreign Relations of the United States Senate. *Inter-American Relations Report: A Collection of Documents, Legislation, Descriptions of Inter-American Organization, and Other Material Pertaining to Inter-American Affairs.* Washington, D.C.: Government Printing Office, December 1988.
CONCLAP, *Carta Econômica de Teresópolis, Documento da Conferência das Classes Produtoras do Brasil.* Rio de Janeiro, 1945
Confederação Nacional da Indústria. *Análise e Perspectivas da Indústria Automobilística.* Rio de Janeiro, 1960.
Conselho do Desenvolvimento. *Documento de Trabalho. Número 1. Relatório Reservado.* Rio de Janeiro: Presidência da República, April 1956.
———. *Documento Agricultura e Alimentação.* Volume I. Rio de Janeiro: Presidência da República, 1957.
———. "Relatório das atividades do GEIA." In *Plano de Desenvolvimento Econômico Industrial de Base.* Volume 1, Indústria Automobilística. Rio de Janeiro: Presidência da República, 1957.
———. *Relatório sobre a Meta 27: Indústria Automobilística.* Rio de Janeiro: Presidência da República, Serviço de Documentação, 1959.
———. *Relatório Geral para o Exercício 1959.* Rio de Janeiro: Presidência da República, 1960.
———. *Relatório Geral para o Exercício 1960.* Rio de Janeiro: Presidência da República, 1961.
Conselho Nacional de Economia, *Exposição Geral da Situação Econômica do País.* Rio de Janeiro: Presidência da República, 1956.
———. *Exposição Geral da Situação Econômica do País.* Rio de Janeiro: Presidência da República, 1959.
———. *Exposição Geral da Situação Econômica do País.* Rio de Janeiro: Presidência da República, 1960.
———. *Exposição Geral da Situação Econômica do País.* Rio de Janeiro: Presidência da República, 1961.
Department of State. *Nationalism in Brazil.* Intelligence Report No. 8002. Washington, D.C., Bureau of Intelligence and Research, July 24, 1959.
Export-Import Bank. *Semiannual Report.* Washington, D.C., 1953.
Governo do Estado de Minas Gerais, *Plano de Recuperação Econômia e Fomento da Produção.* Belo Horizonte, 1947.
Grupo Misto de Estudos BNDE-CEPAL. *Análise e Projeções do Desenvolvimento Econômico.* Rio de Janeiro: BNDE, 1957.
Institute of Inter-American Affairs, Foreign Operations Administration. *Report of the Joint Brazil-United States Technical Commission.* Washington, D.C., 1949.
———. *The Development of Brazil: Report of the Joint Brazil-United States Economic Development Commission.* Washington, D.C., 1953.
Kubitschek de Oliveira, Juscelino. *Ao Povo Mineiro: palestra lida pelo rádio no transcurso da metade do mandato governamental.* Belo Horizonte: Imprensa Oficial, 1953.

———. *Palestras Dirigidas ao Povo Mineiro pelo Rádio em 1951–1952*. Belo Horizonte: Imprensa Oficial, 1953.
———. *Realidades e Perspectivas: discursos dos 4 anos de governo em Minas Gerais, 1951–1955*. Belo Horizonte: Coleção Cultural, 1955.
———. *Discursos proferidos no primeiro ano do mandato presidencial, 1956*. Rio de Janeiro: Presidência da República, 1956.
———. *Mensagem ao Congresso Nacional*. Rio de Janeiro: Departamento de Imprensa Nacional, 1956.
———. *Mensagem ao Congresso Nacional*. Rio de Janeiro: Departamento de Imprensa Nacional, 1957.
———. *Discursos proferidos no segundo ano de mandato presidencial, 1957*. Rio de Janeiro: Serviço de Documentação da Presidência da República, 1958.
———. *Exposição da Operação Pan-Americana `as Forças Armadas no Palácio do Itamaraty, no dia 17 de julho de 1958*. Rio de Janeiro: Ministério das Relações Exteriores, Seção de Publicações, 1958.
———. *Industrialização: batalha pela própria sobrevivência da nacionalidade*. Speech given at the graduation ceremony of the School of Industrial Engineering of the Industrial Federation of São Paulo, May 1958. São Paulo: FIESP/CIESP, Serviço de Publicações, 1958.
———. *Mensagem ao Congresso Nacional*. Rio de Janeiro: Departamento de Imprensa Nacional, 1958.
———. *Operacion Pan Americana: Compilacion de Documentos—I*. Rio de Janeiro: Servicio de Documentacion de la Presidencia de la Republica, 1958.
———. *Discursos proferidos no terceiro ano de mandato presidencial, 1958*. Rio de Janeiro: Serviço de Documentação da Presidência da República, 1959.
———. "Mensagem Presidencial XXVIII." In *Discursos*. Rio de Janeiro: Imprensa Nacional, 1960.
———. *O Avanço do Brasil: o governo e os problemas do desenvolvimento econômico brasileiro*. Speech given at the National Economic Council, January 16, 1961. Rio de Janeiro: Departamento de Imprensa Nacional, 1961.
Ministério da Fazenda, *Programa de Estabilização Monetária para o Terceiro Quadrimestre de 1958 e Ano de 1959*, Vol. I, Rio de Janeiro, 1958.
Ministério do Planejamento. *Índices de crescimento econômico médio do produto real na indústria*. Brasília: 1967.
Ministério do Planejamento e Coordenação Geral. *Programa Estratégico de Desenvolvimento, 1968–1970*. Vol. 2. Brasília, 1968.
———. *A Industrialização Brasileira: Diagnósticos e Perpectivas, Estudo Especial do Programa Estratégico de Desenvolvimento, 1968–1970*. Brasilia, 1969.
Presidência da República. *As Metas do Governo: 50 anos em 5*. Rio de Janeiro, 1959.
———. *Relatório Geral de Exportações e Importações, 1947–1960*. Rio de Janeiro, 1960.
———. *Relatório Geral do Conselho do Desenvolvimento*. Four volumes. Rio de Janeiro, 1960.
———. *Resenha do Governo do Presidente Juscelino Kubitschek*. Four volumes. Rio de Janeiro: Presidência da Republica, Serviço de Documentação, 1960.
Sindicato da Indústria de Tratores, Caminhões, Automóveis e Veículos Similares no Estado de São Paulo. *Indústria automobilística: esboço histórico de suas origens e desenvolvimento no Brasil*. São Paulo, 1960.
Superintendência da Moeda e do Crédito. *Relatório do Banco do Brasil*. Rio de Janeiro, 1964.

United Nations. *Post War Price Relations in Trade between Under-Developed and Industrialized Countries*. New York: Economic and Social Council, 1949.

———. *International Co-Operation in a Latin American Development Policy. Preliminary Report of the Secretariat of the United Nations Economic Commission for Latin America Prepared for the Meeting of Ministers of Finance at the Fourth Meeting of the Inter-American Economic and Social Council of the Organization of American States to be held in Rio de Janeiro, November 1954*. New York: United Nations, 1954.

———. *International Cooperation in Latin America: A Development Policy. Preliminary Report of the Secretariat of the United Nations Economic Commission for Latin America Prepared for the Meeting of Ministers of Finance at the Fourth Meeting of the Inter-American Economic and Social Council of the Organization of American States to be held in Rio de Janeiro, November 1954*. New York: Economic and Social Council, 1954.

Vargas, Getúlio D. *Mensagem ao Congresso Nacional*. Rio de Janeiro: Departamento de Imprensa Nacional, 1951.

PERIODICALS EXAMINED

The list of the periodicals examined includes:

A Voz do Metalúrgico, Published by the Metalworkers' Union of the city of Rio de Janeiro (SindMet/RJ)

Boletim DIEESE
Published by Inter-Union Department of Economic Studies and Statistics (DIEESE)

Boletim Informativo da FIESP
Published by the Industrial Federation of the State of São Paulo (FIESP)

Boletim Sindicalista do Brasil.
Published by the Regional Inter-American Labor Organization CIOSL-ORIT

Conjuntura Econômica
Published by the Getúlio Vargas Foundation

Desenvolvimento & Conjuntura
Published by the National Industrial Confederation (CNI)

Novos Rumos
Published by the Brazilian Communist Party (PCB)

O Metalúgico
Published by the Metalworkers' Union of the city of São Paulo (SindMet/SP)

Revista da Associação Comercial
Published by Commercial Association of Rio de Janeiro

Revista do Conselho Nacional de Economia
Published by National Economic Council (CNE)

Revista do Serviço do Público
Published by the Administative Department of Public Servants (DASP)

Revista Industrial de São Paulo
Published by the Industrial Federation of the State of São Paulo (FIESP)

Sesi Jornal
Published by the Social Service of the Industry (SESI/CNI)

Tribuna Sindical
Published by the National Confederation of Industrial Workers (CNTI)

SECONDARY WORKS CITED

Abreu, Alzira Alves de. "Nationalism et Action Politique au Brésil: Une Étude sur L'ISEB." PhD diss., Université René-Descartes, Paris V, 1975.

———. "Os suplementos literários: os intelectuais e a imprensa nos anos 50." In *A Imprensa em Transição: O Jornalismo Brasileiro nos Anos 50*. Edited by Alzira Alves Abreu. 13–60. Rio de Janeiro: FGV, 1996.

Abreu, Alzira Alves de, and Israel Beloch, eds. *Dicionário Histórico-Biográfico Brasileiro Pós -30*. Rio de Janeiro: Editora da FGV, 2001.

Abreu, Marcelo de Paiva, ed. *A Ordem do Progresso: Cem Anos de Política Econômica Republicana, 1889–1989*. São Paulo: Campus, 1990.

———. "Crise, Crescimento e Modernização Autoritária: 1930–1945." In *A Ordem do Progresso: Cem Anos de Política Econômica Republicana, 1889–1989*, edited by Marcelo de Paiva Abreu, 73–104. Rio de Janeiro: Campus, 1990.

———. *The Brazilian Economy, 1945–1964*. Texto para Discussão, no. 414, Departamento de Economia. Rio de Janeiro: Catholic University, 2000.

Abreu, Marcelo de Paiva, and Dionísio Dias Carneiro. "1944–1994: 50 anos de política econômica no Brasil." In *50 anos de Brasil, 50 anos da Fundação Getúlio Vargas,* edited by Bolivar Lamounier, et. al. 113–80. Rio de Janeiro: FGV, 1994.

Addis, Caren. "A Clash of Paradigms: Recent Interpretations of Brazilian Development." *Latin American Research Review* 32, no. 3 (1997): 123–39.

———. "Cooperação e desenvolvimento no setor de autopeças" In *De JK a FHC: a reinvenção dos carros*, edited by Glauco Arbix and Mauro Zilbovicius. 133–58. São Paulo: Scritta, 1997.

———. *Taking the Wheel: Auto Parts Firms and the Political Economy of Industrialization in Brazil.* University Park: Pennsylvania State University Press, 1999.

Ahn, Yeonmi. "The Political Economy of Foreign Aid: The Nature of American Aid and Its Impact on the State-Business Relationship in South Korea, 1945–1972." PhD diss., Yale University, 1992.

Alexander, Robert J. "Juscelino Kubitschek de Oliveira: Interview to *O Jornal do Brasil* in July 17, 1959." In *Artigos e Entrevistas Sobre a Operação Pan-Americana.* Rio de Janeiro: Ministério das Relações Exteriores, Seção de Publicações, 1960.

———. *Juscelino Kubitschek and the Development of Brazil.* Athens: Ohio University Center for International Studies, 1991.

———. *A History of Organized Labor in Brazil.* Westport: Praeger, 2003.

Almeida, Cândido Mendes de. *Perspectiva Atual da América Latina.* Rio de Janeiro: ISEB, 1960.

———. *Nacionalismo e Desenvolvimento.* Rio de Janeiro: Instituto Brasileiro de Estudos Afro-Asiáticos, 1963.

Almeida, Lúcio Flávio R. de. *Uma Ilusão de Desenvolvimento: Nacionalismo e Dominação Burguesa nos Anos JK.* Florianópolis: Editora da UFSC, 2006.

Almeida, Paulo Roberto de. "Uma política externa engajada: a diplomacia do governo Lula." *Revista Brasileira de Política Internacional* 47 no. 1 (2004): 162–84.

———. *Brazil as a Regional Player and an Emerging Global Player.* Friedrich Ebert Stiftung Briefing Papers No. 8. São Paulo, July 2007.

Amsden, Alice. *Asia's Next Giant: South Korea and Late Industrialization.* New York: Oxford University Press, 1989.

Andrade, Ana Maria and José Cardoso. "Aconteceu, virou manchete." *Revista Brasileira de História* 21, no. 41 (2001): 243–64.
Anfavea. *Indústria Automobilística Brasileira: uma história de desafios*. São Paulo: DBA, 1994.
Antunes, Luanda Pereira. "Legislativo e Desenvolvimento no Governo JK." MA thesis, IUPERJ, 2002.
Antunes, Ricardo. *Classe operária, sindicatos e partidos no Brasil*. São Paulo: Cortes Editora, 1982.
Armijo, Leslie E. "Public Policymaking in a Semi-Autonomous State: Brazilian Financial Modernization, 1950 to 1987." PhD diss., University of California Berkeley, 1989.
Arndt, H.W. *Economic Development: The History of an Idea*. Chicago: University of Chicago Press, 1987.
Ayittey, George B.N. "The Failure of Development Planning in Africa." In *The Collapse of Development Planning*, edited by Peter J. Boettke. 146–81. New York: New York University Press, 1994.
Baer, Werner. *Industrialization and Economic Development in Brazil*. Homewood, IL: Irwin, 1965.
———. *The Development of the Brazilian Steel Industry*. Nashville: Vanderbilt University Press, 1969.
———. "Import Substitution Industrialization in Latin America: Experiences and Interpretations." *Latin American Research Review* 7, no. 1 (Spring 1972): 95–122.
Balandier, Georges. "Contribution a une Sociologie de la Dépendance." *Cahiers Internationaux de Sociologie* 12 (1952): 47–69.
Barbosa, Francisco de Assis. *Juscelino Kubitschek, uma revisão na política brasileira*. Rio de Janeiro: Jose Olympio, 1960.
Belluzzo, Luis and Renata Coutinho, *Desenvolvimento capitalista no Brasil: Ensaio sobre a crise*. São Paulo: Brasiliense, 1982.
Benevides, Maria Victoria de Mesquita. *O governo Kubitschek: desenvolvimento econômico e estabilidade política, 1956–61*. Rio de Janeiro: Paz e Terra, 1976.
Bergeron, Suzanne. *Fragments of Development: Nation, Gender, and the Space of Modernity*. Ann Arbor: University of Michigan Press, 2004.
Bhabha, Homi. "Remembering Fanon: Self, Psyche, and the Colonial Condition." In *Colonial Discourse and Postcolonial Theory*, edited by Patrick Williams and Laura Chistman. 112–23. New York: Columbia University Press, 1994.
Bhattacharya, Rajesh. "Ethics and Economic Development: Why Developmentalism Prevails as an Ideology." In *Beyond Developmentalism*, edited by Nilanjan Dutta. 23–50. Kolkata: Sherya Publications, 2010.
Bielchowsky, Ricardo. *O Pensamento Econômico Brasileiro: O Ciclo Ideológico do Desenvolvimentismo*. Rio de Janeiro: Contraponto, 2004.
Boito, Jr., Armando. *Sindicalismo de Estado no Brasil*. Campinas: Ed. Unicamp, 1991.
Bojunga, Cláudio. *JK: O Artista do Impossível*. Rio de Janeiro: Objetiva, 2001.
Bonilla, Frank. "A National Ideology of Development: Brazil," In *Expectant Peoples: Nationalism and Development*, edited by K.H. Silvert. 232–64. New York: Random House, 1963.
Boschi, Renato. *Elites Industriais e Democracia*. Rio de Janeiro: Graal, 1979.

Bradley, Mark P. "Decolonization, the Global South, and the Cold War, 1919–1962." In *The Cambridge History of the Cold War*, edited by Melvyn P. Leffler and Odd Arne Westad. 464–85. Volume 1. Cambridge: Cambridge University Press, 2010.
Braillard, Phillipe, and Mohammed-Reza Djalili. *The Third World and International Relations*. Boulder: Lynne Rienner Publishers, 1984.
Bresser-Pereira, Luis Carlos. *Desenvolvimento e Crise no Brasil*. Rio de Janeiro, Zahar, 1968.
———. "O Conceito do Desenvolvimento do ISEB Rediscutido." *Dados—Revista de Ciências Sociais* 47. no. 1 (2004): 49–84.
———. "De la Cepal y el ISEB a Teoría de la Dependencia." *Desarrollo Económico* 46, no. 183 (Oct/Dec 2006): 419–39.
———. "From the National-Bourgeoisie to the Dependency Interpretation of Latin America." *Latin American Perspectives* 38, no. 3 (May 2011): 40–58.
Bresser-Pereira, Luiz C., and Marcia Van Dyke. "Six Interpretations of the Brazilian Social Formation." *Latin American Perspectives* 11, no. 11 Brazil in Crisis (Winter 1984): 35–72.
Bueno, Clodoaldo, and Amado Cervo. *A Política Externa Brasileira, 1822–1985*. São Paulo: Ática, 1986.
Bulmer-Thomas, Victor. *The Economic History of Latin America since Independence*. Cambridge, UK: Cambridge University Press, 2003.
Burns, E. Bradford. *Nationalism in Brazil: A Historical Survey*. New York: Frederick A. Praeger, 1968.
Cabot, John M. *Letter to Secretary Dulles, 28 March 1953* In Department of State Bulletin, Volume 6. Washington, D.C.: Department of State, Agency for International Development, Overseas Loans and Grants, 1954.
Caldas, Ricardo W. *A Politica Externa do Governo Kubitscheck*. Brasilia: Thesaurus, 1996.
Campos, Francisco L.S. *O Estado Nacional: sua estructura e seu conteúdo ideológico*. Rio de Janeiro: José Olympo, 1940.
Campos, Roberto de Oliveira. "Cultura e Desenvolvimento." In *Introdução aos Problemas do Brasil*, 221–33. Rio de Janeiro: ISEB, 1956.
———. *Economia, Planejamento e Nacionalismo*. Rio de Janeiro: APEC, 1963.
———. *Ensaios de História Econômica e Sociologia*. Rio de Janeiro: APEC, 1963.
Cano, Wilson. *Raízes da concentração industrial em São Paulo*. São Paulo: Difel, 1977.
Cardenas, Enrique, José Antonio Ocampo, and Rosemary Thorp, eds. *An Economic History of Twentieth-Century Latin America: Industrialization and the State in Latin America: The Postwar Years*. Volume 3. London: Palgrave Macmillan, 2000.
Cardero, Maria Elena. "Estructura monetaria y financiera de Mexico: 1932–1940." *Revista Mexicana de Sociología* 41, no. 30 (Jul-Sep 1979): 729–68.
Cardoso, Fernando Henrique. "Desenvolvimento Econômico e Nacionalismo," *Revista Brasiliense* 12 (Jul/Aug 1957): 88–99.
———. *Empresário industrial e desenvolvimento econômico*. São Paulo: Difel, 1964.
———. "Associated-Dependent Development: Theoretical and Practical Implications." In *Authoritarian Brazil*, edited by Alfred Stepan, 142–78. New Haven: Yale University Press, 1973.
———. *Autoritarismo e Democratização*. Rio de Janeiro: Paz e Terra, 1975.
Cardoso, Fernando Henrique, and Enzo Faletto, *Dependencia y Desarrollo en America Latina*. Buenos Aires: Siglo XXI, 1969.

Cardoso, Miriam Limoeiro. *Ideologia do Desenvolvimento, Brasil: JK-JQ*. Rio de Janeiro: Paz e Terra, 1978.
Cardoso de Mello, João Manuel. *O Capitalismo Tardio: constribuição à revisão crítica da formação e desenvolvimento da economia brasileira*. São Paulo: Brasiliense, 1982.
Carew, Anthony. "Towards a Free Trade Union Centre: The International Confederation of Free Trade Unions (1949–1972)." In *The International Confederation of Free Trade Unions*, edited by Marcel van der Linden. 287–339. Bern: Peter Lang, 2000.
Carone, Edgar. *A Quarta República, 1945–1964*. São Paulo: Difel, 1980.
Carvalho, Maria Isabel Valladão de. "A Colaboração do Legislativo para o Desempenho do Executivo durante o Governo JK." MA thesis, IUPERJ, 1977.
Castro, Antonio Barros. "Renegade Development: Rise and Demise of State-Led Development in Brazil." In *Democracy, Markets, and Structural Reform in Latin America: Argentina, Bolivia, Brazil, and Chile*, edited by William Smith, Carlos Acuna, and Eduardo Gamarra. 183–213. Miami: North/South Center, University of Miami, 1982.
Chatterjee, Partha. *Nationalist Thought and the Colonial World: A Derivative Discourse*. Minneapolis: University of Minnesota, 1993.
CEPAL, *La creación de la industria automovilística brasileña analizada como un caso de programación sectorial*, Studios de Cepal (Santiago: Cepal, Juño 1961).
Chibber, Vivek. *Locked in Place: State-Building and Late Industrialization in India*. Princeton: Princeton University Press, 2003.
Ciambarella, Alessandra. "A tradição abre as portas à modernidade: o Rio de Janeiro e a transferência da Capital Federal (1956–1960)." In *O Rio de Janeiro nos Jornais: ideologia, culturas políticas e conflitos sociais (1945–1964)*, edited by Jorge Ferreira. 136–53. Rio de Janeiro: 7 Letras, 2011.
Colistete, Renato P. *Labour Relations and Industrial Performance in Brazil: Greater São Paulo, 1945–1960*. New York: Palgrave, 2001.
———. "A Força das Idéias: A Cepal e o Industrialismo no Brasil no Início dos Anos 50." In *História Econômica do Brasil Contemporâneo*, edited by Tamas Szmerecsanyi and Wilson Suzigan. 121–45. São Paulo: Hucitec, 2002.
———. "Productivity, Wages, and Labor Politics in Brazil, 1945–1962." *Journal of Economic History* 67, no. 1 (March 2007): 93–127.
Collier, David, ed. *The New Authoritarianism in Latin America*. Princeton: Princeton University Press, 1979.
Connell-Smith, Gordon. *Los Estados Unidos y la America-Latina*. Mexico City: Fondo de Cultura Economica, 1977.
Conniff, Michael, ed. *Latin American Populism in Comparative Perspective*. Albuquerque: University of New Mexico Press, 1982.
———. *Populism in Latin America*. Tuscaloosa: University of Alabama Press, 1999.
Cony, Carlos Heitor. *JK, como nasce uma estrela*. Rio de Janeiro: Ed. Record, 2002.
Corbisier, Roland. "Situação e Alternativas da Cultura Brasileira." In *Introdução aos Problemas do Brasil*. 187–218. Rio de Janeiro: Instituto Superior de Estudos Brasilieros, 1956.
———. *Formação e Problema da Cultura Brasileira*. Rio de Janeiro: ISEB, 1959.
———. *Brasília e o Desenvolvimento Nacional*. Rio de Janeiro: ISEB, 1960.
———. *JK e a luta pela Presidência*. Rio de Janeiro: Duas Cidades, 1976.

Corrêa, Maria Letícia. "Estado e desenvolvimento no Brasil: um estudo de caso sobre engenheiros e economistas (1956–1961)." *Revista Intellectus* 6, vol. I (2007): 1–15.
Costa, Celia Maria Leite, et al. *Impasse na Democracia Brasileira, 1951–1954: Coletânea de Documentos*. Rio de Janeiro: Editora de Fundacao Getulio Vargas, 1983.
Costa, Emilia Viotti da. *The Brazilian Empire: Myths and Histories*. Chicago: University of Chicago Press, 1985.
Costa, Hélio da. *Em busca da memória*. São Paulo: Scritta, 1995.
Couto, Ronaldo Costa. *Brasília Kubistchek de Oliveira*. Rio de Janeiro: Record, 2001.
D'Araújo, Maria Celina. *O Segundo Governo Vargas 1951–1954: democracia, partidos e crise política*. Rio de Janeiro: J. Zahar, 1982.
Darnton, Christopher. "Assymetry and Agenda-Setting in U.S.-Latin American Relations: Rethinking the Origins of the Alliance for Progress." *Journal of Cold War Studies* 14, no. 4 (Fail 2012): 55–91.
Dean, Warren. *The Industrialization of São Paulo: 1880–1945*. Austin: University of Texas Press, 1969.
Delgado, Lucília de Almeida Neves. "Nacionalismo como projeto de nação: a Frente Parlamentar Nacionalista (1956–1964)." In *Nacionalismo e Reformismo Radical (1945–1964)*, edited by Jorge Ferreira and Daniel Aarão Reis. Vol. 2, 358–76. Rio de Janeiro: Civilização Brasileira, 2007.
Di Tella, Torquato. *Para uma política latino-americana*. Rio de Janeiro: Paz e Terra, 1969.
Dinius, Oliver J. *Brazil's Steel City: Developmentalism, Strategic Power, and Industrial Relations in Volta Redonda, 1941–1964*. Stanford: Stanford University Press, 2011.
Diniz, Eli. *Empresário, Estado e Capitalismo no Brasil, 1930–1945*. Rio de Janeiro: Paz e Terra, 1978.
Draibe, Sonia. *Rumos e metamorfoses: um estudo sobre a constituição do estado e as alternativas da industrialização no Brasil, 1930–1960*. Rio de Janeiro: Paz e Terra, 1985.
Duarte, Regina Horta. " 'It Does Not Even Seem Like We Are in Brazil': Country Clubs and Gated Communities in Belo Horizonte, Brazil, 1951–1964." *Journal of Latin American Studies* 44, no. 3 (Aug 2012): 435–66.
Dunn, Christopher. *Brutality Garden: Tropicália and the Emergence of a Brazilian Counterculture*. Chapel Hill: University of North Carolina Press, 2001.
Eakin, Marshal C. *Brazil: The Once and Future Country*. New York: St Martin's Griffin, 1998.
———. *Tropical Capitalism: The Industrialization of Belo Horizonte*. New York: Palgrave, 2002.
Erickson, Kenneth P. *The Brazilian Corporative State and Working-Class Politics*. Berkeley: University of California Press, 1978.
Escobar, Arturo. "Imagining a Post-Developmental Era? Critical Thought, Development and Social Movements." *Social Text* no. 31/32, Third World and Post-Colonial Issues (1992): 20–56.
———. *Encountering Development: The Making and Unmaking of the Third World*. Princeton: Princeton University Press, 1995.
Evans, Peter. *Dependent Development: The Alliance of Multinational, State, and Local Capital in Brazil*. Princeton: Princeton University Press, 1979.

———. "Predatory, Developmental, and Other Apparatuses: A Comparative Political Economy Perspective on the Third World State." *Sociological Forum* 4, no. 4, Comparative National Development Theory and Facts for the 1990s (Dec 1989): 561–87.

———. *Embedded Autonomy: States and Industrial Transformation.* Princeton: Princeton University Press, 1995.

Evans, Peter, and Gary Gereffi, "Foreign Investment and Dependent Development: Comparing Brazil and Mexico." In *Brazil and Mexico: Patterns in Late Development*, edited by Sylvia Ann Hewlett and Richard S. Weinert. 116–68. Philadelphia: Institute for the Study of Human Issues, 1982.

Fanon, Franz. *Les Damnés de la Terre*. Paris: Galimard, 1961.

Faoro, Raymundo. *Os Donos do Poder.* Porto Alegre: Ed. Globo, 1984.

Faro, Clóvis, and Salomão da Silva. "A Década de 50 e o Programa de Metas." In *O Brasil de JK*, edited by Angela de Castro Gomes. 44–70. Rio de Janeiro: FGV, 1991

Fassy, Amaury S. *JK: O Maior Estadista do Século XX*. Brasilia: Thesaurus, 2000.

Fausto, Boris. *O Brasil Republicano: Economia e Cultura (1930–1964)*. Coleção História Geral da Civilização Brasileira. São Paulo: Difel, 1984.

Fernandes, Florestan. *A Revolução Burguesa no Brazil: Ensaio de Intepretação Sociológica*. Rio de Janeiro: Zahar, 1981.

Ferreira, Jerusa, ed., *Editando o Editor - Ênio Silveira*. São Paulo: Edusp, 2002.

Ferreira, Jorge. *Trabalhadores do Brasil: O Imaginário Popular*. Rio de Janeiro: Editora da FGV, 1997.

———. ed. *O populismo e sua história*. Rio de Janeiro: Civilização Brasileira, 2001.

———. *Prisioneiros do Mito. Cultura e imaginário político dos comunistas no Brasil (1930–1956)*. Rio de Janeiro/Niteroi: Eduff/Mauad, 2002.

———. *O Imaginário Trabalhista: getulismo, PTB e cultural política popular, 1945–1964*. Rio de Janeiro: Civilização Brasileira, 2005.

Ferreira, Marieta de Moraes, and Claudia Mesquita. "Os anos JK no acervo da Biblioteca Nacional." In *Biblioteca Nacional: 500 anos de Brasil na Biblioteca Nacional*, edited by Paulo Pereira. 76–82. Rio de Janeiro: Fundação Biblioteca Nacional/Nova Fronteira, 2001.

Figueiredo, Ana Cristina Camargo Moraes. *Liberdade é uma calça velha, azul e desbotada: Publicidade, cultura de consumo, e comportamento político no Brasil, 1954–1964*. São Paulo: Hucitec, 1998.

Figueiredo, Argelina Cheibub. *Democracia ou Reformas? Alternativas Democráticas a Crise Política, 1961–64*. São Paulo: Paz e Terra, 1993.

Fiori, José Luis. *O Vôo da Coruja: uma leitura não-liberal da crise do Estado Desenvolvimentista*. Rio de Janeiro: EdUERJ, 1995.

Fishlow, Albert. *Some Reflections on Comparative Latin American Performance and Policy*. Helsinki: World Institute for Development Economics Research, 1987.

Fonseca, Pedro C. Dutra. *Vargas e o Capitalismo em Construção, 1906–1954*. São Paulo: Brasiliense, 1989.

Fontes, Paulo. *Trabalhadores e cidadãos: Nitro-Química, a fábrica e as lutas operárias nos anos 50*. São Paulo: Annablume, 1997.

———. "Centenas de estopins acesos ao mesmo tempo—a greve dos 400 mil, piquetes e a organização dos trabalhadores em São Paulo (1957)." In *Na Luta por Direitos: Estudos Recentes em História Social do Trabalho*, edited by Alexandre Fortes, et al. 145–72. Campinas, 1999.

Fortes, Alexandre, et al. *Na Luta por Direitos: Estudos Recentes em História Social do Trabalho*. Campinas: Editora da Unicamp, 1999.
Franco, Maria Sylvia Carvalho. "O tempo das ilusões." In *Ideologia e Mobilização Popular*, edited by Marilena Chaui and Maria Sylvia Carvalho Franco. 151–209. São Paulo: Paz e Terra/Cedec, 1978.
Freixo, Adriano de, et. al. *Política externa brasileira na era Lula: um balanço*. Rio de Janeiro: Apicuri, 2011.
French, John. *The Brazilian Workers' ABC. Class Conflict and Alliances in Modern São Paulo*. Chapel Hill: University of North Carolina Press, 1992.
Furtado, Celso. *A Economia Brasileira: uma contribuição à análise do seu desenvolvimento*. Rio de Janeiro: Editora A Noite, 1954.
———. *Manual of Programming and Economic Development Promotion*. Rio de Janeiro: Economic Commission for Latin American, 1956.
———. "O Desenvolvimento Econômico e suas Ilusões." *O Observador Econômico e Financeiro* no. 256 (June 1957): 32–38.
———. *Perspectiva da Economia Brasileira*. Rio de Janeiro: DASP, Ensaios de Administração, no. 15, 1958.
———. *Formação Econômica do Brasil*. São Paulo: Fundo de Cultura, 1959.
———. *Desenvolvimento e Subdesenvolvimento*. Rio de Janeiro: Fundo de Cultura, 1961.
———. *A Pré-Revolução Brasileira*. Rio de Janeiro: Fundo de Cultura, 1962.
———. *Dialética do Desenvolvimento*. Rio de Janeiro: Fundo de Cultura, 1964.
———. "Political Obstacles to Economic Growth in Brazil." In *Obstacles to Change in Latin America*, edited by Claudio Veliz. 145–61. Oxford: Oxford University Press, 1965.
———. *The Diagnosis of the Brazilian Crisis*. Berkeley: University of California Press, 1965.
———. *Formação Econômica da América Latina*. Rio de Janeiro: Lia Editores, 1969.
———. *A Fantasia Organizada*. Rio de Janeiro: Paz e Terra, 1985.
———. *A Fantasia Desfeita*. Rio de Janeiro: Paz e Terra, 1997.
Gattas, Ramiz. *A Indústria Automobilística e a Segunda Revolução Industrial no Brasil: Origens e Perspectivas*. São Paulo: Prelo, 1981.
Gaylord, Donald R. "The Instituto Superior de Estudos Brasileiros (ISEB) and Developmental Nationalism in Brazil, 1955–1964." PhD diss., Tulane University, 1991.
Geddes, Barbara. *Politician's Dilemma: Building State Capacity in Latin America*. Berkeley: University of California Press, 1994.
Gereffi, Gary, and Donald L. Wyman, eds. *Manufacturing Miracles: Paths of Industrialization in Latin America and East Asia*. Princeton: Princeton University Press, 1990.
Germani, Gino. *Política y sociedad en una época de transicion: de la sociedad tradicional a la sociedad de masas*. Buenos Aires: Paidos, 1962.
Gerschenkron, Alexander. *Economic Backwardness in Historical Perspective*. Cambridge, MA: Belknap, 1962.
Gomes, Angela de Castro, ed. *Burguesia e Trabalho. Política e Legislação Social no Brasil, 1917–1937*. Rio de Janeiro: Campus, 1979.
———, ed. *O Brasil de JK*. Rio de Janeiro: FGV, 1991.
———. *A Invenção do Trabalhismo*. Rio de Janeiro: FGV, 1994.
———. *Minas e os Fundamentos do Brasil Moderno*. Belo Horizonte: Editora UFMG, 2005.

Gordon, Lincoln. *A New Deal for Latin America: The Alliance for Progress*. Cambridge: Harvard University Press, 1963.

Gordon, Lincoln, and Engelbert L. Grommers. *United States Manufacturing Investment in Brazil: The Impact of Brazilian Government Policies, 1946–1960*. Cambridge, MA: Harvard Graduate School of Business Administration, 1960.

Guerreiro Ramos, Alberto. "A Problemática da Realidade Brasileira." In *Introdução aos Problemas do Brasil*. 13–32. Rio de Janeiro: Instituto Superior de Estudos Brasilieros, 1956.

———. *A Redução Sociológica*. Rio de Janeiro: ISEB, 1958.

———. *O Problema Nacional do Brasil*. Rio de Janeiro: Saga, 1960.

Guillerme dos Santos, Wanderley. "Desenvolvimentismo: Ideologia Dominante." *Tempo Brasileiro* 2 (Dec 1962): 155–92.

Haggard, Stephan. *Pathways from the Periphery: The Politics of Growth in the Newly Industrializing Countries*. Ithaca, NY: Cornell University Press, 1990.

Hagopian, Frances. *Traditional Politics and Regime Change in Brazil*. Cambridge: Cambridge University Press, 1996.

Haines, Gerald K. *The Americanization of Brazil: A Study of U.S. Cold War Diplomacy in the Third World 1945–1954*. Wilmington: SR Books, 1989.

Harding, Timothy Fox. *The Political History of Organized Labor in Brazil*. Palo Alto: Stanford University Press, 1973.

Hilton, Stanley. "The United States, Brazil, and the Cold War, 1945–1960: End of the Special Relationship." *Journal of American History* 68, no. 3 (Dec 1981): 599–624

Hirschman, Albert O. "Ideologies of Economic Development in Latin America." In *Latin American Issues: Essays and Comments*, edited by Albert O. Hirschman. 3–42. New York: The Twentieth Century Fund, 1961.

———. *Journeys Toward Progress: Studies of Economic Policy-Making in Latin America*. New York: W. W. Norton, 1963.

———. *The Strategy of Economic Development*. New Have: Yale University Press, 1965.

———. "The Political Economy of Import-Substituting Industrialization in Latin America." *Quarterly Journal of Economics* 82, no. 1 (Feb 1968): 1–32.

———. *A Bias for Hope: Essays on Development in Latin America*. New Haven: Yale University Press, 1971.

Hirst, Monica. *Vargas-Peron Y Las Relaciones Brasil-Argentina*. Série de Documentos e Informes de Investigacion no. 32. Buenos Aires: FLACSO, 1985.

———. "O Pragmatismo Impossível: A Política Externa do Segundo Governo Vargas (1951–1954)." *Cena Internacional* 1, no. 3 (2003): 1–33.

Hollanda, Sérgio Buarque de. *Raízes do Brasil*. São Paulo: Cia das Letras, 1995.

Holloway, Thomas H. *Immigrants on the Land: Coffee and Society in Brazil, 1886–1934*. Chapel Hill: University of North Caroline Press, 1980.

Holston, James. *The Modernist City: An Anthropological Critique of Brasilia*. Chicago: University of Chicago Press, 1989.

———. "Autoconstruction in Working-Class Brazil." *Cultural Anthropology* 6, no. 4 (Nov 1991): 447–65.

Huddle, Donald. "Balanço de pagamentos e controle de câmbio no Brasil: diretrizes, políticas e história." *Revista Brasileira de Economia* 18, no. 1 (Mar 1964): 5–40.

———. "O Sistema Brasileiro de Taxas Cambiais Flutuantes: Sua Equidade Distributiva, Suas Relações com a Inflação e Sua Eficiência." *Revista Brasileira de Economia* 24, no. 4 (1972): 149–68.
Humphrey, John. *Capitalist Control and Worker's Struggle in the Brazilian Auto Industry*. Princeton, NJ: Princeton University Press, 1982.
Huntington, Samuel P. *Political Order in Changing Societies*. New Haven: Yale University Press, 1968.
Ianni, Octavio. *Industrialização e desenvolvimento social no Brasil*. Rio de Janeiro: Civilização Brasileira, 1963.
———. *Crisis in Brazil*, New Yok: Columbia University Press, 1970.
———. *O Colapso do Populismo no Brasil*. Rio de Janeiro: Civilização Brasileira. 1978.
———. *O Ciclo da Revolução Burguesa*. Petropolis: Vozes, 1984.
———. *Estado e planejamento econômico no Brasil*. Rio de Janeiro: Civilização Brasileira, 1986.
IBGE. *Estatísticas Históricas do Brasil: Séries Socio-Econômicas, Demográficas e Sociais, 1950–1988*. Rio de Janeiro: IBGE, 1990.
Indian Economic Journal. "Plurality as Underdevelopment. Editorial Section. 6 (1958): 73–88.
Ioris, Rafael R. "*Fifty Years in Five* and What Is in It for Us? Development Promotion, Populism, Industrial Workers and the Case of *Carestia* in 1950s Brazil." *Journal of Latin American Studies* 44, no. 2 (May 2012): 261–84.
IPEA. *A Controvérsia do Planejamento da Economia Brasileira*. Rio de Janeiro: IPEA/INPES, 1977.
Jaguaribe, Hélio. "A Crise Brasileira," *Cadernos do Nosso Tempo* 1, no. 1 (Oct/Dec 1953): 120–60.
———. "Três Etapas do Comunismo Brasileiro." *Cadernos do Nosso Tempo* 1, no. 2, (1954): 123–38.
———. "Situação Política Brasileira." *Cadernos do Nosso Tempo* 2, no. 2 (1954): 101–22.
———. "Sentido e Perspectivas do Governo Kubitschek." *Cadernos do Nosso Tempo* 1, no. 5 (Jan/Mar 1956): 1–18.
———. *Condições Institucionais do Desenvolvimento*. Rio de Janeiro: ISEB, 1958.
———. *O Nacionalismo na Atualidade Brasileira*. Rio de Janeiro: ISEB, 1958.
———. *Desenvolvimento Econômico e Desenvolvimento Político*. Rio de Janeiro: Fundo de Cultura, 1962.
———. "ISEB e o Desenvolvimento Nacional" In *Intelectuais e política no Brasil: a experiência do ISEB*. Edited by Caio Navarro de Toledo. 31–42. São Paulo: Revan, 2005.
Johnson, Chalmers. *MITI and the Japanese Miracle: The Growth of Industrial Policy, 1925–1975*. Stanford: Stanford University Press, 1982.
Jordan, Thomas M. "Contesting the Terms of Incorporation: Labor and the State in Rio de Janeiro, 1930–1964." PhD diss., University of Illinois Urbana-Champaign, 2000.
Kay, Cristobal. *Latin American Theories of Development and Underdevelopment*. London: Routledge, 1989.
Kohli, Atul. *State-Directed Development: Political Power and Industrialization in the Global Periphery*. Cambridge: Cambridge University Press, 2004.
Kubitschek de Oliveira, Juscelino, *Diretrizes Gerais do Plano Nacional de Desenvolvimento*. Belo Horizonte: Livraria Oscar Nicolai, 1955.

———. *Discursos proferidos no primeiro ano do mandato presidencial, 1956*. Rio de Janeiro: ISEB, 1958.
———. *Quatro Anos no Governo de Minas Gerais (1951–1955): Síntese das Realizações do Governador Juscelino Kubitschek de Oliveira*. Rio de Janeiro: José Olympio Editora, 1959.
———. *A Marcha do Amanhecer*. São Paulo: Bestsellers Livros, 1962.
Lafer, Celso. "O Planejamento no Brasil—Observações sobre o Plano de Metas (1956–1961)." In *Planejamento no Brasil*, edited by Betty Mindlin Lafer. 29–50. São Paulo: Perspectiva, 1970.
———. *JK e o Programa de Metas (1956–1960): Processo de planejamento e sistema político no Brasil*. Rio de Janeiro: FGV, 2002.
Lamounier, Bolivar. "O ISEB: notas `a margen de um debate." *Discurso* no. 9 (Nov 1979): 153–58.
Latini, Sydney A. *Suma Automobilística*. Rio de Janeiro: Editora Tama, 1984.
Leal, Victor Nunes. *Coronelismo, Enxada e Voto*. Rio de Janeiro: Forense, 1948.
Leff, Nathaniel. *Economic Policy-Making and Development in Brazil, 1957–1960*. New York: Wiley, 1968.
Leite, Rogério Proença. *A Dupla Face do Nacionalismo: Ideologia, Discurso e Dominação em Kubitschek e Medice*. Recife: Editora da UFPE, 1995.
Leopoldi, Maria Antonieta P. "O difícil caminho do meio: Estado, burguesia e industrialização no Segundo governo Vargas (1951–54)." In *Vargas e a Crise dos Anos 50*, edited by Angela de Castro Gomes. 160–203. Rio de Janeiro: Relume Dumara, 1994.
———. *Política e Interesses na Industrialização Brasileira: As associações industriais, a política econômica e o Estado*. São Paulo: Paz e Terra, 2000.
Lerner, Daniel. *The Passing of the Traditional Society*. Glencoe, IL: The Free Press, 1958.
Lessa, Carlos. "Fifteen Years of Economic Policy in Brazil." *Economic Bulletin for Latin America* 9, no. 2 (Nov 1964): 153–214.
Lewis, W. A. *The Theory of Economic Growth*. London: Allen & Unwin, 1955.
Leys, Colin. *The Rise and Fall of Development Theory*. Bloomington: Indiana University Press, 1996.
Lima, Hermes. "Significação do Nacionalismo." *Cadernos do Nosso Tempo* 4, no. 3 (Apr/Aug 1955): 85–100.
Limoncic, Flávio. "A Civilização do Automóvel: A instalação da indústria automobilística no Brasil e a via brasileira para uma improvável modernidade fordista, 1956–1961." MA thesis, URFJ, 1997.
Lipset, Seymour M., and Aldo Solari, eds. *Elites in Latin America*. New York: Oxford University Press, 1967.
Loomba, Ania. *Colonialism/Postcolonialism*. London: Routledge, 1998.
Lopes, Carmen Lúcia E. "A Organização Sindical dos Metalúrgicos de São Paulo." PhD diss., University of São Paulo, 1992.
Lopes, Juarez Rubens Brandão. *Sociedade Industrial no Brasil*. Sao Paulo: Difel, 1964.
Lopes, Rodrigo. *Sonho e Razão: Lucas Lopes, o Planejador de JK*. São Paulo: Arx. 2006.
Lopez-Maya, Margarita. "The Change in the Discourse of US-Latin American Relations from the End of the Second World War to the Beginning of the Cold War." *Review of International Political Economy* 2, no. 1 (Winter 1995): 135–49.
Loureiro, Maria Rita. *Os Economistas no Governo: gestão econômica e democracia*. Rio de Janeiro: FGV, 1997.
Louzeiro, José. *JK: o otimismo em pessoa*. Rio de Janeiro: Ediouro, 1996.

Lovatto, Angelica. *A Utopia Nacionalista de Helio Jaguaribe: os tempos do ISEB.* São Paulo: Arte Scritta, 2010.
Love, Joseph L. *A Construção do Terceiro Mundo: Teorias do Subdesenvolvimento na Romênia e no Brasil.* São Paulo: Paz e Terra, 1998.
Lowy, Michael, and Sarah Chucid. "Opiniões e atitudes de líderes sindicais metalúrgicos." *Revista Brasileira de Estudos Politicos* 1, no. 13 (1962): 132–69.
Luz, Nícia Vilela. *Aspectos do Nacionalismo Econômico Brasileiro: os esforços em prol da industrialização.* Coleção Revista Brasileira de História, volume XVI. São Paulo: Coleção Revista Brasileira de História, 1959.
Macarini, José Pedro. "A política econômica do governo Médici: 1970–1973." *Nova Economia* 15, no. 3 (Sep–Dec 2005): 53–92.
Maia, João Marcelo Ehlert. *Estado, território, e imaginação espacial. O caso da Fundação Brasil Central.* Rio de Janeiro: FGV, 2012.
Malan, Pedro S. "Relações Econômicas Internacionais do Brasil, 1945–1964." In *O Brasil Republicano: Economia e Cultura* (1930–1964), edited by Bóris Fausto. 51–106. Coleção História Geral da Civilização Brasileira. São Paulo: Difel, 1984.
Malan, Pedro S., et. al. *Política econômica externa e industrialização no Brasil, 1939–52.* Rio de Janeiro: IPEA/INPES, 1977.
Mantega, Guido. *Desenvolvimento e Política Econômica no Brasil: Os Anos 50.* Relatório de Pesquisa, no. 22. São Paulo: Escola de Administração de Empresas de São Paulo, Fundação Getúlio Vargas, 1982.
Maram, Sheldon. "Juscelino Kubitschek and the Politics of Exuberance, 1956–1961." *Luso-Brazilian Review* 27, no. 1 (Summer 1990): 31–45.
Maranhão, Ricardo. *Sindicatos e Democratização. Brasil, 1945–1950.* São Paulo: Brasiliense, 1979.
Marques, Alexandre Rios. *Evolução Histórica do Planejamento Econômico no Brazil e em Minas Gerais—do Nacional-Desenvolvimentismo ao Neo-Liberalismo.* Belo Horizonte: Fundação João Pinheiro, 2002.
Martins, Heloísa de Souza. *O Estado e a Burocratização do Sindicato no Brasil.* São Paulo: Hucitec, 1979.
Martins, Luciano. "Formação do empresariado industrial no Brasil." *Revista do Instituto de Ciências Sociais* 3, no. 1 (1966): 91–138.
———. *Industrialização, burguesia nacional e desenvolvimento.* Rio de Janeiro: Saga, 1968.
———. *Pouvoir et Développement Économique: Formation et évolution des structures politiques au Brésil.* Paris: Éditions Anthropos, 1976.
Martins Filho, Amilcar Vianna. *O Segredo de Minas: a origem do estilo mineiro de fazer política (1889–1930).* Belo Horizonte: Crisálida, 2009.
Mauss, Marcel. "Essai sur le don: Forme et raison de l'échangé dans les sociétés archaïques. "In *Sociologie et Anthropologie.* 149–279. 4th edition. Les Presses Universitaires de France, 1968.
Meira, Lúcio. "A indústria do automóvel no Brasil." *Revista do Conselho Nacional de Economia* 6, no. 48 (Nov–Dec 1957): 41–47.
———. *A Industrialização e o Problema Agrícola no Brasil.* Belo Horizonte: UFMG, 1960.
———. "A Industrialização." In *JK: O Estadista do Desenvolvimento*, edited by José Aparecido de Oliveira. 117–30. Brasília: Memorial JK, 1991.
Mendonça, Sônia Regina de. *Estado e Economia no Brasil: Opções de Desenvolvimento.* Rio de Janeiro: Graal, 1988.

Miranda, Wander Melo, ed. *Anos JK: Margens da Modernidade*. São Paulo: Imprensa Oficial, 2002.
Morton, Adam David. *Revolution and State in Modern Mexico: The Political Economy of Uneven Development*. London: Rowman & Littlefield, 2011.
Mota, Carlos Guilherme. *Ideologia da cultura brasileira*. São Paulo: Ática, 1985.
Moura, Gerson. "Avanços e Recuos: a política externa de JK." In *O Brasil de JK*, edited by Angela de Castro Gomes. 23–42. Rio de Janeiro: FGV, 1991.
Muniz, Clélio Campolina. "Estado e Capital Estrangeiro na Industrialização Mineira." MA thesis, University of Campinas, 1978.
Myrdal, Gunnar. *Economic Theory and Underdeveloped Regions*. London: Duckworth, 1964.
Napoleão, Aluízio. *Juscelino Kubitschek: audácia, energia, confiança*. Rio de Janeiro: Bloch Editores, 1988.
Nascimento, Benedito H. *Formação da Indústria Automobilística Brasilieira: Política de Desenvolvimento Industrial em uma Economia Dependente*. Série Teses e Monografias, Instituto de Geografia, no. 24. São Paulo: Universidade de São Paulo, 1976.
Negro, Antonio Luigi. *Linhas de Montagem—o industrialismo nacional-desenvolvimentista e a sindicalização dos trabalhadores*. São Paulo: Boitempo, 2004.
Negro, Antonio Luigi and Fernando Teixeira da Silva. "Trabalhadores, sindicatos e politica (1945–1964)," In *O Brasil Republicano*: *o tempo da experiência democrática, da democratização de 1945 ao golpe civil-militar de 1964*, edited by Jorge Ferreira and Lucilia de Almeida Neves Delgado. 47–96. Rio de Janeiro: Civilização Brasileira, 2003.
Neves, Santuza Cambraia. "Os novos experimentos culturais nos anos 1940–50: propostas de democratização da arte no Brasil." In *O Brasil Republicano: o tempo da experiência democrática, da democratização de 1945 ao golpe civil-militar de 1964*, edited by Jorge Ferreira and Lucilia de Almeida Neves Delgado. Vol. 3: 273–99. Rio de Janeiro: Civilização Brasileira, 2003.
Nkrumah, Kwame. "African Prospects." *Foreign Affairs* 37, no. 1 (Aug 1958): 45–53.
Nunes, Edson de Oliveira. *Dilemmas of State-Led Modernization in Brazil*. Série Estudos, no. 39. Rio de Janeiro: IUPERJ, 1985
Nunes, Edson de Oliveira, and Barbara Geddes. "Dilemmas of State-Led Modernization in Brazil." In *State and Society in Brazil*, edited by John Wirth, et al. 103–45. Boulder: Westview Press, 1987.
O'Brien, Thomas. *The Century of U.S. Capitalism in Latin America*. Albuquerque: University of New Mexico Press, 1999.
———. *The Making of the Americas: The United States and Latin America from the Age of Revolutions to the Era of Globalization*. Albuquerque: University of New Mexico Press, 2007.
O'Donnell, Guillermo. *Modernization and Bureaucratic-Authoritarianism: Studies in South American Politics*. Berkeley: University of California Press, 1973.
Oliveira, Francisco. *Crítica à Razão Dualista & o Ornitorrinco*. São Paulo: Boitempo Editorial, 2003.
Oliveira Vianna, Francisco de. *O Idealismo da Constituição*. Rio de Janeiro: Terra de Sol, 1927.
———. *Instituições Políticas Brasileiras*. Rio de Janeiro: José Olympo, 1949.
———. *História Social da Economia Capitalista no Brasil*. Niteroi: Editora da UFF, 1988.

Oliveira, José Aparecido de. *JK: O Estadista do Desenvolvimento*. Brasília: Memorial JK, 1991.

Oliveira, Lúcia Lippi de. "A redescoberta do Brasil nos anos 1950: entre o projeto político e o rigor acadêmico." In *Descobertas do Brasil*, edited by Angélica Madeira and Mariza Veloso. 139–61. Brasília: Editora da UnB, 2001.

———. "Tempos de JK: a construção do futuro e a preservação do passado." In *Anos JK: Margens da Modernidade*, edited by Wander Melo Miranda. 31–44. São Paulo: Imprensa Oficial, 2002.

Orenstein, Luiz, and Antonio Claudio Sochaczewski. "Democracia com Desenvolvimento: 1956–1961." In *A Ordem do Progresso: Cem Anos de Política Econômica Republicana, 1889–1989*, edited by Marcelo de Paiva Abreu. 171–95. Rio de Janeiro: Campus, 1990.

Ortiz, Renato. *Cultura brasileira & Identidade nacional*. São Paulo: Brasiliense, 1985.

Owen, Jenkins Rhys. *Dependent Industrialization in Latin America: The Automotive Industry in Argentina, Chile, and Mexico*. New York: Praeger, 1977.

Owensby, Brian P. *Intimate Ironies: Modernity and the Making of Middle-Class Lives in Brazil*. Stanford: Stanford University Press, 1999.

Parada, Maurício Barreto. "A Fundação do Museu de Arte Moderna do Rio de Janeiro: a Elite Carioca e as Imagens da Modernidade no Brasil dos Anos 50." MA thesis, PUC-RJ, 1993.

Pecaut, Daniel. *Os intelectuais e a política na Brasil*. São Paulo: Brasiliense, 1990.

Pelaez, Carlos Manuel. *História da Industrialização Brasileira: crítica a teoria estruturalista do Brasil*. Rio de Janeiro: APEC, 1972.

———. *História Econômica do Brasil*. São Paulo: Atlas, 1979.

Pempel, T.J., "The Developmental Regime in a Changing World Economy." In *The Developmental State*, edited by Meredith Woo-Cumings. 137–81. Ithaca: Cornell University Press, 1999.

Penna Filho, Pio. "A Política Externa Brasileira do Governo Juscelino Kubitschek (1956–1961)." *Cena Internacional* 1, no. 1 (1999): 121–40.

Pereira, Simone Maria Andrade. "Os Anos Dourados: Copacabana e o Imaginário Urbano dos Anos 50." MA thesis, UFRJ, 1991.

Picolin, João Carlos. "Juscelino para presidente: As estratégias de comunicação política na campanha eleitoral de JK em 1955." Paper presented at the Twentieth National Conference of Communication Sciences. Salvador, 2002.

Piñeda, Yovanna. *Industrial Development in a Frontier Economy, The Industrialization of Argentina, 1890–1930*. Palo Alto: Stanford University Press, 2009.

Pinheiro, Letícia. "Ação e omissão: A ambiguidade da politica brasileira frente ao processo de descolonização africana, 1946–1960." MA thesis, PUC-RJ, 1988.

Prado, Jr., Caio. *História Econômica do Brasil*. São Paulo: Brasiliense, 1970.

Prado, Maria Emilia. "Os intelectuais e a eternal busca pela modernização do Brasil: o significado do projeto nacional-desenvolvimentista das décadas de 1950–60." *História Atual Online* no. 15 (2008): 19–27.

Prebisch, Raul. *Interpretacion del proceso de desarollo latinoamericano*. Santiago: Comision Economica para America Latina, 1949.

———. "O desenvolvimento econômico da América Latina e seus principais problemas." *Revista Brasileira de Economia*. 3, no. 3 (Sept 1949). 47–111.

———. *The Economic Development of Latin America and Its Principal Problems*. New York: United Nations Department of Economic Affairs, 1950.

———. "Commercial Policy in the Underdeveloped Countries." *American Economic Review, Paper and Proceedings* XLIX, no. 2 (May 1959). 251–273.

———. *Dinâmica do Desenvolvimento Latino-Americano*. Rio de Janeiro: Fundo de Cultura, 1964.

Presidência da República, *Plano Trienal de Desenvolvimento Econômico e Social, 1963–65*. Rio de Janeiro, 1962.

Queiroz, Maria Isaura Pereira de. *O Mandonismo local na vida política brasileira*. São Paulo: Alfa e Ômega, 1976.

Queuille, Pierre. *Histoire de l'afro-asiatisme jusqu'à Bandung*. Paris: Payot, 1965.

Rabe, Stephen G. *Eisenhower and Latin America: The Foreign Policy of Anticommunism*. Chapel Hill: University of North Carolina Press, 1988

Rabelo, Ricardo Fonseca. "Plano de Metas e a consolidação do capitalismo industrial no Brasil." *E&G Economia e Gestão vol.* 2 & 3, no. 4 & 5, (Dec 2002/July 2003): 44–55.

Ramalho, Jose R. G. *Estado Patrão e luta operária: o caso FNM*. Rio de Janeiro: Paz e Terra, 1989.

Ramirez, Miguel D. "Public and Private Investment in Mexico, 1950–90: An Empirical Analysis." *Southern Economic Journal* 61, no. 1 (Jul 1994): 1–17.

Ramos, Ricardo. *História da Propaganda no Brasil*. São Paulo: Edusp, 1972.

Reidinger, Edward A. *The Making of the President, Brazil 1955: The Campaign of Juscelino Kubitschek*. Chicago: University of Chicago Press, 1978.

Revista da Indústria Automobilística, *O Problema da Mão-de-Obra para a Indústria Automobilística*, São Paulo, 1958,

Rocha, Amara Souza. "Nas Ondas da Modernização: Uma História Social do Rádio e da Televisão no Brasil nos Anos 1950–1960." PhD diss., UFRJ, 2004.

Rodrigues, Georgette. "Ideologia, propaganda e imaginação social na construção de Brasília (1956–1960)." MA thesis, University of Brasilia, 1990.

Rodrigues, José Albertino. *Sindicato e Desenvolvimento no Brasil*. São Paulo: Difel, 1968.

Rodrigues, Leôncio Martins. *Conflito Industrial e Sindicalismo no Brasil*. São Paulo: Difel, 1966.

———. *Industrialização e Atitudes Operárias: Estudo de um grupo de trabalhadores*. São Paulo: Brasiliense, 1970.

Rodrigues, Marly. *A década de 50: populismo e metas desenvolvimentistas no Brasil*. São Paulo: Atica, 1994.

Rodriguez, Otávio. *Teoria do Subdesenvolvimento da Cepal*. Rio de Janeiro: Forense Universitária, 1981.

Rostow, Walt W. *The Stages of Development: An Anti-Communist Manifesto*. Cambridge, UK:Cambridge University Press, 1960.

Roxborough, Ian. *Theories of Underdevelopment*. London: Macmillan, 1979.

Royal Institute of International Affairs. "Final Communiqué of the Bandung Conference." In *Documents on International Affairs, 1955*. 429–36. Oxford: Oxford University Press, 1958.

Sachs, Ignacy. *Capitalismo de estado e subdesenvolvimento*. Petropolis: Vozes, 1969.

Saldana-Portillo, Maria Josefina. *The Revolutionary Imagination in the Americas and the Age of Development*. Durham: Duke University Press, 2003.

Salm, Cláudio. "Estagnação Econômica, Desemprego e Exclusão Social." In *Novo-desenvolvimentismo: um projeto nacional de crescimento com eqüidade social,*

edited by João Sicsu, et al. 189–216. Rio de Janeiro: Fundação Konrad Adenauer, 2005.
Sandoval, Salvador A. *Social Change and Labor Unrest in Brazil since 1945*. Boulder: Westview, 1993.
Santana, Marco Aurélio. "Partido e militância sindical: a atuação comunista no Sindicato dos Metalurgicos do Rio de Janeiro, STIMMMERJ, 1947–1964." MA thesis, UFRJ, 1992.
———. "Entre a Ruptura e a Continuidade: Visões da Histórica do Movimento Sindical Brasileiro." *Revista Brasileira de Ciências Sociais* 14, no. 41 (1999): 103–20.
———. *Homens Partidos: comunistas e sindicatos no Brasil*. Rio de Janeiro: Boitempo, 2001.
———. "Trabalhadores e militância sindical: a relação partido/sindicato/classe no Sindicato dos Metalúrgicos do Rio de Janeiro, 1947–1964." In *Trabalho e Tradição Sindical no Rio de Janeiro a Trajetória dos Metalúrgicos*, edited by José Ricardo Ramalho and Marco Aurélio Santana. 165–212. Rio de Janeiro: DP&A, 2001.
———. "Bravos companheiros: a aliança comunista-trabalhista no sindicalismo brasileiro (1945–1964)." In *Nacionalismo e reformismo radical (1945–1964)*, edited by Jorge Ferreira and Daniel A. Reis. 238–77. Civilização Brasileira, volume 2. Rio de Janeiro: Civilização Brasileira, 2007.
Santos, Joaquim Ferreira dos. *Feliz 1958: O ano que não deveria terminar*. São Paulo: Record, 1997.
Santos, Pedro Augusto Gomes. *A classe média vai ao paraíso: JK em Manchete*. Porto Alegre: EDIPUCRS, 2002.
Saretta, Fausto. "O Governo Dutra na Transição Capitalista no Brasil." In *História Econômica do Brasil Contemporâneo*, edited by Tamas Szmrecsanyi and Wilson Suzigan. 99–120. São Paulo: Edusp, 2002.
Sartre, Jean-Paul. "Le Colonialisme est un Système." *Les Temps Modernes* no. 123 (Mar–Apr 1956): 1371–86.
Scaletsky, Eduardo Campos. "Dois projetos para o Brasil: 1945–1954: uma análise dos projetos da Missão Abbink, da Comissão Mista Brasil-Estados Unidos e do Grupo Misto BNDE-CEPAL." MA thesis, UFRGS, 1988.
Schmitter, Phillipe C. *Interest Conflict and Political Change in Brazil*. Stanford: Stanford University Press, 1971.
Schneider, Ben Ross. "The *Desarollista* State in Brazil and Mexico." In *Developmental State*, edited by Meredith Woo-Cumings. 276–304. Ithaca: Cornell University Press, 1999.
Schwartzman, Simon. "Desenvolvimento econômico e desenvolvimento político: do nacionalismo ao desenvolvimentismo." *Revista Brasileira de Ciências Sociais* 3, no. 1, (March 1963): 271–82.
———. *O Pensamento Nacionalista e os Cadernos de Nosso Tempo*. Brasília: UnB, 1981.
Scott, James C. *Seeing Like a State: How Certain Schemes to Improve the Human Condition Have Failed*. New Haven: Yale University Press, 1998.
Segatto, José Antonio. *Reforma ou revolução: as vicissitudes políticas do PCB, 1945–1964*. Rio de Janeiro: Civilização Brasileira, 1995.
Shapiro, Helen. "State Intervention and Industrialization: The Origins of the Brazilian Automotive Industry." PhD diss., Yale University, 1988.
———. "Determinants of Firm Industry Entry into the Brazilian Automobile Manufacturing Industry, 1956–1968." *Business History Review* 65, no. 4, The Automobile Industry (Winter 1991): 876–947.

———. *Engines of Growth: The State and Transnational Auto Companies in Brazil.* Cambridge, UK: Cambridge University Press, 1994.

Sheahan, John. *Early Industrialization and Violent Reaction: Argentina and Brazil.* Discussion Paper 176. University of Sussex: Institute of Development Studies, 1982.

Sikkink, Kathryn. *Ideas and Institutions: Developmentalism in Brazil and Argentina.* Ithaca: Cornell University Press, 1991.

Silva, Adriana Hassin. "A Modernidade em Alvorada: Brasília e a imagem do Brasil moderno no fotojornalismo d'O *Cruzeiro* e da *Manchete* (1956–1960)." MA thesis, UFRJ, 2003.

Silva, Alexandra Mello e. "A Política Externa de JK: a Operação Pan-Americana. MA thesis, PUC-RJ, 1992.

Silva, Fernando Teixeira da. *A carga e a culpa: Os operários das Docas de Santos: Direitos e Cultura de Solidariedade, 1937–1968.* São Paulo: Hucitec, 1995.

Silva, Hélio, and Maria C.R. Carneiro. *Os Presidentes: Juscelino e o Desenvolvimentismo 1956–1961.* Rio de Janeiro: Grupo de Comunicação Três, 1983.

Silva, Patrício. "State, Public Technocracy and Politics in Chile, 1927–1941." *Bulletin of Latin American Research* 13, no. 3 (Sep 1994): 281–97.

Simão, Azis. *Sindicato e Estado no Brasil.* São Paulo: Dominus, 1966.

Simonsen, Mario Henrique, and Roberto Campos. *A Nova Economia Brasileira.* Rio de Janeiro: José Olympo, 1974.

Simonsen, Roberto C. *A Evolução Industrial do Brasil e outros estudos.* São Paulo: Cia Editora Nacional, 1973.

Skidmore, Thomas E. *Politics in Brazil, 1930–1964—An Experiment in Democracy.* Oxford: Oxford University Press, 1967.

———. *A Case Study in Comparative Public Policy: The Economic Dimensions of Populism in Argentina and Brazil.* Working Paper No. 3. Washington, D.C.: The Wilson Center, 1978.

Soares, Walmer Jacintho. *Os Interesses Industriais na Consolidação do Nacional-Desenvolvimentismo.* Rio de Janeiro: IUPERJ/PUC, 1994.

Sodré, Nelson Werneck. *Raízes Históricas do Nacionalismo Brasileiro.* Rio de Janeiro: ISEB, 1960.

———. *A verdade sobre o ISEB.* Rio de Janeiro: Avenir, 1978.

Sola, Lourdes. *Idéias Econômicas, Decisões Políticas: Desenvolvimento, Estabilidade, Populismo.* São Paulo: Edusp, 1998.

Souza, Luis Eduardo Simões de. "Políticas Públicas em São Bernardo do Campo no Pós-Guerra: 1945–1964." MA thesis, University of São Paulo, 2002.

Stein, Stanley J. *The Brazilian Cotton Manufacture: Textile Enterprise in an Underdeveloped Area, 1850–1950.* Cambridge, MA: Harvard University Press, 1957

Stepan, Alfred, ed. *Authoritarian Brazil.* New Haven: Yale University Press, 1973.

Stuart, Lisa. "A atuação dos conselhos sindicais na indústria metalúrgica do Rio de Janeiro, de 1953 a 1964." MA thesis, Universidade Federal Fluminense, 1992.

Suzigan, Wilson. *Indústria Brasileira: Origem e Desenvolvimento.* São Paulo: Hucitec, 2000.

Szusterman, Célia. *Frondizi and the Politics of Developmentalism in Argentina, 1955–62.* Pittsburgh: University of Pittsburgh Press, 1993.

Taffet, Jeffrey F. *Foreign Aid as Foreign Policy: The Alliance for Progress in Latin America.* New York: Routledge, 2007.

Tavares, Maria da Conceição. *Da Substituição de importações ao capitalismo financeiro.* Rio de Janeiro: Zahar, 1973

Teixeira, Alberto. *Planejamento Público: de Getúlio a JK (1930–1960)*. Fortaleza: IPLANCE, 1997.
Toledo, Caio Navarro de. *ISEB: Fabrica de Ideologias*. São Paulo: Atica, 1977.
———. "ISEB Intellectuals, the Left, and Marxism." *Latin American Perspectives* 1, no. 98 (Jan 1998): 109–35.
———, ed. *Intelectuais e política no Brasil: a experiência do ISEB*. São Paulo: Revan, 2005.
Topik, Steven. *The Political Economy of the Brazilian State, 1889–1930*. Austin: University of Texas Press, 1987.
Touraine, Alan. "Industrialisation et conscience ouvriere à São Paulo." *Sociologie du Travail* III, no. 4 (1961): 77–95.
Touraine, Alan, and David Pecaut. "Working-Class Consciousness and Economic Development in Latin America." In *Masses in Latin America*, edited by Irving Louis Horowitz. 59–93. New York: Oxford University Press, 1970.
Trevisan, Maria J. *50 anos em cinco: a Fiesp e o desenvolvimentismo*. Rio de Janeiro: Vozes, 1986.
United Nations Economic Commission for Latin America. *Economic Bulletin for Latin America* 3, no. 2 (Oct). Santiago: 1958.
———. *La creación de la indústria automovilística brasileña analizada como un caso de caso de programacion sectorial*. Estudios de Cepal. Santiago: Cepal, Juño 1961.
———. *Development Problems in Latin America*. Austin: Institute of Latin American Studies, University of Texas Press, 1970.
Valdivia-Machuca, Arnulfo. *State and Business Groups in Mexico: The Role of Informal Institutions in the Process of Industrialization, 1936–1984*. New York: Routledge, 2005.
Vargas, Getúlio. *A Campanha Presidencial*. Rio de Janeiro: José Olympio, 1951.
———. *O Governo Trabalhista no Brasil*. Rio de Janeiro: José Oympio, 1952.
Veliz, Claudio. *The Centralist Tradition in Latin America*. Boulder: Westview Press, 1981.
Versiani, Flávio Rabelo. *A Década de 20 na Industrialização Brasileira*. Rio de Janeiro: IPEA, 1987.
Versiani, Marian O. "Cotton Textile Industry of Minas Gerais, Brazil: 1868–1906." PhD diss., University College of London: 1991.
Vianna, Sérgio Besserman. *A Politica Econômica no Segundo Governo Vargas (1951–1954)*. Rio de Janeiro: BNDE, 1987.
———. "Duas Tentativas de Estabilização, 1951–1954." In *A Ordem do Progresso: Cem Anos de Política Econômica Republicana, 1889–1989*, edited by Marcelo de Paiva Abreu. 123–50. Rio de Janeiro: Campus, 1990.
Vianna, Sérgio Besserman, and André Villela. "O Pós-Guerra.' In *Economia Brasileira Contemporânea (1945–2004)*, edited by Fábio Giambiagi, et. al. 21–59. Rio de Janeiro: Campus, 2005.
Vieira Pinto, Alvaro. *Ideologia e Desenvolvimento Nacional*. Rio de Janeiro: ISEB, 1960.
———. *Consciência e Realidade Nacional*. Volumes 1 and 2. Rio de Janeiro: ISEB, 1962.
Vigevani, Túlio, and Gabriel Cepaluni. "Lula's Foreign Policy and the Quest for Autonomy through Diversification." *Third World Quarterly* 28, no. 7 (2007): 1309–26.

Villela, Anibal, and Werner Baer, *O Setor Privado Nacional: Problemas e Políticas.* Rio de Janeiro: IPEA, 1980.

Vinhas, Moises. *O Partidão: a luta por um partido de massas, 1922–1974.* São Paulo: Hucitec, 1982.

Vizentini, Paulo G.F. *As Relações Exteriores do Brasil:1945–1964.* Petrópolis: Vozes, 2004.

Wade, Robert. *Governing the Market: Economic Theory and Role of Government in East Asian Industrialization.* Princeton: Princeton University Press, 1990.

Walker, Michael. *The Cold War and the Making of the Modern World.* London: Fourth State Press, 1993.

Wallerstein, Immanuel. "The Concept of National Development, 1917–1989: Elegy and Requiem." *American Behavioral Scientist* 35 (1992): 517–29.

Wallerstein, Michael. "The Collapse of Democracy in Brazil: Its Economic Determinants." *Latin American Research Review* 15, no. 3 (1980): 3–40.

Watson, T.J. *O novo Presidente to Brasil Visita aos Estados Unidos da América: Visita de Sua Excelência o Doutor Juscelino Kubitschek de Oliveira Presidente do Brasil.* New York: World Trade Corporation, 1956.

Weffort, Francisco C. "Classes populares e politica: contribuição ao estudo do populismo." PhD Diss., University of the São Paulo, 1968.

———. *Origens do Sindicalismo Populista no Brasil: A Conjuntura do Após-Guerra.* No. 4. São Paulo: Estudos Cebrap, 1973.

———. "Democracia e movimento operário: algumas questões para a história do período 1945–1964." *Revista de Cultura Contemporânea* no. 1, (1978): 3–11.

———. *O Populismo na política brasileira.* Rio de Janeiro: Paz e Terra, 1978.

Weinstein, Barbara. *For Social Peace in Brazil: Industrialists and the Remaking of the Working Class in São Paulo, 1920–1964.* Chapel Hill: University of North Carolina Press, 1996.

Weis, W. Michael. *Cold Warriors & Coups D'Etat: Brazilian-American Relations, 1945–1964.* Albuquerque: University of New Mexico, 1993.

Welch, Cliff. "Labor Internationalism: U.S. Involvement in Brazilian Unions, 1945–1965." *Latin American Research Review* 30, no. 2 (1995): 61–89.

Westad, Odd Arne, ed. *The Global Cold War: Third World Interventions and the Making of the Our Times.* Cambridge: Cambridge University Press, 2005.

Wiarda, Howard J., ed. *Politics and Social Change in Latin America: Still a Distinct Tradition.* Boulder: Westview Press, 1992.

Willis, Eliza J. "Explaining Bureaucratic Independence in Brazil: The Experience of the National Economic Development Bank." *Journal of Latin American Studies* 27, no. 3 (1995): 625–61.

Wolfe, Joel. *Working Women, Working Men: São Paulo and the Rise of Brazilian Industrial Working Class, 1900–1955.* Durham: Duke University Press, 1993.

Woo-Cumings, Meredith, ed. *The Developmental State.* Ithaca: Cornell University Press, 1999.

Young, Jordan. *Brazil: 1954–1964, o fim de um ciclo civil.* Rio de Janeiro: Nova Fronteira, 1973.

Appendix
Specific Goals and Achievements of the Targets Plan

Area I—Energy Production: This area would receive close to 43 percent of all funds invested during the plan implementation and included the following targets:

1) Electricity: Increased production from 3,500,000 kW in 1956 to 5,000,000 kW in 1960, and 9,000,000 kW in 1965. In December 1960, production had reached 4,770,000 kW, which represented 87 percent of the initial target and within the next year production reached 5,205,000 kW.
2) Nuclear Energy: Included training of technical personnel to implement a national program of nuclear energy and installation of a nuclear energy facility in the country. Insofar as its results, these were hard to measure but a reactor was installed at the University of São Paulo, some educational fellowships were given to Brazilian researchers to study abroad, and the Nuclear Energy Council began production of atomic fuel material at a state-owned unit.
3) Mineral Coal: Increased production to 3,000,000 tons in 1960. This goal was partially achieved as production peaked at 2,199,000 tons. This was still considered a success as the consumption of coal decreased given the conversion to diesel-run engines used in the railroad system.
4) Oil (production): The specified target was for reaching a domestic oil production of 100,000 barrels a day in 1960, primarily by expanding production via the new state-owned oil company Petrobrás. This objective was only partially met (75 percent as production reached 75,000 barrels a day in that same year). In 1961, production peaked at 95,000 barrels a day.
5) Oil (refining): Originally planned to reach 175,000 barrels a day, the target was revised to 300,000 barrels a day in 1960. The results exceeded the target as 309,000 barrels were refined daily by the end of that year.

Area II—Transportation: Received about 30 percent of investments and included the following targets:

6) Railroads (renovation): Consisted of the acquisition of 400 diesel-run locomotives, 1,086 passenger wagons, and 10,943 cargo wagons, goals that were only partially met.
7) Railroads (construction): The goal was to build 1,500 km of new tracks, and only 50 percent of these were constructed as of 1960; representing an expansion of only 3.5 percent of new tracks into the national railroad network system.

8) Roads (paving): The initial aim was to pave 3,000 km, but the goal was expanded to close to 6,000 km in 1959 and by late 1960, the paved roads network had doubled.
9) Roads (construction): The initial goal was to open 10,000 km of new unpaved roads. This target was later revised to 12,000 and then again to 13,000 km. By the end of 1960, close to 15,000 km of new roads had been built, representing one of the highest success rates of the plan.
10) Port Network: The target was to double the naval transportation system by investing in the reformation of old harbors and the building of new ones, but only about half of this target was met.
11) Merchant Fleet: Aimed at acquiring new vessels to the government-owned merchant company in order to increase the fleet by about 30 percent. The rate of completion was close to 70 percent of the initial target.
12) Air Transportation: The subsidized acquisition of 45 new airplanes was planned; only 13 were added.

Area III—Food Production and Distribution: Received only about 3 percent of the funds disbursed and include the following targets:

13) Wheat Production: The target planned was to reach a domestic production of 1,500,000 tons of wheat by the 1960 mid-year harvest. This was the target with the most dismal results considering that the actual production that year was of 370,000 tons, less than what had been produced in 1955.
14) Warehouses: The target of reaching a storage capacity of 800,000 tons was met by about 70 percent by the end of 1960.
15) Meat Warehouses: Only 18 percent of the goal of achieving a storage capacity of 100,000 tons was met.
16) Industrial Slaughterhouses: The original aim was to be able to slaughter about 4,000 cows and 1,500 pigs daily in government-run facilities. These numbers were revised to about 2,750 cows and 1,100 pigs in 1958, and only 80 percent of this new target was reached.
17) Mechanization of Agriculture: The goal was to have about seventy-eight thousand tractors working in the fields by the end of 1960; this number was surpassed by about 7 percent.
18) Fertilizers: The target of having 290,000 tons of fertilizer used in agricultural production by the end of 1960 was surpassed by about 40 percent.

Area IV—Basic Industries: Received about 21 percent of all investments and was centered on increasing production of various industrial products, as follows:

19) Steel: The initial goal was to increase steel production to about 2,000,000 tons in 1960 from about 1,300,000 in 1955. The target was surpassed as production reached 2,279,000 tons in 1960.
20) Aluminum: The goal was to increase domestic production to 20,000 tons in 1960, a figure that was only partially reached (about 16,0000 tons).
21) Minerals Processing: Expansion in the refining process of copper, lead, and tin was close to the assigned targets.
22) Concrete: The initial goal was met by about 90 percent; the target was to increase production to about 5,000,000 tons a year.

23) Alkali: Production peaked at 212,000 tons in 1960 (94 percent of the target).
24) Cellulose and Paper: The initial goal was to produce 200,000 tons of cellulose and 450,000 tons of paper in 1960. Both targets were met.
25) Rubber: The targets were for producing 40,000 tons of synthetic rubber and 25,000 tons of natural rubber by 1960. The goal for the first item was met in 1961, but production of natural rubber did not improve from the 1955 figure.
26) Mineral Exports: In 1960 the country exported 8,000,000 tons of minerals, about 62 percent of the assigned target.
27) Automotive Industry: The initial target was to produce 130,000 vehicles in Brazil in 1960. Actual production reached 230,000 that same year, well above the revised target of 170,000 set in 1958.
28) Naval Construction: The target was to increase the production of ships by about 30 percent, which was achieved in 1960.
29) Electrical Equipment: No specific targets were set but results were very positive as the amount of electrical equipment produced in Brazil doubled between 1955 and 1960.

Area V—Education and Technical Qualification of Labor: Received only about 3 percent of all investments and consisted of only one vaguely specified target:

30) Training Technical Personnel: The goal was to improve the training of laborers who were expected to work in the new industrial plants. As no specific numbers to be reached in this target were set, it is impossible to define a rate of achievement for this target. What is clear however is that despite being a promise made during Kubitschek's presidential campaign, this area was not a priority for the administration and only very small results could be shown in the area.

Index

Kubitschek during his presidential campaign in 1955. (CPDOC Archive).

Kubitschek and Lucas Lopes at a ceremony inaugurating a hydroelectric power plant. (CPDOC Archive).

Vargas (left) and Kubitschek during the former's presidency (1951–1954). (CPDOC Archive).

Lucas Lopes at a presentation of the Targets Plan, sometime between 1956 and 1958. (CPDOC Archive).

For Product Safety Concerns and Information please contact our EU representative GPSR@taylorandfrancis.com
Taylor & Francis Verlag GmbH, Kaufingerstraße 24, 80331 München, Germany

www.ingramcontent.com/pod-product-compliance
Ingram Content Group UK Ltd.
Pitfield, Milton Keynes, MK11 3LW, UK
UKHW022117190926
475702UK00013B/1493
9781138651500